The 4-H Harvest

POLITICS AND CULTURE IN MODERN AMERICA

Series editors:
Margot Canaday, Glenda Gilmore, Michael Kazin,
Stephen Pitti, Thomas J. Sugrue

Volumes in the series narrate and analyze political and social change
in the broadest dimensions from 1865 to the present, including ideas
about the ways people have sought and wielded power in the public
sphere and the language and institutions of politics at all levels—local,
national, and transnational. The series is motivated by a desire to reverse
the fragmentation of modern U.S. history and to encourage synthetic
perspectives on social movements and the state, on gender, race, and labor,
and on intellectual history and popular culture.

The 4-H Harvest

Sexuality and the State in Rural America

Gabriel N. Rosenberg

PENN

UNIVERSITY OF PENNSYLVANIA PRESS

PHILADELPHIA

Published by
University of Pennsylvania Press
Philadelphia, Pennsylvania 19104-4112
www.upenn.edu/pennpress

Printed in the United States of America
on acid-free paper
1 3 5 7 9 10 8 6 4 2

Library of Congress Cataloging-in-Publication Data
Rosenberg, Gabriel N., author.
The 4-H harvest : sexuality and the state in rural America / Gabriel N. Rosenberg.
    pages cm. — (Politics and culture in modern America)
Includes bibliographical references and index.
ISBN 978-0-8122-4753-4 (alk. paper)
1. 4-H clubs—United States—History.   2. United States—Rural conditions—
History—20th century.   3. Sociology, rural—United States—History—20th
century.   4. Agriculture—United States—Social aspects—History—20th century.
I. Title.   II. Series: Politics and culture in modern America.
S533.F66R67   2016
630.6073—dc23   2015006404

For Ruth Farrell and Selma Rosenberg

CONTENTS

ABBREVIATIONS

AAA	Agricultural Adjustment Act of 1933
ABA	American Bankers Association
ADT	Agribusiness Development Team
AFBF	American Farm Bureau Federation
AIA	American International Association
ATP	Agricultural Training Program
CCC	Civilian Conservation Corps
CES	Cooperative Extension Service
CORDS	Civil Operations and Revolutionary Development Support
FTD	Foreign Training Division
GVN	Government of the Republic of Vietnam
IFYE	International Farm Youth Exchange
IICA	Inter-American Institute of Agricultural Sciences
LGCA	Land Grant College Association
National Committee	National Committee on Boys and Girls Club Work
PIJR	Programa Interamericano para la Juventud Rural
SCS	Soil Conservation Service
SDE	Southern Directors of Extension
USAID	United States Agency for International Development
USDA	United States Department of Agriculture
USOM	United States Operations Mission to Vietnam
VES	Vietnamese Extension Service
WFA	War Food Administration

Signs of the State

Fretting about the countryside is a great American pastime. And contemporary anxieties about the state of rural America run as high as ever. Current worries range from industrial meat production and use of pesticides to depopulation and the scourge of methamphetamines, and they issue from across the political spectrum. Despite this anxious mood, politicians of all stripes and most voters are still deferential toward agrarian political rhetoric: the Jeffersonian ideal of the small, independent yeoman farmer and the belief that a virtuous rural past offers a model for a better future. In a time when increasing globalization pushes people to focus on local and small-scale action, the rhetoric of family farms is appealing. Yet that rhetoric sidesteps how, when, and why the current rural idyll came to such prominence. This book revises that political mythology by providing an overdue history to a key piece of agrarian Americana: 4-H, the homespun youth clubs that, over roughly a century of existence, taught millions of rural children how to be farmers and homemakers.

For my own part, rural places have rarely been a source of anxiety. Growing up in the Midwest, I was never a member of 4-H but was also never far from farms. Many of my most cherished experiences with the countryside, however, were linked to family vacations. Every summer, my parents hauled my siblings and me to a remote rented cabin near the western shore of Michigan for a week or two of swimming in frigid lake waters. We drove in the family minivan on U.S. 31 to a little town called Montague, cutting through endless fields of corn and soy on the way but missing any cities larger than South Bend. Travel with young children being what it was (and is), my parents made ample stops in the towns and businesses scattered along our route. We ogled an enormous stuffed steer in Kokomo—the world's largest!—and paused for ice cream in Rochester. My mother still swears that we stopped at corn stands—sweet corn, boiled, dipped in butter, salted, and served hot enough to burn your fingers—but I don't remember that. I do recall the many fresh produce stands as we drew closer to our destination in the heart of Michigan fruit country. At those stands, my mother bought enough tart cherries to bake a half-dozen pies and pints and pints of blueberries that we promptly devoured. At the cottage, I split time between the beach and riding my bicycle on country back roads, where I lost myself in the late summer fields of wheat and corn and occasional orchards. My sense of what was "beyond the city" was formed in this delightful milieu of lush agricultural landscapes, scrumptious treats, frenzied excitement, and the asphalt lanes that stretched to the horizon, dotted occasionally with peculiar road signs emblazoned with four-leafed clovers.

Deciphering those signs tells us much about the complicated political culture that guides their placement. Across the country, rural communities welcome visitors with signs much like the one in Tillman County, Oklahoma: "Tillman 4-H Club Welcomes You." The term "4-H" and its emblematic clover appear ubiquitously in American popular culture as quiet totems of rural life. Many readers of this book will be familiar with 4-H. Some may have been part of the 70 million Americans who, in the past century, joined a 4-H club. Other readers may have had only a vague understanding of the organization. 4-H clubs are voluntary associations for youth between the ages of ten and twenty. Through most of 4-H's history, the clubs were predominantly rural and focused on agriculture and home economics. 4-H'ers, the term for club members, worked hard on a specific project through spring and summer, with the ambition of producing something—a hog, a bushel of corn, a dress, a can of tomatoes—to show at the county fair at the end of the growing season. And if they produced something of exceptional quality, they might even win a ribbon and the chance to compete at the state fair. 4-H'ers, as both spectators and participants, are a ubiquitous presence at state fairs. Some may even be garbed in paraphernalia featuring the clover. Given the number of signs along county roads, 4-H and its clover stand not just narrowly for the club but for a broader sense of rural authenticity and pride, so much so that farm towns across America choose to express their civic identity in 4-H's voice.

If you look closely at an official 4-H clover, you will find the mysterious characters "18 USC 707" in the lower right-hand corner of the emblem. "18 USC 707" refers to the portion of the federal code that gives the United States Department of Agriculture (USDA) full ownership of the 4-H name and emblem. It is this portion of the federal code that makes the unauthorized use of that name and emblem a felony. 4-H is a USDA program, now administered by the National Institute of Food and Agriculture. At a time when rural political culture has become synonymous with skepticism of Big Government, the most ubiquitous symbol of rural civil society is the full legal property of an immense federal bureaucracy. How could this relationship between an icon of rural America and the leviathan of the American state be hidden so effectively?

The existence of this relationship is not exceptional but rather constitutive of the modern rural world. Contrary to the assumption that rural communities are the last bastions of an authentic American culture untainted by government bureaucracy, you can see the imprint of the state on every rural landscape. Rows of subsidized cornfields, once homesteads, are crisscrossed by interstate highways. They grow from hybrid seeds using technologies developed at public land-grant universities, purchased through a subsidized credit program, and vouchsafed by federal crop insurance. Along those highways, semis roll past federal penitentiaries and U.S. army bases, and they roll over irrigation ditches fed by massive dams. The semis are loaded with surplus commodities, purchased for distribution abroad under the USDA's Food for Peace program. Each of these images summons an intimate connection to state infrastructure that punctures cherished national myths about the American heartland—its robust independence, its nostalgic embodiment of a purer past. Rural America is not a resistant rump to the state's modernizing impulses; it is the outcome of those impulses. Yet in rural America, the state still hides in plain sight.

Seeing rural America as an embodiment of modern political economy structures my approach to 4-H's history. I take rural people and culture seriously, not as the remnants of a decaying past but as the keystones of modern industrial agriculture. At times, this demands accounting for 4-H's relationship to broader structures of violence related to commercial agriculture, racialized patterns of farm tenancy, and labor exploitation. At other times, however, it means examining how 4-H was positioned as a way to avoid direct violence—how 4-H worked as a strategy of alliance, an object of affection, and an instrument of sociability mutually constituted among rural people, urban capitalists, and federal bureaucrats. In all these instances, 4-H functioned as a mode of governance implemented through the bodies of participating children. In this, 4-H's iconic clover unlocks the unexpected history of the American biopolitical state. By biopolitics, I mean the political strategy that takes the management of life as both its fundamental object and means.[1] By tracking the 4-H clover, inscribed on the chests of millions of youth around the world, we find the American state insinuating itself into the intimate spaces of the rural world and connecting national projections of population and crop yields to the vigor and health of individual bodies. Far from a benign feature of a bucolic past, 4-H is a sophisticated biopolitical apparatus—a state infrastructure built out of youth instead of concrete.

This book tells three stories as one. First, it is an institutional history of 4-H. Readers curious about the most critical dates, names, and events in 4-H's history will find them in this book. Given the size of the program, its centrality to the social experiences of many people, and its colorful and fascinating history, this is a task I tackle with pleasure. Notably, this is a task never before undertaken by a professional historian.[2] Second, the book offers a cultural interpretation of the history of the political economy of agriculture in the United States.[3] By this, I mean broadly the process of producing and regulating markets for agricultural commodities. My cultural perspective on political economy attends to structures of governance and capital, material conditions, labor relations (informal and formal, public and private), particular technologies of capital production and reproduction, and the gendered assumptions that formed and conditioned those various factors. Third, this book is a history of a biopolitical apparatus—how it came to be assembled and to what ends. I map the interlocking series of biopolitical units produced by and constitutive of that apparatus in an arc that proceeds successively from the gendered bodies of rural youth, to the familial and community bodies in which their productive and reproductive capacities were elaborated, and to the national and global bodies that defined their reproductive horizons. To comprehend 4-H's status as biopolitical apparatus, we must first locate it within a broader transformation of agricultural production and rural communities across the United States in the twentieth century.

*   *   *

At the turn of the twentieth century, most farming in the United States still obeyed a simple maxim of production: labor poor, land rich. Abundant land in the western United States, guaranteed by federal military power, and patterns of internal migration led landowners to develop particular labor strategies. Small farmers in the North, the Corn Belt, the Upland South, and the High Plains made extensive use of familial labor. The resulting operations frequently mixed some amount of subsistence farming with commercial-oriented staple production. Early twentieth-century Americans rarely, if ever, used the term, but such farms loosely resembled the contemporary ideal of "family farms," though the families in question—sprawling, contingent, and multigenerational—bore little resemblance to a nucleated "farmer and farmer's wife" model that featured rigid divisions of gendered labor. Regardless, even by the late nineteenth century, most Northern farmers had integrated into commodity markets of varying scales with non-market-oriented and subsistence farming appearing only at the margins. Meanwhile, in the South, the crop lien system, discrimination in hiring and public accommodations, sanctioned vigilante violence, and pervasive vagrancy laws constrained black labor mobility. By the turn of the twentieth century, Southern land tenure had stabilized around tenant farmers and sharecroppers, forming the basis of a "neo-plantation" system that matched and then exceeded the South's prodigious antebellum cotton output.[4]

Although relatively limited at the twentieth century's turn, agriculture in the Far West offered the key to farming's future in the United States. While the South concocted an extensive legal regime to retain its agricultural labor force, Californian landowners sought workers from Central America, China, and the Philippines (and then supported legal measures to constrain the employment opportunities of their new labor force). With productive land clustered primarily around costly irrigation systems in the Central Valley, California reversed the usual maxim of production. California was land-poor and labor-rich: its farms mechanized first and were soon viewed as sound investment vehicles by bankers and speculators.[5] In other regions, such as the High Plains, similar experiments in capital-intensive farming proved less successful. Nevertheless, massive, highly mechanized farms stoked the imaginations of investors, reformers, and technocrats, who idealized "large scale production, specialized machines, standardizations of processes and products, reliance on managerial (rather than artisanal) expertise, and a continued invocation of efficiency as a production mandate." Proponents of this "industrial ideal" invoked "efficient," "progressive," "businesslike," and "scientific" agriculture nearly interchangeably to describe this prescriptive model of agriculture that privileged capital- and technology-intensive modes of production.[6]

Wealthier landed farmers—those who could most easily absorb capital costs and afford luxuries that better accorded with reformers' sense of order, aesthetics, and hygiene—joined the fold first. Initially, poor farmers, including tenants, sharecroppers, and wage laborers, critiqued the enterprise vociferously and used the vestiges of the populist movement as a vehicle for structural reform of the agricultural economy that, in turn, vexed reformers and investors alike. Whatever momentum structural reforms like the nationalization of the railroads enjoyed in the first two decades of the twentieth century, however, the agrarian Left had lost momentum by the 1920s. Instead, a legislative "farm bloc" coalesced around the American Farm Bureau Federation (AFBF), an organization that further institutionalized capital-intensive modes of production and made them central to the collective political identity of farmers. By the end of the 1920s, the notion that farming should be organized primarily along industrial lines had achieved broad consensus among both farmers and reformers. Southern farm owners, however, evinced a notorious lack of interest in capitalization, and Southern agriculture remained predominantly labor-intensive until the development of the mechanical cotton harvester and the transition to industrial poultry production after World War II.[7]

4-H developed as an integral part of this broader push toward mechanized, industry-backed agriculture and the politics of progressive agricultural reform that eventually rendered rural America safe for agribusinesses. Stymied by adult farmers, agricultural progressives targeted rural youth through clubs, contests, and home demonstrations. These youth-oriented methods were flexible enough to be used in racially and geographically diverse communities, and their emphasis on voluntary labor enrolled local allies and provided an organic, nonthreatening image for technocratic expertise. On the strength of this system of "agricultural extension," Congress created a permanent appropriation for the USDA's Cooperative Extension Service (CES) in 1914. By the 1920s, 4-H clubs were circulating the USDA's preferred technical farming methods and had created robust alliances of technocratic expertise, private capital, and local voluntary labor in every corner of rural America.

Buoyed by its relationship to the farm bureau and champions of progressive agriculture, 4-H grew considerably between 1914 and 1930. 4-H's prevalence in areas with the most labor-intensive agriculture reflected its transformational role in guiding farmers from labor-intensive methods to capital-intensive mono-cropping. With the farm bureau's support, 4-H aimed to take youth laboring on inefficient farms and teach them how to farm—and live—like businessmen. 4-H provided the technical details and mental instruments necessary for capital-intensive production. 4-H also provided local spaces where rural youth could network with farmers, businessmen, and agricultural experts. In these spaces, the USDA sponsored the circulated information, subsidized the salaries of county agents, and provided training for club leaders. In return, rural youth became accustomed to accepting the expert prescriptions of state agents as trustworthy and public-minded. In the wider community, the successes of club members advertised the advantages of scientific agriculture as well as the authority of the USDA. Club activities—daily labor, public demonstrations, fair exhibits, and community talks—constituted a form of everyday state building. Quotidian activities long accepted as constitutive elements of rural living, such as raising calves or sewing dresses, slowly and subtly insinuated state expertise into communities.

4-H clubs, and agriculture extension more generally, enjoyed their greatest influence in regions where rural populations were densest and where agriculture was most labor-intensive. In those communities, shorter travel times gave extension agents more contact with community members and made attendance at regular meetings manageable for club members. In addition, extension agents drew from larger target populations. 4-H clubs enrolled the highest percentages of rural youth in New England, states in the Deep South, and eastern Corn Belt states. The states ringing the Great Lakes, in particular, achieved impressive club enrollments, enrolling, on average, between a quarter and a third of farm youth by 1940. As the scale of farming increased west of the Mississippi and the land was less densely populated, club enrollments shrank—hovering in the Dakotas, for example, at less than 15 percent of the farm youth. Additionally, some western states with highly concentrated farm populations and efficient extension services—Oregon and Nevada, most notably—managed to enroll high percentages of their farm populations, even though, in raw numbers, their enrollments were comparatively smaller.[8]

4-H organizers believed that they could better secure the attention and cooperation of rural people if they catered to the gendered interests and labor of farm youth. Accordingly, and with increasing uniformity from the 1920s on, most 4-H projects were segregated by sex. Few girls participated in male agricultural projects that focused on revenue production. Even fewer boys learned about home economics. Organizers encouraged girls to enroll in homemaking projects, which could hypothetically provide valuable knowledge to the entrepreneurial girl. But by the late 1920s, they were focusing primarily on the relationship of domestic labor to the care and cultivation of the self and family. By contrast, male 4-H enrollments clustered almost exclusively around crop and animal husbandry projects. While boys spread their attention among the various agricultural projects, there was almost no male involvement in home economics projects.[9]

That sex-segregated structure allowed club organizers to turn their attention from the technical details of agriculture and home economics and to focus on the gendered bodies and psychologies of their youthful charges. By the 1930s, 4-H health programs had pushed rural youth to produce healthy bodies capable of laboring and reproducing for the nation and had positioned technocratic authority at the center of rural family life and social reproduction. 4-H material idealized the economic and biological union between a revenue-producing male "farmer" and a nurturing "farmer's wife" and promoted it as the normal form of organization for rural life. In rural communities, in the national media, and on the floor of Congress, the USDA and advocates of club work advertised the virtues of federal planning, using images of wholesome, white 4-H'ers conducting gender-appropriate labor on family farms. At the close of the 1930s, 4-H citizenship programs merged this vision of rural normalcy with American nationalism and the language of civic obligation, casting white, commercial family farmers as the backbone of the nation.

The lily-white public presentation of 4-H conflicted with the racial diversity of the organization's members. According to USDA statistics, African American enrollments were concentrated almost entirely in the states of the Confederacy and Kentucky, West Virginia, Missouri, and Maryland. In those states, the extension systems were segregated with a "negro" extension service, run out of each state's African American agricultural college, supervising a separate system of extension agents. Serious financial disparities between the systems left black extension grossly understaffed and black extension agents poorly equipped and ill-compensated. In many counties, where insufficient funds existed to hire a black county agent or home demonstrator, white extension agents were given responsibility for serving both black and white populations, although many white extension agents simply neglected black farmers altogether. Despite regular criticism from civil rights organizations and from African American extension pioneers like Thomas Campbell, financial disparities persisted. Even by 1946, black county agents were earning, on average, only 60 percent of what their white counterparts were earning. A racial ideology that cast African American farmers as genetically incapable of mastering the complexities of scientific farming informed this financial neglect of African American extension.[10]

Even when figures within the extension service rejected the notions that African Americans were genetically incapable of practicing scientific agriculture or were prone to superstition, explanations of Southern race relations tended to elide the economic consequences of white racism and place unreasonable expectations on the education of "backward" black farmers. African American extension agents also tended to be constrained by this racial ideology. They focused their efforts on "break[ing] down superstitions" among black farmers and publicizing "outstanding" examples who defied the crude stereotype of the backward black tenant farmer, efforts that consistently focused on black self-improvement rather than white racism. 4-H material perpetuated that stereotype, presenting club work as a scientific curative for crippling superstition. African American extension services did their best to circulate the stories, real and fictional, of 4-H members who improved their homes and lives through club work and shattered the grip of the previous generation's ignorance. African American extension material in the inter-war period also never questioned the basic racial division foisted by white supremacists in the Jim Crow South. In Alabama, for example, the extension service insisted on printing separate runs of material for white and black 4-H clubs. Despite being otherwise identical to the white club version, ledgers for African American livestock club members came emblazoned with the word "Negro" on the cover.[11] Similarly, African American 4-H members were excluded from the national 4-H events—the National 4-H Congress in Chicago and the National 4-H Camp in Washington, D.C. In general, while Southern white 4-H'ers enjoyed subsidized access to camps and social outings, there was no parallel structure for African American members. As a result of financial disparities, inattention from white extension agents and obvious racism, and despite large rural black populations throughout the South, white youth were disproportionately active in 4-H clubs.[12]

The Great Depression did nothing to dislodge the industrial ideal from 4-H or among farmers more broadly. The most costly and enduring component of the New Deal agricultural program, the Agricultural Adjustment Act of 1933 (AAA), enjoyed the enthusiastic support of the farm bureau. The AAA sent billions of dollars in price supports to farm operators by 1940 and integrated them soundly into the emergent corporatist New Deal state. These shifting links between capital-intensive agriculture and the American state placed the USDA at the center of the New Deal political coalition. It also situated 4-H as a key instrument of state power. The New Deal and World War II emerged as two key moments of emergency for the USDA, moments when the regulation of agriculture became inseparable from broader understandings of collective social and political health. In these moments, 4-H'ers performed vital services for the state. They rallied rural folk behind government programs at public meetings. They explained to their parents and neighbors how to fill out AAA contracts. They planted trees for the Soil Conservation Service (SCS). They mapped their communities for the Rural Electrification Administration. At war, they organized resource campaigns and provided vital agricultural labor.[13]

In fact, World War II shifted 4-H's focus from the task of producing farm families to the task of cultivating healthy bodies capable of laboring and sacrificing in the war effort. "4-H Club work in its daily program is building men and women to live," declared one USDA official at the 1940 National 4-H Club Congress, "and to live the great life here and now. Its first purpose is not soldier building but man building. But, if the Nation needs men for its defense, it will find that in 4-H Club work men and women trained to live are unafraid, if need be, to die."[14] Participation in 4-H became proof of civic virtue and able-bodied sacrifice for the nation. Despite vocal protests from African Americans, the USDA circulated a public image of 4-H that elided the wartime sacrifices of nonwhite 4-H'ers and thus cemented the links between authentic, rural citizenship and healthy, white bodies.

4-H's deployment as a selectively embodied tactic of state power coincided with the near-total integration of national corporations into the production and consumption of foodstuffs. Agribusinesses sold hybrid seeds, petrochemicals, and mechanical implements to farmers, and farmers sold unprocessed agricultural commodities to agribusinesses. Prewar reformers dreamed of a managed countryside that was politically compatible with and economically integrated into an urban capitalist order. By 1960, that dream had become reality, and the model of vertically integrated agribusinesses had come to shape every corner of life in the rural United States. Small farmers were more obsolete than ever, but the family farm enjoyed greater cultural idealization than ever before in the American popular imagination. Less a relic of an agrarian past, the family farm was now just an idealized link in an agribusiness chain that stretched from the American heartland to markets and farmers around the world. 4-H was an apparatus keeping those links in place.[15]

*   *   *

It is inadequate to tell 4-H's story as one only concerned with the normalization of state-subsidized, capital-intensive agriculture in rural America. A history of 4-H must also be a history of sexuality, gender, and the body: a story about the gendered production of desirable bodies through heteronormative family farms. Neither of those histories is intelligible without the other. When articulated together, these histories raise crucial questions about the means and ends of biopolitics, as well as the history of state power in the United States. I interpret 4-H as a governing network dedicated to the orchestration of both nonhuman and human bodies within the framework of agriculture, a framework that is necessarily biopolitical. In doing so, this book places two seemingly different objects—the politics of gender and sexuality as well as the politics of food and agriculture—into a single biopolitical frame.[16]

This move has important consequences for the objects in question as well as for the underlying political theories and disciplinary practices that have previously divided them. For scholars of the history of political economy and state building, the book demonstrates the vital necessity of an engagement with feminist and queer theories, as well as increased attention to the roles that embodiment, intimacy, and seduction play in the actual logistics of governance. For historians of gender and sexuality, it marks the urgency of connecting the gendered reproduction of human life to the dramatic transformations of the global food system. For theorists of biopolitics, it provides a precise, empirical account of how knowledge about the reproduction of nonhuman life conditions how actors approach the governance of human reproduction.

Agriculture is the governance and orchestration of life—plant life, animal life, and human life—to produce more life. In this, agriculture is one of the oldest and most ubiquitous forms of biopolitical governance. Today, agriculture's objective is the production of life at multiple scales. Individuals must eat or perish. Communities risk hunger. Nations obtain food security. And the globe has a food system. Each of these statements registers a problem of governance and a logistical challenge for the maintenance of life at its variously conceived scales: individual, communal, national, and global. Governing programs identify bodies at each scale in need of sustenance and management. Food stamps and agricultural education treat consuming and producing bodies, respectively, while crop subsidy regimes target a food supply that gives vitality, in turn, to aggregated national and global populations. The production of food is arraigned as a crucial factor in projections of growth, and, similarly, projected growth shapes agricultural practices, sometimes cloaking the bucolic in a shroud of apocalyptic urgency. This procedure links the quotidian practices of individual farmers, like plowing and spraying fields, to the growth and sustenance of life in its various collective configurations. The biopolitics of agriculture exists not just within each scaled entity. It dwells in the interstices and in the labors through which those scales are constituted and coordinated. A biopolitical history of agriculture thus reveals a state anatomy in which the governance of agriculture "orchestrate[s] the conduct of the body biological, the body social, and the body politic," to quote political theorist Wendy Brown's description of biopolitics.[17]

Agricultural governance is never merely a question about how best to grow food and, thus, to produce life.[18] It is also a constant calculation and negotiation of life's value and what sorts of lives are worth living. At an intimate scale, agriculture coordinates between life and death through the obvious fact that some life—both the hog and the nubbin for its slop—is only produced to ultimately die. Farmers systematically extinguish other life, such as pests and weeds, to preserve fragile monocultures and the precarious ecosystem of industrial agriculture. The geopolitics of agriculture is just as inextricably wound into this dialectic of life and death. Driven by the demands of U.S. Cold War foreign policy objectives, the Food for Peace program and the subsequent Green Revolution moved millions of subsistence farmers throughout the global South into precarious cash cropping and urban wage labor, rendering them dependent on the importation of food stuffs. Escalating petroleum prices in the 1970s and the Soviet purchase of American crop surpluses, sealed by the sudden diplomatic urgency of détente, caused massive increases in food prices and generated deaths from famine and political instability.[19] Similarly, for the last half-century, the production of food for consumption in the global North depended on the widespread use of toxic petrochemicals in the global South. That dynamic placed the cause of life's attrition in the water, air, and soil of some communities so that other communities might consume what they liked.[20]

The historical trajectories of 4-H, agribusinesses, and the reproduction of the American state illustrate precisely how agriculture is biopolitical and, in doing so, identify neglected biopolitical valences to state power and capitalist agriculture that I call "agrarian futurism." Historians have cataloged the influence of agrarian ideas, language, and politics in the American past but have tended to characterize agrarians as antimodernists—individuals on the margins of American political culture dedicated to protecting a vanishing agricultural past from an encroaching urban, industrial future. By contrast, American agricultural expansion often produced agrarianism that was radically modernist and futurist in its orientation and that enjoyed powerful influence in centers of government well into the twentieth century. I define agrarian futurism as an ideology linking the governance of human social and biological reproduction to the practice, theory, and language of agriculture. It is agrarian in the sense that it privileges tropes, technologies, and knowledge derived from plant and animal agriculture. It is futurist in the sense that it links the intensive governance of the present in an aspirational vision of the future. To understand the powerful influence that agrarian futurism holds in American political culture—conditioning debates on topics as diverse as development programs, reproductive rights, farm policy, and estates taxes— this book locates it in the powerful fusion of agricultural expertise and modernist ambitions in the modern American state.

Agrarian futurism is conceptually, rhetorically, and materially invested in the concept of generation as an instrument of biopolitical development. The context of nineteenth-century "improved" agricultural practice acutely informed how agrarian futurists sought to manage human reproduction. Beyond the gaze of the husbandry expert, human reproduction often seemed ill timed, like a field gone to seed or planted too late in the season. In nineteenth-century agriculture, the synchronization of reproduction brought uniform plants and animals, as well as paths to enhanced future prosperity. Like most farmers throughout history, nineteenth-century farmers manipulated nonhuman reproduction according to seasonal rhythms that created discrete generations of plants and animals. A hog farmer had the sows farrow at the same time so that their offspring would be of uniform size for market. The ability to organize reproduction also enabled farmers to selectively breed and, thus, to transform animal and plant bodies for human economic purposes over ensuing generations and time scales that exceeded the span of a single human life. In both cases, generational differences—differences between parents and offspring—offered a way for farmers to coordinate between banal present tasks and future bounties, especially when the agricultural present was often impoverished.

A futurist orientation, of course, eased some of the contradictions between America's mythological origin among independent Jeffersonian homesteaders and the material reality of the United States as a settler-colonial project. Westward expansion and settlement of North America required one of the most successful projects of planned land reform in human history: the calculated dispossession of indigenous populations, redistribution of land to European populations practicing settled agriculture, and, finally, integration of settled agriculture into Atlantic trade networks. Contrary to the rhetoric of individualistic independence and self-sufficiency, this project necessitated that rural spaces be laboratories of effective governance. The largely rural West, to quote historian Richard White, was "the Kindergarten of the American state."[21] Modernist political projects ran directly through American hinterlands: innovative state-building programs, communication networks, public health initiatives, and regulatory mechanisms all emerged out of efforts to govern peripheral agricultural spaces.[22] In the twentieth century, rural America served as a vital staging ground for international development programs, neoliberal economics, and the transition to the post-Fordist service economy.[23] In all these cases, the guiding conflict was rarely between urban visions of change and a bitter and unified rural resistance. Rather, conflicts often pitted rural economic and racial classes against one another and designated some rural people as important components of governing coalitions. Indeed, many agrarian movements were modernist and utterly enamored of the ability of collective institutions to unleash powerful economic and political change.[24] Farm folk, despite the homespun rhetoric, have possessed expansive political imaginations. Their work and their lives crystallize agrarian futurism.

Tasked with improving the impoverished spaces of America's sprawling agrarian empire, USDA experts turned to these generational logics for animals, plants, and humans alike. These technocrats placed the improvement of seemingly marginal locales and bodies at the core of the nation's reproductive future. Although these technocrats diverged in fundamental ways from the agrarian modernists of the populist rebellion, they shared populism's confidence that the nation's future hinged on the transformation and budding prosperity of nonmetropolitan spaces. This inverted the typical narrative of urban modernity in which movement into the future coincided always with movement to the city.

To map 4-H as a biopolitical apparatus makes this book a work of queer political history, a declaration that may seem initially counterintuitive, given that it makes no direct comment on the histories of sexual minorities.[25] The history of 4-H challenges depictions of nonmetropolitan family life as more authentic or normal than its metropolitan counterparts. Instead, I embed the material production of youthful bodies and the reproduction of rural society squarely within the historical development of state power and capitalist agriculture in rural America. The nucleated family farm was the cultural effect of the managed industrialization of the American countryside. This site of healthy social and biological reproduction in the countryside was ever fragile, faltering, and in need of federal assistance. Such an explanation makes normalized relationships between rural people and the American state rural heterosexuality's prerequisite.

Just as the body of the 4-H'er allows us to historicize heteronormativity in rural America, it also illustrates the assembly of the American state. In other words, as the American state produces heterosexuality in rural America, heterosexuality also produces the American state.[26] In rural America, we find the state assembled out of unexpected materials. 4-H was an infrastructure composed of prized calves, symmetrical ears of corn, hand-sewn dresses, cans of tomatoes, bags of seed, precise record books, and, most important, the gendered bodies of rural youth—these all testified to rural people on the state's behalf. They endowed it with credibility and insinuated its physical presence into barns, fields, and parlors. In those locations, through the bodies of 4-H'ers, the state became an object of desire and affection and operationalized that desire and affection in its governing technologies. This infrastructure, along with its affective products, became an indispensable part of the American state's functioning and capacity, rendering vital service at moments of historical necessity such as the New Deal and World War II. Burdened with the agricultural and military demands of the wartime state of emergency, 4-H's infrastructure clarified the biopolitical stakes of agricultural production. 4-H offered healthy, vigorous bodies—individual and collective—ready to live and die for the American state.

In identifying this infrastructure, I am referencing the historical sociologist Michael Mann's concept of "infrastructural power," originally defined by Mann as "[t]he capacity of the state to actually penetrate civil society, and to implement logistically political decisions throughout the realm."[27] His concept shifts attention from the sovereign rights of the state to the technologies that actively and materially constitute governing networks; he pushes historians of the state to move from problems of law to problems of logistics and thus makes possible an empirical approach that historian William Novak calls a "bottom-up" history of governing and statecraft. 4-H'ers entered into alliance with the state, but their value to that alliance depended on their simultaneous ability to embody an innocent future; 4-H's political efficacy hinged on its political innocence. 4-H's state/civil status was always fluid, contingent, and contextual.[28] At some moments, 4-H'ers embodied the state; at other moments, they embodied its antithesis, civil society. This ambiguity was not a problem to be overcome. It was, to the contrary, a strategic asset and the very root of 4-H's political power.

* * *

This book is organized into six chapters that proceed chronologically and thematically. Just as the chapters move in a generally chronological fashion, each chapter also maps a particular biopolitical unit. The book moves in an arc from a broad regulative field of discourse (rural degeneracy and agrarian futurism in Chapter 1) to particular localized embodiments of gender (rural boys in Chapter 2 and rural girls in Chapter 3) to the idealized reproductive units assembled from those local bodies (farm families in Chapter 4) to the aggregated bodies that harnessed and redirected the labor of those reproductive units (nations and global communities at war, hot and cold, in Chapters 5 and 6).

Chapter 1 begins by tracing the development of the 4-H movement from its origins in early twentieth-century rural reform movements to its central role in the creation of the USDA's CES in 1914. Progressive Era reformers believed that the countryside—and, with it, the nation—had entered a stark and dangerous decline. Many rural communities and households, they argued, corroded body and soul, driving the fittest to cities and leaving the countryside teeming with the infirm, foolish, and deviant. For a nation rooted in agrarian virtues and a "native" population demographically dependent on the fecundity of rural families, these facts boded ill for rural populations, imagined racial futures, and national bodies alike. Faced with intractable stubbornness of ignorant, lazy farm patriarchs, reformers turned increasingly to children as instruments of transformation. Youth clubs departed dramatically from previous methods of agricultural reform because they gave government agents direct access to rural homes, educated the next generation of farmers and homemakers, and allowed rural youth to carry the banner of rural modernization. Buoyed by reports of healthy, radiant youth canning tomatoes and growing corn, Congress created the CES with the passage of the Smith-Lever Act in 1914. The legislative debate around that act crystallized the assumption that rural youth, when allied with the technocratic expertise of a federal bureaucracy, could bypass faltering rural fathers, transform rural households, and restore vigor to the national body.

Chapter 2 explores the intertwined growth of 4-H, capital-intensive agriculture, and technocratic expertise in the decade after the passage of the Smith-Lever Act. During that period, 4-H developed from an inchoate set of loosely affiliated clubs and contests to a well-organized network unified by a standard set of methods, symbols, and institutions—most notably, the National Committee on Boys and Girls Club Work (National Committee), a private, not-for-profit organization that handled 4-H's national fundraising and lobbying. Through an alliance of state expertise, local voluntary labor, and private capital, the 4-H clover sprouted in communities around the nation, enrolling more than 800,000 youth by the end of the decade. By providing rural youth with an arena for cooperation, club organizers enticed participation and habituated club members to accepting the USDA as a reliable source of knowledge and advice. By enlisting a diverse array of private local actors as the face of the 4-H program and by tightly coordinating with county farm bureaus, the USDA packaged 4-H'ers as authentic representatives of rural communities and the apotheosis of a cooperative spirit. Crucially, this cooperative spirit critiqued extant rural masculinity: the stubborn rural patriarchs who, lacking the masculine self-discipline to run their farms like businesses, begged like dependents for public relief. 4-H's allies and advocates contended that through the clubs, rural boys could develop into farmer-businessmen: men characterized by both their homespun folksiness and economic self-possession; men as comfortable at barn raisings as at financial conferences; men for whom capitalist competition was a gate to rural cooperation rather than a barrier.

The gendered reform of rural households also had significant implications for the hundreds of thousands of rural girls engaged in club work. As Chapter 3 explains, 4-H programming encouraged rural girls in the 1920s to minimize strenuous revenue-producing labor and to concentrate on cultivating beauty, health, and careful consumption in rural homes. Like the businesslike agriculture taught to rural boys in 4-H clubs, modern homemaking required the acceptance of objective, quantifiable standards provided by external technocratic expertise. Advocates of club work, both public and private, used the health of 4-H'ers to promote a variety of different, occasionally contradictory, ends: for technocrats at the USDA, robust 4-H bodies advertised the benefits of the broader extension program; for the cluster of commercial interests organized under the auspices of the National Committee, 4-H bodies advertised the advantages of robust rural consumerism. In 1926, the National Committee initiated a sophisticated lobbying campaign for legislation to increase federal appropriations for extension. This campaign focused on the benefits of club work and, in particular, the healthy, attractive youth produced by 4-H. Even as the National Committee corralled support for the legislation from across the spectrum of commercial agriculture, maternalist activists raised concerns about the organization's exploitative and pecuniary interests. The debate surrounding the Capper-Ketcham Act of 1928 ultimately hinged on a question of expert biopolitical authority: Who was best situated to protect and cultivate the health of rural youth? Resolution of that debate pitted the production-minded agricultural modernizers of the National Committee against the authority of the science of motherhood: home economics. Crucially, that debate designated the bodies of rural youth as the territory to be won.

The Great Depression and the New Deal placed 4-H at the center of rural family life, national service, and new federal programs. Chapter 4 explains how the increasing material and symbolic value of 4-H pushed the USDA to regulate the National Committee and safeguard rural youth from the corrosive effect of urban commercialism. From 1930 to 1940, 4-H expanded from about 800,000 members to more than 1.4 million, growing in visibility and reach. During that period, the variety of activities available to 4-H members and the concomitant connections between technocratic expertise and rural youth also multiplied. By the end of the decade, 4-H members were serving their communities by cooperating with the Agricultural Adjustment Administration, the SCS, the Rural Electrification Administration, and a host of cultural programs designed to edify entire rural communities. The sum of these activities "conserved the youth," as one USDA expert put it, and reinforced links between the bodies of 4-H members, farm families, rural communities and landscapes, and the modern bureaucratic state. Even as mechanization and "production control" weakened the economic justification for the farm family, club experts at the USDA presented the wholesome 4-H movement as a reason for and a means to conserve the family farm, rural society, and national fertility. Just as perfected 4-H specimens advertised the broader extension program in the 1920s, the belief that 4-H created happy marriages and healthy heterosexual relations offered powerful proof of the wisdom of federal authority in 1930s rural America. Emboldened by this cultural force, club experts finally moved to protect 4-H clubs at the end of the decade from the crass commercialism and "exploitative" behavior of the National Committee that threatened to upend federal authority and its conservation of rural youth.

The growing threat of totalitarianism and probability of war in the late 1930s led the USDA to ponder how 4-H could prepare rural America for war and inoculate rural Americans against the virus of totalitarianism. As Chapter 5 shows, by the beginning of the 1940s, many states had launched 4-H citizenship programs and sought to provide rural youth with democratic practice. Citizenship programs mixed democratic procedure with nationalist ritualism and emphasized that rural youth needed to be ready to make bodily sacrifices for the good of the nation. With the outbreak of World War II, 4-H programs encouraged rural youth to cultivate healthy bodies and copious agricultural commodities as proof of national allegiance and good citizenship.

Contrasts between the fit, vigorous bodies of all-American, white 4-H'ers and depleted foreign bodies continued in the immediate postwar moment and provided embodied evidence of the virtue of American leadership in a global age. Even as such contrasts strengthened the case for American postwar hegemony, they also shifted the focus of rural youth away from pervasive inequalities in the United States. African American critics identified the hypocrisy of promoting democracy abroad while countenancing segregation at home, and they pilloried 4-H in the national press for racial exclusion at national 4-H events. In contrast to their vigorous efforts to contain the gendered threat of the National Committee in the previous decade, USDA officials hid behind a states'-rights argument when faced with criticism from leading African American civil rights activists. Although this criticism did little to change 4-H's policies, it revealed the larger symbolic politics at work in public discussions of 4-H, which, by 1950, had become synonymous with authentic rural living and white, middle-class commercial farmers.

In the postwar period, the USDA parlayed its modernizing expertise into a broad agenda of anticommunist development in the global South. Chapter 6 surveys the growth of international 4-H programs after World War II and contends that youth-oriented development programs constituted a vital piece of that broader agenda. Based on the precedent of 4-H's experiment in the rural U.S., American-trained and -financed development technicians crafted 4-H programs for the developing world that imagined American capital, technology, and knowledge flowing into and enriching the bodies of rural youth in the global South—the fecund soil from which a cultivated future would blossom. In seventy-six countries, on every inhabited continent, 4-H programs created robust alliances between modernizing technocrats, agribusiness firms, the U.S. military, and millions of rural youth. The chapter explores three particular international 4-H programs in detail: the Japanese Agricultural Training Program, a youth exchange program that brought thousands of rural Japanese youth to labor on farms in rural America; the Programa Interamericano para la Juventud Rural, a development agency financed by the American International Association that coordinated 4-H programs across Latin America; and 4-T, the Vietnamese 4-H affiliate financed and run by the U.S. military. Across the vast expanses that separated these three Cold War battlegrounds, the unique pliability of 4-H members promised to coordinate between the contradictory elements of America's modernizing agenda: agribusinesses premised on both capitalist enterprise and statist technocracy; democracies built on both liberal tolerance and violent anticommunism; and an international order structured by both the equality of nations and U.S. interventionism. Youth's coordinating power served as a black box through which development technicians could bridge the gaps between the contradictions of the impoverished present and the prosperity of an imagined future.

4-H aspired to crossbreed technocratic expertise with country life—scientific agriculture with rural social reproduction—to produce a countryside both fertile and modern and a state both powerful and hidden. A 1909 article in the farm journal *The Homestead* described the agricultural and homemaking clubs being organized by Oscar Benson, then-superintendent of schools for Wright County, Iowa, but soon to be a paid agent of the USDA, charged with organizing 4-H clubs across the Northern states. The article laid out 4-H's agrarian futurist agenda in no uncertain terms. Benson could "give the entire corn belt pointers on how to raise a crop of young farmers who will increase the fertility of the soil and solve the problem of how to keep farm boys and girls on the farm."[29] By imagining Benson as a breeder selecting for the countryside's future and fertility, the article exposed a raw reproductive concern. That anxiety, in turn, forged a tangled relationship between 4-H's futurist ambitions and a commitment to farming as a privileged occupation in American life that persists.

Driving on U.S. Route 31 now, my eyes catch things I missed as a youth. We once drove past Grissom Air Base, just outside Kokomo. Today, the air base has been shuttered and converted into a prison. Most of the small towns I drive through are economically depressed. Northern Indiana and southern Michigan still suffer from some of the highest unemployment rates in the nation. The last three decades have been unkind to automobile manufacturing and agricultural production in this corner of the Rust Belt. There are still fruit stands, but some operators will candidly tell you that they are selling produce grown in California or abroad and shipped in at prices that undercut locally grown produce. If grown locally or in California, Latino migrant laborers, many of them undocumented, do most of the fruit picking. (The proliferation of Mexican bars and restaurants in small Indiana towns subtly signals this fact.) Aside from these new details, there is, however, a constant. Those same signs—the ones with the four-leafed clover—cheerfully greet travelers up and down U.S. Route 31. Agrarian futurism still binds peripheries and centers, humans and animals, reproduction and governance even as the American century now fades beyond the last row.

CHAPTER ONE

Agrarian Futurism, Rural Degeneracy, and the Origins of 4-H

For this educational work now being carried on through the Department of Agriculture will be like leaven in the meal, leavening the whole lump; for new ideas have the quality of reproduction. . . . We are just at the beginning of this movement, which will make a transformation in the minds of young men equal to that which machinery has made in the methods of older men.

—"A Little Child Shall Lead Them," *Wallaces Farmer*, December 3, 1915

Will Otwell built a pyramid of corn. In the Palace of Agriculture of the 1904 World's Fair in St. Louis, the commissioner of education for the Illinois World's Fair Commission arranged ears of corn into a great ziggurat ten thousand ears large, each ear gathered from the prizewinning entries of the Illinois boys' corn contests that Otwell had been organizing in Illinois since 1901. In front of this pyramid, perhaps as homage to an Egyptian obelisk, Otwell erected a single towering ear of corn assembled from the same entries. Thousands of fairgoers passed through the Palace and marveled at King Corn given architectural form, and Otwell's exhibit invited each spectator to take home a packet's worth of fine seed corn. Through these careful arrangements, Otwell made a monument "to the industry and intelligence of 8,000 Illinois farmer boys," one representative of the USDA remarked, on witnessing the exhibit.[1]

The exhibit, like the World's Fair around it, exposed the agrarian futurist impulses underwriting America's burgeoning empire. Framed around the hundred-year anniversary of the Louisiana Purchase, the fair commemorated a century's worth of agricultural expansion and visually linked the nation's rise as an international power to the successful internal conquest of nature

Figure 1. The Illinois Boys' Corn Exhibit at the 1904 St. Louis World's Fair.

through settled agriculture. Near exotic ethnological exhibits of primitives drawn from far-flung colonial possessions and peripheries, individual states displayed bounties in the Palace of Agriculture grown on their most impressive, modern farms. For Illinois, the intricate corn structures, built from ears selected for their even rows and plump kernels, figuratively testified to the enduring virility of Illinois's corn farmers. Through its hopeful invocation of youth, the exhibit envisioned a national future of abundance bred of technocratic expertise and rural fertility. Alongside that figurative assertion of virility, the accompanying seed samples intended a literal dissemination—a plan for the strong seed of the Illinois farmer boys to impregnate fertile soil from Grand Island to Canton.

At the turn of the twentieth century in America, such hopeful visions for the countryside mingled with disturbing reports of growing depravity, criminality, and venereal disease in decaying rural quarters previously toasted as holdfasts of national virtue and healthy reproduction. Witnessing rural "degeneration and demoralization" in 1893, Social Gospel activist Josiah Strong warned that if rural out-migration continued unabated, he could "see no reason why isolation, irreligion, ignorance, vice and degradation should not increase in the country until we have a rural peasantry, illiterate and immoral, possessing the rights of citizenship, but utterly incapable of performing or comprehending its duties." In 1897, the poet Walter M. Rogers eulogized "the strong Green Mountain boy" in a poem called "Vermont's Deserted Farms," a demise marked on the landscape by "the shattered homes/ all crumbling to decay,/ like long-neglected catacombs/ of races passed away." Reports of rural degeneracy were the nightmarish underbelly of agrarian futurism's cheerful utopianism. Too many rural communities fell prey to out-migration and inbreeding, rural reformers complained. Rather than questioning agrarian futurism's focus on the fertile possibilities of youthful rural bodies, tales of rural degeneracy assumed them—with a twist. If the reproductive possibilities of rural youth could be harnessed to produce a better future, what frightful perils attended their neglect? Where had the youthful virility of "the strong Green Mountain boy" gone? And would the Illinois farmer boy join him in this racial passing, littering the Corn Belt with the same "shattered homes"?[2]

In a moment when the future of agricultural landscapes was linked so intimately to healthy racial reproduction, Will Otwell's efforts were poised to render all those questions moot. He directed the construction of the corn exhibit but had also pioneered the youth contests and clubs that had produced the corn—associations that were years in the making and that Otwell reported dramatically improved interest in the scientific cultivation of corn among boys as well as adult farmers. His approach was effective but was hardly unique. Across the Corn Belt and Deep South, a similar complex of clubs and contests blossomed throughout the first decade of the twentieth century. Educators, bureaucrats, bankers, and reformers alike identified youth clubs as an effective way to reach rural youth and, through them, farmers. Propelled by the success and notoriety of youth-oriented workers like Otwell, the U.S. Congress moved to formally subsidize agricultural extension and agricultural youth club work in 1914, with the passage of the Smith-Lever

Act. Debate on Smith-Lever revealed that, more than simply a system to promote scientific agriculture, youth clubs were also intended to husband the nation's future in a time of reproductive uncertainty. On the floor of Congress, advocates of the extension bill identified clubs as a powerful tool to stanch the dysgenic flow to the city and, with it, rural degeneracy. Through such strategies, early advocates of agricultural youth clubs aligned a vision of normal racial reproduction with the presence of diffuse federal power in the countryside.

* * *

Federal interest in agricultural youth clubs initially emerged out of efforts to materially improve conditions in America's rapidly expanding farmlands in the late nineteenth century, but it was tied as well to efforts to reconcile the nation's seemingly urban destiny with its agrarian past. The increase of cultivated acreage and production across the United States during this period brought attendant concerns about pervasive rural poverty, moral and physical degeneracy, and inefficient farming techniques that complicated equally pervasive celebrations of the homesteading farmer as the source of national character. Middle-class reformers, both urban and rural, promoted "progressive" and "scientific" practices in the countryside, intending to improve rural living conditions, increase the nation's agricultural bounty, and safeguard the countryside's reproductive future. By the early twentieth century, agricultural progressives like Seaman Knapp were contending that existing means of rural reform—farmers' institutes, pamphlets, and agricultural colleges—were insufficient, particularly in the impoverished South. Knapp argued that proponents of progressive country life needed to journey to the afflicted communities and farms to demonstrate their findings. He built an alliance among state experts, commercial interests, and farm families, using a method that became known as cooperative agricultural extension. Extension placed an agent of the state agricultural college in rural communities and among farmers, bringing the insights of scientific agriculture directly to farmers without intermediaries. No longer would farmers need to seek out the insights of the USDA and land-grant colleges. Agricultural extension would bring it to their doorsteps and into their homes.

In the second half of the nineteenth century, primarily through the USDA and the Department of the Interior, the federal government subsidized agricultural expansion in a number of ways. The USDA directly assisted farmers by distributing millions of seeds, free of cost. Federal monies helped to establish a network of universities partially dedicated to agricultural research and education through the Morrill Acts of 1862 and 1890. After the 1887 Hatch Act, agricultural scientists conducted research at experimental stations in every state. The Department of the Interior dispersed millions of acres of land to homesteaders and underwrote sundry and ambitious irrigation schemes. Congress granted millions more acres of land to railroad companies to finance the construction of a rail network that could cheaply and quickly transport agricultural commodities from remote farmlands to eastern markets. As some federal agencies provided direct and indirect subsidy for agricultural expansion in the West, federal military power worked to remove any indigenous population that threatened the power of white settlers.[3]

Between 1850 and 1900, the total number of farms in the nation quadrupled and total land in farms grew from 293 million acres to 841 million, primarily driven by vast agricultural expansion west of the Mississippi. The transformation of the prairies, plains, and deserts of the West into farmland provided new opportunities for families willing to endure backbreaking labor and the grueling deprivations of homesteading. Over the second half of the nineteenth century, the average size of farms in the North Central census region—an area encompassing all states north of the Mason-Dixon line from Ohio to Kansas—hovered between 121 and 145 acres, as tens of thousands of families took advantage of the cheap acreage offered by the Homestead Act and helped to create nearly 1.5 million new small farms. In the Western census region, where vast tracts of arid land could ill support more than cattle grazing absent large-scale, capital-intensive irrigation, larger farms were the norm. Nevertheless, the 1900 census recorded 242,000 farms in the Western census region, where just more than six thousand had existed in 1850.[4]

Even as federal largesse helped push millions of acres into farm production, advances in agricultural technology and agricultural practice—tractors, commercial fertilizers, more widespread observance of crop rotation, and improved seed and animal selection—enabled some farmers to improve yields and easily farm larger tracts of land.[5] Highly mechanized operations required a large initial investment, so smaller farms frequently did without them. As a result, scientific agriculture was frequently both a cause and an effect of affluence: only the wealthiest farmers could afford to innovate, and thus, only the wealthiest farmers could enjoy the benefits of innovation. Nevertheless, the progressive agricultural movement of the late nineteenth century—a movement of agriculturalists, scientists, and commercial farmers who planned to modernize American agriculture through improved planning, education,

and technology—touted agricultural innovation as a path to wise management and moral virtue. Unproductive farms, their thinking went, were symptomatic of the ignorance, sloth, and greediness of operators unable to read
up on modern practices, too content to fish rather than toil, and too willing
to sacrifice the long-term health of their land for one bumper crop. By the
turn of the twentieth century, innovations in plant biology, animal breeding,
and farming technology were encouraging agriculturalists at land-grant colleges, in the agricultural technology industry, and in the farm press to talk of
a science of farming in which experts could objectively describe the correct
methods to maximize yields and profit from a particular crop, as well as to
organize and manage an entire farm household. Despite the lauded objectiv-
ity of their methods, poorer farmers frequently chafed at the condescension
of agricultural progressives, derisively dismissing it as mere "book farming."[6]

Scientific farming, mechanization, and the massive expansion of crop-
land bolstered the nation's agricultural output but did little to improve living conditions across rural America relative to the cities. Throughout the
settled North, many farmers barely scraped by, mixing subsistence farming
with commercial farming. Homesteaders found frontier life hard and new
land less fecund than promised. Even the modest amenities of rural living
in the East, such as roads, common schools, and proximity to established
communities were altogether absent across much of the West. Years of hard
labor in miserable conditions—chronic hunger, pervasive squalor, great
distances to potable water, rampant disease, and social isolation—were frequently required to turn a prairie into a profitable field. Many farmers abandoned or sold their holdings rather than persevere, or went into heavy debt
to finance and modernize their operations. In large portions of the arid West,
homesteaders sold their farms to holding companies when they discovered
that they lacked, even collectively, the capital necessary to irrigate their land.
Individuals and companies with the resources to mechanize farm operations
gobbled up cheap land from the bankrupt, only to retain the broken farmers
as tenants or wage laborers. Tenancy and sharecropping characterized the
bulk of Southern agriculture. African American farmers toiled under the
weight of vicious racism, intense poverty, and constrained labor mobility.
Poor white Southern farmers fared only slightly better. In 1900, agricultural
labor was abysmally compensated relative to other labor: a year of farmwork earned an average income of $260, while nonfarmworkers averaged
$622.[7] These factors contributed to substantial rural out-migration, particu-
larly as rising prices for arable land in the West squeezed opportunities for
rural resettlement. Growth in number of farms, cultivated acres, and rural

population slowed considerably from Gilded Age breakneck paces, and the 1910 census ominously reported that, while national and urban populations had grown at 21 percent and 35 percent, respectively, the rural population had grown only 11 percent, and it was "probable that the agricultural population had increased even less rapidly." States ringing the Great Lakes reported slight declines in rural populations for the first time in their history.[8]

For many elite commentators, the rough truths of rural poverty made fine clay for more sensational narratives about a civilizational decline rooted in the reproductive implications of urbanization. Capturing this perspective in a 1901 essay in the *Annals of the American Academy of Political and Social Science*, prominent sociologist Edward Alsworth Ross coined the term "race suicide" to describe a reproductive crisis in which the "higher [Anglo Saxon] race quietly and unmurmuringly eliminates itself" by failing to procreate as prolifically as members of the "inferior race[s]." Ross's position took historian Frederick Jackson Turner's influential "frontier thesis," which held that access to the Western frontier provided both stability and dynamism to American society, and stretched it into a commentary on the invidious demographic effects of frontier closure and accompanying urbanization.[9] As Ross explained it, once acclimated to the luxuries of the city, the white, middle-class "gradually delay[ed] marriage and restrict[ed] the size of the family," allowing urban immigrants from inferior races to demographically eclipse "the prudent, self-respecting natives." Ross consoled readers that, in the United States, recent experiences on the frontier might stave off race suicide for a time. "The American . . . has been chiefly a farmer and is only beginning to expose himself to the deteriorating influences of city and factory," he wrote.[10] Warnings of race suicide received wider public attention when, beginning in 1902, President Theodore Roosevelt used the term in letters and speeches to condemn those who shirked their reproductive duties and became "criminal against the race."[11] In April 1903, when Roosevelt embarked on a Western speaking tour, historian Gail Bederman notes, he "grabbed the chance to encourage the American race to breed" and placed the menace of an urbanization-driven race suicide in the headlines of many American newspapers.[12]

Historians have often filed these sentiments under the pervasive anti-urbanism of the early twentieth century in the United States, but this particular brand of anti-urbanism depended upon concomitant tales of rural degeneracy.[13] The dangers to gendered and racial order posed by urbanization reiterated a well-established nostalgic agrarianism that traced back, at least, to Jeffersonian celebrations of yeoman farmers, and it capitalized on the white middle class's discomfort with the visible ethnic and racial diversity abounding in the nation's bustling metropolises. But for Roosevelt, Ross, and many other prophets of race suicide, the countryside's presumed fecundity went hand in hand with the need for rural reform, and proponents of rural reform usually assumed rural degeneracy and decline in its absence. Aside from being an inveterate proponent of race suicide and eugenic theory, Roosevelt was also the nation's most powerful rural reformer and the convener of the National Commission on Country Life in 1908, arguably the climax of the progressive agricultural movement. In the same article in which he coined "race suicide," Ross complained about "the listlessness and social decay noticeable in many of the rural communities and old historic towns on the Atlantic slope." For Roosevelt and Ross, concerns about the vice and immorality of the city fueled the urgency of rural reform. The ailments of city and country reinforced a downward spiral in which excessive rural to urban migration created parasitic dependencies between a decadent metropolis and its degenerate hinterlands. "Cities have the best of the human material," complained Orator Fuller Cook, a prominent eugenics advocate and plant scientist at the USDA, in an essay arguing for rural educational reform. "But [cities] spoil [human material] in the making, and must continue to import rural talent to make good the deterioration."[14]

"Folk depletion," as Ross would later call that "import [of] rural talent" to cities, proceeded precisely because of the abundant, fecund possibilities of rural bodies assumed by nostalgic agrarianism. By folk depletion, Ross meant the tendency of the best rural youth to abandon country life for excitement and profit in the city. Those who remained on the farm, according to this narrative, were typically the least intelligent and moral, and rural isolation did little to improve the situation. Ross memorably quoted one rural informant who scoffed at the supposed "purity of the open country.... The moral conditions among our country boys and girls are worse than in the lowest tenement house in New York." On long and lonely winter nights, the informant continued, "What is more natural than that the boys should get together in the barn and while away the long winter evenings talking obscenity, telling filthy stories, recounting sex exploits, encouraging one another in vileness, perhaps indulging in unnatural practices?" What could it mean for the farm boys to behave "naturally ... unnatural"? Agrarianism held that farms were naturally more fecund and conducive to reproductivity than the sterile mechanization of the city. But, as Cook warned, "the instincts which lie at the basis of the family and the preservation and development of the race are likewise capable of endless perversions." As uncontrolled out-migration disrupted social constraints, it also eroded the outlets that guided farm boys' surging libidos to fruitful marriage and procreation. The natural desires of farm boys thus gave way to unnatural practices. But the situation was remediable, Ross argued, by rationalizing and managing rural out-migration. Ross's informant's perspective, like Cook's, contained the seeds of both modernist and agrarian logics: they reaffirmed the countryside's unique reproductive potential even as they insisted that such human fertility be larded as jealously as the soil's.[15]

Ross's concerns about farm boys' "unnatural practices" dovetailed with broader worries about the mounting perversity and degeneracy of the white, rural poor. Rather than calling attention to the extreme material deprivations of rural life, these narratives often reframed the unsightliness of rural poverty as a moral, mental, and genetic pathology. A host of eugenic family studies depicted the rural remnants as thoroughly perverse and degraded, partly to justify the more rational governance of human desire and reproduction. Studies of the Jukes (1877 and 1916), the Kallikaks (1912), the Nams (1912), and the Hill families (1912), among others, identified white, poor rural families as wellsprings of congenital "idiocy," criminality, and mental disease wrought of extensive incest and poor breeding.[16] In their 1919 study of Ohio country churches, Gifford Pinchot and Charles Otis Gill echoed concerns about inbreeding when they noted pervasive sexual immorality in rural communities with "inefficient churches." Pinchot and Gill warned: "Syphilitic and other venereal diseases are common and increasing over whole counties. While in some communities nearly every family is afflicted with inherited or infectious disease. Many cases of incest are known, inbreeding is rife. Imbeciles, feebleminded, and delinquents are numerous."[17] Doctors also pointed to the surprising prevalence of venereal diseases among rural residents. One study of Michigan, for example, found that syphilis infections were present in nearly a third of all the autopsies of rural residents, a rate of prevalence considerably higher than those found in urban communities. (Other doctors argued that the study's conclusions were an artifact of a less rigorous diagnostic standard.) By 1920, medical authorities cited pervasive degeneracy and venereal disease to explain why, during World War I, rural men had been disproportionately found unfit for military service.[18]

Although such reports of rural degeneracy made broad generalizations about the collective pathologies of rural spaces, rural reformers typically used tales of malformed reproduction to justify personal rather than structural reform. "These sad stories of rural degeneracy must not make us pessimists," warned George Walter Fiske, a junior dean at the Oberlin Theological Seminary, in The Challenge of the Country (1912). "These communities

however warn us that even self-respecting rural villages are in danger of following the same sad process of decay unless they are kept on the high plane
of wholesome Christian living and community efficiency."[19] Fiske linked the
"rural problem" to "social and economic adjustment," noting that degeneracy was most acute "in the isolated places among the hills or in unfertile
sections which have been deserted by the ambitious and intelligent, leaving
a pitiable residuum of 'poor whites' behind." Solutions to rural degeneracy
encompassed a broad variety of rural reforms, from encouraging scientific
agriculture to better recreational opportunities in rural communities. At
the heart of all these efforts, however, resided the unifying assumption that
personal transformation was both the object and the instrument of rural
reform. As Liberty Hyde Bailey, a leading agricultural progressive and dean
of the College of Agriculture at Cornell University, wrote in *The State and the
Farmer* (1908): "The great country problems are now human rather than tech-
nically agricultural." To ensure that the rural labor force could meet the needs
of progressive agriculture, reformers schemed to modernize all elements of
rural living—first and foremost, through education. "We much need to know
how to use our increasing technical knowledge," Bailey continued, "and to
systematize it into practical ideals of personal living."[20]

Such a strategy of education hinged on the transformative possibilities
of youth. Uprooted youth were at the heart of Ross's theory of folk depletion. Turn-of-the-century education reformers and child-development theorists spoke of youth as the key moment of personal development, the period
when individual personality was cast irrevocably toward normalcy or aber-
rance, health or perversion.[21] Their supposed flexibility made young people
both ideal subjects for personal reform and potent threats to social stability, and that double bind only intensified the focus on youth in discussions
of the "rural problem." For example, Fiske emphasized youth by including
"the country boy," smiling and towheaded, in *The Challenge of the Country's*
frontispiece. "Why does he want to leave his father's farm to go to the city?"
wondered the picture's caption. "He ought to be able to find his highest happiness and usefulness in the country, his native environment, where he is sadly
needed." Fiske summarized his youth-oriented approach to the "peril of rural
depletion and threatened degeneracy" as a call to "consecrated young manhood and womanhood" to become the agents of a "reconstructed rural life."[22]

A reconstructed rural life might keep the best youth on farms, but it
demanded better methods that extended expert lessons into rural communities and homes. Proponents of agricultural extension argued that their innovative methods effectively circulated the advice of university professors and

THE COUNTRY BOY

Why does he want to leave his father's farm to go to the city? He ought to be able to find his highest happiness and usefulness in the country, his native environment, where he is sadly needed. Can we make it worth while for this boy to invest his life in rural leadership?

Figure 2. "The Country Boy," frontispiece to George Walter Fiske's *The Challenge of the Country* (1912).

USDA officials in rural communities and, in the process, discredited their homespun skeptics, scoffers, and critics. Federal support for agricultural extension was eventually forthcoming, thanks in no small part to the work of Seaman Knapp. Knapp was born in upstate New York in 1833 and educated at Union College. Over the course of five decades, he became one of the nation's most prolific agriculturalists. He served as the second president of Iowa State Agricultural College before leaving the position in 1886 to operate a rice plantation in Louisiana. His time in Iowa also introduced him to "Tama" James Wilson, the future secretary of agriculture in the administrations of William McKinley and Theodore Roosevelt. In 1898, Knapp journeyed to Japan, China, and the Philippines on behalf of the USDA to gather exceptional rice seed and study rice cultivation practices. He made similar trips to East Asia for the USDA in 1901 and to Puerto Rico in 1902. In 1902, he was appointed "Special Agent for the Promotion of Agriculture in the South" for the USDA.

Knapp believed that educating Southern farmers about correct agricultural practices could ensure prosperity even amid the boll weevil blight. He established an experimental farm in Terrell, Texas, where local farmers could cultivate plots using his methods. Local elites contributed to a guaranty fund that would cover the risks for participants, while Knapp and the USDA provided advice and instruction. The scheme worked beautifully. One demonstrator, Walter Porter, claimed a $700 profit, a result that was widely publicized. Wilson solicited an emergency appropriation from Congress for $40,000—loosely justified by the continuing advance of the boll weevil—which Knapp spent, with Wilson's approval, on the creation of more demonstration farms and the hiring of "cooperative demonstration agents." Knapp built an ambitious network of agricultural extension throughout the South, broad enough to reach all rural residents, young and old, white and black. He also hired African American home demonstrators, starting with Thomas Campbell of Alabama. By 1910, the General Education Board, flush with Rockefeller money, had matched the USDA's contributions, which it eventually exceeded, all the while leaving Knapp fully in control of the administration of the network. In 1911, when Knapp died, the USDA employed 450 cooperative demonstrators in twelve states.[23]

Knapp instructed his agents to work with youth in addition to adults. Such an approach attended to the problem of restless farm youth and offered satisfaction to those boys and girls most likely to contribute to Ross's folk depletion. But it rested as well on the strategic possibilities of targeting youth. Knapp recognized that, by working with youth, his agents could bypass his most resistant rural critics altogether. He hired county superintendents to oversee youth clubs at the local level and enlisted other educators to organize club work across entire states. In 1909, for example, he hired Luther N. Duncan, a young professor of agriculture at Alabama Polytechnic, to supervise club work across the state. In 1913, the USDA claimed seventy thousand "boy demonstrators" and thirty thousand "girl demonstrators" in the South working under the supervision of O. B. Martin, the agriculturalist in charge of boys' and girls' club work. As political scientist Daniel P. Carpenter notes, "Knapp set out to transform southern agriculture through the systematic education of farm youth."[24] It is the "through" in Carpenter's description that needs emphasis. In its fully developed form, extension made rural youth into conduits for federal power and capital-intensive agriculture. In that scheme, a focus on children created a peculiar dependency. By firmly planting children in country soil, a government agency promised healthy reproduction to rural America. But the multiplication of healthy boys and girls on American farms also multiplied points of contact, allies, and agents for an expanding technocratic state, extending its reach into scattered parlors, orchards, and barns. As youth became a strategy of development in those spaces, normal social reproduction increasingly aligned with the robust capacity of the federal state, particularly the USDA.

*   *   *

Cultural anxieties about rural degeneracy and dreams of perfected futures converged in the figure of the rural child, and they took shape as practical problems of the education, rearing, and development of rural children. The first rural youth clubs emerged from an alliance drawn from school superintendents, wealthy farmers, country bankers, and university professors, with the USDA only later joining as the institution best situated to mediate among the potentially conflicting interests of those varied players. In the earliest, experimental iterations, rural youth clubs supplemented ailing country schoolhouses, to the delight of agricultural and educational reformers. In addition to blending agricultural and educational expertise in a single unified network, rural youth clubs depended upon a reexamination of rural homes, families, and parenting: What role did the internal dynamics of rural families play in the problem of rural degeneracy? Were rural parents to blame? How could reformers correct parents already unwilling to accept the tested, profitable wisdom of agricultural experts? Rural youth clubs promised to bypass two rotten players driving rural degeneracy: bad parents and bad schools.

Seaman Knapp's focus on rural youth offered the first federal support for rural youth clubs. He expanded on a class of programs in which agricultural progressives proposed to address two lingering problems: the reluctance of farmers to accept the suggestions of agricultural experts; and the inability of rural schools to meet the vocational needs of rural youth. Agricultural progressives tended to regard these problems as interrelated. Because rural schools failed to address the needs of rural youth, farmers dismissed the insights of education in general and the rigorous scientific thinking required of modern agriculture. Because farmers sneered at book farming, they also refused to recognize the potential of a comprehensive education system. While rural public schools could hardly be done away with, agricultural extension programs could reach rural youth on the farm directly. Extension programs for youth began with the notion of attracting youth through contests but quickly expanded into more comprehensive club programs in which rural youth gathered in small groups to receive instruction in agriculture and home economics. Through these programs, agricultural progressives believed that they could insinuate themselves into ordinary farm households that were otherwise resistant to modern methods, create new allies, and shape the next generation of rural people.

By 1900, Will Otwell had witnessed the frustrating apathy of farmers in his community toward the recommendations of scientific agriculture. As secretary of his county farmers' institute in central Illinois, he assisted the president of the institute in organizing a meeting. After running ads in thirteen papers throughout the county, the president opened the doors several hours early in anticipation of a great audience of farmers. Attendance disappointed. The institute chaplain led the crowd of three, a count that included Otwell, the president, and the chaplain, in "a fervent prayer for the officers of the organization." For the next meeting, the president changed tactics. He commissioned the printing of five hundred "gilt-edged programmes" and mailed them, "like wedding invitations, in nice square envelopes," to the farmers of the county. Attendance improved to only two dozen. The president resigned in embarrassment.[25]

Otwell succeeded to the presidency of the institute and tried an entirely different approach. First, he contacted successful corn growers from around the region and "procured 12 samples of first-class seed corn." Next, he summoned the leading farmers of the county and arranged for them to produce from the samples, at two dollars per bushel, a supply of seed corn. After some fund-raising, Otwell offered as much of the seed as could be sent for one cent of postage to any boy under eighteen, with the promise of forty one-dollar premiums and one two-horse plow awarded to the most outstanding results. The boys were instructed to attend the farmers' institute so that they could have their corn scored by a professor from the college at Champaign. The entire county buzzed in anticipation of the institute. When the appointed day arrived, scores of boys with bushels of corn and more than five hundred adult farmers flooded the meeting. The next year, Otwell repeated the contest—this time, with more lavish prizes. Fifteen hundred boys competed for the prizes in each of the successive years, and Otwell's contest drew attention and praise all over the state. His method attracted to the institute farm boys and "[f]armers who two years before would not attend, and who boldly asserted that 'they had forgotten more than those speakers would ever find out.'" The USDA's Dick Crosby glowed that "the problem of arousing an interest in farmers' institutes . . . has been solved. The farmers were reached through their children, and the interest thus aroused will be handed down to their children's children."[26] While corn contests were not Otwell's unique innovation, his experiences were representative of many agricultural progressives who found children more receptive to their lessons than parents were.

Educational reformers identified rural schools as an unusually thorny problem in the national educational landscape. Because of low population density, rural schools usually enrolled fewer than several dozen students spread over twelve grades, all of whom were instructed by a single teacher in a single room—frequently a dilapidated room. As late as 1920, half of the nation's schoolchildren lived in rural sections; in the same year, nearly 200,000 one-room schools still operated in the American countryside.[27] The low pay, unattractive living conditions, and even more miserable working conditions associated with rural teaching made attracting and retaining qualified educators difficult. Desperate for teachers, Horace Culter and Julia Madge Stone lamented in 1913, rural schools often employed newly minted educators who, "if they are successful . . . go into the city, simply because the city would pay more than the country was willing to pay."[28] Even with competent teachers, rural schools often focused only on a curriculum of writing, reading, and arithmetic. Educational reformers derided that focus as inadequate for the needs of rural students and as unlikely to attract their interest. To accommodate demand for child labor on farms, many country schools were in session for only twenty to thirty weeks during the year. To make matters worse, distances and parental apathy meant that some farm children avoided school altogether. Even as educational reformers identified serious problems with rural schools, their solutions—school consolidation, mandatory attendance, professionalization, and more extensive state and federal oversight—expanded the prerogatives of agents of the state at the expense of parental and local control. As educational reformers depicted their programs as technocratic, apolitical solutions to rural social problems, many rural people bitterly resisted them as the political encroachments of meddling outsiders.[29]

Rural reformers comfortable with increasing the state's rural reach, however, found convenient common cause with school reformers. For example,
the National Commission on Country Life placed the improvement of rural
schools at the forefront of its recommendations to the nation. President
Theodore Roosevelt asked Liberty Hyde Bailey to chair the commission
and appointed to it sundry prominent agricultural progressives, including
"Uncle" Henry Wallace, a successful Iowa commercial farmer and publisher
of *Wallaces Farmer*; Kenyon Butterfield, president of the Massachusetts Agricultural College; and Gifford Pinchot, the prolific chief of the U.S. Forest Service and later coauthor of *Six Thousand Country Churches* and governor of
Pennsylvania. The commission solicited input from around the nation, sending out half a million circular letters and holding public hearings in thirty
locations across the country. In January 1909, it issued its findings. "The subject of paramount importance in our correspondence and in the hearings is
education," stated the commission. "In every part of the United States there
seems to be one mind, on the part of those capable of judging, on the necessity of redirecting the rural schools. There is no such unanimity on any other
subject." Poor rural schools, the commission reported, were responsible for
virtually all the problems of rural life, "ineffective farming, lack of ideals, and
the drift to town."[30]

Rural schools were not deteriorating, the report contended; rather, they
were in a state of "arrested development" and were failing to adapt themselves
to the evolving needs of rural people. This was most acutely apparent in the
absence of instruction in agriculture and home economics in rural schools.
The commission recommended several changes to address these problems.
There would need to be a greater curricular emphasis on the "real needs of
the people" in rural schools—agriculture and the "home subjects," in particular. A significant part of the solution would also come from restructuring the
system of rural education entirely, making rural schools only a small part of
a larger comprehensive educational program. Rural educators needed to tear
down the barrier between homes and schools and the similarly false division between work and learning. Rural educational reformers should better
integrate schoolteachers into rural communities and create a complementary
system of "continuing education" outside schools through extension. The
USDA, the commission concluded, provided the "best extension work now
proceeding in this country," and its program, including "boys' and girls' clubs
of many kinds," should be emulated and systematized nationwide.[31]

The "boys' and girls' clubs" that the report referenced had initially blossomed without the benefit of explicit federal support but had instead been

the innovation of rural school superintendents. By the time the Louisiana Purchase Exposition asked Will Otwell to hold a statewide contest and to exhibit the results in the Palace of Agriculture in 1904, eight thousand boys were enrolled in his corn contests. Educators quickly recognized that these contests offered an entry point for a more elaborate vocational education in the form of regular youth clubs. "The State College of Agriculture, the Illinois Farmers' Institute, and the county institute secretaries and county superintendents of schools" encouraged corn contestants to form clubs where they could meet to discuss their methods and results under the supervision of master farmers and expert agriculturalists. O. J. Kern, a school superintendent in Winnebago County, founded the first such club in the state in February 1902 and attracted thirty-two members.[32] By 1905, two thousand boys across the state belonged to "corn" or "experiment" clubs. The clubs connected promoters of progressive agriculture with individual farmers and rural youth. Traveling libraries regularly visited the clubs and offered the boys access to a "liberal sprinkling of standard agricultural books, and the bulletins and other publications of the State experiment station and of the United States Department of Agriculture." Club leaders invited successful farmers, professors of agriculture, and other agricultural experts to speak to their members. Clubs also toured the more prosperous farms in their counties and occasionally embarked on longer trips to institutes, experiment stations, and agricultural colleges. At the conclusion of the year, club leaders awarded exemplary members a "diploma or other certificates" to mark their efforts. While most clubs focused on the cultivation of corn, the clubs also provided a venue to discuss other crops and more generic farming issues. Though organized in coordination with educational professionals, the early Illinois boys' club movement fused state subsidies with private support to promote progressive agriculture outside the benighted country schoolhouse.[33]

Similar efforts developed simultaneously across the Corn Belt and in the Deep South, winning attention and support from Seaman Knapp.[34] While early clubs were similar to "nature study" clubs in some ways, they focused on practical problems involved in agricultural production. A. B. Graham organized corn and tomato clubs in western Ohio, holding the first meetings in the basement of the Springfield public building in January 1902. He explained that the clubs would teach boys "elementary knowledge" about agriculture, just as girls would learn "the simplest facts of domestic economy," and would "inspire young men and young women to further their education in the science of agriculture or domestic science."[35] William H. Smith, superintendent of education in Holmes County, Mississippi, organized corn clubs for boys and "culture study" clubs for girls in 1906. His work caught Knapp's eye, and, after 1907, Knapp promoted similar programs in all states where his cooperative demonstrators worked.[36]

From the start, the Southern clubs interested adults in the agricultural activities of their children and created a new channel of communication between farmers and agricultural experts. Earlie Cleveland of Decatur, Mississippi, reported that his previously indifferent father was now invested in the practices of scientific agriculture. Papa Cleveland could be found "hustling Round for seed corn" to help his son improve his contest acre of corn. The Boykin brothers of Maury, Virginia, wrote that "Papa and Mama are both interested in this work. They both help us and are proud of our efforts." Loucas Puckett of Dresden, Tennessee, proudly announced that he had his "father and mother interested in the Agricultural work" through his club activities. At other times, the corn clubs pitted rural children *against* their parents. Perry T. Dill of Taylor, South Carolina, provided Knapp with his father's address and requested that, though his father was not in demonstration work, the Department of Agriculture should write to him and give him "any thing you have to help him in his farm work." Though Paul Burtner's father was "simply not on our side," the Harrisonburg, Virginia, boy thought that his father would "gratefully receive any bulletins or other literature. . . . I am hopeful of winning him over." In these cases, the clubs created persistent allies inside rural homes.[37]

Although Knapp's support was important, Oscar Herman Benson, the USDA's club expert in the Northern states, honed Knapp's philosophy further by explaining how youth work, more than any other phase of extension, had the potential to convert farmers to the gospel of scientific agriculture. Benson played a crucial role in the early formation of the agricultural youth club movement, presiding over Northern club work for almost a decade before leaving to run the Junior Achievement Bureau in 1920. Benson, born and raised on a farm in southwest Iowa, studied at the University of Iowa, Iowa State Teachers' College, and, eventually, the University of Chicago.[38] At the turn of the century, the University of Chicago was a hive of progressivism and home to some of the leading advocates of educational reform, including John Dewey, George Herbert Mead, and Colonel Francis Parker. Dewey and other progressive education reformers rejected the distinction between "ethical consciousness (concerned with ends)" and "practical execution (the employment of means)" in education.[39] Upon his return to Iowa as superintendent of education for Wright County, Benson merged some of Dewey's principles with the teachings of "corn evangelist" P. G. Holden, using the "club acre" on the farm to be "the laboratory for the rural school."[40] William J. Spillman, the head of the Office of Farm Management for the northern and western states at the USDA, impressed with Knapp's work in the South, hoped to replicate a similar extension system across the North, including the now-famous Southern corn and canning clubs. Benson captured Spillman's attention and, in 1910, Benson was hired by the Bureau of Plant Industry to supervise and promote club work throughout the North. Working in cooperation with county superintendents of education, USDA field agents, and agricultural specialists at land-grant colleges, Benson concentrated on spreading corn clubs for boys and canning clubs for girls.[41]

According to Benson, corn clubs advanced a host of objectives, both practical and abstract. He argued that corn clubs promoted efficient, profitable corn agriculture by stimulating the competitive interests of rural boys and providing them with the needed intellectual and material support. Boys were urged to cultivate no less than one acre of corn and to lavish it with as much care, attention, and fertilizer as they could spare. They were also required to "follow instructions," regularly attend club meetings and sponsored talks, and keep detailed records of their work, which would be submitted to club organizers. The results would be placed in competition and premiums awarded on the basis of a formula that took into account yield, profit, quality of their county fair exhibit, and quality of their project records. Exceptional results would be entered in a national contest, known as the "All Star Corn Clubs." Benson believed that the competitive instincts of participants would push them to integrate "the best known methods of soil-building, selection of seed, [and] seed tests" to secure the highest yield and greatest profits. The practice of scientific agriculture could then "offer a medium through which interest, inspiration, and careful direction can be given to the average boy now in rural life." More abstractly, corn clubs "adapt[ed] the boy to his agricultural environments and ma[d]e him capable of self-expression within th[o]se environments." Clubs provided "intellectual guidance" and promoted "careful observation, cultural comparison and investigation." Together, these features transformed education previously defined by sterile lectures into a dynamic experience that spanned schoolhouse, farmhouse, and field. "The 'club interest,'" Benson wrote, "becomes the connecting link between parent and teacher, farm and school, and last but not least it forms a cooperative atmosphere in which rural boys may be saved to the highest ideals of rural life."[42]

Unlike reformers who sought to remasculate the increasingly urban American white, middle class through sport, conservation, and wilderness excursions, Benson promoted rural-focused solutions to the drift to the city, grounded in his abiding faith in scientific agriculture and Christian devotion. "I am a profound believer in the sacredness of God's earth," he told a gathering of the South Carolina State Teachers' Association in 1911. "My kind of religion means a consecration of our 'acres of soil,' our bodies, and the soul within. And this kind of religion will not permit the continuation of our national waste in soil fertility and the criminal desecration of our great agriculture." This "desecration of 'Holy Ground'" proceeded, Benson argued, because the "depopulation of rural communities and the rapid growth of our already congested centers of population" had left few desirable youth to take over farming. Rather, the ignorant and ignoble tended crops as farms increasingly drew their labor from a "few technical schools in large cities, reformatories, [and] penitentiaries." "[I]t would seem impossible," Benson complained, "to conserve our industrial interests and our American agriculture without increasing in youthful crime." Rural youth needed to be educated in practical agriculture and to be taught the values that would make them excellent farmers. Anything less risked not only the health of the countryside but the vitality of the entire American civilization.[43]

Rural parents—particularly, stubborn farm fathers—posed a serious obstacle to Benson's planned "conservation" of rural fertility. "You may work with the father from now until doomsday and never wholly succeed in changing his bad habits and getting him to adopt 100 percent value of your recommendations," Benson complained in 1915. "[The farmer] will vote for you," he continued, "endorse what you say, and go right back to his home farm and barnyard, put into practice perhaps a part of your instructions, but in the main he will cling to many of his old ones." Adult educational programs unaccompanied by club work, according to Benson, were "a great waste . . . because after you have spent your millions of dollars to train the adult farmer and his wife you will have to begin all over again in the next generation."[44]

When Benson noted the intractable stubbornness of farmers, he invoked a stock figure from progressive agricultural literature: the stubborn rural patriarch who mistreated his son and drove him to the city. In this figure, agricultural progressives slyly moralized poor farming practices, casting them as a sure route to the exploitation of rural children and the dissolution of rural families. Inefficient dairy operations, complained Wilbur Fraser in the *Berkshire World and Corn Belt Stockman*, generated drudgery that "drives all the bright boys from the farm. . . . The only way a man with a herd as poor as this can hold the business together at all is by having his children do a large amount of work . . . for which they receive no compensation." A 1910 article in the *Prairie Farmer* quoted a number of city-bound country lads.

One blasted "the narrow-minded and selfish attitude of farmers toward their sons." Another young man complained about overwork, noting that it was "not the fault of farm life" but of rural fathers who practiced "unbusinesslike management and unscientific operation." A third young man indicated that he would like to stay on the farm, but his "unresponsive . . . very poor" father "could not agree" to his modern techniques, and so he departed. A short narrative called "Why One Boy Left the Farm" dramatized the situation succinctly. Jim, a boy with a particularly tyrannical father, fled to the city, though his "whole nature revolted against the surroundings." Physically depleted by the bad air and dim light of a tenement house and morally depleted by his job delivering ice to saloons, Jim nevertheless had the financial independence that his father had denied him. Concluding his narrative, he wrote to his mother and suggested that he might return only "if father will do the right thing by me."[45]

Jim's story underscored how, as rural reformers saw it, negligent rural parents interfered with even the most basic elements of rural reproduction and contributed to rural degeneracy. By impoverishing and degrading their sons, stubborn fathers made it impossible for them to court young ladies and create their own families. City-bound boys—at least, the adults who spoke for them in the progressive agriculture press—complained frequently about the hopeless conditions for romance on the farm. For example, Jim reported that his family had become disgusted when he scraped together enough money to purchase a Christmas gift for a "little black-eyed miss." The present "made hard feelings at home" because his sister, Florence, "had no beau" and Jim was expected to "act in that capacity." With hardly enough money or time to court any other girls, Jim felt pressured to romance his sister, a twist to the story that simultaneously deployed the twin rural menaces of incest and poverty. Rural reformer Warren H. Wilson implied a different unsavory outcome. Noting the widespread exploitation of the countryside's "crop of boys," he relayed the story of one "exploiting father" who refused to let his son marry "because the old man was accustomed to collect the boy's wages. . . . [The boy] had to become a woman's husband to escape from being his father's property." Wilson suggested that treating boys like "work-cattle" in this way had disturbingly literal consequences: "When a boy smells like a cow every time he comes into a closed room his mother, instead of scolding him, should help him to find associates among ladies rather than bovines. That boy is in danger of leaving the farm for hatred of it, or sinking to an animal level and ceasing to care. In the former case the farm loses him. In the latter case the church loses him; the school, the grange and the social gathering lose him, and the stable gets him." Wilson posited a startling trade-off: boys could have romance "among ladies" or associations in the stables, but never both. Rural romance battled in a zero-sum game with a exploitative, parent-driven bestialization, the stakes of which were healthy boys and healthy rural repro-duction. A 1912 article in *Wallaces Farmer* explicitly linked the absence of social interactions among rural boys and girls through planned recreation and amusements back to the greatest rural menace, warning that "a playless countryside marks the beginning of degeneracy in that section."[46]

Rural reformers could not remove the menace of bad rural parents entirely, but Benson reasoned that youth clubs, at the very least, could entice parental cooperation. Without youth clubs, Benson memorably put it, the county agent was worse off than the greenest traveling salesman. Salesmen always knew to "first give attention to the children as they enter the door yard or the household by chanting to, rocking and kissing the babies, before the[y] introduce themselves and their subject to the adult members of the family." This approach was commonsense enough to be called "orthodox business practice." It was difficult "to go direct to the farmer and convince him of the necessity for a change of practice." If the farmer is "approached through his boy or girl," however, "a welcome is at once extended" because "every normal parent loves the man or woman who will give attention, direction, and lead-ership to the children." Some would call this "exploitation," Benson noted, but club work brought "maximum returns in net profits, yields, [and] eco-nomic adjustment of project[s] into the farm unit." While it advanced the goals of the USDA and agricultural progressives, it did so, according to Ben-son, through bettering the participant, the family, and the community.[47]

Working with youth offered an immediate entry point for reformers, but the structure of the corn contest promised a longer-term pecuniary inter-est to skeptical farmers. The "corn club acre" could valuably, and deceptively, advertise the USDA's preferred agricultural methods. Benson insisted on one-acre clubs as the basis for corn work because it would "limit work to a piece of land that can be properly prepared, fertilized, and managed dur-ing the growing season."[48] This limiting principle enabled one-acre projects to be intensively farmed in ways that were not feasible or efficient for larger plots. Seduced by premiums and promises of impressive yields, farmers often offered their sons their best acre and ample fertilizer to farm it. Club organiz-ers secured adequate supplies of premium seed. The boys, for their part, lav-ished far more attention on their single acre than most farmers could afford to spend on any individual acre. The results were corn yields that simply could not be replicated on a larger scale. A Monroe County, Indiana, corn club, for example, managed an average yield of 91 bushels per acre in 1918. The statewide average for corn yields was only 35 bushels per acre in the same year. A 1911 issue of *Ohio Farmer* boasted that the hundred best corn-club boys from around the nation had achieved an average yield of 133.7 bushels per acre, with the nation's yield champion, Jerry Moore of South Carolina, obtaining an astounding yield of 228.7 bushels per acre. Prizewinning one-acre yields like those, circulated widely in newspapers, provided valuable publicity for progressive agriculture, though they seldom revealed the limitations implicit in the one-acre method. Club organizers hoped to impress or shame farmers into adopting their preferred methods, as well as to curry favor with other farmers by directly assisting their children. When the promise of amazing yields faltered, donated prizes and awards, worth $40,000 in 1911 alone, incented boys—and their fathers—to participate.[49]

The astounding yields of the club acre were only the means; "a man for every boy," as Benson put it, were the ends. For every child that was enrolled in club work, organizers endeavored to interest a parent or neighbor in club work and to have that adult regularly attending meetings and reading club literature. In this way, club work could accomplish more than simply improving the local school system. More ambitiously, club work transformed rural children into extensions of the USDA and made any adults who assisted them the same. "The boy, as a corn club member," wrote Benson, "is a demonstrator for the State and the United States Department of Agriculture. . . . [T]he cooperator is a man who will agree to cooperate with the boy and the State and Government authorities in getting the best possible results from this club work." By 1914, O. B. Martin's clubs in the South and Benson's clubs in the North and West enrolled more than 120,000 boys and girls and provided the USDA with access to farm households across the nation.[50]

Club work evolved as a strategic adaptation for the promoters of progressive agriculture as well as a vital supplement to the troubled country schoolhouse. Club work gave educators access to entire rural families and blurred the boundaries between agricultural and educational expertise. While those same families, particularly adult males, might reject the USDA's book farming, club work enticed them by appealing to their pride and pocketbooks. Agricultural progressives hoped that club work could save households impoverished by the ignorance of negligent farm patriarchs. As debate surrounding the 1914 Smith-Lever Act makes clear, concern about rural social reproduction licensed and shaped the expansion of state authority in rural

America. If agricultural extension was to reverse the withering of the countryside and carve out the rot of the cities, it would do so only by providing
what rural fathers did not, remaking the fragile rural home, and bringing the
state back into the farm.

                                *   *   *

The publicity and achievements generated by Benson's and Knapp's clubs
helped agricultural progressives make the case for an institutionalized system
of agricultural extension subsidized by federal monies. On the floor of the
U.S. Congress, their congressional allies echoed Benson's formulation of the
problem, noting that, through agricultural extension, scientific agriculture
could reach entire rural families. Congressmen argued that other efforts to
promote scientific agriculture faltered because they could not penetrate the
farm household and, thus, left the next generation of rural citizens unpre-
pared for farmwork and unhappy with country living. Both advocates and
critics of agricultural extension cited the ability of government agents to supplement patriarchal authority in rural communities. Its advocates did so by
gesturing to the revolutionary potential of youth clubs; its critics, by decrying
the bill's "paternalism." Frank Lever, the House sponsor of the Smith-Lever
Act, announced in his committee report to the House, "If rural life is to be
readjusted and agriculture dignified as a profession the country boy and girl
must be made to know . . . that successful agriculture requires as much as
does any other occupation in life. . . . The farm boy and girl can be taught that
agriculture is the oldest and most dignified of the professions."[51]

In 1914, a bipartisan alliance of legislators overcame a decade's worth of
opposition and finally passed the Smith-Lever Act through the United States
Congress. The Smith-Lever Act provided the first standing federal appropriation for agricultural extension and, through it, for agricultural youth clubs.
Pressure had been building on Congress to provide a regular appropriation
for agricultural extension for several years. Knapp and Spillman had received
public accolades for their extension work and eventually commanded the
support of both agrarian and labor interests. Western populists worried that
an extension system that traded on the USDA's reputation but was financed
with Rockefeller money gave private interests undue influence.

Multiple extension bills had floated through the 61st and 62nd Congresses—most notably, the McLaughlin Bill in 1909, the Dolliver Bill in 1910,
and the Page Bill in 1912—but the chambers never managed to agree on a

single piece of legislation. After Democrats ascended to control of the House, the Senate, and the presidency in the 1912 elections, supporters of extension in both chambers rallied around a bill authored by South Carolina Democrat Frank Asbury Lever. Lever first introduced his bill in 1913. It passed both chambers but died in conference. In 1914, he reintroduced it with additional support from Senate Republicans. The bill passed the House and Senate overwhelmingly and was signed into law by Woodrow Wilson on May 8, 1914. In the first year, it appropriated a flat sum of $10,000 to each state, as well as an additional $600,000 that would be distributed proportionate to each state's share of the total national rural population. In seven succeeding years, the appropriation for the "proportionate" pool would increase by $500,000, until it reached a permanent annual appropriation of $4.1 million. In addition, states were required to appropriate matching funds to have any access to the proportionate pool. The total amount of funding was significant, given the size of the federal budget in the early twentieth century. The ultimate $4.7 million per annum price tag of extension amounted to around 2.1 percent of the $226 million in federal outlays, excluding defense and pension spending, in 1914. Because of the rapid expansion of federal budgets during and after World War I, the actual percentage of spending on extension was considerably less—only around 0.6 percent of federal spending, excluding defense and veterans' pensions in 1923—but in 1914, the cost of extension constituted a considerable federal outlay.[52]

In its final form, Smith-Lever provided for an extension system that largely institutionalized Knapp and Spillman's existing program. The bill contained several controversial provisions that departed significantly from previous extension legislation. First, the administering department for the bill was the USDA rather than the Department of the Interior. Second, the bill authorized a cooperative demonstration agent system over a "farmers' institute" model. (In the latter model, farmers traveled to an institute, usually at the state agricultural college, for a short course taught by professors of agriculture.) Third, rather than a model organized around towns, districts, or even states, the organizing unit for extension would primarily be the county—ideally, every county would have its own extension agent. Fourth, the bill excluded a broader program of vocational education, which had been present in earlier bills. Finally, while the extension system was to be administered in cooperation with the land-grant colleges, the colleges needed budgetary and programmatic approval from the USDA. Departments at the land-grant colleges managed day-to-day operations of the extension service, but the USDA retained ultimate control over the system. The legislation was a vital piece of state building that provided early twentieth-century national government with a means to monitor and regulate America's sprawling rural spaces.[53]

From its inception, supporters of a national agricultural extension program touted extension's ability to transform rural society by reaching inside the farm household. County agents would become members of local communities, diagnosing its unique needs, forming deeper relationships with neighbors than professors could with students, and, generally, using their proximity to farmers as a way to strengthen the reputation of extension. This method relied on a collapse of the public and private and a desire to bring the forces of education directly into the home of the farmer to reach his wife and children. Club work exemplified this approach because it provided the apostles of progressive agriculture with access to individuals who, according to republican ideology, were excluded from public life. The state's previous access to rural children had been strictly mediated by rotten country schoolhouses. If, as those apostles also held, the rural home was the fundamental unit of both agricultural production and rural social reproduction, reformers needed to insinuate themselves into farm households to reform not only agricultural practices but also domestic labor, hygiene, child rearing, and a host of other activities that determined the wholesome nature of the rural home.

The leading proponents of Smith-Lever in Congress emphasized that extension touched the farmer's wife and children. Frank Asbury Lever contrasted this approach with previous efforts at agricultural education. "We have been spending 50 years trying to find an efficient agency for spreading this information throughout the country," he complained before the House. "We have tried the Farmers' Bulletin. We have tried the press. We have tried the lecture and the institute work." These had "done good" but always fallen short of the desired end. By contrast, the bill would "set up a system of general demonstration" that addressed itself to the entire farm household. The genius of this approach was that it did not depend upon "writing to a man and saying that this is a better plan than he has or by standing up and talking to him and telling him it is a better plan." Rather, agents of progressive agriculture proceeded "by personal contact." They traveled to the farmer and "under his own vine and fig tree" demonstrated correct practices to "the man and woman and the boy and girl."[54] Citing boys' corn clubs and girls' tomato clubs, Lever argued that extension reached rural youth directly, without interference from adults and parents. His gendering of this dynamic was highly revealing. Previous efforts—the bulletin, institute, and press—had failed partly because they were directed only to adult males. Those males resisted or ignored the knowledge provided by scientific agriculture, and their families suffered as a result. Agricultural extension, however, considered the fathers as only a single piece of the puzzle. Successful agricultural education would supplement patriarchal authority, reach women and children, and effectively address the fulcrum around which rural societies pivoted: the farm family.

Other advocates of the bill emphasized that only assistance to all members of farm households could stanch the drift to the city. Echoing concerns about rural degeneracy, Representative John Adair of Indiana noted that "many farms have already been deserted," a serious cause for concern, considering the centrality of country life to human civilization. "You may burn down and destroy our splendid cities," he said, paraphrasing William Jennings Bryan's "Cross of Gold" speech, "and the wealth of the farms will rebuild them more beautiful than before; but destroy our farms, and our cities will decay and our people will starve." Rural life needed to be "revolutionize[d]." It needed to be made "as attractive and as profitable as city life and this can be done only through a systematic effort to redirect rural methods and ideals." Agricultural scientists possessed sufficient knowledge to enact the needed reforms but had no way of communicating it to rural people. This, Adair announced, was the genius of cooperative extension. Through "personal contact," it "carr[ied] the truths of agriculture and home economics to the door of the farmer" and "ma[de] the field, the garden, the orchard, and even the parlor and the kitchen the classrooms." The county agent and demonstrators would provide "leadership . . . along all lines of rural activity—social, economic, and financial" and become "the instrumentality through which the colleges, stations, and Department of Agriculture will speak."[55]

Opponents of the bill chafed at the alleged "paternalism" of government agents entering rural homes. Senator John Works of California worried that recent trends in legislation would produce a "spineless citizenship" utterly dependent upon "paternalistic aid." Proponents of the bill, Works charged, were erecting a "paternalized government" and the United States was "on the downward road, not only to paternalism, but ultimately to socialism."[56] Senator Frank Brandegee of Connecticut called it "paternalism" and an unprecedented exercise of federal power.[57] Representative John Joseph Fitzgerald, a conservative Democrat from New York, had no great objection to the idea of "a man of scientific attainments" going to farms and teaching agricultural techniques there. He objected, however, to a plan "by which an agent of the Federal Government shall be sent to every farm in the United States . . . to go into the farmer's household and there to demonstrate, for his wife or for other female members of his family in charge of his household, the most practical and best methods of promoting domestic economy." Fitzgerald considered such a plan "wholly obnoxious to our theory of government."[58]

By inveighing against government access to rural women and children, opponents of the act suggested that the "paternalism" that rankled was not simply government treating farmers like children but government supplanting farmers as the fathers of rural society. The farmer, Senator Franklin Lane quipped, "does not need some scientific person to come around and teach his wife how to stretch the beefsteak for supper in order to meet the demands of the family so much as he needs free access to the markets of the country and a fair price for his product after he raises it."[59] Senator Thomas Sterling of South Dakota fumed about the bill's displacement of rural paternal authority, calling the bill "the extreme of paternalism. . . . [N]othing like it has ever been attempted in Federal legislation." Federal agricultural extension would "permit the enforced interference of the Federal Government in problems so commonplace, so everyday, so local and so individual as knowing how to plow and plant and fertilize, and knowing how to cook and sew and having a care for cleanliness and sanitation." Government ownership of railroads was a minor intrusion by comparison. "The Government," announced Sterling, "will not in owning and operating any railroad be in the business of fathering the enterprise and directing the conduct and work of the individual citizens."[60]

If few legislators found this argument compelling, it was perhaps because proponents of the legislation deployed even more dramatic gendered appeals. Like Adair and Lever, Representative Dudley Hughes of Georgia believed that extension would manifestly improve all elements of rural living because it reached entire households. Like other supporters of the legislation, Hughes worried about the deterioration of rural masculinity implicit in boys leaving farms for the city. But in that migration, Hughes also saw a profound threat to rural femininity, which he made clear in an extended meditation on the status of Southern soil. The "fertility" of "the mother of all" had been deteriorating because of poor practices and now needed to be "impregnated with artificial fertility." Hughes identified the agricultural practices of African American farmers as the gravest threat to the "conservation of the soil." African American farmers, he argued, cared little about the health of the soil, since they could leave the soil "denuded" and simply move to a different plot. "The soil is deteriorating rapidly for want of intelligent care, and it would be criminal on the part of those with whom the very destiny of the people rests to continue to delay and finally realize that they have been aroused too late," announced Hughes. "The soil—the land—is an inheritance, handed down to man for humanity," he concluded. "It belongs to future generations." He articulated a gendered rationale for both Smith-Lever and an expanded federal presence in rural America: the failure of white, rural masculinity to preserve the fertility of the feminized landscape heralded civilizational decline and justified the state assuming the neglected prerogatives of farm patriarchs.[61]

Hughes's confidence that extension would benefit African American farmers was, at best, misplaced and, at worst, disingenuous. Many of the bill's chief advocates in the Senate—Hoke Smith of Georgia, Furnifold Simmons of North Carolina, and James K. Vardaman of Mississippi—were also architects of black disenfranchisement and Jim Crow in their states. Rhetoric about assisting African American farmers belied their efforts to degrade and impoverish African American extension. Corn Belt senators, led by Albert Cummins, a leading progressive Republican from Iowa, argued that extension funds should be distributed according to the number of acres of improved farmland in a given state—a formula that would benefit northern and western states at the expense of labor-intensive Southern agriculture. Hoke Smith, the bill's sponsor in the chamber, proposed that the funds should be released according to the size of a state's rural population. Cummins countered that, since funds would only be spent to educate white farmers, such a formula was unjust.[62] Smith's funding formula prevailed, but several other amendments attempted to direct funds to African American extension as well. Wesley Jones of Washington introduced an amendment, supported by the NAACP, that explicitly directed some of the appropriations to African American land-grant institutions. Gilbert Hitchcock of Nebraska successfully introduced an amendment to have the work conducted "without discrimination as to race."[63] From there, the debate quickly devolved into a discussion of the "backward, uninitiative, unintelligent, incapable black race," as John Sharp Williams of Mississippi put it, and the eventual removal of language protecting African American extension.[64] The cityward drift of rural youth was too dire a threat—the greatest "menace" to "our civilization," according to Minnesota senator Moses Clapp—to be derailed by sectional jockeying. "The great city," Clapp reported, "is the place where vice feeds upon itself, like a great festering sore thriving upon its own rottenness." If a federally sponsored extension program could keep rural youth out of the city, it was money worth spending.[65]

As the debate on Smith-Lever unfolded, proponents and opponents of the bill agreed to a series of revealing propositions: that the rural household was in disarray and rural fathers were an impediment to scientific agriculture; that this disarray fed the drift to the cities, rural degeneracy, and threatened the nation's social reproduction; that the situation portended ill for American civilization; that the crisis demanded federal attention; and that the proposed plan of agricultural extension addressed itself precisely to that root ailment. At this point, legislators began to part ways. Opponents of the bill claimed that farmers were competent to rectify the situation if the state could ensure a fair market for agricultural products. Plans by the federal government to meddle directly in rural households, then, were unnecessary and potentially invidious. By usurping the role of the farmer as the father of rural society and possessor of uncontested authority within the rural home, government agents risked paternalism and the further degradation of the rural family. In contrast, supporters of the legislation considered the household-centered approach of extension one of its greatest virtues and accordingly emphasized the role of club work and domestic science in extension. From this perspective, male farmers had been obviously negligent and needed to share their authority with government agents, granting them access to their wives and children.

*   *   *

Dudley Hughes's celebration of Southern soil located profound reproductive power beneath the cotton fields, orchards, and pastures that dotted the region's countryside—a fecundity that needed to be jealously husbanded. This fertility crept into rural spaces and bodies, and in this way sustained alike the nation's agriculture and vitality. Critics of the bill might quibble about who should do the husbanding, but they never contested this geography of social reproduction. With that point conceded, Smith-Lever's proponents offered a vision of a rural future in which agricultural experts and state authorities worked with rural households to correct the damage done by negligent rural fathers. Truly unlocking the countryside's fertility, however, was a generational project: a new generation of rural citizens was required, a generation amenable to scientific agriculture and state authority, and youth clubs for rural boys and girls were the surest means of producing it.

     Proponents of agricultural youth clubs shared their confidence in the pliability of youth and the efficacy of this generational project with numerous other movements dedicated to guiding the development of American youth in the early twentieth century. Many other major American youth organizations—Scouting, YWCA, YMCA, the Camp Fire Girls—emerged as the part of Progressive Era reform movements directed at the character and bodies of middle-class youth. Most of those organizations focused on structuring the leisure time of youth to avoid the perils of vice and unwholesome associations in the city. Athletics, crafts, and supervised recreations provided youth with social interactions that the largely white, middle-class reformers found morally and gender-appropriate. Many youth organizations used engagement with the natural world through camping and nature study as a means of reforming the character of their members, reasoning that pristine nature could counteract the corrosive effects of city life. In this way, youth organizations hoped to escort the urban middle class through troubled adolescence and into maturity.[66]

The agricultural youth clubs that eventually developed into 4-H started with the notion that youth were a vital component of a larger unit of economic production and social reproduction: the farm family. They addressed themselves first and foremost to the laboring bodies of rural youth to influence that larger unit. Other youth organizations focused on reforming the leisure activities of their participants, but agricultural youth clubs were addressed to farmwork, and their appeal was partly based on the promise of greater revenue for participants. By improving the labor practices of rural people, agricultural youth clubs could harness the true productive power of the country, stanch the drift to the city, and secure the civilization built on that labor. All participants in the debate on Smith-Lever agreed that rural society and American civilization were failing to adapt to the crucible of modernity. A crisis of modernity also mobilized other youth organizations: the notion that urban, industrial life was degraded and unwholesome was central to the missions and appeal of nearly all the organizations. Agricultural youth club work, however, depended upon a vision of that crisis focused on the countryside rather than on the city. Unlike other youth organizations, 4-H addressed itself exclusively to rural youth and concerned itself with the rural world as a physical place rather than as a nostalgic foil to urban life. Advocates of agricultural youth club work may have indulged in nostalgic agrarianism but not without being tempered by a personal knowledge of rural life: nearly every organizer hailed from the countryside and had worked on or operated a farm. Their vision emphasized that rural America could become modern and that a healthy modernity was necessarily one that integrated the knowledge and expertise that agriculturalists had developed. Rather than using the countryside as a therapeutic instrument to edify city dwellers—a taste of the premodern to make modernity bearable—agricultural youth clubs were intended to transform the countryside into a site of modernity and to retain and grow rural populations.

More than merely a personal transformation, agricultural youth clubs were designed to effect a much broader collective transformation of rural

America. The ambition of that transformation demanded state action and support. It envisioned state power as an enduring and pervasive influence over rural life and in farm households, enacted by agricultural youth clubs, the USDA, the extension service, and land-grant colleges. Not surprisingly, while other youth organizations abetted government schemes over the years—all major youth organizations, for example, participated in wartime resource drives—no other major youth organization was directly administered by a federal agency nor was any predicated on the fundamental ideological acceptance of state authority and expertise. Whether it was appropriate for the state to intervene in rural households was the most basic and divisive question for those debating Smith-Lever. The passage of Smith-Lever—and the very existence of 4-H—affirmed the proposition that the federal government should be a source of scientific and cultural authority for rural Americans and that the vitality of American civilization depended upon that affirmation.

Six years after the passage of Smith-Lever, the national conversation was still dominated by pervasive fears of the degeneracy of rural society and the reproductive decline of white American civilization. In late September of 1920, the Census Bureau announced that the urban population had, at last, surpassed the population of the countryside, according to the results of the decennial census. This announcement unleashed another wave of worry and anxiety about the health of the countryside and the nation. "Evidently something is wrong with country life, its occupations and amusements, when so many cannot resist the 'lure' of the city," opined the *New York Times*. Others wondered if the rise of the cities also meant the political ascendance of immigrants. The *Chicago Daily Tribune* "hope[d] that the balance of power in the affairs of the nation may remain for some time in the hands of a class of citizens of proved stability, strong in national feeling, not carried away by waves of alien sympathies."[67] Frederic J. Haskin, writing in his regular column for the *Los Angeles Times*, was less oblique. "The America of our grandfathers," he asserted, "was a land of blond men of Nordic or so-called Anglo-Saxon blood, who lived outdoors, herded cattle, tilled the soil, hunted, fished and sailed the seas from Arctic to Antarctic." The new America, he continued, would be "a heavily populated country of short dark-skinned men, living . . . [in] crowded, complicated and enormous cities." This was America's troubling destiny, Haskin claimed, unless "the government gets down to the necessary work of creating more farms."[68]

Haskin would find little disagreement from club work experts at the Department of Agriculture. By 1920, the USDA employed a national staff of seventeen full-time specialists dedicated to club work, even as hundreds of county agents around the nation directly supervised club work increasingly under the name "4-H" and the symbol of the four-leafed clover. Led by Benson and O. B. Martin, club work specialists concurred with Haskin's assessment that rural society was in decline and argued that the government needed to remake the rural home in order to save it. They concentrated their efforts on improving the agricultural practices of rural boys and the homemaking labor of rural girls, operating under the theory that even if adults dismissed their lessons, youth would adopt them and create healthy and attractive households where the previous generation had failed. To make this operation as effective as possible, however, club specialists argued that they needed to make club work more uniform. The following decade witnessed efforts to expand 4-H club work and, at the same time, to strengthen the USDA's power in the American countryside.

CHAPTER TWO

Financial Intimacy and Rural Manhood

I pledge my head to clearer thinking . . .
　　　　　　　　　　　　　—The 4-H Pledge

Where did the name "4-H" come from? Although the iconic clover and the "H" mnemonic originated in Iowa, before World War I the clubs were still referred to as "Boys' and Girls' Clubs" or "Junior Extension Clubs." At a club conference in 1913, Mrs. Jane McKimmon, a North Carolina club organizer, pointed out the need for a catchier "brand name" that would help club members market their products to consumers. The conference pondered the question until Oscar Baker Martin, the USDA's club agent for the South, suggested the moniker "4-H clubs." Martin's suggestion met with "unanimous approval," and shortly after, an "artistic tomato label" with the name was created. "From that it was extended to other labels," explained Martin, "not only in the Girls' Work, but on the boxes of potatoes, seed corn, and other such thing which the boys had to sell. Then began the systematic campaign to raise and maintain standards in order that the 4-H brand might become favorably known."[1]

The term caught fire. USDA specialist Gertrude Warren used the term in a USDA pamphlet for the first time in 1918; by 1924, the USDA had trademarked "4-H" and its four-leafed clover symbol. During the 1920s, "4-H" appeared regularly in USDA literature, congressional hearings, and the press. Meanwhile, emblazoned "upon myriads of badges, caps, aprons, pennants, flags and standards," the 4-H clover proliferated as the symbol of the movement "to make the best better." That motto, suggested by USDA extension specialist Carrie Harrison and in wide use by 1919, provided only a minimal description of the program's aim. In 1927, a national assembly of club leaders offered a clearer explanation in the form of a standard national 4-H pledge: "I pledge my head to clearer thinking, my heart to greater loyalty, my hands to larger service, and my health to better living for my club, my community, and my country."[2]

The widespread adoption of the term "4-H," as well as national club mottos, pledges, and symbols, was emblematic of a broader trend toward expansion and standardization of club work in the decade after the passage of the Smith-Lever Act. During that period, 4-H developed from an inchoate set of loosely affiliated clubs and contests to a well-organized network unified by a standard set of methods and symbols. Over the same period, the USDA also helped establish a set of institutions to supplement its own educational activities with fund-raising, lobbying, and leader training. These institutions—most notably, the National Committee on Boys and Girls Club Work (National Committee)—fused the publicly financed technocratic expertise of the USDA with the commercial capital of bankers, railroads, mail-order retailers, and agricultural technology firms. Through this alliance of state expertise, local voluntary labor, and private commercial capital, the 4-H clover sprouted in communities around the nation, enrolling more than 800,000 youth by the end of the decade and visibly "demonstrating" the USDA's preferred brand of capital-intensive, debt-financed agriculture in every rural county.

Far from an incidental detail, the famous moniker's genesis explained much about how 4-H functioned in the decade after the passage of Smith-Lever. Despite 4-H's avowed educational and public-spirited purposes, profit motives and commercial transactions were integral components of 4-H's identity. 4-H was a marketing device designed by state experts to help farm kids sell agricultural products to the rural public. Experts at the USDA also used 4-H to "sell" capital-intensive, debt-financed agriculture and technocratic expertise to rural Americans. And bankers and businessmen gave cheap loans and prizes to 4-H in the belief that it would prime the sale of financial products to the next generation of farmers. Among the various actors enticed by the 4-H movement, the clover planted visions—and seeds—of multiplying transactions from which future rural prosperity would grow. All these "sales" depended upon and reproduced a range of intimate registers—trust, loyalty, friendship, and affection—that were typically re-coded through the ubiquitous buzzword "cooperation." By offering rural youth an arena for cooperation, club work cultivated spaces where the rising generation would be brought into proximity and contact with community members, bankers, merchants, and agricultural experts. Crucially, the cumulative effect of this combined economic and cultural project provided what I call "financial intimacy" or, in other words, intimacy—in the form of knowledge and social bonds—with and through capital. Financial intimacy entailed sustained relationships with numerous adults—primarily the bankers, businessmen, and county agents who arranged and supervised loans—but it also meant intimate familiarity with financial instruments. 4-H clubs offered rural youth the opportunity to practice their finances: practical experience with capital accumulation, manipulation, and mastery.

In the context of the critique of rural degeneracy and corresponding efforts to reform rural masculinity outlined in the previous chapter, the stakes of 4-H's project of cultivating financial intimacy are clear: although 4-H broadened financial opportunities for farm girls, 4-H's finance programs primarily benefited rural boys. Boys tended to enroll in the most capital-intensive projects, and club organizers usually presented the ideal subjects of loan programs as male. As controlled entrepreneurial simulations that concealed capitalist agriculture's vices and proclaimed its virtues, 4-H projects also worked as gendering instruments. They offered everyday practices for masculine self-making and idealized specimens of adult masculinity. Loans provided rural boys with the means to buy a pig or calf, and the imperative to repay the loan encouraged efficiency, discipline, and precise financial record keeping, all characteristics deemed essential to propertied manhood. But commercial loans also laid the groundwork for sustained personal relationships with the fine examples of manhood that boys could not find at home. Club work vitally expanded the social universe of rural boys and exposed those boys to the example and influence of bankers, businessmen, and bureaucrats. From these intimacies, 4-H's boosters dreamed, a generation of farmer-businessmen would grow.

For many rural Americans, two words defined the decade preceding the Great Depression: crisis and cooperation. Crisis was the economic and social blight that afflicted rural America throughout the decade, with an intensity not seen since the agricultural depressions of the 1890s. Cooperation, a ubiquitous buzzword of the age, was the tonic for that malady, prescribed by countless, breathless technocrats at the USDA and in the agricultural progressive press. Many historians have noted the explosion of cooperative agricultural marketing organizations in the 1920s, but cooperation functionally encompassed a much broader variety of social forms for rural Americans. Cooperation did mean engaging in collective economic action. However, it also required openness to various elite actors who, in previous decades, had provoked anger and skepticism from rural people. In 1919, leading agricultural progressive and president of the Massachusetts Agricultural College, Kenyon Butterfield, famously characterized this openness to the complementary interconnections of modern life as the "New Day" in American agriculture. The dawn of the New Day would bring professionals, experts, bankers, managers, and marketers into the fabric of everyday rural life through a variety of cooperative economic and civic organizations. Once embedded within communities, cooperative institutions would also quiet the radical and populist political agitation. By aligning farmers with urban business interests and the agents of the technocratic state, cooperation promised to make the American countryside safe for capitalism.[3]

Agricultural depressions in the late nineteenth century precipitated a swell of political unrest emanating from epicenters in the rural South and West. Farmers formed the core of the populist movement through agrarian organizations like the People's Party and the Farmers' Alliance. Populists were not reactionary antimodernists; rather, they promoted a striking agrarian futurist reform agenda. They envisioned a powerful governing network independent of metropolitan capital that was accountable to the interests of rural white landholders and integrated their knowledge and expertise in regulatory institutions. Nor were most populists anticapitalists. Rather, they hoped to reorient national institutions to create more favorable market conditions for agricultural commodities and to reinforce their own political influence. Populists, however, did agitate vociferously against urban capitalists. They accused bankers, railroad barons, major industrialists, and political toadies—often correctly—of graft, corruption, collusion, monopoly, and price-fixing. Populists sought electoral reforms to increase their own political clout and regulatory measures that would ease the terms of loans and rail-fare schedules.[4]

The legacy of the populist rebellion conditioned how agricultural progressives approached reform in the New Day. The modernist ambitions and populist rhetoric of agricultural progressives may have had superficial appeal for poorer farmers who, only two decades earlier, supported populist candidates. But the agricultural progressive vision fundamentally diverged from the populist vision in crucial respects. While populists sought to construct an alternative modernity around the political and economic influence of white rural smallholders, agricultural progressives sought to integrate the agricultural sector with the existing metropolitan order. In this, agricultural progressives presumed shared interests between rural and urban elites. Populists promoted a silver standard to remove the financial yoke borne by farmers, but agricultural progressives designed programs to educate and encourage debt-financed mechanization and expansion. If populists had been openly antagonistic to urban capital, agricultural progressives preached amicable relationships between town and country, farmers and bankers. The primary structuring division of the populist rebellion had been the diverging interests of rural debtors and urban lenders. By contrast, the terrain of rural reform after World War I pitted the most affluent rural (and former rural) people against the rural poor. Targets of reform included those smallholders and tenants whom the populists had once mobilized and the marginal nonwhite tenants, sharecroppers, and wage laborers whom the populists had excluded. By the 1920s, the rural poor often instead gravitated toward radical agrarian political movements like the Nonpartisan League, the Farmers' Union, and the Farm-Labor Party. Despite a similarly modernist orientation, these organizations levied critiques of urban capital that placed their members in uneasy alliance with Socialist Democrats and communists rather than the bankers and businessmen whom agricultural progressives hailed.[5]

Even as enthusiasm for the New Day swelled, agricultural progressives argued that the success of this strategy would hinge on the personal transformation of rural men. In contrast to rugged, atomized pioneers and stubborn patriarchs, new rural men needed to be intensely social creatures—men who could swim with ease through the labyrinthine channels of knowledge and capital that modern agriculture demanded. "Leaders of this awakened rural manhood," proclaimed Albert Mann, dean of the College of Agriculture at Cornell University, "must be clear-thinking, direct, and of superior intelligence; and their foundations must be laid in a sure understanding of economic and social laws and of folk psychology superimposed on reliable farm knowledge." The new rural man would be a community and church leader, a learned correspondent of professors of agriculture and economics, and a friend of bankers and merchants. He mixed the characteristic practical experience and folksy charm of the farmer with the "clear-thinking," rational efficiency of the businessman. He could as easily hold court among a council of economists as at a county fair. In the blossoming of those expanded relationships, new rural men could take real responsibility for the affairs of their communities and cease to demand special privileges from the state. "The sound farmer-businessman does not seek legislation to fix prices or regulate details," Secretary of Agriculture William Jardine explained in 1925, for he knew that "legislation cannot annul economic laws." The farmer-businessman, steeped in the ever objective and rational laws of economy, demanded only what was due to him as an adult male. "The farmer does not want to be a ward of the state," Jardine continued. "He doesn't want to be babied or pitied by other people."[6]

Jardine's rhetoric elided the degree to which legislation, more than personal failings, had played a dramatic role in creating the dismal rural conditions of the early 1920s. In 1917, anticipating the strategic military value of crop surpluses, Congress enacted a series of measures to boost agricultural production, among them a large emergency appropriation for extension. With $6.8 million in emergency wartime appropriations in 1918 alone, the CES dramatically expanded its operations. In 1914, the CES employed about 2,600 persons; by 1918, it had grown to about 6,700. The CES encouraged farmers to do whatever they could to increase production, whether it meant taking out loans to mechanize or employing short-term labor. Under the authority of the Lever Food and Fuel Control Act of 1917, county agents purchased and distributed fertilizer to farmers free of charge. The U.S. government, the largest domestic consumer of agricultural commodities during the war years, intentionally paid above-market prices, a policy that effectively acted as an indirect system of price supports. Wartime policies, a decline in European production, and the contraction of Atlantic shipping lanes all caused agricultural commodity prices to skyrocket between 1917 and 1919.[7]

This wartime agricultural boosterism set the stage for a stark and painful reversal. Following peak prices during and immediately following World War I, prices for agricultural commodities cratered, precipitating a "farm crisis," as some newspapers dubbed it. In 1920 alone, the price of wheat, for example, crumbled by 85 percent. Many farmers had responded to high wartime prices, cheap credit, and the USDA's insistent nudges by borrowing heavily to expand production. The ensuing price collapse scuttled overleveraged farms and sent other farmers scrambling to boost production to make up for lost income. Faced with tightening budgets, rural people—particularly, rural women—searched for work in nearby towns. Others fled farms altogether, intensifying both the "drift to the city" and anxieties about rural degeneracy. Farmers abandoned 2 million acres of land by the middle of the decade, and the farm population had declined from one-third to one-quarter of the nation's population by 1930.[8]

Many elites, like Jardine, merely shrugged at the structure of economic incentives that had induced the spiraling price situation. The more proximate problems, they reasoned, were ignorance and a lack of organization: farmers failed to understand how to use credit responsibly, to record their expenses properly, to monitor market conditions, to grow crops suitable for both soil and market, to take advantage of premiums, value-added crops, and niche marketing possibilities, and, most crucially, to engage in cooperative economic endeavor where it might pad their margins and stabilize prices. This elite consensus held that, far from being farmer-businessmen, few American farmers knew how to run their farms like businesses. As historian Deborah

Fitzgerald argues, the USDA and agricultural progressives doggedly promoted an "industrial ideal" as a tonic for the farm crisis under a variety of
deceptive monikers. Extension officials and the farm press used "efficient,"
"progressive," "businesslike," and "scientific" agriculture nearly interchangeably to describe a prescriptive model that privileged capital- and technology-
intensive agricultural practices.[9]

This industrial model shared important rhetorical and intellectual similarities to the prevailing reform rhetoric in the previous three decades. In particular, industrial idealists in agriculture evinced a lockstep enthusiasm for
technical fixes and expert knowledge that hardly distinguished them from
earlier proponents of scientific agriculture. However, in privileging large-scale
agricultural operations, proponents of the industrial ideal diverged from earlier thinkers who contended that scientific agriculture could save any farm,
large or small, and who, indeed, had considered small farms the greatest ben-
eficiaries of their insights. The industrial model, by contrast, designated atomized small farmers as destined for failure because of the laws of the market.
Small farms could not capture the economies of scale to compete with larger
operations, nor could they afford the expensive "specialized machines" that
would minimize production costs. Without cooperation, farmers could never
effectively curb overproduction but would be forever at the mercy of the market's whims. Absent cooperation, farms would stay small and would die small.
This recognition, so central to elite advice to farmers in the 1920s, hinted at
an important ideological development. When previous generations spoke in
hushed tones of scientific farming, they tended to narrowly mean methods
informed by the natural sciences. By contrast, with the launch of agricultural
economics, rural sociology, and farm management, agricultural progressives
increasingly capitalized on a rural turn in the social sciences. These subdis-
ciplines emphasized that agricultural and rural community improvement
depended upon fostering the correct relationships more than merely the adoption of up-to-date technical advice. Agricultural economics, farm management, and agricultural marketing focused on economic relationships between
creditors and borrowers, between producers and consumers, and among producers of common crops. Rural sociologists described rural collective and
relational units—villages, towns, and families, primarily—and offered recommendations about how to cooperatively restructure those units to promote
healthier and more efficient communities. Cooperation provided a flexible
rhetorical framework that encompassed a diverse swath of institutions with
remarkably different goals—from agricultural cooperatives designed to lower
production costs to civic organizations that offered Christian fellowship.[10]

Historians have correctly emphasized that agricultural marketing cooperatives were among the more popular palliatives prescribed by the USDA during the farm crisis. In 1900, the USDA had recorded only 1,167 agricultural cooperatives nationwide. By 1924, twelve thousand agricultural marketing cooperatives did business worth $2.5 billion. With the pretext of creating economic opportunities for farmers, the cooperative turn circulated the industrial ideal among smaller producers and defused radical political challenges to capitalist agriculture. Unlike their nineteenth-century predecessors, most new marketing cooperatives integrated managerial strategies predicated on profit, efficiency, standardization, and capital-intensive production. As a result, new marketing cooperatives had a variety of institutional characteristics that ensured that they would be governed like businesses and managed exclusively for profit maximization. "There must be no politics in it—nothing but straight business from the ground up," explained Aaron Sapiro, a prolific evangelist of the cooperative turn. "We don't permit discussions on subjects that have nothing to do with our commercial problem. . . . The cooperative associations are composed wholly of business interests and are organized exactly like a bank." The Capper-Volstead Act (1922) expanded agricultural antitrust exemptions by allowing marketing cooperatives to issue stocks and bonds and thus to finance mechanization and the hiring of marketing and management experts. The agricultural cooperatives envisioned by the USDA and the agricultural press were not so much ways for farmers to band together and defend themselves from predatory firms and the caprices of the market; they were instruments to ease farmers into management models suitable for an economy dominated by large, efficient, highly mechanized firms.[11]

Beyond marketing cooperatives, the cooperative turn found its clearest expression in the explosive growth of farm bureaus. Beginning in upstate New York in 1911, county extension agents and chambers of commerce urged the creation of these voluntary farmers' associations or clubs. Ultimately, farm bureaus served simultaneously as locally rooted clearinghouses for businesslike agriculture; cooperative purchasing and marketing organizations; political muscle for the CES, USDA, and agricultural progressives; and community organizations for rural people. The Smith-Lever Act fueled the farm bureau's flame with an accelerant of public subsidies. County extension agents—salaries and expenses paid by federal, state, and municipal agencies—did the organizational legwork and often gave free office space to farm bureaus. In return, farm bureaus provided the USDA with grassroots allies and acted as extension's civil-society partner. On the High Plains, extension and the farm bureau allied to rout the Nonpartisan League, a radical agrarian political movement. In the South, the two broke labor and tenant organizations. By the advent of the farm crisis, the farm bureau emerged as a national political power. At its founding meeting in 1919, the American Farm Bureau Federation (AFBF), the national umbrella organization for county and state-wide farm bureaus, claimed an initial membership of more than 300,000 farmers. Within five years, membership topped 1.5 million and the AFBF was the most formidable agricultural lobby in Washington.[12]

Farm bureaus gave the USDA and the CES consolidated access points for personal contact, further multiplying the extension's potential for personal transformation. New York extension official and farm bureau pioneer Maurice Burritt laid out that case in his book *The County Agent and the Farm Bureau* (1922). Farm bureaus, by Burritt's reckoning, permitted collective economic action but also offered a "common meeting ground" where "the farmer and the government's agricultural employees" could be "brought closer together." In the farm bureau office, ordinary farmers, middlemen, financiers, agricultural experts, and county agents would all commingle, "sharing agricultural statistics and records" and "information and advice as to what the best practices and methods" were. Burritt's emphasis on shared social space underscored the trust and intimacy that farm bureaus fostered between farmers and sometimes distant sources of capital, knowledge, and technology. That cooperative spirit was also highly infectious beyond the confines of the meeting room. Describing the cooperative activities of a Maryland farmers' club, B. H. Crocheron noted that the greatest benefit of the organization was to circulate among "the people of the country-side a concrete example and ideal of fine American citizenship and strong country manhood." If proximity in cooperative spaces produced the necessary masculine self-possession, rationality, and comfort with external expertise and capital needed for rural leadership, that exemplar of manhood could be translated further through the daily interactions between members and the rest of the community.[13]

To complement the promise of better men, rural cooperative institutions also promised to improve the lot of women and children. The CES, of course, employed female home demonstration agents and invested a third of its resources in 4-H clubs. Mirroring this strategy, farm bureaus featured "home bureaus" for rural women and a variety of planned activities and events for rural youth. Beyond ensuring that the personal contact of cooperation was gender-appropriate, such activities provided additional access points, allowing the farm bureau to appeal on multiple fronts, not just to rural patriarchs. It also made use of the labor and activism of rural women, who, according to Burritt, gave their "natural" attention to "rural social and community problems and to the needs of children." In deploying this familial rhetoric, advocates of the cooperative turn appealed to female reformers concerned with the relationship between rural family life and poor rural health. The alleged causes of poor rural health were numerous. Reformers rightly noted that distance to potable water and medical care in rural communities drove the countryside's comparatively higher morbidity rates. Reformers pointed out that rural women engaged in strenuous labor during and immediately after pregnancies, which undoubtedly posed a serious danger to mothers and infants. But they also blamed the consequences of poverty and racism on ignorance and bad "mothering" skills. The ideal of the "farmer's wife" circulated by home economists encouraged rural women to abandon revenue-producing labor and focus on domestic consumption, nurturing, health, and aesthetics—changes that essentially sought to transform farmwives into rural analogues of urban, middle-class housewives.[14]

As with male-focused agriculturalists, cooperation's promise of enhanced social connectivity and multiplying personal contacts offered female reformers a number of new tools. Cooperation could mean broader public support for rural infrastructure improvements that shrank distances to clean water and medical care. Farm organizations worked with public health agencies on campaigns and initiatives. And women's rural organizations provided grassroots workers for those campaigns that could do the taxing organizational and persuasive labor in scattered communities where male public health officials would not deign to travel. But social connectivity also enhanced the educational opportunities that female reformers hoped would transform coarse rural women into efficient "farmers' wives." Just as cooperation expanded the reach of the CES's county agricultural agents, it did the same for their home demonstration agents, who introduced USDA-approved homemaking techniques into rural communities through public demonstrations, home visits, and clubs. Cooperation promised to break the boredom, monotony, and lonesomeness that many women candidly admitted drove them from farms to city. In this, justifications for cooperative social forms circled back to the specter of rural-to-urban migration. By making rural life more socially fulfilling for rural women, reformers could hope to retain the countryside's most eugenically fit. For the many female rural reformers enamored of eugenics, cooperative institutions provided the means to assess and voluntarily regulate reproductive fitness. Female health reformers organized "better baby" contests at state and county fairs not far from stalls promoting cooperative livestock marketing organizations. Such a juxtaposition of standardized animal and human bodies was far from accidental. Rather, those reformers transposed to the problem of rural health the grammar, values, and organizational techniques of the industrial ideal.[15]

For all its victories, proponents of the cooperative turn recognized a fundamental obstacle to their ambitions: the atomized patriarchs most in need of the cooperative spirit were also those most unwilling to enter the institutions that fostered it. Experts at the USDA, such as William Lloyd, the USDA's representative at the organizational meeting of the AFBF, worried that adult farmers, poorly educated and accustomed to the social isolation of rural living, would never accept the USDA's recommendations, no matter how many pamphlets county agents pushed into their hands or how much they promoted farm bureaus. A decade earlier, the conflict had focused on the integration of modern planting techniques; now agricultural progressives bemoaned the overly individualistic, stubborn farmers who refused to "cooperate" or who, in the case of the Nonpartisan League and the Farmers' Union, cooperated in ways dangerous to capitalist enterprise. As with scientific farming before it, the acceptance of a cooperative spirit would require serious cultural work beginning in youth, when rural residents were most pliable. According to Lloyd, club work was essential to effective cooperation and farm bureaus. Part of the solution to stubborn patriarchs was to train a generation of boys in "community leadership and cooperative efforts" that combined cooperation with "self-reliance" and the rudiments of business-like agriculture. Like Mann, who announced an "awakened rural manhood," Lloyd envisioned 4-H boys grown into splendid manhood as the key to future rural leadership. But producing such splendid manhood required a careful balance: on the one hand, boys needed to be trained to participate in collective action; on the other, they needed to cherish the spirit of commercial competition. Even by 1920, the USDA believed that 4-H, with an approach both competitive and cooperative, trained rural boys to be the extraordinary examples of rural capitalism who would, in time, grow into a generation of farmer-businessmen drawn from Jardine's dreams.[16]

Before 4-H could be expected to promote cooperation, businesslike agriculture, and awakened manhood in rural America, the club system needed to be reinforced. In fact, the events of World War I had dangerously overextended the 4-H network and left it in need of serious organizational attention from the USDA. In the decade after World War I, experts at the USDA and the land-grant colleges attempted to "standardize" club work, particularly through the introduction of what O. H. Benson, the USDA's 4-H architect, termed the "club cycle." Experts at the USDA hoped to create "standard" 4-H clubs at the local level—clubs that shared a uniform structure and set of goals in every rural community in America. To ensure that 4-H clubs were locally supported and considered organic elements of their communities, organizers also worked hard to enroll individual farm bureaus in the organization and operation of the clubs. Within a decade of the Smith-Lever's passage, the USDA had created a network of standard clubs, interwoven with the farm bureau, that were conducive to financial intimacy and the promotion of healthy rural manhood.

The sharp increase in agricultural production during World War I created a rural labor shortage and pulled millions of youth into agricultural production. Given considerable wartime migration to urban areas and the enlistment of potential agricultural workers, the CES recognized the need to access new sources of labor beyond just gardening. To that end, the CES focused on utilizing the labor of youth, both rural and urban. As a part of that wartime food-production program, the CES encouraged youth to enroll in a variety of agricultural clubs, framing agricultural labor in the language of national service. Many youths tended small victory gardens of produce for subsistence and local sale, but the program was often even more elaborate. To promote club work, O. H. Benson envisioned a massive "mile-long" "Boys' and Girls' Club Interstate Pageant." The pageant would feature farm machinery presented as "Our 4-H Machine Guns" and the "Corn Club Cavaliers"—"40 boys mounted on horse back . . . bedecked with corn stalk gun, ear of corn pistol tied to belt and corn husk decorations of uniform arrangements on hats." Youth from towns and cities also joined the effort, by converting open urban lots into gardens or by taking a work holiday in the country to help with the harvest. "Boys of Connecticut! Help the farmers with the harvest!" implored a propaganda poster. In total, more than a million youth joined clubs organized by the USDA in 1918, including more than 364,000 in garden clubs, and hundreds of thousands of urban youth traveled into the countryside at the harvest.[17]

Like high commodity prices, massive club enrollments were an artifact of war and fell back to earth with peace. Recognizing that the appropriations would not survive the war, many agricultural colleges had employed temporary or part-time club agents with limited experience in extension work and virtually no experience with club work. This "constantly shifting personnel," in turn, had constructed ad hoc "costly" and "ruinous" club organizations that diverged broadly from club to club.[18] Training new leaders was laborious and expensive. Inexperienced leaders made more mistakes, and too many mistakes could damage the broader reputation of the program. A bad calf club might produce a dead calf. "It takes a long time to overcome the prejudice thus established," pointed out one Wisconsin club leader. As nationalist sentiments began to recede and the extension service laid off its temporary agents, club enrollments sank to prewar levels. The war brought an enormous expansion of club enrollments but had left the program badly overextended, even as the deteriorating agricultural situation demanded, more than ever, a vigorous and efficient club network.[19]

Extension officials in Washington and club workers in the states argued that the club network needed structural improvement and that individual club workers needed better training. After a conference on club standardization in 1918, the USDA circulated a definition of a "standard" club to bring clubs in line with its educational philosophy. A "standard" club required a minimum of five members "working on the same project" under the charge of an adult leader. Each club would elect a set of officers from its members, and the clubs would follow a program of work over the course of the year. If the club achieved that basic standard, the USDA issued it an official charter. Clubs might also acquire a "seal of achievement" if they met an even more rigorous standard. To acquire the seal, clubs needed to hold a minimum of six meetings, to publicly exhibit project results, and to organize a team to give "public demonstrations" of the club's production methods. The club needed to secure a project completion rate of 60 percent from its membership, to file a concluding report with the extension service of its activities, to organize "a judging team" for fair competitions, to host "an achievement day program," and to integrate its members "in the farm bureau or other county extension organization."[20] The USDA circulated material that defined the standard components and practices involved in club work.[21] In addition to this uniform structure, the more rigorous training of leaders established a standard procedure, or club "cycle," as O. H. Benson put it.[22]

The USDA insisted that the clubs be organized according to "democratic" principles that emphasized the clubs' voluntary nature and their deliberative structure. Farm youth joined individual clubs organized on a community-by-community basis by state club specialists, county extension agents, or, in counties that employed one, a club agent. The organization of a club began early in the year, with an enrollment campaign by county agents. Once a base level of enrollments had been achieved, club members elected officers—usually a president, vice president, treasurer, secretary, and historian—who were charged with running individual meetings and keeping collective records (individual club members were responsible for keeping personal project records). The club elected the voluntary adult leader, a responsible adult who attended meetings, regularly checked in with the county agent, distributed material provided by the CES to club members, planned and chaperoned club social events, and regularly made home visits to check the progress of projects. "A carefully planned system of follow-up work contemplates a visit from a leader not less than once a month, [and] a brief letter, giving timely advice should be sent by the local leader to each member," Benson explained.[23] In the first decade of club work, teachers constituted a large portion of club leaders. By 1925, fewer than a quarter of club leaders were teachers, as farmers, bankers, merchants, and homemakers replaced them.[24]

The decreased reliance on schoolteachers was due, in no small part, to the growing role of the farm bureau in organizing and running 4-H clubs. In the early years of the farm bureau, county agents had considered the farm bureau an entirely distinct project from agricultural clubs. By 1920, however, county agents were working to integrate clubs and farm bureaus, reasoning that they were mutually reinforcing institutions. By then, most county agents worked closely with local farm bureaus as they established clubs, depending on farm bureau members to volunteer as leaders and to recruit their own and neighbors' children to join. To facilitate that process, county agents asked older 4-H members to sit on county agricultural planning councils. Some club organizers went so far as to consider club work as a direct feeder for farm bureau membership. "If we are going to make club work permanent our boys and girls must be club members until they are 18 years old and then they will step right over to be farm bureau members," explained one Colorado extension official.[25] Even when clubs failed to accomplish that ambitious goal, close coordination was the norm.

Such close coordination permitted county agents to effectively integrate club work with the county farm bureau's agricultural plan. Project selection was an important process, since it dictated how member labor would be directed, what sort of instruction would occur, what supplies would be needed for the year of work, and what methods would be demonstrated to the wider community. Projects varied widely by state and region, depending on the local patterns of agriculture—the types of agriculture practiced and the types of agriculture that the extension service wished to see practiced. Cotton projects, for example, were common across the South but almost entirely absent in the North. Nearly all states, however, offered a basic core of projects: core agricultural projects included corn, pig, cattle, and garden projects; core home economics projects included meal preparation, canning, and sewing. In theory, a club's project selection would be the result of deliberation between the club, the leader, the county agent, farm bureau members, and county agricultural planning councils, a deliberative process that would ensure that the project complemented the agricultural plan of the county. To assist that process, the clubs in a single county often elected representatives to form a county 4-H council. In practice, however, county agents, farm bureaus, and local leaders decided in advance what projects would be most appropriate and guided the club to select them. The CES warned leaders against domineering behavior and encouraged leaders to have clubs vote on all major decisions. Club experts noted, however, that a tactful adult could guide deliberation to preferred outcomes, an observation that echoed the broader philosophy of extension. "That local leader governs best who appears not to govern at all," wrote Gertrude Warren. "Carefully guide the group into making just decisions by placing the responsibility upon them."[26]

The "common ground" of the farm bureau enabled county agents and home demonstration agents to better integrate the frequently distinct male and female components of the 4-H program. 4-H clubs were usually de facto sex-segregated by projects. Even when a single club ran male "agricultural" projects and female "home economics" projects, the club would break into smaller sex-segregated groups for project instructions. However, some amount of intermingling between the sexes was both unavoidable and desirable. In the early 1920s, many of the most popular agricultural projects— garden and poultry projects, for example—attracted both male and female enrollments. Even when clubs were entirely sex-segregated, they often coordinated to plan outings, picnics, and other joint social activities with clubs composed of the opposite sex. Given those complex needs, farm bureaus and county planning councils frequently provided a venue for leaders focused primarily on just one sex to coordinate with leaders of other clubs.[27]

Having decided the type of project, the club leader prepared a syllabus of meetings based on material provided by the extension agent, which offered lesson plans for the individual meetings. The plan of work often laid out club meetings for an entire year, but in areas where travel was difficult, it might squeeze all six mandatory meetings into a span of three months. Clubs met at a private home or a centrally located public space such as a school or civic building. Meetings also convened in "demonstration" spaces—a barn, field, or kitchen—where the club could watch as a leader or member worked through a recommended practice. For projects with no seasonal specificity, such as sewing, meeting plans developed basic skills in the initial meetings and introduced more advanced methods in successive meetings. For projects that were seasonally sensitive, like most agricultural projects, syllabi patterned lessons around the demands of the calendar. The extension service offered introductory, intermediate, and advanced syllabi for most types of projects, and a given club might enroll a mix of members with different levels of competency. Introductory sewing projects, for example, focused only on teaching the basics of garment repair, while advanced projects instructed girls on fabricating entire wardrobes. Similarly, introductory pig-club syllabi concentrated on the care and feeding of pigs, while advanced pig-club syllabi introduced the intricacies of breeding, farrowing, and herd development.[28]

Once a club was organized and had adopted its line of work, club leaders staged regular meetings. At these meetings, club members reported on their progress, and the club leader or a guest speaker demonstrated timely project-related methods. Clubs often met for purely social occasions, such as picnics, parties, and dances. In the fall, club leaders and county agents introduced club members to the "standards" and "quality of products" that would be used to evaluate their club projects. Club results were presented first to the club and then at the county fair or a 4-H "achievement" day. Club leaders were expected to fully catalog project results and forward their reports to the county, district, or state leaders. The club leader coordinated with community members and organizations to recognize the accomplishments of club members.[29]

The standard method called for club members to demonstrate promising agricultural and homemaking techniques to the public. Club demonstration teams refined a particular innovative agricultural or home economics practice with the goal of popularizing it in communities through staged regular demonstrations. New Hampshire 4-H clubs spread the word about successful iceberg lettuce cultivation.[30] In Arizona, teams of rural youth raised the long-staple pima cotton and gave presentations about their results and methods through farmers' organizations and at fairs and civic gatherings.[31] In other cases, youth demonstrations pushed farmers to rethink how they used traditional commodities. "Caponizing" or castrating roosters had fallen out of practice in Essex, Massachusetts, because of the high level of skill required for the surgical procedure. Fourteen-year-old James Reed, a skilled poultry demonstrator, popularized the craft in his community by informing Essex farmers about the lucrative value-added product.[32]

With responsibility for staging demonstrations, organizing clubs, and conducting home visits, 4-H-related activities consumed a considerable portion of any county agent's time. Although extension and home demonstration agents rarely led clubs, they dedicated, on average, slightly under a third of their time to 4-H. This commitment of time included visits to club meetings and farms to check the results of projects; the demonstration of techniques to club members and, frequently, curious parents; and the organization and

judging of countywide 4-H contests, usually at the county fair. Agents collected and evaluated the records of the individual clubs, organized events
such as picnics and "rally days" for club members from multiple clubs, and
recruited new members and leaders.[33] County agents and state specialists
acted as the primary publicists for 4-H by drafting press releases for local
papers or by assisting club members in doing the same. State extension services and the USDA noted that newspapers were more willing to give free
publicity to extension if the copy mentioned 4-H.[34]

By standardizing club work, experts at the USDA and at the land-grant
colleges hoped to create a network of clubs organized according to a uniform
set of methods and symbols that was nevertheless locally embedded and
well adapted to the needs of individual rural communities. Club organizers
believed that standardization would ensure higher-quality instruction and
more stability for clubs. Nevertheless, standardization needed to be tempered
by the unique needs of each county. "I am not so especially interested in the
machinery, as to whether it has two cog wheels or five, as to how many club
members there are on the executive committee or on the community committee," warned William Lloyd at a conference of club organizers. "Let's not so
far standardize the machine that we think only of it and not the work."[35] The
farm bureau provided a space where county agents could gather allies for club
work, coordinate club leaders, and work out how club work fit into the larger
county extension program. Even as the USDA worked to standardize organizational methods and the symbols of club work, it also took steps to ensure
that 4-H clubs were firmly embedded in local institutions and communities.

As standardization created a uniform method for organizing and conducting club work at the local level, experts at the USDA worked to ensure
that 4-H clubs also created a spirit of cooperation that connected individual
clubs to commercial capital and technocratic authority. By "cooperation,"
these experts meant more than the ability of club members to work together
on common projects. More important, these experts envisioned club work as
the local access point for a national network that connected rural youth and
communities to far-flung sources of finance and knowledge. Experts at the
USDA and the land-grant colleges argued that, through local clubs, 4-H'ers
would learn to cooperate not just with one another but with banks, railroads,
implement and input retailers, and agricultural experts. Cooperation with
these actors required iterative practices that encouraged thrift, efficiency,
discipline, responsibility, and scrupulous accounting, all characteristics that
agricultural progressives deemed essential both to manhood and profitable

farm management. Cooperation generated financial intimacy and blazed a healthy trail to manhood for rural boys.

Cooperative potential and financial intimacy distinguished 4-H from other forms of agricultural vocational education, which focused on technical instruction. 4-H's cooperative potential facilitated a private funding structure for the most costly components of club work, the livestock and crop projects that enrolled mostly boys. The funding structure, in turn, built trust between farm boys and businessmen that primed the boys to reliably consume a variety of financial products. Such personal relationships exposed rural boys to examples of manhood beyond just their own fathers. Consistent with agricultural progressives' skepticism of rural patriarchs, 4-H's proponents argued that the cooperation facilitated by club work allowed for the interwoven economic development of rural communities and the gendered development of rural boys. Boys banqueted with bankers and "unconsciously" absorbed their "influence" and "viewpoints." 4-H's supporters invested those personal relationships with the power to cultivate a new generation of farmer-businessmen even if rural patriarchs remained hopelessly wedded to their "old man's method."[36]

Experts at the USDA and voices in the agricultural press lauded 4-H's dual commitment to cooperation and competition. Club work "developed local leadership and a habit of cooperation through the club group," explained O. H. Benson, but it also trained for "self-reliance" and "matters of thrift and economy by showing [club members] how to make profits on their own investment of time, money, and energy. . . . It teaches business methods and management in farming and home making."[37] Similarly, Gertrude Warren extolled 4-H's ability to foster teamwork.[38] The effect of this teamwork inculcated "faith in industry" and led to both personal and collective profit. As one USDA manual from 1925 put it, "4-H club boys and girls earn money and acquire property" even as they "meet together, work together, play together, cooperate, achieve." 4-H clubs promoted a capitalist vision of cooperation that valorized the accumulation of private property through industrious, businesslike agriculture and emphasized that voluntary, private associations had the power to solve many of the social and systemic problems that plagued rural America.[39]

Advocates of club work charged that the dual competitive and cooperative nature of 4-H elevated it above competing educational ventures in rural America. In 1917, Congress passed the Smith-Hughes Act, which appropriated funds for vocational agriculture classes at high schools and junior colleges and, after 1928, for Future Farmers of America clubs. In theory,

Smith-Hughes substantially expanded the federal government's role in education; but in practice, the breadth of its mandate and the scarcity of its funds meant that the federal board depended on state educational bureaucracies for administrative oversight and had little tangible influence.[40] Still, many prominent educators favored Smith-Hughes vocational education over 4-H. Some critics of 4-H, like David Snedden, dismissed it as merely an "amateurish" social club that lacked the disciplinary environment that successful vocational education required. Mabel Carney and Fannie Wynch Dunn complained that 4-H utilized county agents trained as agriculturalists rather than educators and was, as a result, too focused on "economics," competition, and profits.[41] In response, 4-H's defenders argued that club work's ability to hone and mobilize the competitive and profit-oriented instincts of rural youth within a cooperative space was precisely what elevated it above traditional school-bound education. As Robert Foster of the USDA argued in direct response to Carney and Dunn, 4-H taught "young people how to conduct business meetings, how to handle their own affairs, how to cooperate and work together and certainly cooperation is one of the most needed traits of our generation."[42]

Although Foster focused on cooperation between club members, 4-H also fostered a kind of cooperation that paralleled the relationships created by farm bureaus among farmers, financiers, businessmen, and technocrats. The CES and state and local sources paid extension agents' salaries but did not cover the expenses of individual projects. For some families, the costs of fertilizer, cloth, or a purebred hog were easily absorbed, but, for poorer families especially, diverting money to an untested educational project was a risky investment. To address capital costs, extension agents worked to enroll local businesspeople in club work, usually by asking them to provide "loans at reasonable interest rates directly to club members," as C. B. Smith, an extension official and 4-H booster, put it in a speech to the American Bankers Association.[43] Extension officials argued that the participation of the business community was good for all parties concerned. It offered the business glowing publicity, just as it habituated local youth to purchasing their wares or taking their loans. For the youth, building relationships with bankers and retailers not only allowed them to participate in club work; it also gave them vital experience managing the financial side of a farming operation. As A. C. True explained, club work taught rural youth "the value of money or other property earned by productive work, the functions of the banker and insurance company, and the importance of wise expenditures to make possible a good income from work."[44]

Organizers praised 4-H's encouragement of "ownership" among rural boys, partly because it promised to release those boys from the grips of their miserly fathers. "Too many of the boys of yesterday had no proprietary interest in the farm," noted a 1920 article in *Wallaces Farmer*. "They worked, and worked hard, but got very little out of it. All too often they had no live stock of their own." By contrast, the growing availability of livestock breeding and crop clubs offered boys the opportunity to own livestock and captain their own business venture. A 1919 article in *Farm Home* hailed the end of the "days of penury" for rural youth. "Johnnie Jones," the author's archetypal rural boy, was no longer "penniless . . . dependent on his father's generosity." Thanks to 4-H and the USDA, Johnnie was "a young man of financial standing who owns property and has money in the bank." It was not yet farm ownership, but club work set the boys to become farmer-businessmen by cultivating "proprietary interest[s]" in farming through small infusions of capital. Nor was Johnnie alone. The agricultural press abounded with similar tales, some fictional, but others extensively documented, of rural youth—usually boys—finding financial independence through 4-H clubs and overturning, as an article in *Prairie Farmer* put it, the days of "Frank's colt and father's horse."[45]

Girls, too, appeared in these accounts, but articles usually emphasized the novelty of female participation in animal breeding or field crop projects. A characteristic blurb in the *Chicago Livestock World* about an Iowa 4-H delegation at the International Livestock Exposition announced, "32 Young Farm People, Including Two Girls, Are Headed to the Show." Rather than subverting the increasingly ironclad bifurcation of masculine revenue-producing agricultural labor and feminine homemaking labor, the marked "exceptional" girls stabilized the emergent gendered division of labor. Even in cases where club work created paths to financial autonomy for rural girls, exceptional accounts were usually accompanied by testaments to the very gendered norms that the exceptions punctured. For example, Caroline Eyring, a nineteen-year-old Arizona club girl, amassed a remarkable $1,000 in assets through her homemaking club work. "Much of my little feat I attribute to my training in club work," she wrote, "for efficiency is taught in keeping records and in leading clubs." Yet Eyring also assured her readers that her enviable resources would not mean that she planned to pursue future riches in the city. Rather, she cited her mother's advice: "Let choose who will a city life; I will be a farmer's wife." O. C. Croy, Ohio's 4-H assistant state leader, offered an even more conventional account in his explanation of 4-H's contributions to "the proper development of [Ohio's] boys and girls." Among the girls, Croy lauded Mary Staker, a girl who, while serving on the Muskingum County farm bureau's club committee, had still done "all the housework at home." By contrast, Croy celebrated Pern Woodman for collaborating with his father to "establish a herd of purebred hogs and is now starting with purebred Short-horn cattle."[46]

Tales of boys like Pern Woodman reflected the tightening links among revenue production, debt consumption, and rural masculine identity; they also proposed that such financial intimacies worked *as* gendering instruments that guaranteed boys' healthy ascents into rural manhood. As John-nie Jones's growth into propertied maturity suggested, the opportunity for ownership as a boy ensured a responsible, profitable attitude toward finances as a man. A 1928 article in *Wallaces Farmer* warned parents about the alternative. The article cited one mother who begged a newspaper not to print her thieving son's name. He had been "an awfully good boy," but his father's tight fist had driven him to a life of crime. The father "never [gave] him any money to buy gasoline for his car to use going to school six miles away, and altho the boy worked hard, he didn't get anything for his labor, and so stole." The article contrasted the criminal boy with a boy who was a model student and the star of his football team. His father gave him "an allowance" and had made him a "partner . . . in the business of farming." Similarly, "club boys who raise poultry or livestock have a home interest and are not found loafing in town," the article noted. An article in *Banker Farmer* relayed a similar, if less sensational, contrast. One boy, Jimmy, had asked his father for a pure-bred pig, only to receive mockery and the offer of a scrub. Rebuffed, Jimmy left the farm to work at a garage in town, and his father was baffled, unaware, as the article put it, that "the time to interest the boy in the farm is when he is a boy—not a man." Another boy, John, joined a pig club and took a loan from a local banker, Mr. Brown. In a year's time, he repaid the loan, deposited $117 in his account, and invited Mr. Brown to speak at his club's banquet. The future of Mr. Brown's community justified his interest in the pig club. Even if it was "small business," one day the "six pig club boys will probably be the six wealthiest farmers in the community. . . . Boost the boys and they will boost the banks." Such articles reformulated the problem of rural progress as a complicated intergenerational melee, as scoffing, skinflint fathers battled rural bankers for the next generation's destiny—for the right to shepherd boys on their path to propertied manhood.[47]

Extension agents concentrated their efforts on local bankers to secure financial support for club work. Noted agriculturalist Seaman Knapp designed his original system of demonstration work with the enrollment of bankers and merchants in mind, partly in the interest of crafting better relations between farmers and businessmen. Banks had responded with enthusiasm to the possibility of improving their standing with farmers and embraced the opportunity to help finance extension programs. Taking note in 1912 of a sudden swell of support for scientific and businesslike agriculture in the banking industry, the *New York Times* went so far as to describe a "great movement" for "better farming ... head[ed]" by thirty state banking associations and the American Bankers Association. Bradford Knapp, Seaman Knapp's son and the head of Southern extension at the USDA, urged the ABA at an "agricultural rally" during its annual meeting to extend loans to agricultural club members. He argued that youth, unlike their parents, would adopt "progressive" practices and that club work could habituate them to the use of credit and amicable relations with local bankers.[48]

The banking industry heeded Knapp's call. "Bankers and businessmen have taken more direct interest in this phase of our extension work than any other," reported C. B. Smith.[49] In 1920 alone, bankers provided over $1.6 million in loans to club members.[50] By 1925, thirty-six state banking associations were actively supporting club work with prizes and encouraged their members to provide loan service.[51] Typically, bankers offered a loan of as little as ten dollars, cosigned by a parent, which was sufficient to cover project expenses and due to be repaid, with interest of 5 percent to 10 percent of the principal, at the time of the county or state fair. For livestock clubs, bankers and merchants sometimes arranged for club members to carry insurance policies on their livestock in case of disease or poor care. Loan contracts frequently encouraged boys to deposit any profits from their project with the bank that offered the financing.[52]

The idea that country banks should be a primary source of capital for club projects was so well institutionalized that industry publications identified support for club work as a foundational element for agricultural finance departments.[53] E. B. Harshaw, in a series of articles for *Bankers Magazine*, quoted favorably an assessment that 4-H clubs were "the most important phase of extension works" and urged that, if a community did not have a club, bankers should work with the county agent to organize one. Bank-backed club work, Harshaw glowed, kept youth in rural communities, improved agricultural practices, familiarized future farmers with account and record keeping, and improved the standing of the bank in the community.[54] By funding clubs, businessmen would convince rural residents that they were "public-spirited." In addition to loans, local merchants and bankers provided prizes and premiums for outstanding club work. In Arizona, the ABA transported outstanding club members to Tucson for an annual short course, while local creameries, dairy magazines, and packers all donated prizes to support Wisconsin 4-H clubs.[55]

Banking industry publications emphasized that commercial loan transactions underwrote ever more binding forms of intimacy, such as friendship and mentoring. The pig-club banquet, then, was an especially prime site in the intergenerational melee—a space where Mr. Brown and John assembled their relationship with "roasted weinies" and good cheer. An editorial in *Wallaces Farmer* explained that a small loan "secur[ed a] hold on these boys that will surely tie them to his bank when they get into business for themselves. [The banker] has been their friend, and they have learned to trust him." But beyond businessmen simply opening their coffers, 4-H boosters also emphasized that they needed personal proximity and intimate contact with rural youth. Country bankers must "cultivate the acquaintance of the boy and girls. . . . Get in your automobile, drive through your community or county with your county agent, call on some of these boys and girls." Club promoters argued that boys needed contact with the businessmen of their communities because, to be successful farmers, boys needed the financial skills and sober judgment that their fathers so manifestly lacked. Interesting boys in modern farming, *Banker Farmer* explained, could not just be entrusted to the farmers alone but was "the specialized duty of every man in the community." J. D. McVean, an animal husbandry specialist with the USDA, expanded on the advantages that accrued when bankers embraced this "duty" and forged "close personal relations" with youngsters. "The personal interest of the banker in his young patrons has a very valuable influence," wrote McVean, "and can be made a big factor in character building—then, too, the youngsters being close imitators will unconsciously attain the business man's viewpoint through their association with him—a point all too often lacking in our farmers." Similar to Maurice Burritt's contention that the intimate connectivity of farm bureaus generated amicable relations among businessmen and farmers, McVean's idea was that clubs allowed bankers to play an important role in the gendered development of rural boys by exposing boys to the sobriety, diligence, and efficiency that their fathers lacked.[56]

Neither the boys nor their fathers were always inclined to follow this script. Sometimes, it seemed, the boys disregarded good examples set by the businessmen and emulated their shiftless fathers. In Polk County, Wisconsin, for example, County Agent F. C. Claflin awarded Harold Larson, a local club boy, seventeen dollars to cover his attendance at the state fair in Madison. Rather than attending, the boy pocketed the money. Claflin confronted Harold and his father, but Harold's father "insist[ed that] the boy should have the money."[57] Observing the case, the state leader of Wisconsin 4-H, T. L. Belwick, could "not blame the boys" for dissembling. "I blame the fathers. The farmers today are so grasping that they would even train their sons in dishonesty rather than to lose even a dollar that doesn't belong to them."[58] Club organizers sometimes grumbled that the most rotten patriarchs infiltrated clubs with the sour hopes of exploiting club work's financial benefits for their own enrichment. "Some men are unscrupulous enough to try to use club members as a means of selling livestock, seeds, or other products at high prices or to use their boys or girls as a so-called club member in order to buy high class products which some good breeder or crop men is willing to sell to the club members at a price lower than the established price," complained E. L. Austin, an Indiana club leader. Despite ongoing problems with such unsavory behavior, local bankers and businessmen continued to finance many club programs.[59]

After O. H. Benson's departure from the USDA in 1921, Clarence Beaman Smith took primary responsibility for ensuring that the 4-H program prepared its members for the demands of modern agriculture. Smith was a leading voice for the cooperative turn in the USDA—he attended the 1919 organizational meeting of the AFBF with William Lloyd—and his vision for 4-H directly reflected that passion. Born in rural Michigan in 1870, Smith carved a four-decade career out of extension work. First employed as an accountant in the Office of Experiment Stations in Washington, D.C., Smith transferred to the Office of Home Management under his mentor William J. Spillman in 1907. From there, he slowly worked his way up through the extension bureaucracy, eventually becoming assistant director of extension, until his retirement in 1938. Throughout his career, he was a tireless advocate of club work and took a great interest in its expansion and operation. As a CES administrator, Smith directed official extension policies concerned with club work and supervised the specialists in the Office of Cooperative Extension whose work touched on 4-H, including Milton Danziger, George Farrell, Ray Turner, and, most significant, Gertrude Warren.[60]

Smith praised 4-H's unique ability to promote cooperation and to "unit[e parents and children] in the work of solving the economic and social problems of the community as a whole."[61] Club work, Smith believed, was the best means to promote the most important "end" of agricultural extension, "helping the farmer farm more efficiently." Smith analogized the situation to the advent of prohibition. Preaching to adults had accomplished little. Prohibitionists had only managed to amend the constitution after they had "put the evil effects of alcohol in the textbooks of our schools, and the generation of boys and girls thus taught reached manhood and womanhood." Youth exposed to cooperation through 4-H clubs "g[o]t a bigger vision of agriculture and rural life during their early years which stay[ed] with them to their profit all the days of their lives." They would "at the outset access the sources of agricultural information and help they will want to consult all their years on the farm." Armed with that information, "they begin their farm and home careers with a knowledge of an experience in <u>cooperation</u> and group action, one of the most vital needs of farmers." Smith defined cooperation, then, as not merely collective work among rural youth but collective work that built relationships between rural youth and those external sources of "consult[ation]." Given that definition, Smith noted that 4-H'ers offered members experience in cooperating with businessmen. Businessmen, Smith boasted, were so enthusiastic that they had "form[ed] an independent, private National committee to encourage and help public agencies in carrying on the work."[62]

Smith alluded to the National Committee on Boys and Girls Club Work (National Committee). Although the National Committee vowed to "'sell' the club idea to business men all over the United States," its initial formation came at the USDA's behest.[63] At the 1920 National Swine Show in Des Moines, Milton Danziger, then working as a demonstration specialist for the USDA, approached Guy Noble, an employee of the Armour Packing Company. In 1919, Noble, on his own initiative, had obtained a set of prizes for club work from Armour and even organized a tour of the International Livestock Exposition for the prizewinners. Danziger asked Noble if he would be interested in organizing a group of like-minded businessmen to assist in the promotion of club work. Noble accepted.[64] The organization held a charter meeting in December 1921 and, thereafter, raised private funds for club work, lobbied Congress for more public support, and acted as the primary retailer of 4-H paraphernalia.

The National Committee quickly gathered an impressive coterie of supporters. In addition to giving assistance to the USDA, the committee would "coordinate and unify the efforts of bankers, manufacturers, merchants, chambers of commerce, packers, farm organizations, fair associations, livestock associations, farm papers and others supporting boys and girls club work in any way."[65] To accomplish this task, early organizational meetings of the committee were attended by a mixture of businessmen, representatives of the USDA, and well-placed agricultural progressives. Woodrow Wilson's second secretary of agriculture, Edwin T. Meredith, initially served as chairman of the committee; after 1924, meatpacking magnate Thomas E. Wilson steered the committee, with Noble's assistance. In 1921, Noble left his position with Armour and worked exclusively as managing director of the National Committee out of offices provided by the AFBF. John Coverdale, then the AFBF's national secretary, also joined the committee and attended the initial organizational meeting, along with representatives of most of the major livestock exposition and fair associations. In short order, other luminaries joined, bringing contacts that spanned banking, agribusiness, electoral politics, and the federal government: Alexander Legge, president of International Harvester and former vice chairman of the War Industries Board during World War I; Cully A. Cobb, publisher of *Southern Agriculturalist* and an extension veteran; Melvin Traylor, president of First National Bank; Walter William Head and John Huegin Puelicher, bank executives and successive presidents of the ABA; former Illinois governor Frank Lowden; and Senator Arthur Capper, a farm press baron, former Kansas governor, and an influential figure on national agricultural policy. In 1923, Calvin Coolidge accepted a position as the "honorary" chairman of the committee, a designation later offered and accepted by Presidents Hoover, Roosevelt, and Truman.[66]

With the National Committee providing political and financial support for club work, the USDA created supplemental institutions that offered training for club leaders and local organizers. Milton Danziger left the USDA to found the International 4-H Leadership Training School in Springfield, Massachusetts. Financed primarily by contributions from Horace A. Moses, a paper magnate and prolific philanthropist who also served on the board of the National Committee, the Leadership School met at the Northeastern Livestock Exposition in Springfield, beginning in 1923, and provided adult leaders with free instruction and training. USDA club specialists regularly gave lectures at the Leadership School. Individual state extension services also conducted their own 4-H leader training programs, usually running them out of the state's land-grant university. Volunteer local club leaders journeyed from around the state to receive instruction from extension specialists and professors at the agricultural college.[67]

As the USDA worked hard to present 4-H clubs as local, organic extensions of rural community spirit, club work functionally connected rural people to a vast national network of commercial interests and technocratic expertise. This network allied private bankers and retailers with public agricultural experts and county agents, shattering tenuous divisions between public and private agencies. In this sense, the spirit of "cooperation" fostered by 4-H clubs directly mirrored the cooperative spirit of the farm bureau. More than simply cooperating with one another, 4-H clubs taught rural youth to work with, rather than against, the mavens of commerce and finance. This cooperation was more than philosophical; it was visceral and intimate. The 4-H network created concrete and personal relationships between rural youth, agricultural experts, and the business community. By design, these personal relationships transmitted a new view of rural masculinity and exposed rural boys to male role models other than their fathers. From the titans of industry on the National Committee to Mr. Brown the country banker, bankers and businessmen rallied to the idea of shaping the next generation of farmers as they developed into manhood, a vision of rural progress that conflated the gendered development of boys with the expansion of capital-intensive, debt-financed agriculture. Put differently, justifications for 4-H's micro-finance programs reversed the usual announcement that a thriving, modern agriculture needed farmer-businessmen. Beyond that predictable narrative, the 4-H's financial components detailed how capital-intensive, debt-financed agriculture could itself be a gendering instrument.

*   *   *

At every level, 4-H organizers focused their efforts on ensuring that all 4-H members produced two classes of objects that could be examined and marveled over by the community: commodities and records. Whether it was a sewing, nutrition, or potato project, syllabi structured projects to ensure that the labor invested produced at least one tangible item suitable for demonstration and that club members recorded the process of producing that item through exhaustive record keeping. It was these items, the focus of club labor, that members showed to the community, entered in competitions at the fair, and ultimately hoped to sell for a tidy profit. "Each member conducts a substantial piece of work," a 1926 USDA manual noted, "designed to show some better practice on the farm or in the home or community; keeps a record of results; explains the work to others, and makes a final report on the work."[68]

Emphasis on records and the act of "recording" fit seamlessly with the broader ambition of 4-H organizers to habituate rural youth to ways of thinking consistent with the demands of capital-intensive, debt-financed agriculture. Keeping tidy records was the very definition of "businesslike" in 4-H clubs. "The first thing in being businesslike is to keep records," noted Harold Carmony, a celebrated Ohio 4-H'er, in the pages of *Ohio Farmer*. "A great many people fail in business and in life simply for lack of adequate and available records to give them the constant knowledge of where they stand.

Each of the various clubs requires a careful record of such items as costs, time, value and profit. These simple records instill in the conscientious member a businesslike aspect." As Carmony's comments suggested, this businesslike aspect guided youth "in business and in life." More than a narrow set of technical guidelines meant to regulate club practices now and farm practices later, record keeping, along with the "businesslike aspect" it instilled, constituted a system of decision making that guided agriculture as a profit-making venture. As O. H. Benson put it, 4-H meant "more than the mere management of and growing of a crop." 4-H should also instruct members in "preparing, grading and crating the products for the market, and how to secure and maintain a profitable market. . . . All club members should be taught the relation of producer to consumer, the best means of transportation, the value of the honest pack. . . . All over the United States today there are thousands of young men who have thus been benefited by this . . . *industrial education*, and it gives evidence of its efficiency in . . . opening the way for constructive and permanent interest and efficiency in the problems of farm management."[69]

Keeping accurate records and accounts permitted a transition from a particular wise practice to a more systematic effort at "farm management." The process of record keeping enabled rural youth to calculate costs, revenue, and profitability, to aggregate that information, and to make collective decisions on its basis. Instruments like scorecards, ledgers, and record books trained 4-H members in a broadly applicable way of gathering, organizing, and deploying knowledge. This epistemology of industrial agriculture structured an individual 4-H member's interaction with the world through processes of quantification, standardization, historicization, and monetization.

4-H material taught that the ambition to produce a perfect result was a noble one. "To aim toward a perfect type of animal or of crop, to a perfect type of home making," wrote Charles J. Galpin, "perfectly adjusted to the capacities of the community, and likewise perfectly adjusted to the needs of the State and Nation, is to take an unquestioned place among all privileged persons and classes who aim at attainment of 'the good, the beautiful, the true,'—an aim which, according to the standards of all ages, of all civilized peoples, is as high an aim as humans rise to."[70] In this way, 4-H material enabled a single object to express the "dignity" of rural life—a tomato, dress, bushel of corn, or calf—and channeled potentially alienating labor into a celebration of ageless agrarian ideals. As C. B. Smith described the potential inspiration of 4-H, "Ordinary tasks, done in ordinary ways, are simply work; but ordinary tasks, done in a better way, spell growth and satisfaction and make a contribution to life."[71] Even when the result of a project was not intended for the market, club material emphasized producing objects of at least a commercial quality that could be publicly displayed. In the case of home furnishing projects, for example, girls were encouraged to create visual representations of their refurbished rooms—through models, dioramas, posters, or photographs—or to present individual pieces from the room like a cabinet, lamp shade, or quilt.[72]

To assist club members in reaching "the good, the beautiful, the true" and producing the "perfect" specimen, most clubs included a scorecard that dissected complex objects into a series of quantifiable metrics. Scorecards could be used to compare a particular product with an ideal standard, a product with itself over time to demonstrate progress or regress, and one product with another product of the same class. Scorecards served the dual purpose of allowing club members to evaluate their products according to objective standards and preparing club members for the competition of the contest, fair, and, eventually, market. The scorecard provided an unofficial way for club members to compare themselves with their peers and, by the logic of the manuals, to motivate their best performances. As one Wisconsin circular put it: "The score card is more than a standard for competition in fairs and club work. . . . Competition is the lifeblood of business. It compels a search for better methods."[73] Scorecards acted as an ever-present reminder of the commercial future always implicit in 4-H's educational endeavors. In searching for the "State Egg Champion," Arizona poultry clubs balanced the pedagogic priorities of club attendance and record keeping with production metrics such as "flock size" and "average egg production."[74]

Because of their simplicity and flexibility, club organizers included scorecards in every facet of club work and thus rendered every facet of club work potentially competitive. Club material suggested that any characteristic could be usefully quantified, measured, and compared with objective external norms. Demonstration teams could be scored not just in terms of their project results but also by quantifications of their presentation skills.[75] Health projects typically provided scorecards to club members that encouraged "each club member [to] score herself at the beginning of the club year and again at the end."[76] Some nutrition projects encouraged members to score their own eating habits as well as those of their parents and siblings, allowing external experts to evaluate and adjust the behavior of entire rural families.[77] Bordering on parody, Robert G. Foster's 1926 manual on club organization demonstrated the usefulness of the scorecards by scoring George Washington on a set of "leadership" metrics. Foster concluded that, while earning a perfect 10 in both "War" and "Government," poor performance in the categories of "Charity," "Arts," "Education," and "Science" earned Washington a total score of only 78 out of a possible 120. Bringing things full circle, Gertrude Warren provided extension workers with a scorecard with which to evaluate the organizational abilities of local leaders in her 1925 guide to club leadership.[78]

While scorecards permitted club members to quantify their accomplishments, club material also emphasized the importance of recording the process of club work. The keeping of records, club experts argued, encouraged literacy without embracing a stilted pedagogy. Rather, recording the process through account books, ledgers, and a concluding narrative history made club members the authors of their labor. "The work is an educational process, dealing not with books, of which the child is frequently tired, but with the things out of which books are made. It is *doing something* rather than learning about doing something," explained one USDA manual. The doing something, in this case, depended on exhaustive record keeping of "time spent, materials used, costs, etc.," as well as making reports on "the progress of their work at club meetings . . . [and] to their leader summarizing their whole season's work."[79] Club records were proof of the "doing something." They provided both a visual trace of the something done—examinable by club leaders, county agents, and, potentially, state and national club experts—and a means to replicate the doing again. That twofold potential was crucial to preparing club members for work on a modern farm—where the operator precisely recorded practices, costs, and revenue to distinguish the profitable from the unprofitable. "Every boy and girl ought to keep a record of everything that he or she does," explained George Farrell. "When I say to a boy, 'How did you grow that pig?' he has his record, and can tell me what he fed that pig on last Monday morning. He knows what that pig had for breakfast, absolutely. The members need that record work."[80]

State extension services created a ledger for each type of project offered and made one available for every club member enrolled. A typical "poultry" manual, for example, provided a ledger to track all expenses and profit associated with a poultry production project. The manual's "final report" was a basic grid spreadsheet, with "month" rows along the y-axis and columns for "Eggs Produced," "Hens Sold or Used," "Grain Used," "Mash Used," "Milk Used," "Labor," and "Miscellaneous Items" along the x-axis further itemized by number/amount and value. At the bottom of the page, ten steps allowed club children to calculate the "net returns" over the course of the entire project.[81] Extension agents argued that these sorts of exhaustive, precise records enabled club members and their parents to assess the profitability of different farming practices. A. B. Ballantyne, the assistant club leader of Arizona, relayed a tale of an Arizona club member whose father owned a large dairy herd. When his son had initially enrolled in a dairy project, the county agent, checking on the boy's progress, had challenged the father to explain how he knew which of his cows turned him a profit. The farmer had dismissed record keeping, replying, "Oh, I can tell. I milk the cows." After two years of witnessing his son's results and after substantial hectoring from the county agent, the farmer began to keep production records and quickly sent unproductive members of the herd "to the butcher's block."[82]

This probably apocryphal interaction between the county agent, the 4-H boy, and the farmer revealed the deeper purpose of record keeping. Of course, the county agent helped the farmer make his operation more efficient and profitable, but he also encouraged him to assemble a written account of his farm—a quantitative map of his dairying—that made an expert analysis possible. The extensive and exhaustive keeping of records familiarized rural youth with the fundamental accounting tasks of commercial agriculture. They permitted 4-H members to accurately calculate the costs, revenue, and profit involved in each project, skills that extension agents hoped youth would carry with them as adult farmers to ensure that their future farms were efficient. On the other hand, as much as records were personally useful, they also rendered the farmstead "legible" to a variety of outside observers. Efficiency could be assessed only if a farm operation could be quantified. Records permitted agricultural experts and county agents to assess how an agricultural operation functioned as a business and to offer advice to improve that functioning. Experts at the state colleges and the USDA could compile those records to create aggregate pictures of the agricultural economy and to proffer recommendations about which crops to grow and how to market them. Records formed a financial history of a farm operation and provided a way for financiers to assess its future prospects. The world of finance also depended on this copious record keeping to build a complex picture of the agricultural economy, to inform banks and investors about the wisdom of investing in agricultural operations, land, or commodity futures. These economic maps depended on the process of collecting, assembling, and aggregating information from diffuse locations spread across a continent, a monumental task that required an alliance between state power, commercial interests, and individual farmers. Focused ever intently on the work of quantifying and recording, 4-H prepared rural youth to labor efficiently in full sight of experts and financiers. Record keeping was intimately wound into the larger project of cooperation—a means to permit rural youth to communicate with both sources of technocratic expertise and private commercial capital.

*   *   *

4-H's ability to acclimate rural youth to cooperation elevated it above alternative schemes to promote vocational education in rural America. In 4-H, rural youth worked with bankers, bureaucrats, and businessmen and created a seemingly grassroots movement for cooperation in communities across rural America. Cooperation exposed rural boys to sterling examples of awakened rural manhood, and, through accompanying financial intimacies, it imparted to boys the important manly characteristics that their fathers often lacked. But cooperation entailed more than personal contact. Records and account books traveled from local communities to state colleges and eventually to Washington, where, in aggregate, they offered officials like C. B. Smith and other advocates of club work a bird's-eye view of the 4-H network. By pulling such a broad array of actors into the 4-H network, the mantra of cooperation sometimes flattened a remarkably diverse set of interests. In this sense, the benefits of club work came to mean very different things to different actors, even as they cooperated in an ostensibly unified project.

For the USDA, cooperation with the National Committee promised additional political support for expansion of the 4-H network and agricultural extension. In 1925, Smith instructed agents of the extension service to give more attention to 4-H and to spend more time organizing new clubs and boosting enrollments. His enthusiasm was palpable. "[W]hat an opportunity is ours in developing this work. How big it is! How worth while! How significant for agriculture and the home! How promising for youth!" Smith gushed to a conference of club workers. "We can not let it stand still," he continued. "We must toll its value to the world. We must place it within reach of every rural boy and girl."[83] Of course, Smith knew that extension agents could only do so much, given Smith-Lever's appropriation. To expand further, the CES needed a larger budget and the ability to hire more agents. To surmount the legislative process, the USDA and the Land Grant College Association schemed with the National Committee to mount a lobbying campaign that would focus public attention on the benefits of 4-H.

Alliance with distant industrialists also carried serious gendered perils for 4-H. Perhaps businessmen set good examples for rural boys—though this, too, was debatable—but surely, they could not be trusted with rural girls. The milieu of interests milling about in 4-H's cooperative spaces, brushing against boys *and* girls, left unresolved important questions. Did the mavens of industry have the interests of rural youth in mind, or were they driven only by a profit motive? Were they even competent to understand what those interests were, let alone balance them appropriately against their own pecuniary interests? And how might an imbalance warp the gendered development of rural youth?

More than a decade before the National Committee initiated its lobbying campaign, America's most famous agriculturalist, chairman of the Commission on Country Life, and founder of the College of Agriculture at Cornell University, Liberty Hyde Bailey, succinctly identified the risks incumbent to careless cooperation in club work. Less than six months after the passage of Smith-Lever, Bailey gave a perspicacious speech to the Forest City, New York, Grange on the perils and possibilities of a national system of club work. While praising 4-H in general, Bailey scorned club "rewards out of proportion to effort expended" and 4-H contests that "inflated the child and g[a] ve him undue and untruthful estimates of his own importance." Most of all, he worried that 4-H'ers were "likely to be used in the making of political or other public reputation, or in accomplishing advertising and propaganda for institutions, organizations, publications, commercial concerns, and other enterprises." That was inadvisable. Extension agents should place the healthy development of their charges above the economic development of their counties, Bailey implored. "It is legitimate to use domestic animals and crops for the primary purpose of improving and advertising the agriculture of a region; but we must not use children in this way," he concluded. "Animals and crops are agricultural products; children are not agricultural products."[84] Bailey's comments punctured the agrarian futurist pretenses of 4-H's backers. Children were not agricultural products. They were not grown like corn or raised like calves. Children would not be jarred, milked, or husked. And a program that relied only on agricultural expertise, when applied to children, might damage those children. Agricultural expertise, especially expertise that considered farming strictly as a commercial endeavor, was hardly sufficient to produce healthy children. But what room did this leave for the USDA or the National Committee?

Bailey's warnings were prophetic but largely unheeded. Even as experts in the USDA plotted 4-H's expansion, the bounties of the cooperation proved less substantial than advertised. As the agricultural slump dragged across the decade, various commentators argued that recommendations by the USDA had actually only intensified the problems of average farmers. Outside of niche and perishable commodities, cooperatives did little to minimize costs. Instead, the cooperative turn had accelerated the trend toward mass-scale, input-intensive agriculture, which had further defaced commodity prices. Cooperation had boosted agricultural production, but its contributions to rural welfare were murkier. Similarly, 4-H had extended the USDA's reach and circulated scientific and businesslike agriculture. For the commercial interests that flocked to the National Committee's banner, 4-H offered a fine business opportunity. But what did all this mean for the welfare of the youth? If the rewards reaped by the USDA, National Committee, bankers, and industrialists came at the cost of maladjusted rural youth, it was all merely exploitation in the trappings of public service. Extension promised to extend the state's reach into rural homes and to displace stifling rural patriarchs, but the cooperative turn brought the corrosive touch of urban commercialism and other unsavory forces that, in rendering the countryside productive, might deplete its fertility and corrupt the gendered division of labor in rural households. Did the USDA have the ability to balance the healthy gendered development of rural youth with the demands of capitalist agriculture? The viability of both 4-H and agrarian futurism turned on that question's resolution.

CHAPTER THREE

4-H Body Politics in the 1920s

... my health to better living ...
—The 4-H Pledge

"The automobile, the airplane, the movie, and the radio with its jazz, have multiplied the desire and temptations of the adolescent girl," warned the report of the Committee on Girls' Work of the 1930 White House Conference on Child Health and Protection. The committee, helmed by the Girl Scouts' Jane Dieter Rippin and Gertrude Warren of the USDA, evaluated how voluntary youth organizations aided the imperiled girls of America. New technologies had lured girls from "the wholesome social life around the family table" into a jungle of dangerous materialism and individualism. These influences were precipitating a slide into delinquency, disorder, and lawlessness, evinced by endemic sexual promiscuity and young "sex offenders." Voluntary organizations, the report concluded, guided participating girls away from such "shocking" behavior by "offering more constructive use of leisure time."[1]

Warren, the report's primary author, identified the reproductive potential of farm girls as vital and contested terrain in the nation's ongoing struggle against rural degeneracy. Tired of the poor conditions, stark poverty, and unsatisfying labor on the farm, rural girls fled to the city for excitement, thrills, and romance. Warren told a conference of extension workers in 1927 that rural girls found only moral and social decay in the metropole. Warren announced: "[A]partment life [wa]s lessening home responsibility and in turn that home allegiance which develops character and those family traditions that act as a safeguard in moments of human weakness." Overcrowded housing and "amusements on a commercial scale" had created a "child line in the better sections [of the city] beyond which no children grow." As a consequence, rural youth alone would procreate enough to supply the workforce of an urban civilization, providing a constant influx of population to offset the reproductive slump of the "better sections." 4-H would help prepare rural girls for those responsibilities, as well as ensure that the country home did not lose its "distinct advantages." The farm household was, after all, the hold-fast of American values and virtuous living but was also the literal location of healthy reproduction. Only in rural homes would rural girls bear and rear a sufficiency of children for the nation's future. The future of both urban and rural America depended on encouraging a new generation of girls to become master homemakers—to make healthy and beautiful homes capable of sustaining modern rural living.[2]

Over the course of the 1920s, Gertrude Warren guided 4-H's efforts to prepare rural girls to be the nation's future rural homemakers. If 4-H boys' programming provided spaces for financial intimacy, girls' clubs aimed to reconstruct the intimacy of rural homes, to render those homes healthier and more nurturing and, in the process, to offer neglected rural girls a healthy developmental path. Recognizing what she called the innate feminine "homing" instinct, Warren pushed for programming uniquely fitted to the psychological and physiological needs of female club members. Clubs encouraged rural girls to minimize strenuous revenue-producing labor and to concentrate on cultivating beauty, health, and careful consumption in rural homes. Like the business methods taught to boys, modern homemaking required girls to accept objective, quantifiable standards provided by experts. In contrast to boys' programming, however, the ultimate "product" of girls' labor was rarely for sale. Rather, by the end of the decade, the USDA and the National Committee boldly announced that club work produced rural bodies and homes that were fundamentally healthier and more attractive than those inhabited by urban Americans and rural folk untouched by extension. Advocates of club work used the "health" of 4-H'ers to promote a variety of different, occasionally contradictory, ends: for the agrarian futurists at the USDA, 4-H bodies advertised the benefits of the broader extension program; for the cluster of commercial interests organized by Guy Noble under the auspices of the National Committee, 4-H bodies advertised the advantages of robust rural consumerism and, in particular, the commercial wares hawked in the pages of the National Committee's publications.

These diverging visions of the appropriate use of 4-H bodies came into open conflict on the floor of the U.S. Congress in 1928. In 1926, at the behest of the Land Grant College Association (LGCA) and the USDA, the National Committee initiated a sophisticated lobbying campaign for legislation to increase federal appropriations for extension. This campaign focused on the benefits of club work and, in particular, the healthy, attractive youth produced by 4-H. Even as the National Committee corralled support for the legislation from across the spectrum of commercial agriculture, maternalist activists raised concerns about the organization's exploitative behavior. The debate surrounding the Capper-Ketcham Act of 1928 ultimately hinged on a question of expert authority: Who was best situated to protect and cultivate the health of rural youth? Resolution of that debate pitted the production-minded, commercial agricultural modernizers of the National Committee against the science of motherhood: home economics. Crucially, that debate designated the fecund bodies of rural youth as the territory to be won.

*　　*　　*

By the 1920s, rural reformers and female educators alike had increasingly turned their attention to the status and labor of rural women. Proponents of the newly formed discipline of home economics argued that they could modernize the rural home. With expert guidance, the latest consumer conveniences, and labor-saving technology, farm women could improve efficiency, eliminate onerous chores, and focus on the hygiene and beauty of their homes and children. Home economists joined rural reformers in complaining that the existing hardships of farm life physically and emotionally taxed women and children, sapping rural society of its health and driving its youth to the city. The rural girl emerged as a particularly important figure in this narrative because she was even less satisfied with farm life than her male counterparts and because she was particularly susceptible to the corruption of the city. Thus, the real and imagined decay of rural America—exacerbated by the farm crisis of the early 1920s—prompted home economists to improve the rigor and breadth of their programs for rural girls. In this context, 4-H clubs provided a perfect venue for home economists to supervise the "work" of girls, redirecting their labor from dangerous "overwork" to a variety of socially and aesthetically rewarding activities that, in turn, could narrow the gap between city and country living.

The discipline of home economics grew out of the late nineteenth century "domestic economy" movement. By the end of the nineteenth century, many agricultural colleges and all-women's colleges were providing millinery, sewing, cooking, and other courses in domestic economy designed to teach women how to be ideal homemakers. Prominent reformers like Ellen Swallow Richards argued that those courses could be more rigorously designed and that their instructors could be more professional. In 1899, Richards launched a series of annual conferences to promote "home economics"; in 1908, conference participants founded the American Home Economics Association. At the same time, land-grant colleges created departments of home economics and began to employ full-time female instructors and, eventually, full faculty in the field. The passage of the Smith-Lever Act in 1914 and the Smith-Hughes Act in 1917 offered increased institutional support for home economics research and, in addition, opened up potential career options as home demonstration agents and secondary educators for graduates with home economics degrees. In sum, by 1920, the "science" of home economics fully supplanted the domestic economy movement and endowed expert proclamations about domestic labor with an air of technocratic authority. In 1921, then-president of the American Home Economics Association, Mary Sweeney, remarked that home economics was no longer "the step-child of agriculture and the second wife of industrial training"; rather, it had become an established "science and art of rational living . . . the science of human welfare."[3]

Home economists placed a premium on reaching rural women. Farm women, home economists rightly noted, had a hard lot. The Commission on Country Life lingered on the deplorable conditions of rural women, reporting that no matter what conditions "may exist on any given farm, the burden falls more heavily on the farmer's wife than on the farmer himself. . . . [H]er life is more monotonous and the more isolated."[4] An exhaustive survey of rural women, published in a 1915 series of USDA bulletins, announced that farm women were overburdened with labor-intensive chores and did not have sufficient time or support to properly tend to the health and hygiene of the home.[5] To meet these problems, home economists hoped to introduce farm women to labor-saving technology, to educate them in both the scientific and the aesthetic rudiments of proper housework, and to transform simple homemaking into a "business of home management."[6]

By claiming expertise over domestic hygiene and child rearing, home economists joined broader rural reforms targeting the "overwork" faced by rural youth on farms. Children provided important labor on most early twentieth-century farms, and reformers complained that strenuous farm labor threatened the physical health of country children.[7] "Child labor is not confined to the factory nor the city sweatshop," noted Charles Powlison, general secretary of the National Child Welfare Association, in 1920. "Many a country boy is almost literally 'worked to death' on his father's acres. Many a country girl is prematurely worn and weakened by domestic drudgery in an ill-equipped farmhouse."[8] A 1922 report by the National Child Labor

Committee concurred that there was a "child labor problem on the farms" that was "injuring the health" of some rural children.[9] The cost of rural child labor was not simply broken and infirm bodies; experts also noted that it embittered youth toward farming, and that attitude drove them to cities. As one West Virginia farm boy put it, "I ain't goin' to stay here much longer; I have to work myself to death and don't get nothing out of it; never get to go *nowhurs*. I don't like it and ain't goin' to stay."[10]

Loan services and wages integrated boys into the commercial life of farms, but the perceived tender dispositions and idealized divisions of gendered labor made the situation for rural girls more complicated. Early twentieth-century medical experts warned that overworked girls risked permanent damage to their reproductive systems.[11] But beyond the physical dangers, farmwork also rendered rural girls crude and coarse. Too many farms, William Arch McKeever of Kansas State Agricultural College complained, allowed girls to do a "man's work in the field." Not only were farm girls not physically suited to such work, and thus in danger of harried "overwork," but it was deadly injurious to her "pride and self-respect to be forced to perform farm labor" and robbed her of "opportunities for the practice of the womanly arts."[12] Michigan rural sociologist Roy Hinman Holmes made an identical point in *The Farm in a Democracy* (1922). Holmes relayed a story from an informant of an overworked farm girl who had "a tired, care worn look and might easily [be] taken for a little old woman, when in reality she is just a few years past her teens." The girl "has not had an opportunity to acquire womanly gracefulness, nor taste in dress, and her manners are crude and awkward." The informant reported numerous "instance[s] where young, growing girls were called upon to perform duties entirely too heavy and strenuous," concluding that "a man is not permitted to overload his horse or abuse his hired man, but is permitted to overwork his children to satisfy a greed for profit."[13]

McKeever's and Holmes's comments reflected the practical reality of hard farm living compounded by the broader perception that girls would flee to the city if they could not find delicacy and refinement on the farm. Not only were girls more physically frail, the thinking went, but they needed special cultural and aesthetic stimulation. If girls could not find that stimulation in the country, they would seek it in the unwholesome world of urban consumer culture. Another of Holmes's informants, explaining why she left the farm, commented that in town, "there was leisure and there was money to enjoy that leisure. There was [a] chance to make a home which did not exist in the country."[14] Popular author and influential figure in the back-to-the-farm movement John Herbert Quick satirized the situation in *The Fairview Idea* (1919). In the novel, an old farmer was posed a question by Daisy Wiggins, "the minister's wife," about the health of their country town: "How's the girl crop in Fairview, Uncle Abner?" The question was rhetorical. The "crop," of course, was failing. The town's girls, Uncle Abner learned, were fleeing from the drudgery of farm life to the corruption of city living, a trend embodied by Kate Lutz, a "paint[ed]" girl dressed in "flimsy, sleazy stuff" who returned to Fairview from the city.[15] Early twentieth-century reformers, rural and urban, reported that naive country girls were likely to fall prey to "unscrupulous men and women with evil designs," as social hygiene activist Orrin Giddings Cocks put it. "Foolish girls, with imagined theatrical ability," he continued in his 1912 tract, "are thrown into the midst of terrible sexual temptations while seeking work in large cities."[16] As the farm crisis of the early 1920s accelerated migration from farms and forced many girls to go to work in nearby towns, the sexual threat of urbanity only grew. In 1930, Orie Latham Hatcher famously recorded the sexual threats awaiting country girls in Southern boardinghouses in her landmark study *Rural Girls in the City for Work.*[17]

Child labor posed a thorny problem for rural social reproduction but was nothing that social scientific expertise could not cure. According to rural reformers, addressing intense dissatisfaction with rural life—and the concomitant sexual dangers of rural-urban migration—required the careful management of a girl's time in a way that expertly balanced labor, leisure, and education. To this end, the National Child Labor Committee report drew an important distinction between "child labor" on the farm, which they regarded as taxing to the body, soul, and mind, and rural "children's work" structured by expert supervision. Rather than simply attempting to extract a maximum of productive labor from children, the report contended, supervised "children's work" could take into account the developmental needs of children, ensure that the work was physically, socially, and intellectually stimulating, and, in general, inculcate rural children with valuable lessons about thrift, efficiency, and industry. "With child labor converted into children's work," announced the report, "which means progress in education, promotion of health and physical development, direction of wholesome play and recreation, appreciation of the importance and place of work, acquisition of thrifty habits, and cooperation in community building, we can conceive of no better place for the rearing of children [than the country]." The report recommended the "substitution of children's work for child labor through Four-H Clubs," where rural children could enjoy expert guidance and socialization.[18] John Herbert Quick, in pressing a similar point, focused on what 4-H clubs could provide to dissatisfied girls. Kate Lutz confessed that she hated house-work so much that she "used to wake up in the night to hate it," prompting Uncle Abner to wonder if "a canning club" would have made things more tol-erable. "[W]hy, I think these things would have been fine!" she replied, "Any-thing—oh, lord, anything—to make things sociable, and sort of human!"[19]

As a "science" capable of improving the efficiency, health, and aesthetic sensibility of rural women, home economics provided the most useful frame-work with which to supervise the "children's work" of rural girls. Rural girls required supervision that would preserve their health, take them out of the fields, and find labor better suited to their bodies and temperaments. They also required a "science" sensitive to aesthetics, capable of satisfying the cul-tural interests of restless rural girls. Finally, they required a practical science that could reach the diffuse millions of rural girls, overworked in every region of the nation. Home economics was the only science that could satisfy these demands. It was the only science that focused solely on the labor of women, that cared for the feminine aesthetic sensibility, and that possessed a network of educators spread throughout the nation's rural districts. Home demonstra-tion agents, the ground troops of this practical science, would supervise the work of rural girls in 4-H clubs.

*   *   *

Over the course of the 1920s, the 4-H program for rural girls changed dra-matically, increasingly emphasizing aesthetics and non-revenue-producing "homemaking" labor. Both the broader economic context and a narrower institutional account explain this trend. "Women's work" itself underwent a transition in rural America during the 1920s, driven by a combination of market consolidation, the spread of capital-intensive agriculture, and the prescriptive exhortations of home economists, extension officials, and rural reformers. As rural women and girls observed these broader structural trans-formations in the rural economy and absorbed the recommendations of the CES, they selected preparatory projects accordingly, abandoning "pro-ductive" agricultural labor. The USDA and CES worked hard to make the 4-H program better reflect the "social needs" of rural girls. 4-H organizers like the USDA's Warren, influenced by prominent psychological and child-development theorists, formulated a gender-appropriate program uniquely suited to rural girls—a program that urged rural girls to divert their labor to aesthetics, health, and consumption. In the first decade after Smith-Lever, the 4-H program merely reflected prevailing labor arrangements across rural America; by the end of the 1920s, that program was increasingly directed at transforming those labor arrangements.

In the first decade after the passage of Smith-Lever, the gendered dynamics of club work tended to reflect the flexibility of labor arrangements on American farms. 4-H clubs usually segregated on the basis of sex, and club organizers planned on canning and homemaking projects being appealing to girls, just as corn and other agricultural projects appealed to boys. But a variety of projects—gardening, dairy, and poultry—drew both male and female participants. In the early 1920s, girls constituted an overwhelming majority of enrollments in poultry and gardening projects and nearly a third of all dairy calf projects. In addition, though boys rarely engaged in homemaking projects, as many as one in ten pig club members and one in thirteen corn club members were female. In this sense, club enrollments tended to follow the labor dynamics of many small farms: many girls enrolled in revenue-producing projects that fell within the boundaries of women's work, while a small, but hardly insignificant, number of girls engaged in production projects usually considered men's work.[20]

4-H girls' club literature from this period mirrored the practical realities of women's farm labor with a simple, unadorned aesthetic. It focused on the technical details required to complete each project, providing matter-of-fact explanations of tasks. Clothing project manuals described how to construct individual items of clothing.[21] Meal preparation manuals described how to cook particular meals.[22] Directions were provided in straightforward language with occasional photographic illustrations and tended to emphasize functionality, with little regard for aesthetics.

To Gertrude Warren, the USDA's leading expert on girls' club work, the myopic focus on economic work for girls fed the larger problems of rural society by ignoring the aesthetic and social needs of farm girls. Born on a farm in rural upstate New York in 1884, Warren earned undergraduate and graduate degrees in home economics from Teachers College at Columbia University. In 1917, the USDA hired her to organize girls' canning clubs, then burgeoning with war enrollments. She was asked to stay on after the war and focused her efforts on 4-H club work. Over the next decade, she established herself as the leading club work expert at the USDA and earned the honorific "Mother of 4-H." In addition to overseeing 4-H home economics work and generating material for actual use in clubs, she regularly published articles on 4-H in popular rural magazines and social-sciences journals. In all her writings, Warren emphasized that the success of club work demanded a program

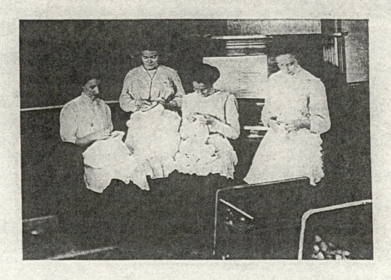

Figure 3. Early Iowa 4-H Girls' Club literature.

tailored to the developmental and psychological needs of youth, a focus that increasingly turned her attention to gendered human psychologies.[23] If attuned to girls' psychological needs, especially "those qualities which we call social," she believed that the 4-H program could shape the "the strategic center of agricultural life—the farm home" and, through it, guarantee that "agriculture [w]as a satisfying type of industry."[24]

Warren distinguished herself from O. H. Benson, C. B. Smith, and most of the male extension officials by regularly invoking the wisdom of the disciplines of psychology and child development in discussions of the club program. Pioneers of educational psychology like Edward Asbury Kirkpatrick, Edward Thorndike, and, most of all, G. Stanley Hall shaped Warren's understanding of gender and childhood and framed how she viewed 4-H's goals. Historian Jeffrey Moran notes that the concept of adolescence as a discrete period in human life emerged fully in 1904, with the publication of celebrated psychologist and president of Clark University G. Stanley Hall's *Adolescence.* The work of Hall and his circle convinced many American intellectuals that youth was "a unique period of life" defined "as a sexually tempestuous period . . . demand[ing] careful and sustained external control."[25] Hall's psychological model of youth emphasized the development of powerful internal sexual urges that were innate, gender-specific, and destructive, absent serious guidance and discipline. By the 1920s, other psychologists had begun to respond to Hall and collectively carve out a notion of normal adolescent psychology. Psychologists, historian Crista DeLuzio suggests, created a model of psychological normalcy for adolescent girls that incorporated a series of contradictory elements: girls were both "individual and female, independent and selfless, sexually confident and sexually vulnerable."[26] Warren's theories existed within that general psychological framework but focused on how adolescence played out for rural girls. She argued that the impulses of adolescence included not only the desire for genital sex but, in addition, the impulse to act out gendered economic desires. For rural girls, this meant a "homing" instinct. Just as the physical union of male and female provided for biological reproduction, the economic union of men and women in the farm family provided for rural social reproduction. But moving from those innate impulses to a fruitful farm family was tricky business. Club leaders needed to be mindful of the inescapable challenges of female adolescence, even as they prepared rural girls to emerge from adolescence as practiced homemakers.[27]

Warren's pamphlet "The Junior Mind in Relation to Boys' and Girls' Club Work" provided a developed explanation of that intellectual framework. Written in 1925 and distributed to extension workers and club leaders as a USDA circular, "The Junior Mind" dissected youth psychology according to a framework proposed by Edward Asbury Kirkpatrick, a professor of psychology at Clark University and an avid promoter of eugenics and social hygiene. Warren, following Kirkpatrick, divided adolescence into three straightforward substages: early adolescence, from twelve to fourteen; mid-adolescence, from fourteen to eighteen; and later adolescence, from eighteen to twenty-four.[28] Warren argued that early adolescence was characterized primarily by the challenges of acclimating to "freakish" growth and "primitive impulses." She stressed the need to recognize and guide those primitive impulses to productive ends, which would also develop proper understandings of familial relationships. Thus, club work should introduce boys to "earning" while steering them from overspecialization and abandoning their education, just as it could help develop girls' impulses for homemaking.[29] Club work should continue to cultivate these healthy outlets throughout mid-adolescence, as youth continued to settle their insecurities and take on "critical" and "idealistic" attitudes. Extension workers should promote projects for youth that integrated ownership, creative self-expression, and service that reflected the gendered desires of club members, but they should also take care to restrain participants from overexertion. Mid-adolescent girls were particularly likely to "overdo" and required "rest, freedom, and a sympathetic understanding."[30]

The rapid physiological and emotional changes of early and mid-adolescence wound down in later adolescence and stabilized in normal, lifelong gendered urges. By then, beliefs, habits, tastes, and even bodies had begun to mature. What had been in early adolescence merely nascent urges—earning and homemaking—blossomed in late adolescence into consuming desires: "The boys are imbued with the desire for independence to earn an adequate living; with girls the desire to have a home reaches its height." These "desires" suggested the normal trajectory for rural youth into stable heterosexual partnerships in which men earned income and women tended the home. If, by later adolescence, a girl was not yet married, Warren wrote, she might attempt to earn income outside the boundaries of the home. Such an arrangement did not accord with normal psychological urges, since, "given an opportunity at home in an interesting environment, more enjoyment consistent with her general makeup is hers, and rural life is enriched accordingly."[31]

By the end of the decade, Warren's vision of a 4-H program tailored to the psychological needs of rural girls was reflected in the selection of club projects by female 4-H'ers and the tone of club literature. In every single project that resulted in a product for market, female participation decreased. Female enrollments in poultry and dairy projects declined dramatically as a percentage of the whole: from 72 percent in 1923 to 54 percent in 1930 for poultry; from 34 percent in 1923 to 14 percent in 1930 for dairy calves. The rare girls who enrolled in agricultural projects became even rarer. By 1930, female enrollments in corn projects as a percentage of the total declined to only 2.6 percent, from about 8 percent in 1923. Similarly, total female enrollments in pig projects declined by almost 25 percent, even as male enrollments climbed. At the same time, female enrollments in home economics projects skyrocketed, drawing the overwhelming bulk of new enrollments (total 4-H enrollments for girls increased over the decade from 270,000 to 490,000). Meanwhile, home demonstration agents provided new social and cultural

Figure 4. The January 1928 issue of *National Boys and Girls Club News* requests more homemakers.

outlets for club girls, providing literature on entertaining guests, hosting parties, and throwing picnics, as well as projects on music and art appreciation.[32] By the end of the decade, enrollments had become substantially more sex-segregated by project, and girls appeared to be heeding the call, illustrated by a cartoon in the *National Boys and Girls Club News*, to become dedicated homemakers.

Girls' club literature became more stylized and removed from the practical realities of farm labor. Rather than providing photographic accompaniment, for example, beginning in 1924 the Iowa Extension Service illustrated the covers of girls' club literature with the "Iowa 4-H Girl," an attractive cartoon girl. The Iowa 4-H Girl wore a dress featuring a large white hoop that formed the infrastructure for four outer petals (intended to be the leaves of a clover). Each petal was embroidered with a large *H*. A 4-H clover crested her breast, and the upper sleeves of her dress puffed to form bulbs, out of which her slender arms emerged. She covered her head in a clover-embla-zoned 4-H cap that barely concealed her soft curls. The 4-H girl occupied the cover of nearly all Iowa 4-H publications directed to female clubs until the 1940s, when illustrations took on a more militant tone, consistent with wartime mobilization.[33] Delicate and demure, the Iowa 4-H Girl, with her unwieldy hoopskirt and awkward sleeves, appeared best suited for only the lightest household chores. Her costume was pristine, and her legs were fre-quently pursed to resemble a ballerina's first position: the Iowa 4-H Girl's stature and costume forbade the strenuous and untidy exertions of field and garden. In this sense, the Iowa 4-H Girl signaled a move from the practical approaches to female labor favored by earlier extension service material to an approach that emphasized cultural idealizations of feminine beauty, health, and cultural sophistication, a trend visible in nearly all 4-H literature.

Rather than dwelling on functionality, 4-H literature increasingly focused on the aesthetic and social dimensions of women's labor in the 1920s. When cooking breakfast, Florence Packman argued in a 1924 pamphlet, it was no longer adequate to simply consider whether the breakfast was palatable and economical, as earlier pamphlets had done. Instead, a 4-H girl needed to con-sider how the aesthetics of presentation might affect the psychological and physical health of her family. A breakfast that "failed to cheer" might "utterly ruin" the day, so the attentive 4-H girl prepared a nutritious breakfast, set an attractive table in a "cheery and bright" place, and donned a crisply pressed dress.[34] A 1928 manual for Alabama food preparation encouraged 4-H girls to adhere to the proper courtesies of a well-laid table. "The most elaborate meal is not an 'occasion,'" explained Mildred Simon, the nutrition expert for the Alabama Extension Service, "if the table is untidy and the food unattrac-tively served." A "tidy" table entailed service on refined and expensive china and silver, as well as linens, glassware, vases, and flowers—elements, in turn, ruled by a variety of aesthetic considerations. Flowers, for example, should be low and spare, since bunched and wedged flowers were unattractive and might distract diners. Rigorous standards similarly dictated the placement and orientation of the dishes, utensils, and equipment around the table, how the girl's body should be maneuvered during service, and how the girl should comport herself during the meal. This final topic received the most exhaustive attention, with thirty-six regulations. Among other things, Simon directed 4-H girls to "keep the feet on the floor . . . keep conversation cheer-ful . . . [and] never mention foods you dislike at the table." "Be careful," she continued, "of personal appearance at all meals, hairs, hands, nails, shoes and dress." And "toothpicks," she concluded, "should be used only in private."[35]

4-H home decoration and garment literature portrayed material possessions as crucial signifiers of aesthetic refinement and "personality," a term
meant to express a girl's unique psychological state. The selection of domestic furnishings and attire required care and aesthetic considerations beyond
mere functionality. These aesthetic considerations required the application
of abstract laws of "harmony," "balance," and "appropriateness" to an individual's personality. Irma Camp Graff recommended in a 1924 pamphlet that,
before deciding on attire, girls "begin right away analyzing themselves."[36]
Through a similar process, 4-H girls could produce a room, wrote Florence
Forbes in an Iowa home furnishing manual in 1931, that would reflect "the
personality of the girl or girls who are to live in the room. . . . [E]ach girl will
express herself in choice of colors, materials and articles." The relationship,
however, between domestic surroundings and personal composition was also
mutually constituting. "Very few people," asserted Forbes, "realize the important part that surroundings play in influencing their character and personality. They fail to see how mere things like wall paper, curtains and furniture
become a part of them whether they will it or not." While a 4-H girl might,
with proper aesthetic training, decorate a room to express the beauty of her
personality, absent that training, a dour, ugly, or cramped room might very
well despoil a girl.[37]

The ostensible product of the project—a canned vegetable, a dress, or a
meal—was often a secondary accoutrement to the project's true goal: a refined
female person. Health information was ubiquitous in all 4-H literature. As
one clothing manual announced, "a bulletin would not be complete if some
consideration to health was not given."[38] An Alabama manual, "Clothing
for Health," included a poster from the National Child Welfare Association
announcing that "good posture means health, beauty, [and] confidence."[39]
Nutrition projects provided extensive information about the health effects
of food, the "keystone of health and strength, self-confidence, beauty and
well-being."[40] Meal planning, similarly, ensured that 4-H girls ate balanced
diets filled with "the minerals and vitamins we must have for perfect health"
and for "abundant living."[41] Interior design and home management specialists insisted that attractive, healthy girls required well-decorated and well-
ventilated rooms in efficiently managed homes.[42] Attractive girls acquired
essential nutrients and vitamins in the winter from canned goods such that
the more mundane-sounding canning project became "4-H Canning for
Good Nutrition." Indeed, the Iowa 4-H Girl's predicament on the cover of the
1930 "4-H Canning for Good Nutrition" manual figuratively suggested the
ultimate goal of canning-club labor. On the cover, she stood staring almost

Figure 5. The Iowa 4-H girl cans herself on the cover
of a 1930 Iowa 4-H manual.

whimsically at the enormous jar inside of which she was imprisoned, pro-
vocatively suggesting that the Iowa 4-H Girl, in order to preserve her own
health, had canned herself.[43]

Home economists tailored girls' 4-H literature to better reflect their understandings of the unique psychological needs of rural girls. The psychological
model promoted by the USDA, particularly in the writings of Gertrude Warren, emphasized that girls possessed an innate "homing" instinct—a desire
to find a mate and create a refined, nurturing home. To meet that instinct,
4-H needed to include social and aesthetic components that guarded girls

from physically "overdoing" it. 4-H literature guided the labor of rural girls in the direction of practiced consumption, physical health, and personal attractiveness. By 1930, responding to these programmatic developments and to structural changes in the rural economy, rural girls had increasingly shied away from production projects, concentrating instead on home economics projects that purportedly provided aesthetic stimulation otherwise unavailable in the countryside.

* * *

Diverting girls from production and toward aesthetic and social projects was only one piece of the puzzle of failing rural health. Extension officials and reformers argued that rural people needed more exposure to medical professionals. By the late 1920s, the 4-H network had parlayed its intimacy with rural youth into health improvement programs in rural communities. These programs featured local health examinations, sustained health education, and county and statewide health contests. The USDA experimented with ways to broaden health education to boys; but in practice, the overwhelming majority of participants in 4-H health programs were female. The examination called for the female body to be the subject of intense and invasive scrutiny, usually by male medical professionals. 4-H health programs, shaped by the discipline of home economics and its priorities, tended to replicate assumptions about the gendered responsibilities of health promotion and conflate health and attractiveness. 4-H health programs encouraged female participants to examine their bodies for "defects," even as they circulated the image of wholesome, attractive rural youth to promote the CES. 4-H health programs generated binding connections among medical professionals, farm-focused capitalists, extension officials, and rural people, connections that traversed and intersected at the intimate, gendered space of youthful rural bodies.

Warren urged county extension and home economics agents to concentrate on health promotion work in 4-H. "In conferences, talks in public, and in publicity articles, emphasize ways in which the health of club members is being looked after through club works," she wrote in a manual on girls' club work in 1925. 4-H promoted good health by "tak[ing] farm girls out of the field [and] into the home," teaching them how "to keep health score cards," and enrolling them in "[h]ealth club contests."[44] In 4-H health contests, doctors and nurses examined club members at county and state fairs, judged them according to a standardized scorecard, deducted points for defects, and, ultimately, selected a winning boy and girl as a perfect "specimen."[45] "The health examinations call attention to defects and help set a standard for positive health," explained an Iowa club organizer.[46] By 1925, building on existing rural enthusiasm for similar beauty contests for babies, women, and livestock, health contests had emerged as one the most highly publicized components of the 4-H program, receiving constant plaudits in newspapers for producing the "perfect boy and girl," as a headline in the *Washington Post* put it.[47]

Iowa 4-H offered one of the earliest templates for a comprehensive health program built around competitive health contests. In 1921, extension officials devised the idea of a statewide 4-H contest to promote better health practices and bring publicity to the extension service's rural health initiatives. The contest called for a boy and girl to be determined the healthiest by each county 4-H organization. The county champions would assemble in Des Moines to be examined by a group of four doctors provided by the Polk County Medical Association, which had agreed to provide a standard scorecard for the contest's use. In its inaugural year, forty-six of the state's ninety-nine counties submitted champions to the state competition, and a boy and girl were named statewide champions. Counties quickly began to adopt the state competition's method of using professional medical evaluations and scorecards. In 1922, seven Iowa counties used the standard scorecard and formal medical examinations to determine which 4-H'ers should be submitted to the state competition. By 1930, ninety-two counties had reported doing so, examining more than 4,400 Iowa girls in the process.[48]

The effectiveness of the health program hinged on the use of a health "scorecard," which permitted medical professionals as well as club members to scrutinize bodies and quantify their copious "defects." The Iowa scorecard comprised more than seventy particular metrics, covering categories as diverse as the flushness of the lips, the symmetry of "sex characteristics," the shape and position of ears, and the quality of posture. Although the scorecard covered health dimensions influenced by habit and behavior, it also deducted points for features outside the youth's control—the presence of "birth marks," flat feet, or an "abnormally shape[d]" skull. A full 13 percent of the total score was governed by an entirely subjective assessment of attractiveness called "general impressions."[49] Although the contest organizers usually awarded first place to the highest scorers, they also recognized members who had improved their scores over the course of successive examinations with a "health improvement" award. This ensured that all participants, even those who were initially infirm or sickly, had motivation to have "some defects corrected [and] bring up her standing for next year."[50] Examinations enabled medical authorities to quantify both the defects and potentials of 4-H bodies and generated valuable bodily knowledge that could be mustered into personal or cooperative health activities executed over the course of months.

Examinations merely provided an entrée for intensive follow-up work on the part of girls, agents, and medical professionals. In Webster County, for example, girls received two examinations over the course of the year. According to the county home demonstration agent, the first examination identified "any bodily defect" and prescribed improved "healthy habits," ensuring that "as much improvement as possible" was made before a county health champion was selected. When some girls were "scored down" for poor posture and skin, a local doctor agreed to talk to them about "physiology and hygiene." Based on the doctor's recommendations, the girls proceeded to score themselves at home for twelve consecutive weeks.[51] After using a similar follow-up system, an agent in Hancock County lauded the results. Thanks to health talks from medical professionals, club girls "striv[ed] to bring their weight to normal. They look much better than they did last spring."[52] With adequate follow-up work by medical experts and extension agents, rural youth could be expected to execute their own private plan for personal health improvement.

Given Iowa's impressive results, similar 4-H health programs soon appeared in other states. Within a year, the Iowa program had inspired health competitions for club members at major livestock expositions in Sioux City and Chicago. The latter competition was integrated into the annual National 4-H Congress and rebranded as the National 4-H Health Competition in 1922. The National 4-H Congress worked with a private philanthropic organization and medical professionals to develop a standard national scorecard in 1924.[53] An American Medical Association survey in 1931 reported that 40 percent of all responding medical associations cooperated with 4-H to conduct medical examinations that qualified members for the national competition.[54] By 1930, more than 100,000 youth were enrolled around the nation in 4-H health projects and examinations. More than 90 percent of those enrollments were female.[55]

Distressed by the paucity of boys in 4-H health programs, USDA specialists devised a human health curriculum suitable for boys' agricultural clubs. Girls' clubs were usually led and organized by women who had received human anatomy and health instruction in home economics curricula. Many county agents and male leaders avoided discussions of health because their training did not directly address human physiology and health, explained Miriam Birdseye, a USDA nutrition specialist.[56] Birdseye encouraged male agricultural agents to make better use of their knowledge of animal and plant biology. She recommended that, when speaking to boys in the context of a dairy or livestock club, club leaders and agricultural agents "us[e] a well-developed club boy, and show how these points parallel the points used in stock judging. . . . Mention parallels between the food-habits scorecard used by club members and good practices in feeding the kind of livestock raised by the club."[57] At 4-H camps and institute, Birdseye suggested that club agents organize a course for club boys taught by "instructors in biology, animal and plant industry, human nutrition and physical training, and . . . a pediatrician." The course would inform club boys that they were subject to "the same laws that govern the growth and development of other living creatures" and thus should accept their personal "responsibility" for "the improvement of the race."[58] At a 1929 extension conference, Birdseye demonstrated her methods to an audience of agricultural agents. She presented a fine calf and "pointed out its many signs of good health." Then, "as the calf was led away, its place was taken by three boys, 10, 12, and 14 years of age, dressed in track pants, with legs, feet, and torso bare." Birdseye scrutinized the boys' physiques in parallel fashion. Though the boys were preselected to display only peak fitness, they demonstrated the "different types of build and coloring" found among white adolescents.[59]

The equation of healthy rural youth with well-bred livestock fit seamlessly into the broader popular celebrations of 4-H health champions as the perfect "specimens" of a wholesome, gender-appropriate middle-class white rural lifestyle.[60] 4-H health competitions, more than any other aspect of the 4-H program, received coverage in local, regional, and even national newspapers, including the *New York Times*, the *Washington Post*, the *Los Angeles Times*, and the *Chicago Daily Tribune*.[61] Newspaper accounts frequently referenced the youth as attractive and fit and provided photographic evidence with the articles. An account of the 1928 National 4-H Health Competition, for example, lauded champion Thelma Svarstad of South Dakota's "blond, clear skinned" appearance, while the *Times* of Alden, Iowa, celebrated Tennessee's Marguerite Martin as the "ideal of perfect health."[62] These media accounts emphasized that this attractiveness was a natural outcome of a wholesome rural lifestyle, one in which boys and girls played their accepted parts. For boys, this meant a robust physique gained from helping out on the farm, playing on athletic teams, or hiking in the woods. For girls, it meant naturally rosy cheeks and no makeup, helping mother in the kitchen, and getting their "beauty sleep." Florence Smock of Florida, the 1929 National 4-H Health champion, "use[d] no rouge nor lipstick but ha[d] rosy cheeks" and, despite going on a "few dates," was always in bed by 9 PM. Harold Deatline, the champion on the "masculine side," had "broad shoulders and [was] strong muscled because of 'plenty of good, hard work' on his father's farm." While Smock enjoyed dancing, Deatline reported that he did not "care for dancing or 'gadding about.' For recreation he [went] hunting and fishing sometimes."[63]

Media accounts focused on the pristine winners of health competitions but ignored the copious supply of defective contest losers and the tens of thousands of nonwhite 4-H'ers who were systematically excluded from competing. Throughout the South, health promotion ranked among the highest priorities for the African American extension services. Nearly 20 percent of all 4-H'ers in the South were African American and regularly received lessons on hygiene and health from black county agents. Similarly, in places like Arizona, the extension service considered health promotion an important component of work with "Mexican" and "Indian" girls. Yet only white 4-H'ers were permitted to compete in health competitions at the National 4-H Congress.[64] Nor did media accounts rhapsodize about perfect nonwhite bodies produced through club work. Instead, media descriptions frequently conflated whiteness and attractiveness when lauding the pristine skin and hair of winners. The publicity associated with 4-H health competitions circulated the ideal 4-H body as white and suggested that state experts, in cooperation with a well-ordered farm home, could produce this perfected white body.

The USDA and the CES intended the image of wholesome white youth to attract the support of rural America, as Gertrude Warren's encouragement to county extension and home demonstration agents indicated. If the reports of Iowa home demonstration agents were any indication, they succeeded in that endeavor. "Parents of club girls have made many favorable comments in regard to the health contest," reported a Sac County agent. Mrs. W. A. Havenhill of Louisa County likewise remarked: "The outstanding accomplishment of our year's work is that we have the mothers and fathers interested in our work the health of their girls."[65] Health work, then, could serve two valuable ends simultaneously: even as club work could create relationships between rural Americans and medical professionals, it could also advertise directly to rural America the benefits provided by extension. By circulating the image of perfected, defect-free youth, 4-H could convince rural America that county agents could be trusted with the most sensitive of activities. And by producing healthy rural youth, the extension service promised to simultaneously protect rural youth from the physically degrading elements of farm life and to shelter them from the sexual depravity of the city.

*   *   *

Although club experts like Warren advised county and home demonstration agents to advertise the benefits of 4-H health work, publicity for the health contest at the National 4-H Congress was handled by Guy Noble and the National Committee. Noble recognized the value of equating 4-H with wholesome, white rural youth and regularly used that rhetorical figure in publicity. By the end of the decade, that publicity had garnered the National Committee substantial private-sector support from firms interested in reaching rural consumers. Noble's activities brought him the political clout necessary to engineer a lobbying campaign for 4-H and the USDA. That lobbying campaign brought Noble and several 4-H members to the floor of the U.S. Senate, where the image of healthy 4-H'ers continued to symbolize club work and the future of rural America. In this, Noble deployed the rhetoric of agrarian futurism to expand the federal commitment to rural youth. Even as he did so, the particular gendered sensitivity of health work brought Noble, the National Committee, and his proposed legislation under scrutiny from maternalist activists, nearly derailing his lobbying effort in the process.

Guy Noble publicized 4-H more aggressively than anyone in the USDA. Born in State Center, Iowa, in 1888 and educated at Iowa State College, Noble witnessed the blossoming of club work firsthand and was duly impressed. But he had little patience for the USDA's deliberate pace, perhaps reasoning that private enterprise could lead the way more effectively than government bureaucrats. In January 1925, he used advertisements in the national farm bureau newsletter to launch a 4-H "one million members" drive without first consulting the USDA.[66] The move earned him a polite but decisive letter from C. B. Smith, pointing out that a million members was "probably beyond what could be achieved with the existing capacity of the extension service."[67] Privately, CES director Clyde W. Warburton fumed to Smith about Noble's "aggressive" behavior, complaining that Noble's scheme would overtax the extension service and be "one of the worst things that could possibly happen to club work." Was "boys' and girls' club work . . . being directed by the National Committee or by the extension service of the Department and the State colleges of agriculture?" Warburton wondered.[68]

Noble's aggression reflected both a burning passion for club work and an obvious pecuniary interest. He was an earnest, resolute, and frequently over-zealous apostle of club work who would ultimately devote his entire professional career to 4-H, retiring only in 1957. His personal passion aside, there were practical reasons for Noble to take a different approach from that of USDA officials. Extension officials at the USDA had the luxury of a permanent, reliable congressional appropriation. The National Committee, however, depended upon constant donations that might dry up at any moment and leave Noble unemployed. While the nuts and bolts of club work could survive on money from the CES and local sources alone, the big-ticket events favored by the National Committee—an elaborate national meeting and a variety of lavish prizes—required contributions from wealthy urban firms. From Noble's perspective, the continued existence of the National Committee depended on finding some support among an urban audience that the USDA had little interest in courting.

Noble's aggressive approach reaped greater financial security for his organization. Under his management, the National Committee continued to attract funds from bankers but also increasingly garnered support from a variety of other firms interested in reaching rural consumers. Mail-order titan Montgomery Ward began sponsoring national club awards through the National Committee in 1922. Sears, Roebuck and Company proposed to underwrite completely the National Committee's operations, provided that the National 4-H Congress be transformed into an elaborate two-week advertising seminar.[69] The National Committee declined that proposal, but in 1925, Sears made a more modest offer to sponsor a contest to promote "the use of mail-order catalogues." To encourage the sponsorship of other mail-order houses, the National Committee arranged to have attendees of the National 4-H Congress tour the offices of the major mail-order firms in Chicago. Through the 1920s, the rules and restrictions associated with sponsored awards were usually left to the sponsoring businesses, which would often structure the contest to encourage the use of a specific product or brand. Agricultural firms such as International Harvester and the Grain Marketing Company, meatpackers such as the Armour, Swift, and Wilson firms, and consumer-goods firms such as Electrolux and Quaker Oats ultimately provided sponsorships through the National Committee.[70] Noble also persuaded dozens of railroads to provide free transportation to club members attending the National 4-H Congress.[71] Smaller firms took the less expensive route of advertising in the *National Boys and Girls Club News*, the monthly magazine that Noble published and circulated to club leaders and members free of charge. Whether large or small, all these businesses hoped to reach rural consumers through the 4-H clover. Through the National Committee, businesses could market directly to club members in advertisements and at sponsored events and, in addition, win the affection of rural people by sponsoring the icon of healthy rural living.

Noble's publicity strategy placed the health benefits of 4-H and wholesome rural living front and center. One National Committee pamphlet, "From Crippled Farm Boy to Agricultural Leader," exemplified Noble's strategy. The pamphlet told the story of Warren W. Simpson of Northfield, Minnesota, who had been "crippl[ed] by infantile paralysis." Simpson "completed his [4-H corn] project by actually crawling through the corn on his hands and knees." The project had won him a "yield of 105 bushels per acre but at the same time his health improved so that he became able to walk." Although usually less sensationalistic than that pamphlet, Noble's press releases about national 4-H health champions made a similar implicit link between 4-H and robust health. Newspaper articles prompted by Noble's press releases frequently ran in major newspapers.[72] Like publicity in local and regional papers, these articles hailed the ideal bodies of participating 4-H'ers. In 1923, Calvin Coolidge accepted the position of "honorary chairman" of the National Committee, and Noble released a press release, then repeated in the *Post* and *Times*, that included a statement from the president lauding "the most virile manhood and womanhood" produced by farm life and 4-H. Another article, following Noble's press release after the 1926 health competition, described the link between this "virile" physique and farm life. "Kentucky, famed for its horses and girls, added to its repute today by giving to the Boys' and Girls' Clubs here . . . the nation's healthiest farmer boy," reported a 1926 edition of the *New York Times*. The "huskiest" lad attributed his impressive physique to hard work on his father's farm and an early bedtime, while the "feminine" cochampion gained the "crown of physical perfection" through "[y]ears of diet and methodical physical training."[73]

A 1925 article in the *Washington Post*, based on Noble's publicity, drew a more explicit parallel between livestock judging and the health contests. The article announced that alongside "grand champion steers, prize porkers, sheared sheep, high-stepping horses" were "the healthiest boy and girl in the United States . . . selected in very much the same manner. . . . Expert judges looked them over, poked them, punched them and put them through their paces." Female health champion Inez Harden, the article continued, was a "beauty" whose "splendid body" was complemented by "so sunny a disposition." When asked about the "opposite sex," Inez deemed "[k]issing games . . .

passe" and said that she would not marry until she was thirty. The article also described the "perfect" body of her male counterpart, Coe Emens: "His eyes, ears, nose and throat are perfect, netting him a total of fourteen points. His head is perfect, too, as are his hair, his scalp, his face, neck, chest, back, abdomen, arms, hands, legs, feet, posture, gait, muscles and nerves. . . . His clean, lean body netted him two more points, and the perfection of his measurements netted him seven." The author of the article was duly impressed with how Coe dealt with "being the most perfect specimen of boyhood," modesty that the author attached to his masculine countenance: "Being a boy, Coe lacks the dramatic instinct to the degree possessed by Inez." Rather, Coe had "poise that could not be shaken" and was "so completely master of himself that it was impossible disturb his equanimity." He had "not the last bit of hunger for publicity." Publicity, it seemed, was best left to Noble. The article included a lengthy quotation from Noble, concluding, "As a result of the work done by the [National C]ommittee, farm boys and girls are better farmers, are better physically and the girls are better housewives."[74]

The USDA was livid about the *Post* article, though not because the article bestialized farm youth. Rather, Warburton and Smith complained that the article had neglected to mention the USDA's role in club work and suggested that Noble was attempting to usurp 4-H altogether. The article, along with the recent million-member drive, prompted a series of heated exchanges between Warburton, Noble, a number of the state directors of extension, and Thomas Wilson, a meatpacking magnate and chairman of the National Committee. Warburton and sympathetic state directors of extension complained that the National Committee "commercialize[d]" club work and induced public confusion with its press releases. (Noble, with characteristic chutzpah, insisted that any confusion was the result of under-publicity on the part of the USDA.)[75] Despite these misgivings, there was little that the USDA or the state directors of extension could do about the National Committee, beyond sharply worded letters. Noble enjoyed the backing and financial support of both the AFBF and influential farm-state politicians like Arthur Capper, who, in turn, provided the most substantial political support for the USDA in Congress. Moreover, even as the conflict between Noble and the USDA unfolded, Noble was in the process of launching a lobbying campaign to increase the CES's federal appropriation, money that both the USDA and the LGCA considered long overdue. Local municipalities and civic organizations like the farm bureau typically contributed as much as half of a county extension agent's salary, effectively tying the continued employment of a given county agent to local political support. USDA officials argued that a larger

extension appropriation would free county agents from local political constraints and let the CES take its message to every county that needed it.[76]

As early as 1921, Noble had begun to engineer support for an increased
federal appropriation. He began by seeking and then circulating supportive resolutions from the AFBF, the LGCA, and a variety of industry organizations.[77] Following a meeting of the executive committee of the LGCA
in November 1926, Noble "initiated" the legislative process by coordinating
between the LGCA, Kansas senator Arthur Capper, and Michigan representative John Ketcham and by circulating the copious private support for
the legislation that he had gathered over the previous six years.[78] Nineteen
national organizations, including the AFBF, National Grange, the ABA,
American Home Economics Association, and the National Dairy Council,
forty-five state associations, and scores of prominent individuals pledged
support for the Capper-Ketcham Bill.[79] Many of those organizations predicated their support on the continued development of 4-H. "The National
Grange favors every movement that will extend the usefulness of boys' and
girls' club work," explained a resolution of the Grange's executive committee. "We favor the Capper-Ketcham Bill recently introduced into Congress to
provide additional funds for this class of extension work."[80]

By 1927, two separate ideas—an expansion of club work and a general
expansion of extension—had become conflated in a single piece of legislation, the Capper-Ketcham Act, which, if passed, would double federal appropriations to the CES. A memo circulated by Noble described the legislation
as the first step in a plan to place a club agent in every county. Clyde Warburton and the USDA, however, supported the legislation because it allowed,
in broad language, a general expansion of extension, only some of which
would be dedicated to club work. Capper and Ketcham, for their parts, gave
statements that only vaguely supported Noble's intent. Though the legislation
explicitly mentioned club work, it contained no specific language to mandate
any spending, leaving it up to the department's discretion. When the legislation was first introduced in 1927, it was passed unanimously out of the House
but stalled in the Senate. In 1928, Capper and Ketcham reintroduced the legislation, with only minor changes.[81]

Despite the USDA's reluctance to view the legislation as exclusively
directed toward club work, Noble's lobbying campaign fundamentally shaped
the terms of the debate on Capper-Ketcham. The *Minneapolis Tribune*
praised the legislation, under the mistaken assumption that it "would provide funds for some 2,000 additional boys' and girls' club agents."[82] During
the bill's committee hearings, legislators peppered witnesses with questions

about club work, and figures like Chester Gray of the AFBF and Frederic Brenkman of the National Grange offered enthusiastic endorsements of the 4-H program. In addition, Noble brought club participants to testify before both committees. Club members Viola Yoder of Cumberland, Maryland, and John Visny of Newtown, Connecticut, praised 4-H to the Senate committee. Yoder stressed that 4-H club work had transformed her family's home and improved her person. Club work had taught her how to sew properly, how to grow fruits and vegetables, and how to prepare better meals for her family. In sum, 4-H had "brought [her] closer to her parents and to [her] home." In addition to imparting him with valuable knowledge, 4-H had entirely changed Visny's attitude toward life on the farm. "I know that if I had my choice to start all over again," Visny announced, "I should want to be born and brought up on a farm, but the most important part of that would be that I be granted an opportunity to take part in 4-H club activities." Other rural youth, without that fortune, would abandon the countryside and make the slow drift to "overcrowded cities." Mrs. D. B. Phillips, a club leader from Forestville, Ohio, also called to testify, expanded on Visny's point. "We do not want to keep everyone of our boys and girls on the farm," she explained. "We want to keep our best boys and girls on the farm, and then you may have the rest of them out in the city." As the Senate hearings wound down, Noble submitted a statement for the record, registering in detail the support of the numerous organizations that had offered glowing praise for 4-H.[83]

Even as the complexities of the legislative process shaped the bill, the public image presented by its supporters coalesced around the agrarian futurist image of robustly healthy, wholesome rural youth. A moment of serendipitous theater brought this rhetorical strategy into focus. As the Senate committee hearing wound down, Alabama senator James Heflin asked how many members of the committee were raised on the farm. After most of the members volunteered that they had been and Senator Capper prepared again to adjourn, Phillips interjected. Asserting her maternal authority and recapitulating the 4-H health examination in a radically different context, she directed those members of the committee who had been raised on the farm to stand so that the audience could "view them." When they did so, she offered her appraisal: "Well that is fine. But I would like to remark one thing, that the farm boys are the best looking members of the committee." Immediately following Phillips's assessment, Brooklyn-born senator Tasker Oddie of Nevada launched into an endorsement of the legislation that emphasized the visceral and bodily contributions of club work. "The boys and girls of our Western States are being developed into better and more progressive citizens," opined

Oddie, "and the result will be a better and stronger America. This is one of the best methods of developing our national defense, making a better class of citizens, and making our country stronger and more self sustaining in every particular." Adding an exclamation point to Oddie's statement, the committee voted unanimously to report the bill to the Senate.[84]

Although Noble's rhetorical strategy corralled support for the bill by appealing to the ingrained assumptions of pervasive agrarianism, it nearly proved to be the bill's undoing. By linking club work to the production of healthy white, farm youth, Noble traded on a gendered trope that was as combustible as it was potent, a fact quickly revealed by opposition from the General Federation of Women's Clubs. The General Federation was a national organization of allied local women's volunteer and charity clubs that had successfully mobilized grassroots support for a number of maternalist reforms throughout the early twentieth century, including the Sheppard-Towner Act (1921), which provided federal funds for maternity education and nurses. The General Federation complained that the Capper-Ketcham Act would allow the USDA to continue to neglect home demonstration work, farm women, and rural girls. Speaking on behalf of the General Federation, its president, Mary Belle King Sherman, explained to the House committee that even though 100,000 more girls than boys were enrolled in 4-H, male agricultural and club agents outnumbered female home demonstration and club agents by a considerable margin. This resulted, she continued, in the distressing "tendency under men agents to divert girls from home making to the raising of baby beef, pigs, and field crops for purely commercial ends." This diversion led to the overproduction of agricultural commodities and a neglect of the rural home. As a remedy, Sherman suggested that the legislation should be amended to ensure that the CES hire equal numbers of home demonstration and agricultural agents.[85]

Sherman explicitly attacked the National Committee, arguing that it encouraged the productionist mentality that degraded rural homes and lured 4-H girls into commercial ventures. The tendency to enroll girls in agricultural projects was "greatly emphasized," Sherman argued, "by the policy of the national committee on boys' and girls' clubs." While Sherman had no qualms with 4-H, she emphasized that farm girls needed the direction of women and thus the legislation needed to focus not just on the promotion of club work but on a broader strengthening of home economics work. In the popular press, she was more explicit. "The General Federation of Women's Clubs," Sherman told the *Atlanta Constitution*, "stands for a square deal for the farm men who are trying to find markets for their products, but it wants to know why women's work and the home are not getting a square deal as was intended under the Smith-Lever law." The National Committee, however, encouraged overproduction and undercut that goal. Her organization, she continued, "also wants to know why the 4-H clubs are being tampered with by an outside committee with the full sanction of the extension heads at Washington. It hopes that congress will inquire in these matters at an early date and clean up the situation."[86]

By focusing on rural girls and dangers to the rural home, Sherman dramatized her case for an expansion of home demonstration agents and appropriated for her own ends Noble's rhetorical focus on the figure of rural youth. The General Federation approved of club work but "favor[ed] the girls being under women," Mrs. John S. Sippel of the Maryland General Federation affiliate testified to the House committee.[87] The image of men directing vulnerable rural girls evoked gendered disarray and portrayed extension as a threat to rural households. In the process, Sherman portrayed the National Committee as a nefarious, sinister organization, a far cry from the image that Noble promoted of a group of public-minded businessmen cooperating to keep the fittest youth on farms. They "tampered" with 4-H, apparently indifferent to the potential damage wrought of their productionist mind-set to farm girls, country homes, and rural communities. In that narrative, the commercial interests represented by the National Committee were willing to exploit rural girls and place them in the care of men—an arrangement as inappropriate as it was ineffective. "What does a man know about teaching a girl home economics?" Representative James Aswell of Louisiana, the General Federation's champion in the House, asked Clyde Warburton. If Noble had hoped to capitalize on broader anxieties about the decline of rural America, Sherman and her allies demonstrated that the gendered complexities of that anxiety could also cut against his schemes.[88]

The resolution of the debate on Capper-Ketcham both vindicated and indicted Noble's chosen rhetorical strategy of promoting the perfected bodies of rural youth. The Senate and House committees adopted the General Federation amendment providing for a "just and fair" distribution of funding between male and female extension workers. The Coolidge administration, however, signaled that it would veto the legislation and encouraged Congress to pare down the price tag. The version of the bill presented to the president eliminated nearly $5.5 million in appropriation authorizations from the original legislation but did secure an increase of $1.5 million in funding for extension and left open the possibility that later Congresses would revisit the issue. Calvin Coolidge signed Capper-Ketcham into law on May 22, 1928. Noble proclaimed the lobbying campaign a singular success and issued a series of letters thanking his various supporters for their contributions to the effort.[89] But the reality behind Noble's public words was surely more mixed. The General Federation's amendment and the Coolidge administration's threat of veto had diluted Noble's vision of thousands of new club agents, marginally strengthening the influence of home economics in the CES. More important, the debate surrounding Capper-Ketcham had accentuated ways in which advertising 4-H through the bodies of rural youth made Noble's private work suspect and potentially dangerous. If 4-H was to produce robust rural bodies and a healthy rural society as a result, it would need expert guidance to temper the commercial agenda that Noble represented.

*   *   *

Although the debate about Capper-Ketcham hinged on whether the extension service was competent to protect the health of rural youth, passage of the act hardly settled the issue. By 1930, Guy Noble recognized that the USDA had not embraced his interpretation of the legislation that made club agents a singular priority. While Capper-Ketcham funds had been used to employ an additional eighty-one county club agents around the nation, twice as many agricultural agents and nearly three times as many home demonstration agents had been hired through the legislation. The USDA's interpretation of the legislation rankled Noble. In a memorandum to members and allies of the National Committee, Noble complained that "the primary purpose of the Capper-Ketcham Act was to strengthen" 4-H but that only 36 percent of the Capper-Ketcham funds had been dedicated to "extension work with boys and girls." A full 50 percent of the funds should be dedicated to club agents, Noble asserted, implicitly criticizing Warburton and the USDA's management of the funds.[90]

Meanwhile, the passage of Capper-Ketcham had dramatically revealed that the USDA reaped a mixed harvest from Noble's work. In his earliest exchanges with Noble, Warburton had stipulated that 4-H's success depended upon "universal recognition of its public and disinterested direction."[91] The National Committee threatened that universal recognition at times. By Warburton's reckoning, the committee generated confusion about what agency was responsible for club work and thus lessened public trust and impaired 4-H's value as source of positive publicity for the USDA. Warburton and Smith bitterly complained that Noble was most interested in currying favor with affluent urban commercial interests that paid for the increasingly lavish trips and prizes awarded by the organization. Feasting farm kids in Chicago might actually complicate the USDA's plans to keep rural youth on farms. Smith's vision of cooperative club spaces imagined 4-H meetings as a way to insert technocratic expertise and commercial capital into distressed rural communities—the USDA would supply the knowledge, and businessmen would help defray the cost of its circulation. In fact, the USDA had created the National Committee to gather and redirect that capital, but Noble and his financial backers had different plans. A network flush with urban capital was also overflowing with urban vice—or, at least, the temptations and desires of urban consumerism. Rather than modernizing rural America, the National Committee intended to exploit it. If the extension service was not careful with 4-H, Liberty Hyde Bailey had warned the Grangers in 1914, "The children are liable to be exploited." The National Committee was Bailey's prophesy given flesh.[92]

The gendered dimensions of this mixed harvest brought the conflict out of the passive-aggressive missives fired between bureaucrats, bankers, and businessmen and into dramatic maternalist politics on the floor of the U.S. Congress. Experts like Gertrude Warren argued that rural decline was not simply a problem of production or marketing. The problems of rural America ran much deeper. Insolvent farms concealed bored and unhappy girls who fled to the city and shirked their vital mothering responsibilities. Reaching those girls—and sheltering them from the corrosive effects of the city—required that extension workers understand the gendered psychologies of boys and girls. Support for extension had always hinged on providing government agents intimate access to rural homes. But it was the specific innovation of Warren and like-minded home economists of the 1920s that pushed the focus from labor in the home to the laborers in the home. Reflected in club work's increasing emphasis on aesthetics, beauty, personality, and bodies, club work was more concerned with what sort of girls farmwork produced than it was with just the efficiency of girls' work.

If the ultimate goal of club work was not only the management of agricultural practices but the perfection of the bodies of rural youth, ever greater vigilance was required of the extension service in guarding rural youth from exploitation and misuse. Knowledge about agriculture and affinity for the progressive agricultural agenda needed to be paired with a basic appreciation for the sensitivity of the program and the fragility of adolescent psychology. Warren carved out a permanent authoritative space within agrarian futurism for experts who claimed domain over the inner workings of rural youth—experts who addressed themselves not just to agriculture practice or cooperative community organizing but also to how farms interfaced with the gendered physiological and psychological health of their youthful charges. As the broader health program demonstrated, the health of 4-H'ers could never be fully isolated from the agricultural context. Indeed, part of the success of maternalist activism in rural spaces hinged on female activists accessing and redeploying agrarian futurist tropes to their own ends. Nevertheless, convincing Clyde Warburton and C. B. Smith that home economists offered crucial insights about the health and well-being of rural youth was one thing, but ensuring the compliance of the entire sprawling, decentralized extension program was another altogether. Policing the behavior of the National Committee, a politically powerful, legally independent entity, proved difficult and, at times, threatened to upend the precarious alliance between the technocratic expertise and commercial agriculture upon which 4-H depended. The Great Depression and the political response to it increased the leverage of the USDA and CES over those commercial interests and heightened the need for 4-H to locate new productive and reproductive outlets for the suddenly devalued bodies of rural youth.

CHAPTER FOUR

Conserving Farm and Family in New Deal 4-H

> . . . my hands to larger service . . .
>
> —The 4-H Pledge

In June 1934, Oliver Edwin Baker, a senior economist at the USDA in the Bureau of Agricultural Economics, told 4-H leaders that the nation faced a dire crisis of reproduction. Less than two years earlier, the eminent economic geographer had offered similar warnings to the American Association of Geographers in his presidential address: "[A] nation must protect and preserve the children. . . . [I]f conditions become unfavorable to the reproduction of the race, the first objective of national policy . . . should be to restore the favorable conditions."[1] Speaking to the adult chaperones of hundreds of rural youth who had traveled to Washington for the National 4-H Camp, he emphasized the role of 4-H members in preventing this reproductive crisis by starting their own healthy farm families. By 1934, 4-H clubs enrolled nearly a million members. Recognizing the popularity of the program, Baker told the assembled leaders that they could help "restor[e] . . . the family as the fundamental institution of society." He believed that 4-H kept rural youth on farms to rear another generation of Americans in the moral, fertile embrace of the countryside. Throughout the 1930s, he peppered 4-H with speeches, pamphlets, and essays about his vision of an agrarian America reinvigorated by the reproductive labor of rural youth.[2]

Baker's vision of 4-H as a reproductive prosthesis for rural America fit perfectly with the growing ambitions of the USDA for the 4-H program. During the 1930s, 4-H expanded from about 800,000 members to more than 1.4 million, growing in both visibility and reach. During that period, the variety of activities available to 4-H members and the concomitant connections between technocratic expertise and rural youth also multiplied. By the end

of the decade, 4-H members were serving their communities by cooperating with the Agricultural Adjustment Administration, the Soil Conservation Service (SCS), the Rural Electrification Administration, and a host of
cultural programs designed to edify rural communities. Justifying this "ever
expanding" program in 1938, C. B. Smith surveyed an agricultural landscape
that was "increasingly mechanized" and marked by "larger farms, larger farm
businesses." Despite this impersonal scale, and thanks to the efforts of 4-H
and the CES, farms would still "be regarded as the ideal place in which to live
. . . because education will be there, culture will be there." Like Baker, Smith
believed that 4-H members would build new families in the countryside and
that generations of "farm families" would populate the nation.[3]

   "Conserv[ing] the youth," as Baker put it, reinforced links between the
bodies of 4-H members, farm families, rural communities and landscapes,
and the modern bureaucratic state.[4] In describing rural reproduction as
another state-run resource management initiative, he articulated the broader
ecological turn of the New Deal USDA. Major New Deal programs like the
Tennessee Valley Authority, Civilian Conservation Corps (CCC), and the
SCS sculpted rural landscapes according to principles borrowed from the
ecological "climax" theory of the day: planners viewed "peak" ecologies as
discrete, static, holistically ordered, and manageable by technocratic expertise. But more than soil whipped about in the wind. New Dealers believed
that the Great Depression had unleashed a whirlwind of demographic, social,
and political chaos. For a windswept national body, permanent agriculture
promised renewed roots—a way both to fix people to soil and soil to earth.
Agrarian futurism had primed rural people for myriad intimacies with the
USDA in the previous two decades and laid the groundwork for the success
of the New Deal rural program. During the New Deal, however, agrarian
futurism also became an apparatus to orchestrate normal sexuality for the
nation as a whole. Rather than a discourse primarily concerned with the relationship between rural reproduction and successful farming, agrarian futurism now concocted portable fantasies of normal family farms and the means
to carve those fantasies into law.

   As Baker's words suggest, 4-H'ers were essential to this fusion of agrarian futurism and the New Deal state. 4-H'ers performed direct service for
government programs like the Agricultural Adjustment Administration,
and the SCS and helped maintain the vital infrastructure of state power in
rural America. Their voices—and bodies—testified to the efficacy of government programs before skeptical audiences of depressed farmers, even
as their hands literally did the work of the state: planting trees, sketching

electrification plans, and filling out adjustment worksheets. But beyond that service, the USDA envisioned 4-H bodies performing reproductive service for the nation. In the 1920s, 4-H connected the gendered bodies of rural youth to progress in the countryside—an argument that had served the USDA well before Congress and the public. In the next decade, the USDA built on that foundation by trying to cultivate a new generation of healthy farm families. Just as perfected 4-H specimens advertised the broader extension program in the 1920s, happy 4-H marriages offered powerful proof of the wisdom of federal authority in New Deal America. Emboldened by this cultural force at the end of the decade, club experts finally moved to protect 4-H clubs from the crass commercialism and exploitative behavior of Guy Noble and the National Committee that threatened to upend federal authority and its conservation of rural America.

*   *   *

The economic, human, and ecological catastrophe sweeping across rural America in the early 1930s generated a massive federal response that provided unprecedented government support for agriculture and positioned healthy rural living as an essential characteristic of authentic American identity. For the New Deal USDA, relief for rural America depended upon using the existing administrative capacities of the CES to advance a set of ambitious new policy ends. The New Deal agricultural program used the CES's expansive human network to enroll millions of farmers in an incentivized, voluntary reduction of acreage, a task that required government persuasion as much as government regulation. Following the initial success of agricultural subsidy programs, the federal government launched a series of initiatives to remake rural America economically, socially, and ecologically. The New Deal agricultural program dramatically expanded the federal government's material investment in rural America but also relied on human capital assiduously developed by the CES over the previous two decades—human capital that could translate a national agricultural program into millions of local quotidian actions. As the CES administered components of the agricultural program, it also circulated an ecological vision of a permanent countryside and reinforced the cultural centrality of the family farm as the preferred system of social and biological reproduction in rural America. New Deal programs established the infrastructure for a system of government-assisted capital-intensive agriculture—a seeming boon to farmers as well as urban consumers—even as they asserted that rural living remained the soul of American civilization. By portraying farm families as the victims of the Depression and dedicating massive reform programs to their salvation, New Dealers cemented ties between agrarian futurism's celebration of white, heteronormative family farms and understandings of modern rural living.

The Depression created extraordinary hardships for average rural families—suffering that surpassed the pains of the disastrous 1920s. What had been merely a farm crisis blossomed into a full-blown farm catastrophe. Prices plummeted, supplemental sources of income evaporated into the broader Depression economy, and farmers faced foreclosures at staggering rates. Compounding the economic crisis, an ecological disaster brewed on the millions of acres of the southern plains that had only recently been swallowed by agricultural expansion. Gaining in frequency and intensity with each passing year, blinding dust storms buried farmsteads and country towns in layers of windswept topsoil, ultimately displacing a half-million individuals from the southern plains in the 1930s. Despite the abysmal conditions throughout much of rural America, many urban unemployed returned to the countryside, seeking to carve bare subsistence from the land or sell their labor in exchange for meals. This momentary pause in America's urbanization added to the 1930 census's finding of a plummeting national birthrate, painting a startling picture of national demographic chaos. The Depression had not only shattered the economy; to many Americans, it seemed poised to reverse the urban industrialism assumed to be at the heart of modernity.[5]

For many agricultural economists, the deteriorating conditions in rural America justified immediate federal intervention in agricultural markets. In addition to its usual bromides about businesslike efficiency and cooperation, the Hoover administration limited its intervention to the creation of the Federal Farm Board and a revolving capital fund of $500 million to be used to purchase and hold surplus commodities and to fund new cooperatives.[6] Agricultural economists such as M. L. Wilson of Montana State University, Rexford Tugwell of Columbia University, and even the Federal Farm Board's assistant chief economist, Mordecai Ezekiel, noted that government efforts to prop up prices through voluntary acreage reduction would only contribute to further spiraling of commodity prices: even if some farmers reduced acreage and prices marginally improved in the short term, other farmers would free ride and increase production to capitalize on favorable prices and worsen the long-term price situation. Sustained favorable prices required that farmers had a unique financial incentive to limit production. Only state financing, planning, and coordination could provide such an incentive.[7]

Franklin Roosevelt's administration warmly received the proposed alternative system, known as "production control" and "domestic allotment." Tugwell, Wilson, and Ezekiel all played crucial roles in drafting what would be the centerpiece of Roosevelt's agricultural policy, the Agricultural Adjustment Act (AAA) of 1933, and, after the election, the three apostles of production control assumed important positions in Henry A. Wallace's USDA. The legislation provided farmers with subsidies to voluntarily retire acreage for a core set of staple crops. The actual formula for the subsidy was opaque and complicated. For the core crops, the USDA would guarantee an elevated contract price for the portion of a farmer's total crop equivalent to the portion of the national crop sold on the domestic market.[8] In return, farmers pledged to retire a certain portion of their acreage, with the added incentive that the contract payment would be calculated as if the farmer had planted to the farm's historical capacity. In 1933, for example, the USDA required participating farmers to retire 15 percent of their wheat acreage but made contract payments to a given farm, based on the average yield of that farm's three prior harvests. Farmers could opt not to participate but would then receive only the market price, which, in the case of wheat, was dramatically lower than the contract price. By the end of the decade, adjustment payments ran to over $1.5 billion.[9]

The complexity and size of the program demanded some level of government oversight. Farmers needed explanations of the program's intricate details and assistance in completing the complicated contracts. Most of all, the USDA needed to guarantee that participating farmers held up their ends of the bargain and complied with the acreage retirements. The USDA hoped that farmers could handle many of the administrative duties through local farmers' committees. But realistically, the existence of farmers' committees created as many governance problems as it solved. Who would train the committees and who would ensure that they adhered to the regulations? The AAA created a government agency, the Agricultural Adjustment Administration, to oversee the program, but the new agency lacked the institutional capacity and national reach to do so without the assistance of another agency. Since county agents with local knowledge and contacts already worked in nearly every rural county in the nation, the USDA used the CES to implement and supervise the AAA.[10] Across rural America, the CES organized mass meetings and met with individual farmers to explain the program's complex rationale and stave off "the prejudices of the rank and file of our people," as Wallace put it.[11]

The CES was particularly well suited to act as a popular advocate for the agricultural program, given its proven ability to coordinate between government agents, farmers, and local political elites. Some directors of extensions, in fact, had parlayed their positions into impressive statewide political power that they subsequently deployed on the AAA's behalf. The director of extension at Alabama Polytechnic Institute and former Alabama 4-H leader, Luther Duncan, used his "political machine" to popularize the agricultural program.[12] By August 1933, the USDA had rented over 800,000 acres of cotton in Alabama, nearly a quarter of the state's total cotton acreage, thanks to Duncan's "4,000 beat committeemen, county agents, and teachers of vocational agriculture." Around the rest of the nation, county agents made similar contributions, persuading millions of skeptical farmers to enroll.[13] Recognizing the obvious value of a network of agents capable of both popularizing and administering federal programs across rural America, Congress in 1935 passed the Bankhead-Jones Act, which, by 1940, had more than doubled extension monies, to about $20 million annually. As historian Brian Balogh explains, involvement in the AAA rendered the CES an indispensable component of national political economy.[14]

As much good as the AAA did, agricultural New Dealers believed that long-term rural prosperity depended on a much broader restructuring of rural resources and landscapes. A host of New Deal programs sought to physically transform the American countryside to push this transition from rapacious cash cropping to "agriculture permanent and lasting," as M. L. Wilson put it.[15] Beginning in 1933, the CCC drew millions of unemployed young adults into largely rural conservation projects, while the Works Progress Administration poured billions of dollars into rural infrastructure as a part of the second New Deal, in 1935. In the same year, the Roosevelt administration launched the Resettlement Administration, the SCS, and the Rural Electrification Administration to transform rural communities and landscapes. The technological modernization of the hinterlands—electrification, mechanization, infrastructural improvement, and dam building—would make rural communities less remote, farms more efficient, and rural people healthier and happier. On their surface, such observations diverged only slightly from what progressive agriculturalists and extension officials had argued for decades. Rather than depending primarily upon efforts to educate rural people about the benefits of modern technology, however, the New Deal state dedicated unprecedented sums of public capital and, when necessary, coercive force to promote its vision of technological modernization.[16]

Among federal planners, ecological thought shaped the conception and execution of these programs. New Dealers frequently asserted that the causes of the rural depression were closely tied to poor soil and land management, not just the market conditions addressed by the AAA. Surveying America's dust-scorched and flood-damaged hinterlands, Henry A. Wallace lamented: "Human beings are ruining land, and bad land is ruining human beings, especially children."[17] Improved ecological planning offered hope. Such planning provided a holistic approach to rural modernization that increasingly blurred the lines between rural sociology, agricultural economics, and the physical sciences. As historian Neil Maher contends, by the middle part of the decade, New Dealers had "incorporat[ed]" a "philosophy of ecology" into national planning based on the "tenets of interdependence, balance, and holism."[18] According to this philosophy, cooperation between farmers and experts could create sustainable biological, economic, and social systems in rural America, but only if it focused on a plan for a restored rural ecology rather than merely a profitable price situation.

The USDA tended to construe this conservation work as men's work, even while reinforcing the idea that farm women should focus on perfecting the rural home. New Deal employment programs concentrated on men: it was primarily men who were expected to be the careful stewards of landscapes and soils, not women. In contrast, New Deal programs urged women to focus on improving their homes, physically and culturally. Home demonstration agents urged rural women to reduce unnecessary purchases, cultivate a hygienic domestic space, and concentrate on cultural enrichment through arts and music education programs. To the extent that rural women were to be engaged in productive labor at all, extension service material contended, it should be directed at producing goods for home consumption, not for the market. This "live-at-home" philosophy imagined that rural women, with the aesthetic and practical assistance of home demonstration agents, could create refined rural homes comparable with homes crowded with mass-produced consumer goods, and at reduced cost. Just as county agricultural agents helped supervise loans issued by the Resettlement Administration and later the Farm Security Administration, home demonstration agents visited rural homes to assist rural women with spending budgets, keeping home accounts, and managing their households. New Deal rural modernization programs redirected male labor toward the physical improvement of the countryside but reinforced the farmer's wife's singular focus on the production of a healthy home.[19]

Guided by warnings from officials like Oliver Baker that American civilization was entering a period of population decline, the USDA's New Deal programs reflected a concern for the ability of the right kinds of rural American to procreate and populate the countryside. In this sense, the Depression and the New Deal did not precipitate a retreat from the particular family farm ideal described in Chapter 3. Quite the contrary: federal agencies became even more invested in the battle to save family farms composed of a male revenue producer and a female homemaker. As historian Sarah Phillips notes, New Deal "agrarian intellectuals," in particular, "wanted to restore and modernize the middle-sized farms of their youths."[20] Most USDA officials, even those beyond the circle of Wilson and Wallace, recognized that smaller, labor-intensive farms were no longer feasible or desirable, but they argued that highly mechanized, small commercial farms could persist with adequate government assistance and that subsistence farming could supplement the income of some laborers. But this enthusiasm for small-scale farming and the resulting government programs had a very particular sort of family farm in mind. The contours of this ideal celebrated white, middle-class rural people and depended upon a much broader effort to bolster the reproductive capacities among those "better sorts" of rural people. Just as agrarianism guided eugenic sterilization campaigns, it also structured "positive eugenic" efforts in the 1930s—efforts to encourage the fittest of society to reproduce more prolifically, in contrast to the "negative" measures of incarcerating and sterilizing the unfit.[21] These programs did less to actually conserve the population of rural America and more to normalize the ideal of white, middle-class rural heterosexuality on farms and in urban popular culture. By working through the specific image of the family farm, USDA programs simultaneously constructed rural heterosexuality, expertly managed rural landscapes, and capital-intensive commercial agriculture.

The New Deal USDA's emphasis on abandoning production maximization in favor of an ecologically informed permanent agriculture required new outlets for the labor and bodies of rural youth. In an era of production control, club organizers struggled to find new directions for club projects that had previously taught members how to squeeze the most profit out of their farms. Ultimately, the CES found that club members could help meet their families' basic subsistence needs through gardening, crop, and livestock projects—production that might previously have been sent to market. But New Deal 4-H also encouraged members to cooperate with the USDA in its broader effort to conserve rural America. 4-H members did so by helping county agents administer the agricultural program and by circulating lessons about soil conservation, land management, and ecological thought. This complex of activities tightened links between federal authority and rural youth by reframing youthful cooperation with federal programs as a form of public-spirited service.

*   *   *

Over the course of the 1930s, 4-H made cooperation with federal rural modernization programs a central component of the service provided by club work. Service projects took on added significance for farm youth, as troubled agricultural markets and the mantra of production control complicated market-oriented projects. Club material frequently alluded to this as service rendered to embattled rural communities, and, surely, rural beautification, conservation, and electrification projects provided tangible benefits to farms and country towns alike. Yet, as much as this was service to particular communities, it was service channeled through the federal government's administrative apparatus and guided by the priorities of federal planners. By presenting cooperation with federal programs in the language of civic duty and ecological holism, New Deal 4-H presented the state as a natural and nonpartisan presence in the American countryside, beyond both politics and private interest.

In the early 1930s, the economic and social unrest fueled serious anxieties about American youth. Young Americans were disproportionately unemployed. "Nearly half of the unemployed are under thirty years of age. The larger part of them have at least high school education and many have college diplomas. They are well equipped in mind and body and can see no good reason why it is so hard for them to find jobs," explained Henry A. Wallace in 1934. Hobos, tramps, and rail riders stoked public fears that unemployed young men would permanently abandon family life and polite society for lives of delinquency—or worse.[22] The radical youth movements popular in Europe figured centrally in the "worse." "There is some danger that these younger unemployed," Wallace continued, "joining hands with farmers who have been in the most serious trouble, and with certain other underprivileged groups, will push the nation so far to the left that we will be headed toward the land of nightmare, even as unemployed youths have succumbed to misguided leadership in certain foreign countries."[23] Roosevelt's solution was employment and, in particular, the CCC. If private industry could not find a use for America's youth, government would, lest youthful energy and passion feed radical politics and demagoguery. In rural America, where production control made the reduction of youth labor official policy, this problem was particularly acute. For the last century, the labor of individuals under thirty—children and hired hands—had been central to the functioning of many farms. What was to be done with all this labor?

4-H grappled with precisely this problem. Club organizers believed that 4-H, as the nation's largest youth organization, could be an effective tool for mobilizing rural youth on behalf of the nation, but they also worried that an organized youth movement could be hijacked for nefarious partisan purposes. Gertrude Warren's 1934 speech to the conference of state 4-H leaders in Washington, D.C, best captured this sense of uneasiness. The speech compared 4-H with the "striking examples of youth movements in a number of countries." It explored the functioning of youth movements all over the world but lingered primarily on the examples in Germany, Italy, and Russia. These movements, suggested Warren, had a "political aspect" that tended to "exploit the high ideals and impressionable nature of youth" for "factional or nationalistic" ends.[24] Youth movements in the "dictatorial nations" had mobilized great "courage, industry, endurance, and skill" only through manipulation, charismatic leadership, and uncritical nationalism. By contrast, she contended, 4-H eschewed partisan or factional thinking and embraced free discussion and democratic deliberation. While foreign youth movements mobilized for destructive, narrow purposes, 4-H was interested only in the public good. The advent of the New Deal introduced a heightened emphasis on the public service done by club members through state-managed rural modernization programs. Rural youth could productively serve their communities not just through economic activities but, as C. B. Smith put it, an "ever expanding program" of rural cultural, ecological, and economic improvement. The scale-traversing New Deal state provided the perfect channel for this service. As federal programs aimed at reforming rural America multiplied during the 1930s, 4-H club members enjoyed new avenues for public service through direct cooperation with these programs. "You are in the midst of . . . revolutionary changes," C. B. Smith told the 1933 National 4-H Camp in reference to the New Deal agricultural program. "Yours is the privilege of taking part in and guiding this great economic and social movement."[25]

Even as 4-H organizers emphasized the organization's public service capacities, AAA responsibilities forced many county agents to neglect the 4-H program in 1933 and 1934. Some USDA officials worried that such neglect would damage the long-term health of extension, and they pushed the

Roosevelt administration and Congress to provide funds to hire additional extension agents. In Arizona, extension organizers repeatedly complained that the new agricultural program had undone much of the meager club organizing that they had already accomplished. Even in states with robust extension services, club work suffered. Alabama's 4-H leader, T. A. "Dad" Sims, reported that, in 1934, 4-H work had "been considerably handicapped" and "neglect[ed]" because of the demands placed on county agents by "the Agricultural Adjustment Program." I. O. Schaub, director of extension in North Carolina, concurred: "Our club work, especially with boys, has almost gone by default" as a result of the AAA. In 1933, total national 4-H enrollments declined for the first time since 1922. They declined again in 1934, before improved conditions in the middle part of the decade enabled county agents to rededicate themselves to club organizing.[26]

Despite their inability to give full attention to 4-H, extension officials recognized that club members could help popularize and administer the federal program. USDA officials encouraged state extension services to circulate explanations of the agricultural program through 4-H clubs, whose members often served as the most persuasive representatives of the extension service. In an effort to increase understanding along these lines, the 1933 National 4-H Club Camp was entirely devoted to the AAA and featured speeches about the relationship of 4-H to the adjustment of the rural home and to hog, corn, and dairy production.[27] "Club forces will be called upon to explain the new law to farmers and to show farmers how they may take advantage of the various provisions of the new Act," Smith told the campers as they prepared to adjourn.[28] State extension services frequently used 4-H members as well as volunteers as local spokespeople for the agricultural program. Warren reported that, in South Carolina, a "club girl explained the cotton program to over a thousand people. In New Hampshire, a club boy similarly explained the dairy situation, while in Kansas, another club boy accompanied his county agent to group meetings throughout his county, explaining in detail, with the use of charts, the wheat situation."[29] George Farrell contrasted the ability of 4-H to promote the new agricultural program with what he considered a meager effort by the public schools, including Smith-Hughes classes. "The schools and colleges have not yet had time to adjust their textbooks and courses of study to the shift in emphasis," he bragged, "but the 4-H clubs have already, in their club meetings and activities, begun to think seriously along lines of controlling production."[30]

Using 4-H to promote a political program fit perfectly into the broader politicization of extension in the previous two decades. For example, by the advent of the New Deal, Luther Duncan had already wound 4-H into his Alabama political machine. T. A. Sims was a close confidant of Duncan's and, according to the accusations of Duncan's critics, one of his chief political lieutenants.[31] Duncan and Sims used their contact with farmers through 4-H to recruit rural Alabamans for political causes.[32] In 1931, Duncan's enemies proposed a bill that would crack down on his politicking. To defeat the bill, Duncan mobilized his political machine and produced an army of farmers to march on Montgomery. His county agents issued letters to 4-H club members urging them to enlist their parents in the cause. "Some mean folks are trying to pass a law to keep the county agent from helping farmers," explained county agent Charles Brockway to the members of the Butler County Boys 4-H Club. "And I want all the farmers in your community to come here Friday to ask the Governor not to pass any such bill. SO MAKE YOUR DAD COME and MOTHER TOO."[33] On May 14, 1931, more than ten thousand men and women flooded the bill's committee hearing, forcing the committee to move the hearing to the nearby Montgomery Bowl. The committee adjourned without action after the angry crowd interrupted the proceedings with an insistent chant of "kill the bill." "We licked the enemy good and proper," Duncan bragged to O. B. Martin, then Texas's director of extension.[34]

Given Duncan's enthusiastic support for the New Deal agricultural program, Alabama extension agents scrambled to find ways for club members to assist with the practical administration of the AAA. Sims and extension agronomist J. C. Lowery designed a program to encourage 4-H members to directly assist their parents with AAA forms. "Record book work has not been so satisfactory," reported Lowery on previous efforts to directly instruct farmers on record keeping. Lowery predicted that "more progress" could be achieved by "us[ing] this record book work as a 4-H club project with the 4-H agents being in position to supervise this project." "Alabama 4-H Club boys and girls will be given credit for keeping AAA record books for their fathers in 1936," explained one Alabama newspaper. On Lowery's recommendation, the USDA distributed tens of thousands of AAA record books directly to Alabama county agents who then distributed many of them to 4-H'ers.[35]

Other states took a similar tack and used 4-H members to assist adults with complicated paperwork. Thanks to club work, many 4-H'ers had extensive experience with calculation and account keeping, precisely the sort of experience that farmers needed to correctly fill out adjustment contracts. The USDA hoped that 4-H members would assist their parents and neighbors in completing the copious forms. As Clyde Warburton explained in a 1934 New Year's radio broadcast to 4-H members, "The farm records many of you have

kept in the past will be very useful to your fathers in making out their pro-
duction-control contracts, and this year I hope many more of you will engage
in this very useful work."[36] Individual states launched 4-H AAA projects,
and county agents distributed AAA account books through 4-H clubs. This
level of coordination often tied the success of the AAA program to the abilities of 4-H leaders and club members. In explaining his county's success in
both club work and AAA hog contracts, an Illinois county agent summarized
his approach: "We have a corps of loyal and outstanding local leaders. . . .
[T]hey have seen that individual members have carried on their share of the
program."[37]

Club account books also linked female 4-H'ers to the CES's live-at-
home program. Home demonstration agents distributed account books to
club members to teach girls how to eliminate wasteful spending. In Iowa,
for example, the extension service distributed personal account books to
female 4-H'ers and directed them to make a precise record of their income
and expenses. Participating girls recorded their every purchase and turned
in completed account books to club leaders and county agents.[38] Literature
explaining how to refine and improve consumption habits, promote wise
purchases, and encourage frugality, thrift, and savings accompanied the
account books. In 1933, twenty-seven states already reported that they were
encouraging club members to keep personal accounts.[39] In this sense, just
as extension literature in production projects encouraged exhaustive record
keeping to ensure efficient, profitable production, other extension material
used the same means to rationalize female consumption and health habits in
line with the Depression emphasis on thrift and economy.

As club enrollments began to rebound in 1935, county agents found
other novel ways to coordinate between club work and the host of New Deal
rural modernization programs. Beginning in 1934, many 4-H clubs began to
offer "conservation" projects. By 1936, more than 100,000 rural youth were
enrolled in projects that required them to design and implement conservation programs on their home farms and in their wider communities. "[W]e
now have a million and forty thousand in various clubs; every one of those
members should be given the opportunity and encouraged to observe and
study nature in all her moods," C. B. Smith urged club leaders at the 1936
National 4-H Camp.[40] Like wildlife appreciation clubs, conservation projects
called for 4-H'ers to map and catalog wildlife near their homes. They also
promoted systematic "fire control" and discouraged the "indiscriminate use
of poison" for pest control. Conservation projects prioritized individual club
members familiarizing themselves with the local and national plans of the

USDA and helping to assist government agencies in all conservation efforts. In contrast to merely appreciating or educating rural youth about wildlife or nature, conservation projects encouraged 4-H members to become active participants in government conservation schemes.[41]

Even when a state did not offer an independent conservation project, existing programs were adapted to fit the ecological priorities of the USDA. Some states expanded existing forestry programs in which 4-H members cooperated with the SCS's Woodland Management division to grow and plant trees in their communities. One Ohio 4-H club, for example, reported that in 1935 alone, its hundred members had planted an astounding 99,000 trees in Tuscaragaw County.[42] After the launch of the SCS in 1935, the Arizona Extension Service combined club work and ecological maintenance by making soil conservation a major point of emphasis in cotton clubs. Roy Westley, the specialist in agronomy and irrigation in Tucson, designed a comprehensive program for cotton clubs that emphasized conserving the state's sandy loam for future generations, deeming club work a crucial element in a larger effort to disseminate information about the conservation program.[43]

Club members received important conservation information at public gatherings and, especially, at 4-H camps. 4-H camps, hosted near wooded ponds, in forest reserves, or in state parks, offered ideal opportunities to expose rural youth to wilderness away from the farm. Representatives of the SCS used captive camp audiences to give presentations on the importance and practices of soil conservation and to explain basic concepts of ecology.[44] Charles Peterson, a member of the Nokay Lake 4-H Club in Minnesota, described the activities of the 1935 Minnesota 4-H Conservation Camp hosted at a forestry school at the end of a "winding forest road . . . on the shores of Lake Itasca." The three-day camp featured wilderness walks, tours of a nursery, and countless talks from "men who are making Conservation their life's work." One Sunday night, camp organizers arranged for a brief ritual to impart to the campers vital ecological lessons. "Each delegate was given a small boat which bore a candle" to be placed "in the current of Mississippi headwaters" as the other campers sang a hymn. "Though they would not travel far in reality," Peterson reported, "they would stand out as a symbol for carrying out conservation spirit the entire length of the Mississippi." Peterson's account, published in the *Brainerd Daily*, ruminated on the historical importance of the New Deal conservation program, of which he saw himself as a part. "We have spent many years in ruthlessly destroying our natural resources," he wrote. "We all now have to spend many years in their reconstruction and maintenance. In the meantime rural youth is thanking the men and women who are contributing to this great cause of providing it with a healthful, mind and body-building work, and aiding our natural resources."[45]

By the late 1930s, 4-H clubs were actively engaged in rural electrification projects conducted by the Tennessee Valley Authority and the Rural Electrification Administration. In 1936, the National Committee, in cooperation with the USDA, the Rural Electrification Administration, and Westinghouse Electric, launched the National 4-H Rural Electrification Contest. To compete for the nearly $1,000 in prize scholarships, club members "ma[d]e surveys of farms and communities . . . [and] provide[d] data valuable in building high lines and in making the most efficient use of electrical power."[46] The winner of the first-place $300 scholarship, Donald Mosher of De Kalb, Illinois, created "detailed plans for complete electrification of his 160-acre home farm" and wrote "a scholarly essay on the benefits of electricity to rural folk." The runner-up, Paul Schaff of Comanche, Iowa, provided electrification plans for "his father's 360-acre farm" and "assist[ed] in planning and staging three local group meetings" in conjunction with the Rural Electrification Administration. In 1939, the USDA announced that forty states had created 4-H electrification programs in which members studied how electricity could be used on their farms and engaged in an "electrical project involving in some cases a study of wiring procedure [and] care and maintenance of electrical equipment." Electrification club members were also expected to give talks and demonstrations in their communities. One Arizona club member screened a film for an audience of two hundred people on the benefits of electrification. In Iowa, "4-H Club members conducted an electrical lunch stand and furnished dinners to around a thousand people." Another Iowa club boy put his expertise to popular use by joining a tour sponsored by the Rural Electrification Administration. Traveling from community to community across Iowa and Nebraska, the boy demonstrated how to use various electrical implements and appliances as "director of machinery operations."[47]

By the end of the decade, the 4-H program was reflecting the increasing presence of federal power in the countryside. To address America's growing youth problem, 4-H organizers found ways to fold club work into the variety of programs directed at the modernization of rural America. 4-H'ers helped their parents and neighbors fill out AAA account books and circulated knowledge about land management and soil conservation. They mapped the wildlife on farms, planted trees, and made plans to electrify farms and towns. They staged musical performances and did their best to elevate the level of cultural literacy in their own communities. The sum of this activity was presented as service—to family, community, and nation. "In these past several years of the depression all of us have been given a much greater chance for service than was ever offered any other 4-H group," explained Maude Wallace, the secretary of agriculture's wife, to the 1935 National 4-H Club Camp. "The broadening influence which comes from the spirit of service developed in the club . . . lift[s] the 4-H club program to a plane on which are all proud to stand with it," she continued. By the end of the decade, 4-H had enabled rural youth to serve their communities, improve rural landscapes, and experience the ennoblement of that broadening influence by cooperating with the federal government's rural modernization programs.[48]

*   *   *

Finding a productive use for the time and labor of rural youth was only part of the solution to America's youth problem in the 1930s. New Deal employment and conservation programs could capture youthful passion and energy, but the source of discontent for many youth was as much emotional as it was economic. As Gertrude Warren explained, the violent, unpredictable behavior of youth—what was exploited by foreign youth movements—was also driven by disintegrating home life and eroding opportunities for emotionally satisfying marriage. Successful marriage and economic security were intertwined, but she argued that, in the long term, successful marriage required the right attitudes as well as emotional and social adjustment. A person in a happy relationship, no matter the immediate economic situation, would be more emotionally stable and less likely to contribute to the youth problem. In this sense, Warren implicitly linked a healthy democracy with heterosexual fulfillment and radical politics with sex delinquency and mental disorder. By training rural youth for marriage, 4-H would render a double service to the nation. 4-H would produce more of the wholesome rural youth who, figures such as Oliver Baker announced, would direct the nation's future. In doing so, 4-H would counter the sort of reproductive disorder that fueled the disintegration of democratic politics. During the 1930s, 4-H organizers focused on how they could train rural youth for healthy, wholesome marriages and heterosexual relations—training that required 4-H members to cultivate pleasing selves and 4-H leaders to cultivate wholesome club spaces conducive to heterosexual romance. By the end of the decade, 4-H literature was educating 4-H'ers about family and marriage, transforming clubs into spaces for sex education. At the same time, popular images of successful 4-H couples bolstered the USDA's claim to help the reproduction of the countryside.

In earlier decades, rural modernizers had hoped to shield rural youth from the dangerous lure of the city; in the 1930s, population trends presented rural-urban migration as an opportunity for rural youth to save the nation from urban decay. "With the population of cities declining and the surplus from rural areas taking their place, will it not be the farm-reared men and women of the future who will eventually dominate the thinking of this nation?" pondered C. B. Smith.[49] Because of the demographic shift announced by O. E. Baker and confirmed by his colleagues in the Bureau of Agricultural Economics, the extension service assumed the responsibility of maintaining both the rural birthrate and a supply of rural youth reared in wholesome farm families. Robert Foster told the 1931 National 4-H Camp that the institution of the family ensured "[t]he reproduction of the race" and was "the best means of securing a satisfactory social control of reproduction." Family life, however, was threatened by modernity. The divorce rate, particularly in urban areas, was "too high." Nevertheless, "most problems of marriage and family life [were] remediable thru education and training" that 4-H could provide to rural youth.[50] Reflecting on the "general decline in the birthrate," Warren agreed that early family education and training were vital.[51] Industrial vocations, she argued, forced men "to search for exciting pleasures to offset the often deadly routine of their daily work," even as it lured women out of the home. In the city, youth were "confronted with the dazzling temptations of commercialized enterprise," all of which had "immeasurably increased . . . youth's desires and secret longings." Given this context, education for healthy family relations needed to occur before families were created. Warren urged extension workers to use club work to fortify the "important institution" of the rural home. Only with a healthy home life and strong family relationships would rural youth be able to resist the temptations of city living. Addressing club members through the national 4-H radio program in 1937, she later explained that "the more we share in making our homes comfortable and enjoyable, the more we are doing in establishing a stable family life which in turn is recognized as basic to national progress."[52] C. B. Smith concurred with her analysis, noting that the demographic trends meant that a monumental "responsibility" was "thus placed on the farm family," as well as "on the 4-H clubs" and various other organizations dedicated to strengthening that institution.[53]

USDA experts placed a special emphasis on reaching older rural youth because heterosexual desire played such a powerful role in shaping youths over the age of fifteen. Extension workers operated from a psychological model that recognized the nascent sexual impulses of adolescents and plotted to redirect those urges into healthy vocational outlets. By the mid-1930s, USDA experts were placing even greater emphasis on what one extension sociologist called the "human mating season."[54] Warren called it an "instinctive desire," while Eugene Merritt pointed out that "all creatures come to a period in their life cycle when they feel a drive or urge to leave their parents, seek someone of the opposite sex, form a new pair and establish a new home or nest."[55] A. B. Graham noted that such biological urges shaped nearly all activities. Boys in their late teens could be expected to try to earn money to impress girls, while girls would seek to improve their physical appearances through careful eating, attire, and exercise.[56] Merritt noted that, in early adolescence, a boy might hope to receive accolades and accomplishments for his dairy club work, but, by his late teens, he would be more moved by the possibility of earning enough money to "buy gas to take his lady friend to a dance."[57]

Ensuring that this nascent heterosexual urge resulted in healthy reproductive outcomes required careful attention on the part of club leaders and organizers. Hedley Dimock told the 1935 National 4-H Congress that mixed-sex activities in 4-H clubs performed the vital service of socializing healthy "heterosexual relations."[58] He argued that, absent the opportunity to meet and interact with members of the opposite sex, youth had no chance to "establish the right attitudes and understandings." Homosocial education and recreation "tragically" ensured that sexual maturation would take place only "in a vacuum" that left boys with distorted understandings of sexual relations. Without the experience of entertaining boys, girls might fall prey to sexually aggressive men and lapse into promiscuity. In the city, where there had been a full breakdown of "old controls and the old ideas," girls might be particularly in danger of "drowning" in a sea of men. 4-H club work, by encouraging the "development of inner controls and of inner ideals," might tame the passions of boys and teach girls to swim.[59]

4-H camp emerged as one arena for such heterosexual socialization. Away from parents and exposed to a host of new friends, camp's emphasis on leisure and socialization offered 4-H youth ample opportunities for flings and romances. As the account of Charles Peterson suggested, the Minnesota 4-H Conservation Camp educated campers about both ecology and heterosexual romance. In fact, camp organizers tended to conflate the two by integrating courtship into nearly all the camp's ceremonies and rituals. Camp organizers paired boys and girls and had them march as "partners from the assembly to the banquet." For the candle-lighting ceremony at the headwaters of the Mississippi that awakened such awe in Peterson, camp organizers directed boys to invite a girl to accompany them. "Emphasis again was placed on companionship," explained Peterson.[60] During the late 1930s and into the early 1940s, Arizona 4-H'ers joked about camp romances in the pages of a brief publication titled the *News*.[61] "Who's the handsome guy, Charlotte? Couldn't be E. M., could it?" wrote Dorothy Ingle and Tommy Patterson from Cochise County, about a budding couple. "Ruth C., can you tell us where tall, dark, and handsome is this year? We hope you haven't been too lonesome!!!" mused Nadene Bishop of Maricopa County, referring to Ruth C.'s past camp romance.[62] "What young man from Mesa," wondered an anonymous writer in the *News*, "takes up so much of a girl's time from Cabin 5 that her mother has to call her to take a shower? B.A. we think." References like these confirmed that relationships, innocently portrayed, blossomed at camp.[63]

Although the excitement of camp seemed especially conducive to romance, 4-H organizers strived to make other components of the 4-H program fruitful for heterosexual romance. Gertrude Warren approvingly reported that a number of state extension services were organizing "more group meetings for both girls and boys" that would keep "the interest of girls in worth-while home-making and community activities" and would offer the "opportunity for them to meet fine, manly young men."[64] Because social interactions in 4-H clubs featured adult guidance, heterosexual relations could be maintained on a "wholesome, constructive basis." Margaret Latimer, a national 4-H fellow at the USDA, identified such activities as absolutely crucial for any program addressed to older rural girls. "Every girl wishes to make herself pleasing to others," she wrote. Girls also wished to "associate with and be popular with boys," which required that 4-H provide girls with "joint meetings . . . and social events . . . to meet fine young men."[65] By 1936, many states were attempting to comply with these recommendations. Elda Jane Barker, a home demonstration agent from Allegheny, New York, reported that the key to her program for older girls had been organizing joint activities with local boys' clubs. One joint event with a livestock club began with "a meat-cutting demonstration, followed by a lesson in various meat cuts and a meat-canning demonstration." A banquet prepared by the girls followed, after which the boys and girls "adjourned to the Wee Blue Inn for a dancing party." G. W. Litton, a county agricultural agent in Tazewell County, Virginia, described his program for older youth based around "the '3 p's,' namely pretty, personality, and parties. Young people are interested in things that pertain to themselves and to the opposite sex."[66]

Litton's inclusion of personality in his "3 p's" reflected how 4-H literature linked a pleasing personality to the maintenance of healthy heterosexual
relations. This link explained that the characteristics that made an individual
immediately desirable to the opposite sex were the same as those that ensured
marital stability and healthy reproduction. Club material asserted that personal attractiveness required social graces and self-control, and it encouraged club members to develop precisely those qualities to help their chances
with the opposite sex. As Virginia state girls' club agent Hallie Hughes noted
at the 1931 National 4-H Camp, club work was oriented toward helping club
members develop a self that was pleasing to others. "The individual self
must be studied, analyzed and trained," she explained. "Self management
must be practiced, but in doing so there must be developed a strong type of
personality that takes proper account of others that they too may grow into
self-directing personalities."[67] At the same camp, Robert Foster linked that
self-control to the ability to attract a mate and to long-term marital success.
He provided campers with a lengthy list of factors that determined marital
compatibility. Although these factors included environmental, biological,
and hereditary influences, he suggested that the success of most marriages
was overdetermined by economic comfort and the ability of the individuals to amicably share domestic space. This latter factor, moreover, could be
addressed through "adjustments in personal relations"—namely, the development of social graces and the maintenance of personal appearance. Because
4-H could help rural youth develop self-control and a pleasing personality, it
was similarly well situated to socializing these healthy family relationships.[68]

Foster's approach laid a conceptual foundation for much of the family
work done by 4-H clubs during the 1930s. Warren praised his efforts, noting that, at the National 4-H Camp and subsequently in local club meetings,
"young people spent considerable time discussing qualifications for successful home partnerships" and "thereby are made more conscious of the desirable qualifications to look for in choosing a mate." Such conversations "have
helped many a 4-H club member to break himself of a habit that heretofore
had proved objectionable."[69] Over the course of the decade, USDA and CES
experts advised club leaders and members on the best routes to developing
precisely these happy family relationships.[70] At the same time, 4-H literature
focused on teaching boys and girls alike how to cultivate a self pleasing to
the opposite sex. The January 1938 edition of the *National 4-H Club News*, for
example, listed for the benefit of its readers "the most frequent failings of boys
and girls," itemized according to "What Boys Dislike in Girls" and "What Girls
Dislike in Boys." The article warned girls about "smart remarks" and "ill-timed

sarcasm," as well as "flashy jewelry," "powdering to cover dirt," and "scorning domesticity." Boys, on the other hand, were cautioned against "staying too long on a date," "talking and gossiping constantly about girls," "telling how shabbily he has treated girls," and the "use of bad smelling hair dressing."[71]

As important as personal appearance and a pleasant personality might be for attracting the opposite sex, 4-H literature also stressed that girls' long-term marital prospects would depend upon their fitness as mothers and wives. In this sense, club literature advanced the proposition that performance of gendered domestic labor was intrinsically linked to a successful marriage and, by implication, to successful heterosexuality. Female club members tested their mothering skills on younger siblings and the children of neighbors—scoring and recording their "mothering" skills just as they would a dress or meal. By the end of the decade, many states had integrated child-care projects into girls' club programs. "Little mothers" Catherine Barnes and Betty Freeman, for example, applied their club lessons to the care of their nephews and nieces, winning national attention and accolades in the process. Barnes, a sixteen-year-old from Florida, "mothered 20-months old nephew Bryant

Figure 6. "Happy Husbands" for 4-H girls from a 1932 issue
of *National Boys and Girls Club News.*

for two weeks last summer while his parents took a much needed vacation."[72] Alabama 4-H provided extensive information on child care and nurturing in senior girls' club literature. "You can make that little fellow who follows you your friend for life," suggested one manual. "He needs your help. Learn how to really help him. It will take a long time for him to grow up. He has so very much to learn."[73]

For 4-H girls, fitness for motherhood meant robust physical health. Although there was little programmatic uniformity from state to state, some 4-H clubs used their entrée with rural girls to launch broader discussions of maternal health that warned against sexual promiscuity. Iowa 4-H, for example, stressed that girls needed to care for themselves with future motherhood in mind. Dr. R. E. Parry, a physician in Scranton, Iowa, addressed the 1936 Iowa 4-H Girls state convention in a talk titled "What Is the Future for the Doctor and 4-H Girl." He praised the 4-H health examinations that he conducted as "an inspiration to the doctor himself" because they were the ideal way of "getting acquainted with the future mothers of our community." Young mothers, he complained, were too "modest." 4-H examinations broke the ice and allowed doctors to "educate the future mothers" and provide a "moral influence." Parry assured his audience that he "put the fear of God in their ears in regard to sex and venereal diseases" and told them of the "actual results of stepping over the moral lines of intimacy between sexes."[74] By 1939, the Iowa state extension staff made sure to include "Mental Hygiene for the Adolescent" and "Venereal Disease Information" for all 4-H leaders to use in clubs.[75]

Discussions of motherhood in health and home economics clubs provided a context to discuss sex education for 4-H girls, but the situation for 4-H boys was more complicated. A study of sex education among 7,500 Wisconsin high school boys from 1939, for example, found that 7 percent of boys received their sex education from 4-H clubs, suggesting that at least some discussion of sexual reproduction in boys' 4-H clubs was common.[76] To be sure, many discussions of human health were likely to involve discussion of reproduction and, depending on the perspective of the club leader, social hygiene. Although 10 percent of the total 600,000 4-H boys were enrolled in health projects by the end of the decade, a significant amount of health information was still being provided in the context of agricultural projects through metaphors of plants and animal biology. Many clubs followed Miriam Birdseye's recommendation to use the agricultural knowledge of male club leaders and county agents to teach 4-H boys about health. One popular graphic developed by Birdseye compared the physical growth and development of boys

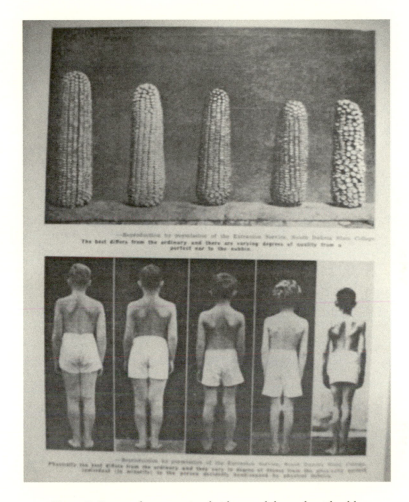

Figure 7. Boys and corn, a visual aid to teach boys about health.

to corn. The graphic circulated throughout the 1930s and 1940s in various club publications.[77] Club leaders often explicitly invoked the example of livestock to communicate health knowledge. Like Eugene Merritt's invocation of animal biology to describe the adolescent mating instinct, Dr. W. W. Bauer, an American Medical Association official addressing the 1933 National 4-H Club Congress, used the metaphor of animal health to describe the challenges of 4-H health education. "He wouldn't start in for a baby beef contest with a scrub animal," contended Bauer, "but he may have to start his life with what amounts to a scrub body."[78]

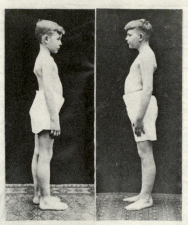

Figure 8. Boys and cattle, a 1929 North Carolina 4-H poster.
Courtesy of the North Carolina State University Library.

Invocations of animal biology in the context of human health did not, in and of themselves, constitute sex education, but they communicated a substantial amount of sexual knowledge by accompanying labor involved in many livestock breeding projects. The most basic 4-H projects allowed boys to purchase baby animals and raise them, but many projects also called for the animals to be bred and for participating boys to go beyond environmental manipulation of animals, to genetic manipulation through animal husbandry. 4-H manuals were often reticent about the logistical details of animal husbandry, but more extensive manuals, produced by husbandry masters at landgrant universities and large corporate farms, provided explicit details about the animal sex act. For pure breeding projects, "hand mating" was preferable because it permitted the breeder more extensive control. When hand mating, breeders selected the animals to be bred on the basis of registered lineage and desirable heredity traits. Breeders monitored a female animal's reproductive cycles, kept undesirable mates away, and, eventually, had her "serviced" by the desirable male animal when she was in heat. Careful observation and segregation of the appointed sire ensured a high sperm count and easier insemination. Simply introducing a female animal in heat to a male was usually sufficient to execute hand mating, but breeders also used "breeding crates" for pigs and sheep to guarantee copulation. No matter what the animal, close observation could guarantee optimal results, and livestock breeders were always encouraged to monitor their animals as they mated.[79]

Some of the very handbooks and manuals that 4-H clubs collected to describe the technical details of husbandry advanced the proposition that nonhuman reproduction provided a useful metaphor for human sexuality. Birdseye's graphic, for example, made an implicit argument about human reproduction. The graphic depicted a hierarchical spectrum of corn from "the nubbin" on the far right—corn fit only for feed—to a "perfect" ear on the left whose kernels could be used as seed for another generation of corn. With this visual grammar transposed to the boys below the corn, the graphic implicitly endorsed eugenic restrictions. By implication, the boy corresponding to "the nubbin"—defective and unhealthy—was unfit to reproduce, while the robust youth below the "perfect" ear provided the seed for the future. Other publications made those connections more explicitly. Harry Cook's *Like Breeds Like*, a 1931 "non-technical treatise," replete with cartoon illustrations, dedicated the first 250 pages to animal breeding and then launched into a lengthy discussion of the dangers of inattentiveness to scientific breeding: "Without intelligent thought and applied science, and the human race continuing to blindly, superstitiously ignore the importance of race improvement, we may find ourselves in the midst of a biological joy ride with a high cliff at the next turn." Among other things, Cook urged the adoption of laws mandating sterilization of the "feeble-minded," the creation of extensive "tabulated pedigree[s]," also by government mandate, and the restriction of marriage licenses on the basis of "genetic compatibility."[80] Another manual, *Heredity in Dairy Cattle*, by New Jersey farmer, 4-H organizer, and geneticist James E. Russell, argued that there was very little difference between human and bovine reproduction. "As long as marriages are fancy free," Russell answered, "the outcome will be a human population comparable to our mixed cattle—scrubs, grades, and pure-breds as they come."[81]

If eugenic advocacy and bestial analogies cast an unsavory pall over club romance, it was not reflected in popular celebrations of club work's procreative possibilities. M. L. Wilson best summarized this attitude in a speech given to the 1937 National 4-H Club Camp. He charted 4-H's role in preserving "rural heritage" and the "unit" of the farm family that "works together at the common job farming for the good of all." 4-H could produce the attitude of simultaneous "cooperation" and "individualism" that composed farm family "solidarity" and the root of rural "character." In calling for the "preservation" of this important and unique element of rural heritage, Wilson identified the farm family as central to rural social reproduction and tied its maintenance to the participation of rural youth in 4-H.[82] Popular magazines echoed his sentiment. A 1937 issue of *The Rotarian* celebrated the specific efforts of the "local 4-H leader," noting that the leader "must be a combined sage, confessor, counsellor, and friend" who could offer wise advice "[n]ot [on] only club work, but also how to act when out on a date . . . what is the best age to get married . . . [and] should a young married couple live with relatives."[83] In 1941, the *Saturday Evening Post* gushed that 4-H was "how to keep them down on the farm," informing readers that most 4-H'ers would stay on the farm and build families there.[84] A later article in the iconic publication offered an allegorical story to explain why. "A Challenge to the Cities" told the tale of a young Kansas couple, Andy Olson and his wife, Helen. Both had been involved in 4-H and had built a successful marriage and family around lessons from club work. They had worked their way from tenancy to full farm ownership.[85]

Just as these depictions of robust rural reproduction traded on long-standing nostalgic agrarianism, they also reinforced new links between state power and the countryside's procreative potential. During the 1930s, club experts and leaders redirected 4-H's existing ability to cultivate healthy rural bodies toward the production of fertile rural families and populations. 4-H's influence and attention leaped from individual bodies to individual "personalities" to healthy farm families and, finally, to rural populations. In the process, club members intermingled, learned about marriage and sex, and built their own rural romances. Of course, the path took unexpected twists and turns, moving from the bodies of animals to the bodies of boys to communicate knowledge about reproduction, for example. But at each step, the optimistic image of the rural future testified to the trust and deference that all Americans owed their government.

*   *   *

By presenting 4-H clubs as wholesome spaces where rural youth could commingle and eventually form new farm families, 4-H organizers implicitly contrasted their preferred vision of rural social reproduction with decadent and decaying city life. This contrast also guided the criticisms that Gertrude Warren and other USDA experts had been directing toward the National Committee since the 1920s. Complaints about exploitative behavior suggested that the National Committee's lavish prizes, elaborate banquets, and mail-order advertisements were importing urban culture to rural communities and thus undermining the CES's public-interest image and undercutting its efforts to conserve the youth. By the end of the 1930s, 4-H's "ever expanding" program required that the USDA do more to restrain the National Committee. 4-H had grown to touch nearly every rural community across the United States, drawing with it the attention and scrutiny of the public. As Arthur Hyde explained to R. A. Pearson, the President of the University of Maryland, justifying a rigorous review of 4-H policies in 1931: "The movement has become so large that educators and the public generally are taking ever-increased interest in it."[86] The New Deal and AAA had proved the CES's worth to the USDA, and, as among the CES's most visible programs, 4-H had similarly proved invaluable as an entering wedge for extension, for building public support for extension programs, and for helping administer federal programs. But 4-H also increasingly played a crucial role in conserving rural family structures and popularizing the USDA's preferred vision of healthy reproduction. The National Committee threatened to corrupt wholesome rural clubs with crass urban consumerism and provide "further embarrassment" to the USDA.[87]

Although the near-derailment of Capper-Ketcham in 1928 had illustrated for the USDA the National Committee's mixed harvest, Noble had nevertheless continued business as usual, arranging sponsorship and contests with major donors without consultation or approval of the USDA. This behavior irritated Warburton and Smith but infuriated Warren. In September 1929, Noble unilaterally approved a "4-H Style Revue" contest sponsored by the Chicago Mail Order Company that called for female 4-H members to assemble a single stylish outfit. Each state would submit its entry to the 4-H National Club Congress. The most stylish outfit would win a trip to Paris for the 4-H member and her club leader.[88] Club organizers and extension workers were aghast at the lavish nature of the prize and the careless indifference to concerns about the corrosive urbanism that Noble seemed to be expressing. Paris was, after all, the subject of the most iconic song on rural-to-urban migration: "How Ya Gonna Keep 'Em Down on the Farm? (After They've Seen Paree)." Despite the fact that the contest was universally condemned, nearly every state submitted an entry. At the National 4-H Club Congress that year, Noble explained that the broader economic problems had crippled the National Committee's financing and made it necessary for him to aggressively pursue any sponsorship offer he could, even those that appeared to use club work as a means of advertising their products. In response, a "Contests and Scholarships" committee, comprising several state leaders and R. A. Turner from the USDA, met at the National 4-H Club Congress. They issued the recommendation that, in the future, Noble should seek the approval of their committee and a representative of the USDA before announcing any contests. Noble accepted the committee's recommendation "in principle" but dismissed it as impractical and likely to result in the "loss of an offer" if followed too doctrinally. In March 1930, Noble proceeded, again without consultation of the USDA or the state club leaders, to announce that the Style Revue would be held again.[89]

As she witnessed these events, Warren worried that Noble's actions exploited rural girls, damaged 4-H's reputation, and generally tainted the 4-H program. Her interpretation was grounded in the belief that club spaces could promote healthy rural reproduction precisely because they excluded the sort of rapacious urban consumerism that Noble was so intent on introducing. Noble's Style Revue, Warren complained in a searing memo to C. B. Smith, exacerbated the "imbalance" of the home economics program by further promoting sewing and dressmaking club work at the expense of the health-focused food-preservation work. By offering such a lavish prize, the contest also promoted the dangerous idea that learning proper homemaking methods was less important than prevailing in a subjective, frivolous outfit-arranging contest. Echoing Mary Belle King Sherman's characterization of the National Committee, described in Chapter 3, as subverting appropriate gender roles, Warren blasted Noble's publicity for its use of titillating "'bathing beach' style headlines" that made rural girls the objects of urban lust. The problem, however, was not confined to the Style Revue but underscored a broader trend subverting the fundamental educational nature of club work. "By allowing club work to be the vehicle by which a commercial company pays to gain publicity, we are subjecting ourselves to severe criticism by educational leaders who are already considering our organization as being subsidized by business interests," wrote Warren, literally underlining her most potent objection for emphasis. "Our relationship with business interests is being brought to the attention of Congress," she continued, and an "outside agency" manipulating club work would "jeopardize the whole movement."[90]

Although Warren implored immediate action, Warburton and Smith were at a loss about what precisely to do. The National Committee was, after all, "outside" the USDA but not outside 4-H. By 1930, the National 4-H Club Congress was the premier national 4-H event. The National Committee provided the only national 4-H publication. And the National Committee's corporate sponsors and banking allies provided 4-H with the capital for many agricultural and livestock projects (and even some home economics projects). The USDA needed a way to regulate the behavior of the National Committee without simultaneously destroying these valuable services. Club experts faced the paradoxical problem of compelling a private entity to voluntarily cooperate with state regulation. This problem was implicit in the entire project of constructing a hybrid network that allied statist expertise, commercial capital, and local voluntary labor. Their solutions to this paradox were, in turn, experimental and haphazard. Extension officials tried several strategies to rein in the National Committee: they complained directly to the organization and attempted to sway its officers with personal appeals; they attempted to rigorously standardize club work in ways that would safeguard the neutrality of the program; and they established standing regulations for how private enterprises could sponsor club work through the LGCA. When these strategies proved ineffective, they took a more assertive stance and simply used the coercive power of the state as a cudgel.

Tense but polite letters had characterized Clyde Warburton's approach to the National Committee in the 1920s; but by the Depression years, he had already exhausted personal appeal as a productive means of constraining Guy Noble. That approach had done little to temper Noble's behavior in 1925. It had similarly accomplished nothing when, in 1929, Warburton had written to Thomas Wilson directly, with concerns about Noble's scheme to secure support from public utility companies by permitting them to sponsor a 4-H playwriting contest, a scheme that "seemed so obviously to exploit club work."[91] When D. P. Trent, the Oklahoma director of extension, complained to C. B. Smith about the growing commercialization of club work in April 1930, Warburton urged the LGCA Committee on Extension Policy to take the matter up directly and to formulate a policy regulating commercial influence. The chair of that committee, Alabama's Luther Duncan, was not disposed to swift action on the matter and simply promised to discuss the issue at the committee's next meeting. The committee, in turn, deferred the issue for another year.[92] In March 1931, Warburton, faced with the committee's foot-dragging, instructed Smith to officially inform the directors of extension that the USDA intended to restrict the use of the 4-H emblem and name to explicitly authorized organizations, a policy change that would adversely affect the ability of state and local 4-H organizations to sell products under their own name and organize sponsored statewide contests. The USDA's threats to exercise the copyright successfully dissuaded companies like Sears, Roebuck from sponsoring independent club contests; but thanks to Noble's long-standing relationships with state-level club organizers and support from the AFBF, the National Committee could afford to simply ignore it. In fact, the move perversely provided the National Committee with a de facto monopoly over club contests. Companies that might otherwise have sponsored independent club contests now worked exclusively through Noble, secure in the belief that the USDA would never sue the National Committee.[93]

Duncan's resistance to the USDA's meddling expressed the attitude of many state directors of extension. Prior to the New Deal, Duncan jealously guarded the rights of state colleges to use the extension system as they saw fit, a perspective that may have made him hesitant to embrace schemes that gave the USDA greater control over the functioning of local 4-H clubs. He believed that the National Committee played a crucial role in the extension system and that very few of its functions could be transferred to the USDA. In fact, he suggested, any matter that required the "handling of money" was better suited to the National Committee, since it did not need to observe "government restrictions and regulations." As for the giving of prizes, Duncan had little interest in the qualms of educational theorists. He believed that prizes, if handled properly, brought out the best in rural youth. He was a realist, if not a cynic, about the intentions of club sponsors. "Every man who advertises expects to get returns," he informed I. O. Schaub, the North Carolina director of extension. Some level of intercourse with business interests was necessary to club work, and, indeed, the business community would only supply such interactions if they believed that they had something to gain. Whether this was exploitation seemed beside the point, since club members also manifestly gained from the experience. Nevertheless, the New Deal agricultural program cemented the relationship between the USDA and individual state extension services. Extension was no longer tasked with just education; it was involved in the administration of billions of dollars in subsidies, a development that strengthened the hand of federal extension officials and enhanced the need for the CES to maintain at least a semblance of neutrality.[94]

In the meantime, the LGCA Committee on Extension Policy initiated a glacial, decade-long process of revising the guidelines regulating prizes and contests, a process significantly impaired by the CES and land-grant colleges' involvement in administering various components of the New Deal. In 1931, the Committee on Extension Policy, then under the chairmanship of I. O. Schaub, conducted a survey of the directors of extension and came to the general conclusion that, while the National Committee performed a vital service for club work, a representative of the Committee on Extension Policy should review prizes and contests before they were approved.[95] In the same year, at the request of Secretary of Agriculture Arthur Hyde, the LGCA organized a separate committee under the direction of C. B. Smith and R. A. Pearson, president of the University of Maryland, to review policies related to 4-H. The earlier recommendation by Schaub's committee was folded into that process and was not approved by the LGCA until 1935; even then, the National Committee failed to abide by the regulation.[96] For the USDA and the LGCA, the problems of the National Committee receded into the background in the face of more practical, pressing problems. Due to the economic crisis and the scarcity of public funds, many land-grant colleges spent the early part of the decade on the verge of insolvency, leading to deep cuts in state and local funding for extension.

With budgetary crises easing after 1935, the USDA and the LGCA returned anew to the National Committee's exploitative behavior. In 1937, the LGCA organized a special subcommittee to deal exclusively with policies related to 4-H, composed primarily of state-level club organizers and representatives from the USDA. By September of that year, that subcommittee released its report, once again criticizing the National Committee for failing to acquire approval for sponsored contests and for running advertisements in the *Club News* that gave the false impression that various products were endorsed by 4-H. By 1937, the National Committee had recovered half the $20,000 cost of the *Club News* from paid advertisements. Circulation of the magazine had grown to more than eighty thousand copies, and the magazine

was distributed free to county agents, club leaders, and members. USDA officials worried that its increasing popularity opened a new front in the commercialization of club work. Thomas Wilson publicly blasted the report at the
1937 National 4-H Club Congress as "manifestly unfair" and "largely unjust,"
but, armed with a critical mass of political capital and will, the USDA would
not be deterred.[97]

The USDA pursued three specific reforms. First, it wanted the National
4-H Club Congress to be planned and supervised by state leaders and representatives of the USDA. Second, it required the National Committee to
seek the permission of representatives of the LGCA and the USDA before
approving interstate contests. The USDA, for its part, would reject any contests that were contrary to the educational goals of the program, that gave the
impression of an endorsement of the sponsor's product, that were contingent
upon an advertising agreement, or that featured a particularly lavish prize.
Third, the USDA sought a broad reform of the management of the *Club
News*. To begin with, it directed county extension agents to cease providing
the National Committee with the names and addresses of club leaders and
members, a practice that, while not universal, was the primary source of the
National Committee's mailing list. The USDA demanded that the National
Committee either change the publication's name and become subscription-
only, or, if the National Committee wished to continue to use the 4-H name
and emblem, they would need to eliminate all advertisements from the publication. To reinforce this demand, the department counsel asked Congress
to give the USDA permanent authority over the 4-H name and emblem. In
1939, Congress acted on the USDA's request and passed legislation that made
the unauthorized use of the 4-H name and emblem a federal crime punish-
able by a fine and six months in prison.[98]

Given the more assertive stance of the USDA and the real possibility of
criminal sanctions, the National Committee began to waver. In 1938–1939, a
series of conferences attended by representatives of the LGCA, USDA, and
the National Committee carved out a compromise fueled almost exclusively
by concessions from the National Committee. Under this compromise, the
National Committee continued to publish the *Club News* but on a subscription basis only. The magazine provided the USDA a free regular one-page
section, titled "Washington Says," and the National Committee independently gathered its subscription list rather than receiving the names of members and leaders from extension agents. The National Committee agreed to a
more rigorous advertising policy that prohibited any advertisement that used
a club member or leader's endorsement in its text. The National Committee

agreed to a series of regular meetings to coordinate with the USDA and LGCA and fully assented to the USDA's demands for a veto over interstate contests. By 1939, the National Committee, which had for nearly two decades disregarded the USDA's constant request for input, was fully cooperating with the USDA and permitting representatives from Washington to rewrite existing contests.[99]

Thomas Wilson and other backers of the National Committee grudgingly stomached the new regulations.[100] By 1944, the National Committee's relationship with the USDA and the Roosevelt administration had soured so substantially that Wilson and Noble tried to coordinate with Thomas Dewey to raise 4-H as a campaign issue in the presidential election that year. In a plan to "assure the election of Governor Dewey to the presidency this coming November," Noble accused Roosevelt of blocking vital legislation and hindering the development of 4-H. With a Dewey victory, Noble argued, 4-H could once again teach rural youth "how to live democracy instead of accepting burocracy [sic] and regimentation." Noble urged Dewey to publicly and vocally endorse legislation proposed by South Carolina Democrat Hampton Fulmer to create a standing $24 million appropriation specifically for 4-H clubs. As a postscript and without a trace of irony, Noble noted that if the Roosevelt administration did support the Fulmer legislation, it would "be only to use it as bait for votes." Exploiters all.[101]

*　　*　　*

Noble's protests against the USDA's encroaching "burocracy and regimentation" suggested that expanding state power was the real threat to rural America, but his complaints fell on deaf ears. To the contrary, by the 1940s, 4-H was synonymous with the wholesomeness of country living, and the ability of the USDA to hide the National Committee's unsavory commercialism only strengthened that connection. In contrast to the National Committee's suggestions, the USDA used 4-H as evidence that federal power was conducive—perhaps even necessary—to a healthy, thriving countryside because of its potential to conserve rural youth and farm families. As if to prove the point, the Jane Withers film *Young America*, screened in country towns across America in 1942, delivered a perfectly distilled narrative of wholesome 4-H romance. Teen star Withers was among the highest box-office earners in 1937 and 1938, and Fox Films contracted her to appear as a "[v]ivacious Jane with her own car, a private aeroplane and her own bank account" who finds romantic fulfillment and personal transformation after an encounter with "the bees and the flowers and the trees." Playing an urban girl forcibly shipped to the country for disciplinary reasons, Wither's character joins a 4-H club. Club work teaches her the error of her spoiled ways and, more important, introduces her to a hunky 4-H boy, played by Robert Cornell. Fox advertised the film throughout the country as a romance and a tribute to 4-H. Like other 4-H material in the early 1940s, the film presented country living as synonymous with heterosexual romantic fulfillment and denigrated urban living as shallow, decadent, and fruitless.[102]

Even as the USDA continued to circulate the image of wholesome, heterosexual 4-H'ers, public health agencies increasingly trusted 4-H clubs to do the practical work of sex education. The American Social Hygiene Society, anxious about an alleged wartime surge in female sexual delinquency, emphasized that 4-H clubs should be used in rural communities to increase awareness about the threats of venereal diseases.[103] The society's local affiliates did just that. In Fulton County, New York, 4-H clubs screened *With These Weapons*, a 1939 film produced by the society, which warned viewers of the scourge of syphilis.[104] The extension service in Puerto Rico arranged to have the blood of a hundred 4-H members examined for syphilis and gonorrhea. "It is a pity to have to say that because of scarcity of personnel and material, due to the war situation, it was impossible to examine the blood of all members belonging to the 4-H Club in Puerto Rico," lamented health and hygiene specialist Elena Bonilla.[105]

These two images provide a powerful contrast. *Young America* represented the potential of 4-H to transform decadent urbanism into wholesome rural heterosexuality, a narrative that echoed interwar pronatalist celebrations of the ideal white farm family. At the same time, sex education programs in 4-H clubs recognized the probability that rural youth would be sexually active. Promiscuous rural youth, contrary to the wholesome romanticism of *Young America*, needed education, restraint, and observation by public health authorities and agents of the state. In Puerto Rico, extension officials used 4-H to directly police the sexual activity of club participants. Far from the bucolic pastoral landscape of 4-H romances, Puerto Rican 4-H reached a population of youth whose wholesomeness, from the perspective of government officials on and off the island, was already called into question by their liminal racial and national status.[106]

The distance between the narrow white public image of 4-H and the racial and ethnic diversity that the program actually encompassed hinted at an unresolved instability in club work. As Chapter 5 argues, club officials used 4-H clubs in the late 1930s and early 1940s to promote tolerant, deliberative democracy in the countryside, a rhetorical posture sharply at odds with the racial inequality that structured life in the rural South. Despite that dissonance, 4-H citizenship programs constructed rural nationalism, strengthened allegiance to the federal state, and promoted what the USDA identified as "democratic practice." During World War II, the USDA used nationalist sentiment and the existing biopolitical capacities of 4-H to transform rural youth labor into valuable wartime commodities. At the conclusion of the war, however, the inequalities to which citizenship programming had weakly gestured loomed larger in the wake of extensive African American sacrifice. Black extension officials and public intellectuals criticized the extension service, Gertrude Warren, and Guy Noble for the unequal treatment of African Americans in 4-H clubs, concentrating, in particular, on the exclusion of black 4-H'ers from the National 4-H Club Camp and the National 4-H Club Congress. By the late 1940s, African Americans were increasingly contesting the all-white public image of 4-H circulated by *Young America*, recognizing the political stakes that the image invoked. 4-H had come to symbolize rural authenticity: white, rural heterosexuals dedicating body and labor to the nation.

CHAPTER FIVE

Citizenship and Difference in Wartime 4-H

> . . . my heart to greater loyalty . . .
> —The 4-H Pledge

In mid-June of 1946, hundreds of delegates and organizers from around the nation braved the steamy Washington summer and convened on the Mall for the first National 4-H Camp since 1941. The delegates represented the most productive, the healthiest, and the best leaders of the nearly 1.5 million rural youth enrolled in club work in 1946. An invitation to the National Camp rewarded their efforts and celebrated the service that millions of other rural youth had contributed during the war through 4-H clubs. Prominent guest speakers encouraged the assembled campers to ponder a pressing set of questions: In a world threatened by wars and depressions that seemed to dwarf all others in recorded history, what did 4-H'ers owe the world, their nation, and their communities? And what were they owed? Arthur Powell Davies, a prominent Washington minister, delivered a talk during the Sunday vesper service and advanced the position that, because of the perils of the atomic age, good citizenship was global citizenship. America needed to use its influence and power to push the world into a new age when "each man must become a member of the world community, a citizen of humanity universal."[1]

Davies's speech underscored more than a decade of "citizenship" programming conducted by 4-H. Beginning in the late 1930s, the USDA urged state extension services to use 4-H to promote democratic practice and symbolic nationalism among rural youth. Consistent with liberal political culture of the period, 4-H literature infused citizenship programming with the rhetoric of inclusion, tolerance, and equality. 4-H clubs adapted that broader message to the specific audience of rural youth and produced a robust concept of rural citizenship that synthesized 4-H's various existing focal points.

Good rural citizenship entailed the able performance of gendered labor on the family farm, active participation in state-directed rural modernization schemes, and the symbolic affirmation of loyalty to the nation and its constitutive democratic values. Citizenship programs also furnished the federal government with an effective tool to mobilize rural youth and advance a host of initiatives that reflected the dynamic needs of the American nation-state. During World War II, the USDA and the War Food Administration (WFA) capitalized on the energy, vitality, and passion of 4-H'ers and routed their labor into prolific commodity production. Just as prewar 4-H clubs had encouraged club members to cultivate healthy, attractive bodies to reproduce rural society, wartime discussions of citizenship encouraged members to maintain bodies capable of laboring, sacrificing, and fighting for the state.

The African American press identified the contradictions at the core of the camp's humanistic pretensions. In describing the camp's "4-H Citizenship Oath," the *Chicago Defender* noted: "Twenty-five young 4-H club members . . . stood at the foot of [the] Lincoln Memorial . . . not a Negro among them. They were excluded by the Department of Agriculture[,] state director[s] of extension[,] and the national extension service." The "Jim Crow Meet," the *Defender*'s headline blared, made a "mockery" of the very oath recited.[2] Like every other National 4-H Club Camp since its inauguration in 1927, the 1946 camp was exclusively white. The South's 300,000 black 4-H'ers were systematically excluded from participating in the Washington camp and in the National 4-H Congress in Chicago. Even as organizers lauded the egalitarian potentials of American democracy, the highly publicized events circulated an all-white image of rural citizenship. This publicity elided the wartime sacrifices of millions of rural African Americans that the events were designed to rhetorically celebrate.

Organizers, activists, bureaucrats, and 4-H'ers parsed the contradictory meanings of citizenship, race, and national identity in 4-H clubs, from the launch of citizenship programming in the late 1930s to the aftermath of the 1948 Southern Regional 4-H Camp. As the USDA successively turned its attention from domestic political reform to national wartime production to postwar international development, the meanings of citizenship mutated to fit shifting national priorities. At each step, however, citizenship material confirmed that the differences that mattered were between America and the world but never between white and black. Whether encouraging democratic practice, nationalist ritual, or wartime commodity production, 4-H citizenship programs taught rural youth that they were the core of the American way. By doing so, citizenship material contributed to an economy of difference that contrasted vigorous American bodies from depleted foreign bodies and obscured manifest racial inequalities in 4-H and the Jim Crow South. By the end of the 1940s, African Americans and racial progressives were pointing to this shift as a glaring, crippling contradiction in the USDA's rhetoric: Could the federal government simultaneously promote an inclusive ideology of global universal citizenship abroad and countenance racial segregation and political inequality at home?

African Americans and racial progressives critiqued 4-H's racial policies because of 4-H's privileged relationship to agrarian futurist definitions of rural authenticity, national identity, and political citizenship. Racial segregation in 4-H promised a rural future in which 4-H's hollow rhetoric of American democracy would continue to paper over the racial inequality lurking beneath the surface of America's agrarian dreams—a kind of "education for fascism," as a July 1946 editorial in the *Chicago Defender* put it. Explaining the stakes of challenging segregation in 4-H, the editorial continued: "4-H clubs have been set up throughout farming areas of the nation as symbols of American enterprise and democracy. They are more than mere scientific clearing houses to train youths in technical agricultural proficiency, they are the one contact numerous lonely farm children have with an American way of life."[3] If 4-H'ers represented ideal rural citizens, the last chance for the imperiled family farm, and hope for the rural future, the full public recognition of African American youth carried with it the chance to upend the lily-white imagery of agrarian futurism.

* * *

At the onset of U.S. involvement in World War II, 4-H was at the vanguard of a broad movement in the CES to create passionate defenders of American democracy in the countryside. In the early 1930s, the specter of European youth movements motivated the federal government to find employment for rural youth. As the short-term domestic economic crisis gave way to a potential international political crisis, federal planners turned their attention away from the labor of rural youth and toward their loyalty. Such plans required that rural youth be passionate believers in American democracy and the forefront of a rural culture resistant to foreign totalitarian impulses. By the close of the decade, thanks to the efforts of agrarian intellectuals like Henry A. Wallace, M. L. Wilson, and Howard Tolley, the USDA had launched a program of democratic education that aimed to generate grassroots reform from within rural America. Consistent with this broader move in the CES, 4-H endeavored to promote citizenship in rural America. "Every 4-H Club leader can be a mighty influence in helping rural youth to meet the present challenge and to gain that spiritual strength and understanding essential for national unity and supremacy," explained Wilson in 1940, then director of the CES.[4]

Efforts to promote democratic practice in 4-H fit into what historians refer to as the "third" or "intentional" New Deal, the policy agenda pursued by the Roosevelt administration beginning in 1937 to effect long-term, rather than immediate, poverty relief. During the late 1930s and early 1940s, agrarian intellectuals-cum-policymakers in the USDA articulated a philosophy informed by pragmatism and drawn from "ideologies . . . that insisted on equality, citizenship and public service." In contrast to approaches that prioritized centralized planning and coercive state power, they organized local planning committees, discussion groups, and traveling philosophy schools. In addition, they allied with other racial progressives in the department to address Southern tenancy with the Farm Security Administration.[5] Explaining his favored strategy, M. L. Wilson encouraged a "cultural approach" to rural reform that worked from within communities rather than from without—an insight that built on two decades' experience in extension and club organizing.[6] More practically, with their focus on the improvement of cross-class intra-community relationships, these sorts of "low modernist" programs were intended to prevent factional political movements that transformed class estrangement into political militancy. Democratic education programs attempted to guide those disagreements into decisively civil, public discussions. This emphasis on discussion expanded on the existing organizational and pedagogical commitments of club experts.[7]

By the end of the decade, club organizers were regarding the discussion of politics in 4-H clubs as vital to a larger project of fomenting a robust democratic culture in rural America. "It is evident that we in 4-H club work are to be called upon to develop citizenship through discussion," explained George Farley at the 1940 National 4-H Club Congress in a speech, "What More Can We Do to Teach Citizenship?" He outlined an ambitious set of topics that would lead club members through the foundational texts of American democracy, to a discussion of recent technological and social developments, and, finally, "to discuss the results upon the individual and therefore upon government of all these modern changes in what way they benefited and what way they made more unhappy the human race."[8] Gertrude Warren recommended a program that similarly integrated the icons of American nationalism with political controversies through orderly discussions in which 4-H members would connect the problems and functioning of government to the canonical documents of American democracy and the "ideals upon which these documents are based and which have made the United States the greatest nation in the world today."[9]

State extension services heeded Warren's call by actively creating new citizenship training programs, expanding existing citizenship programs, and integrating citizenship material into other phases of 4-H club work. In 1941, a report conducted by the LGCA subcommittee on citizenship training found that twenty-three of thirty-three states surveyed had already launched unique citizenship programs through 4-H and that the remaining programs had integrated citizenship material into other facets of the 4-H program.[10] In Iowa, the state extension staff initiated a distinct citizenship program for Iowa 4-H girls in 1937. Using material provided by the Carnegie Endowment for International Peace to prepare attendees, the state extension staff at Ames hosted a panel discussion on "world affairs especially trade relations and the inter-dependence of nations." Club organizers were so pleased with the results that, in 1938, they opened "a two-day training school in discussions" at Iowa State College in Ames and urged graduates to conduct public panel discussions with their local clubs around the state. In 1939, the extension service expanded the program once more, this time hosting another discussion school before the state 4-H convention and organizing a series of public current-event discussion panels, composed entirely of 4-H girls.[11]

The panel discussions in the Iowa program required girls to research and present contrasting political opinions at a large public gathering. Occasionally, an eminent figure would be asked to serve as moderator—a particularly high-profile discussion at the state convention was chaired by the AFBF president—but more often, the "girl herself" led the discussion. Research resources varied widely, depending on the personality, interests, and background of the girls in question. Some referenced mainstream publications like *Reader's Digest*, *Newsweek*, and the *New York Times*. Other girls cited a remarkably heterogeneous set of perspectives: the progressive Charles and Mary Beard's *America in Midpassage*; radical unionist pamphlets from the League of Industrial Democracy; and Kirby Page's pacifist tract *How to Keep America Out of War*. Whether they agreed with their content or not, Iowa 4-H girls prepared for their discussions by reading an ideologically diverse set of works that incited further intellectual curiosity. "It made me want to know more about that topic," explained Betty Plumb of Mills County, Iowa. "I try to read the paper every day. I try to get different ideas from newspapers. . . . I read now not just accepting what the author says but reasoning it and considering it, taking into account the factors influencing it, and reading it critically for propaganda." In the second half of 1940 alone, Iowa 4-H girls organized fifty-nine public panel discussions, attended by nearly twenty thousand people.[12]

Building on the success of the 1940 panel discussions, in 1941 Iowa 4-H augmented its citizenship programming with the offer of an East Coast trip to about twenty lucky 4-H'ers, in the interests of improving citizenship and urban-rural relations. In early March of 1941, the youth headed to New York and Washington, D.C., for ten days packed with a variety of activities and events, accompanied by Edith Barker and Paul Taff, the club work specialists at Iowa State College. The excited farm youth played tourist in the big cities. In New York, they watched *Fantasia* while uptown, took in part of *Madame Butterfly* at the RCA Theater, cheered the New York Giants against the Boston Bees at the Polo Grounds, and ate "little pieces of lamb on a long stick" at a Syrian restaurant in Brooklyn. Taff and Barker also packed the schedules with a host of intellectual activities: a "lecture on Latin American marketing problems" at the New York Port Authority; discussions about labor issues with the iconic organizer Rose Schneiderman of the Women's Trade Union; and a conference led by six officials from the USDA and the Council on National Defense on 4-H's role in preparedness.[13]

The seventeen Iowa youth spent most of their Thursday in New York in a predominantly African American housing project in Harlem, meeting with young inhabitants and listening to a lecture by a prominent African American pastor, James Robinson. Robinson addressed the question of whether "race prejudice" still existed in the United States, a question he answered with emphatic affirmation. "Why aren't we [Negroes] accepted in the United States Marine Corps? Do you expect us to favor a democracy when we have no part in it?" seventeen-year-old Ruth Ann Hermanson reported Robinson to have asked. Addressing health problems among African American populations, Robinson posed, according to Hermanson, an equally provocative question: "Do you expect negroes to go to a hospital where the American Medical Association has approved of the use of experiments on Negroes? A negro would rather die than be used as a guinea pig for testing serums to be used on white [men] when the negro has proved its success or to be discarded when the negro has displayed its failure by suffering or dying."

Not all Robinson's comments seemed to register fully with Hermanson. "To me these problems presented are important and need attention," she wrote in her account of the meeting, before immediately segueing into an observation, mirroring concerns about "race-suicide," that "people who are a success and have proven themselves worthwhile in this world do not reproduce."[14] Nevertheless, she seemed alarmed by the status of race relations, a problem that few rural Iowa youth confronted. When exposed to the problems of inequality, she connected them to her own political context. "I never thought much of or about farm families who were suffering until I saw slums," confided Hermanson, "and then it dawned upon me that we do have similar places in Iowa and it is my duty to have an interest in them."[15]

Ruth Ann Hermanson had a conventional background for an Iowa farm girl, albeit one marked by ambition and accomplishment. Born and raised on a farm in the tiny northwest Iowa hamlet of Ruthven, she ranked in the top quarter of her high school class, was a cheerleader, and appeared in her school play. Her participation in 4-H offered her substantial additional opportunities for accomplishment. After six years in club work, Hermanson had held all the offices in her local club, was the 1941 Palo Alto County 4-H Club president and county health representative to the state contest, and had participated in a number of panel discussions. Her life goals, exceptional for an Iowa farm girl in the 1940s, built on her success as a club leader. She reported that her "ambition [was] to be a lawyer and to devote herself to cases concerning juvenile delinquents." Club work had left her with no short supply of self-confidence, as was made abundantly clear during the trip. After listening to a provocative talk by Eduard Lindeman at the Columbia University faculty club that "attacked youth's apathy toward democratic ideals," Hermanson firmly informed the eminent New School educational theorist that he was in error: "I don't like what you said about the youth of this country not being willing to take the responsibility for democracy seriously. I think you're wrong."[16]

Like other components of 4-H citizenship programs in the late 1930s and early 1940s, the Iowa citizenship program framed political citizenship as a set of practices that were egalitarian and accessible. To the extent that anyone could research a topic at a public library and offer a reasoned opinion, the 4-H citizenship program maintained that everyone could and should participate in public political life, regardless of race, gender, or economic circumstances. Farm girls could trade opinions with esteemed professors and be celebrated rather than scolded. This vision of American democracy was, of course, unrealistic beyond the narrow confines of middle-class white farm youth. Race, class, and gender structured and constrained the institutions that 4-H material identified as sure routes to education and political engagement. Encouraging white farm youth to question authority in the name of democracy worked well enough when those same youth were being toasted as the nation's future. But in the South, encouraging black youth to question authority threatened both political order and the CES's public position that African Americans needed agricultural reform more than political reform to improve their lives. As 4-H material linked citizenship to civic participation, other components of the same programs conceptualized citizenship in terms of fealty to the nation evidenced through ritual and ceremony rather than just through discussion and debate.

*   *   *

In the lead-up to World War II, 4-H ceremonies, rituals, and celebrations of exceptional American values enabled rural youth to publicly affirm their allegiance to the American nation-state. Using the figure of "totalitarians," 4-H material defined "democracy" as much through contrast as through positive description. War sharpened these distinctions and added racial dimensions to discussions of national identity. By the end of the war, 4-H material was encouraging members to practice "global citizenship." The contours of this global citizenship, however, designated America as the first among equals—a nation with an awesome and messianic role to play in the provision of democracy the world over.

By the late 1930s, 4-H clubs had increasingly integrated ritual and symbol into club literature and practice. William F. Ogburn, a leading sociologist at the University of Chicago, encouraged 4-H leaders to emulate the "religious or perhaps the psychological aspects" of European fascist youth movements and to integrate similar "trappings, salutes, songs, uniforms, passwords, [and] fetes."[17] Similarly, the 1939 Committee on 4-H Club Work recommended increasing the ritualism of 4-H activities in its report to the Oregon Extension Conference. "In leading countries," stated the committee, "powerful national influences are constantly directed toward youth movements as the basis for the establishment and maintenance of governmental systems." Given the tumult and chaos of a world at war, the report continued, it was imperative for the state "to train young people in the American concepts of responsibility, tolerance and freedom of action." 4-H was already well equipped for "teaching democracy," but the practice of "ritualistic procedure" could build even greater "enthusiasm for club work." Indeed, the report contended, 4-H ritualism "trains the youth in parliamentary procedure, public speaking, and teaches full respect for the flag of our country." In addition, ritualism could better enable 4-H clubs to fulfill the "psychological" need of youth to belong to "a well-knit group."[18]

Across the country, 4-H clubs promoted citizenship through a variety of ceremonies and rituals that also cemented allegiance to the American nation-state over its totalitarian rivals.[19] By 1940, 4-H had accumulated enough rituals and ceremonies to justify the USDA publishing a booklet compiling the detailed instructions for at least nine ceremonies, including "Ceremony for the Installation of New Officers," "A Service of Dedication to the Building of a Christian Nation," and, most notably, the "National 4-H Citizenship Ceremony." (The USDA republished the booklet again in 1947 and in 1951.) The citizenship ceremony was introduced at the 1939 National 4-H Camp to induct as citizens 4-H members who were of voting age. Undersecretary of Agriculture M. L. Wilson presided over the initial induction of twenty-four new voters, all of whom pledged "to fight for the ideals of this nation" and to "never allow totalitarianism to become enthroned in this, our country."[20] At the 1941 citizenship ceremony, Wilson announced to voters that freedom was under peril but that 4-H leaders had "confidence that you . . . are thankful to God and appreciative of your good fortune in being citizens of the United States of America. We know you have the faith which has made America great." Wilson's comments were doubly suggestive: first, he implicitly located freedom in American traditions and identified American citizenship as uniquely desirable and worthy of thanks; second, he described a moral imperative underlying America's impending involvement in the global conflagration. In so doing, he singled out American citizenry as uniquely charged with the duty to protect freedom and democracy in a global context.[21]

U.S. involvement in World War II—with the "great world conflict" upon it—only heightened the need for citizenship promotion and ceremonial nationalism in club work. Rather than cancel annual countywide 4-H rally-day programs across the state in 1942, the 4-H staff at Iowa State College pushed forward, noting that the rallies were "a vital part of our state and national defense programs." Hitler Youth, the rally-day flyer explained, provided German youth "many dramatic experiences," and the United States could ill afford to "fail in our mobilization of youth." The state staff provided each club with a full script for a heavily choreographed pageant, replete with the performance of four songs, the recitation of the "4-H Girls' Service Creed," the performance of the "4-H Leaders Installation Ceremony," and a "Litany for 4-H Blessings," in which the girls sang "praise" to the "blessings of American girlhood . . . of American homes . . . [and] our democratic community." By listing the various blessings bestowed by life in America and participation in club work, 4-H girls publicly reaffirmed their loyalty to the American nation and posited a common language and history of national identity. The litany announced that the American nation originated in the God-given traditions and freedoms of the American people and in the moral environment of American homes.[22]

The precise meanings of American freedom were frequently underdefined and abstract in 4-H rituals, but some 4-H material occasionally explained democratic liberties in greater detail. The basic liberties, an Alabama 4-H'er explained in a November 1942 Alabama 4-H newsletter, were best expressed by President Roosevelt as the four freedoms: freedom of expression, freedom of conscience, freedom from want, and freedom from fear.[23] According to other 4-H material, the treatment of minorities distinguished democracy from other forms of government. Minorities received full and unvarnished civil liberties, according to one nationally circulated discussion pamphlet in 1941. "These liberties," the pamphlet stated, "are enjoyed by groups differing in religion, race, opinion." Could 4-H'ers recall recent "abuses of civil liberties affecting Negroes, Jews, Catholics, foreign-born? Could they have been better handled? How?" pondered the pamphlet.[24]

The formal declaration of war helped transform abstract totalitarians into concrete Germans and Japanese. Despite its tolerant posture, wartime 4-H material frequently depicted the Japanese in highly racialized terms. Drawing on preexisting racial stereotypes of "orientals" as a subhuman collective, 4-H material often likened the Japanese to insects who would use cunning, subterfuge, "treachery and surprise" to "make us their slaves." P. O. Davis, for example, recalled in his April 1943 letter to Alabama 4-H members a conversation with a friend in the service. "We are doing a lot of night training. We must do this because the Japs do most of their fighting at night," his friend explained. This reminded Davis again "that the Japs are a creepy and crawly people whose military power must be utterly destroyed."[25] This characterization was all the more poignant, given the work associated with 4-H clubs: club material frequently used the Japanese to personify the agricultural pests and diseases that club work was intended to help "exterminate." A suggested program for an Iowa club meeting from 1943, for example, sought to educate club members about the dangers of "livestock diseases." "Diseases that attack livestock are a foe of the farmer," announced the program. "They are a friend of the nations we fight. Livestock diseases are sneaky and won't come out in the open to fight." Instead, they would linger and skulk, waiting for as long as two years to "mobilize and strike." Among other discussion topics, the program suggested that club members ponder, "Why are livestock diseases our national enemy the same as the Japs?"[26]

In lieu of a specific racial or ethnic stereotype for Germans, 4-H material tended to belittle caricatures of Adolf Hitler and the Nazis. "I'm gonna buy a bond that I can call my very own/ A thing that every fellow ought to buy/ And then those Germans and those Japs/ Will be knocked right off the map/ And Hitler will be buried in a trench," sang Ann Barnes, a club member in Henry County, Alabama.[27] A 1943 skit for Iowa 4-H by extension entomologist George Gilbertson depicted a legion of garden insects goose-stepping and *sieg-heiling* to "Adolf Tokyo."[28] By contrast, when describing the behavior of German prisoners of war who had been assigned to harvest cotton and peanuts in southeastern Alabama, P. O. Davis was complimentary. The disciplined German soldiers were "taught to save everything that is useful and use it wisely." Their thrift and industry had earned the admiration of Davis and the farmers for whom they had worked.[29] In the South, where racial difference continued to define the economic and political order of society, the racial demonization of a white European people could prove dangerous. Caricatures of Nazis stood in for a racialized stereotype of Germans and allowed POWs, once removed from the battlefield, to retain some element of racial privilege.

By the conclusion of the war, 4-H material was emphasizing global citizenship, in contrast to provincial or nationalist loyalties, a transition best expressed by the amendment in 1943 of the 4-H club pledge to reflect global responsibilities of club youth: "for my club, my community, my country, *and my world.*"[30] In this construction, America retained a privileged place in the story of human freedom. The United States, 4-H material contended, had an almost messianic role to play. "The first thing to do is to win" the war, explained P. O. Davis to Alabama 4-H'ers, "and the next step is to create conditions throughout the world that will avoid a recurrence." Much of the world, he continued, was looking to America for "light and leadership in this war, and their future." "From us they got their Democracy," he concluded.[31] The "Observance of Rural Life Sunday by 4-H Clubs," an annual program initiated by the USDA in 1940 to strengthen ties between religious ceremony, citizenship, and 4-H club work, similarly reflected this transition by linking the demands of global citizenship to Christian moral duty. Between 1942 and 1944, the USDA promoted "Rural Life Sunday" themes such as "Moral Responsibility and National Unity," "The Spiritual Influence in the American Way of Life," and "Serving God and Country." After the war, the program themes were more explicitly globalist: "Serving as Citizens in Maintaining World Peace" in 1946 and "Working Together for a Better Home and World

Community."[32] M. L. Wilson described the reason for such a transition as being rooted in Christianity in a speech to the 1946 National 4-H Congress. "The weapon of Christian democracy in this ideological struggle ... is not the atomic bomb," he argued. "It is education." 4-H clubs could uphold their moral duties and foster global citizenship, Wilson argued, by cooperating with global educational programs—international youth exchanges, UNESCO initiatives, and, more generally, the United Nations. In 1950, 4-H launched a flag-sewing project to enable club members to display their support for the United Nations. Requests for flag-sewing kits soon exhausted the National Committee's 6,500-kit supply, and they were forced to order an additional 35,000 to meet demand.[33]

The ideological contours of 4-H materials largely mirrored the immediate demands of the national state. As federal authorities came to recognize the likelihood of open war in the late 1930s, they used 4-H to differentiate American democracy from foreign totalitarianism and to cement loyalty to the nation-state. Organizers sought to emulate those psychologically inducing elements of foreign youth movements. But they did so, they consoled themselves, to strengthen democratic practice, not to undercut it. The actual commencement of the war sharpened the need for national unity at the level of abstract ideology and at the practical level of effective coordination. By the end of the decade, 4-H material was articulating the moral necessity for the U.S. to act as the primary steward of world peace.

*   *   *

Faced with extraordinary demands for farm labor and agricultural commodities at the outbreak of World War II, the federal government integrated 4-H citizenship programming into its larger wartime mobilization effort, effectively exploiting the durable sense of nationalist duty that the previous decade of club work had helped develop. Wartime 4-H programming attached citizenship to two priorities: first, the increased production of agricultural commodities through farming projects; and second, the cultivation of vigorous and productive 4-H bodies through health programming. Both goals reflected a unified concern about collective health and vitality: 4-H material emphasized the duty of each rural citizen to cultivate a healthy body so that, collectively, rural America could sustain and feed the nation. If 4-H programs of the early 1940s had offered rural youth the opportunity to practice citizenship through discussion and deliberation, war required rural youth to demonstrate their citizenship through sacrifice and labor. Amid war, good citizenship demanded direct service to the nation-state—being ready and able to do whatever was necessary to prevail over the Axis powers.

The desire to ready the nation for developing conflict drove rural youth to 4-H club work in unprecedented numbers in the early 1940s. Enrollments swelled to a record 1.6 million youth nationwide in 1943, up by more than 200,000 members from 1940. Growing enrollments reflected the society-wide surge in civic-mindedness during the war years and the particular heightened emphasis given to 4-H by war planners, as the USDA urged county agents and local leaders to expand club work. 4-H provided millions of rural youth with a wide variety of possible wartime activities, but most fit into one of four categories: resource-salvage drives (rubber, scrap metal, and so on); bond-sale drives; food-production programs; and health-promotion programs. "There are many different ways that 4-H'ers can help win this war," reported an Alabama 4-H newsletter. "In a democracy it is each person's responsibility to find and do his or her part." Indeed, over the course of the war, 4-H'ers, millions strong, threw their time, money, and bodies into the war effort with abandon. If the nation needed sacrifice, 4-H members were ready to sacrifice. "4-H Club work in its daily program is building men and women to live," declared C. B. Smith in 1940 at the National 4-H Club Congress, "and to live the great life here and now. Its first purpose is not soldier building but man building. But, if the Nation needs men for its defense, it will find that in 4-H Club work men and women trained to live are unafraid, if need be, to die."[34]

The notion of sacrificing for the nation fit seamlessly with the militaristic metaphor of a "4-H army" embraced by 4-H during wartime. "Every one of you is called to be a loyal, effective, and courageous soldier on the home front," directed Secretary of Agriculture Claude Wickard in a message to all 4-H members.[35] 4-H literature urged rural youth to consider 4-H-directed labor as the best way to contribute to the war effort. "Farm labor is needed to grow food," explained a 1942 Alabama 4-H newsletter. "One of the greatest services 4-H club girls and boys can render is producing more good food. Food and feed are as important as tanks and guns. If you really want to do your part in helping to win the war, produce and save all the vegetables, fruit, pork, beef, milk, chickens and eggs possible."[36] Often, 4-H material took the military metaphor even further, depicting agricultural commodities such as pigs and corn marching with rifles.[37] At other times, organizers sought to transform 4-H contribution into the devices of war: forty states participated in a U.S. Maritime Commission program, the "Liberty Ship" program, which allowed state 4-H organizations to name a new military vessel upon the completion of a resource or bond drive. (To the dismay of some state 4-H organizations, some of the vessels were immediately transferred through lend-lease and renamed. Missouri's 4-H's *Henry J. Waters* was sent to the Soviets, renamed the *Rodina*, and never returned.)[38] Similar programs enabled the 4-H name and logo to be inscribed on the sides of combat air-crafts. An October 1943 edition of the *Alabama 4-H News*, for example, excit-edly announced that when Alabama 4-H completed its $1 million bond drive, two heavy aerial bombers would be emblazoned with "Alabama 4-H Clubs." "Wouldn't it look good on a plane fighting for the freedom of our country and the homes we love?" asked the writer of the article.[39]

The 4-H army produced impressive results in its efforts to obtain capital and raw materials for war production. 4-H'ers were hardly unique among the nation's youth in their participation in bond drives—nearly every youth organization participated in bond drives—but some evidence suggests that they were substantially more active. As historian Lawrence Samuel notes, the Treasury Department's Schools at War program was the most significant bond program for American youth during the war. That program, organized in cooperation with the Office of Education, targeted the nation's approxi-mately 25 million enrolled schoolchildren and raised about $2 billion over the course of the war, or approximately $20 per enrolled child per year. By comparison, 4-H members had raised more than $200 million in bonds over the course of the war, or about thirty dollars per member per year. In addi-tion to bond activities, 4-H clubs salvaged hundreds of thousands of tons of scrap material. Further, because of their broad rural base, 4-H'ers could col-lect relatively obscure items, such as milk pods, that were scarce or unavail-able in the city.[40]

While other youth organizations participated in bond and resource drives, no youth organization contributed as prodigiously to wartime commodity production as 4-H. In particular, federal war planners aggressively promoted 4-H agricultural projects as a means to increase youth participation in agri-cultural production during a time of relative labor scarcity. Over the course of the war, 4-H projects produced more than 41 million poultry birds and 2.8 million head of livestock, or enough to satisfy the meat demands of nearly 600,000 servicemen for an entire year.[41] In addition, 4-H members preserved 65 million quarts of fruits and vegetables and farmed nearly 500,000 acres of produce in victory gardens. For the most part, the labor and resources involved in 4-H agricultural projects supplemented any regular inputs that 4-H members had already contributed to their home farms. The results of agricultural projects during the war suggested dramatic increases in the commitment of labor and capital from rural youth to agricultural production uniquely through 4-H. During the war years, for example, each 4-H member produced, on average, 6.63 poultry birds. Between 1937 and 1941, 4-H projects produced an average of only 3.69 poultry birds per club member. In other words, during the war, the average 4-H member produced 80 percent more poultry birds.[42]

To manage wartime agricultural production, the USDA—and, ultimately, the WFA after 1943—needed to systematically analyze the national, state, and local agricultural potentials, calculate realistic production goals, disseminate those goals to farmers, and, finally, ensure that individual farmers participated and met those goals. The WFA primarily incented farmers through price supports rather than direct subsidy, but even generous price guarantees occasionally failed to bring adequate production if farmers were unfamiliar with the WFA's preferred commodity. Some crops, like peanuts, never met production goals, while farmers consistently exceeded goals for common staple crops like corn and wheat. To address this problem, the WFA also depended upon patriotic appeal and persuasion to directly enroll farmers in crop production programs. The USDA hoped to expand acreage by 16 million acres in 1943 alone, bringing the total number of acres under cultivation to a record 380 million. Production did expand considerably during the war—though ultimately, that expansion came from only a 5 percent increase in cultivated acreage. Most of the improvements in agricultural production came from the increased use of fertilizers and mechanization, and some of it from farmers who were using those technological innovations for the first time. The complex nature of the agricultural planning designed by the USDA and its heavy dependence on education required a diffuse network of state actors—primarily county extension agents—to explain the nation's agricultural needs and a compliant and energetic labor force that was willing to integrate their suggestions.[43]

In March 1942, the USDA convened a conference in Washington, D.C., to design a network of volunteers who could serve as local spokespeople and organizers for the USDA's war plan. The National Conference on Voluntary Leadership planned for the USDA to enlist 1.7 million "community and neighborhood leaders" to act as a "direct channel" from the USDA "to all rural families." Each local leader claimed responsibility for ten to twenty rural families and was expected to explain each individual family's role in the war plan and also to monitor their compliance. The network, federal authorities hoped, would efficiently organize vital information about rural labor, map rural populations, and make them comprehensible and useful to government planners. Each leader acted as a conduit for the federal government and relayed local information further up the network, where it could be appropriately collated and redistributed.[44]

4-H members and volunteer leaders played an important role in this network by helping county extension agents, assisting their parents with compliance, and directly relieving farm labor pressures. Federal authorities ambitiously hoped that 4-H'ers could provide "practically all the fruits and vegetables their families need in 4-H Victory gardens," even as rural youth increased their contribution to revenue-producing ventures already in place on farms. In addition, members and volunteer leaders were expected to vigorously recruit unorganized youth, a task that otherwise fell on the shoulders of overtaxed county extension agents. H. W. Hochbaum, chief at the Division of Field Coordination for the USDA, outlined the wartime responsibilities of volunteer 4-H leaders. The sum of these activities enrolled 4-H participants and leaders in the larger network of war planning: the 4-H network offered the extension service a useful medium for communication with rural populations, a way to monitor and direct their agricultural labor, and, given the goal of maximizing production, an enduring means to promote input-intensive mechanized agriculture.[45]

Because this plan relied so heavily on the ability of the rural workforce, already perceived by federal authorities to be physically and mentally deficient, the USDA also hoped to use 4-H clubs to promote good health practices in rural communities. As M. L. Wilson noted in 1943, reports from the Selective Service Administration indicated that men from agricultural backgrounds were found to be disproportionately unfit for military service, a disclosure that hinted at the continued ill health of rural Americans. To help remedy the situation, Wilson listed the promotion of good health practices in rural communities as a top priority for all 4-H clubs.[46] From Wilson's perspective, poor health imperiled not only the ability of men to serve in the military but the ability of the rural workforce to perform the agricultural labor that was so vital to the nation's collective health. 4-H organizers tended to justify programs that would directly promote health practices as well as programs that would increase agricultural productivity in terms of national health. The former directly improved individual health practices, while the latter guaranteed that there would be adequate food to sustain the collective labors of war.

By practicing the "proper care of the body," as Gertrude Warren put it, 4-H members could provide a healthy example for the rest of their community. A 1942 memo, developed by Warren and circulated to state extension

agencies, outlined various aspects of the 4-H defense program addressed
to health. Collectively, they would develop the "individual stamina which
springs from a sense of physical fitness through the improvement of health
and food habits." She included health examinations; projects of food production, preservation, and preparation; recreational activities like camps, trails,
games, and rallies; home nursing and first aid; personal and family hygiene
and cleanliness projects; and clothing care, construction, and repair projects. Across the board, Warren directed, "work in developing good food and
health involving the proper care of the body should be given added impetus."
Thus, she concluded, "the improvement of the Nation's health is our first line
of defense."[47]

4-H material emphasized the importance of health activities by contrasting strong, healthy bodies with the specter of sick and hungry bodies. As
many as a third of all Americans were malnourished, the surgeon general
reported in 1941. Poor diet, particularly in the rural South, was a great con-
tributor to the health defects that prevented national service. "The agricultural extension organization of Louisiana," a radio broadcast from Alabama
announced, "realizes that the way to make <u>America</u> strong is to make Americans strong. We realize that we all can't be airplane pilots, or sailors, or soldiers, but we do have some definite part to play in making Americans strong
and physically fit for the defense of our country." Harriet Elliot, a member
of the Commission to the Council of National Defense, explained, "Hungry
undernourished people do not make for strong defense." An Iowa 4-H circular put it a bit more directly: "Hungry people cannot fight to win a war, hence
FOOD is, literally, ammunition."[48]

At the war's end, the failure to maintain a healthy body implied a serious failure of duty and patriotism. At the 1946 National 4-H Camp, General
Lewis B. Hershey, director of the Selective Service Administration, told the
attending campers that in order to serve the nation, they needed to cultivate
healthy bodies. He noted that while 19 million Americans had undergone
medical examinations administered by the selective service, 4 million had
been determined unfit for military service because of physical defects and
another 2 million because of mental defects. In Hershey's opinion, mechanization had softened too many Americans. Worse, bad parenting had further
sapped the nation's health. "Too much advice and benefit of their parents"
had rendered even those who were physically fit mentally unaccustomed
to the demands of physical labor and thus susceptible to "psychoneurosis."
Health required a physical body capable of laboring for the state, coupled
with the mental and emotional willingness—the personality—to embrace

hard work.[49] A failure of health, Hershey continued, imperiled both the individual and national body. Frailty or an aversion to work wasted time and resources. "As a person dead you will do little," he announced. "As a person ill you will do less than if you are well. As a community, you have got to be able to solve your problems before you will be worth much as an adviser to any community. As a nation, you have got to be able to solve your problem before you can hope to get into any international organization, because if you come as a liability you will find that the international organization is already over-stocked with liabilities. What you have to be, first, is a healthy organization nationally, locally and individually."[50] Hershey applauded the efforts of 4-H, which inculcated in its participants the health habits necessary for good citizenship. His speech equated the maintenance of the healthy body with national service and explicitly tied the promotion of health in 4-H clubs to the promotion of citizenship.

When considered alongside the famine and want that racked much of the world's population during the 1940s, Hershey's conflation of good health with good citizenship implicitly strengthened the case for the moral necessity of American hegemony. "There can be no peace in a Hungry world," the 4-H Girls' World Famine Emergency Bulletin declared. "Starvation diets face[d]" the people of war-torn Europe and Asia. "Mr Herb Plambeck of WHO personally visited homes in Holland where families lived on soup made from tulip bulbs," continued the bulletin. In Asia, where the famine was more intense, the results were ghastly: "Famine is so severe that millions are existing on grass, weeds, foliage, and the bark of trees. The countryside is shaven clean. Children look like old men. Their bodies shrunken, their stomachs swollen." By contrast, explained the bulletin, Americans consumed, on average, 3,360 calories worth of food every day, "11 percent above what was eaten before the war." The bulletin recommended that Americans curb their own consumption—cut back on picky, wasteful, or excessive eating—and redirect food to starving Europeans and Asians as a token of global citizenship.[51]

The altruistic intentions of 4-H postwar activities—very real and very sincere—should not obscure the larger ideological function of health discourses. Discussions of depleted foreign bodies contributed to the self-imagination of the American body and tightened the link between health and American national identity. If strong individual bodies were equated with national vigor, then stricken foreign bodies implied concomitant national weakness. Building on wartime narratives that had equated care of the individual body with the care of the national body, figures of malformed, cancerous, and disease-ridden foreign bodies enabled 4-H organizers to seamlessly transition between national and global concepts of citizenship without revealing the underlying paradox of a world order based simultaneously on universal human equality and American hegemony. In the 1940s, discussions of health in 4-H material provided particularly effective means to mobilize rural youth in defense of their nation because a focus on health enabled rural youth to embody their patriotism—to allow 4-H bodies to become walking significations of American pride, virility, and national virtue. The ideological and practical contours of this virtue and its corresponding notion of citizenship created a complicated and often contradictory image of equality in America. Even as 4-H service and citizenship invested white rural youth with political agency, it simultaneously turned the attention of rural youth outward and abandoned black youth laboring under the weight of Southern racism.

*   *   *

For more than 300,000 African American 4-H members and organizers, the inequality frequently referenced in citizenship material was not an abstract, intellectual problem of a foreign population. It was, rather, a daily fact of life and intimately wound into 4-H programming. Racist assumptions about the ability and intelligence of African American farmers infused the segregated 4-H clubs of the South. Prior to World War II, even racial progressives in the USDA and state extension services tended to support only the most incremental solutions to racial inequality. With regard to agriculture, the ideology of economic racial uplift frequently limited the federal government's role to vague educational efforts. This strategy eschewed more radical proposals to redistribute resources or to actively confront white racism, even as the USDA promoted a limited vision of agriculture that relegated African Americans exclusively to manual labor. Severe financial disparities between white and black extension systems effectively hamstrung even the most milquetoast schemes for racial uplift, leaving African American 4-H clubs without the resources to mount a national gathering to parallel the whites-only National 4-H Camp and Congress.

Although World War II challenged 4-H's racial status quo, it never fulfilled the promise of full equality for black club members implicit in the rhetoric of citizenship programming. By 1948, African American 4-H organizers had surmounted the objections of critics and secured funding for the euphemistically named "Southern Regional 4-H Camp"—a camp for African American 4-H'ers that would supplement the National 4-H Camp in Washington,

D.C. Organizers selected a theme that echoed Lewis Hershey's conflation of health and citizenship—"Creating better homes today for a more responsible citizenship tomorrow"—and designed a program that would mix leisurely tours and discussions with an informative series of lectures on the connections between patriotic duty, nutrition, and domestic hygiene. The camp, to be held at Southern University in the segregated city of Baton Rouge, Louisiana, avoided explicitly addressing the central paradox of its theme: How could 4-H hope to promote citizenship in a community that, as the campers would soon learn, so manifestly denied African American 4-H'ers full citizenship? As one African American extension agent would complain in the aftermath of the camp, organizing a camp around the theme of citizenship and simultaneously exposing campers to obvious discrimination weakened the credibility of the federal government and revealed the multiple "standards of citizenship" at play during the 1940s, a decade that proved precarious for civil rights.[52]

Reactions to the 1948 Southern Regional 4-H Camp evinced a frustrating fate for critics of 4-H's racial politics; but ironically, the paradoxes and pain of the Regional Camp emerged initially from optimism about public responses to black wartime sacrifices and the productive potentials of black citizenship. In lieu of access to the 4-H National Camp in Washington, African American extension leaders such as Thomas Campbell and L. I. Jones, director of Negro extension for Mississippi, desired a national club gathering for black club members to symbolize broader social recognition of African American service and progress. As with public celebrations of labor rendered by white 4-H'ers during the New Deal, black extension officials hoped that a national camp would generate public recognition of African American contributions to the nation. More concretely, it could also offer incentives for the actual club members, promote African American club work across the South, and provide African American extension with a much-needed opportunity for positive publicity. Given the tendency of media to portray rural African Americans as backward and ignorant, African American extension workers craved the opportunity to showcase their best.[53]

African American extension leaders proposed a national camp or congress for African American 4-H in the early 1940s, but the opposition of Southern Directors of Extension (SDE) and the labyrinthine bureaucracy surrounding extension funding continually forestalled their efforts. Reuben Brigham introduced the idea of a national congress for African American 4-H to the Committee on Extension Work with Negroes of the LGCA in late 1940. Campbell and J. B. Pierce, another African American USDA field agent, spurred Brigham to this action, in part by discussing the issue earlier that year with Guy Noble and the National Committee. The Committee on Extension Work with Negroes "questioned the advisability of undertaking such an event at the present time" but promised to give the matter a thorough investigation. At the same time, Brigham pressed L. R. Simons, director of extension in New York and chair of the LGCA's Committee on 4-H Events, to also have his committee consider the event. Ultimately, both committees deferred to the judgment of the SDE, the collective organization of the South's extension directors and a group of men decidedly less sympathetic to the idea of such a gathering.[54]

The idea for the congress came on the heels of a proposed meeting of African American extension leaders to discuss national farm policy and agricultural adjustment in Washington, which the SDE had already sourly received. C. E. Brehm, director of extension in Tennessee, had strenuously opposed the idea. He suggested that a collective meeting for African American extension leaders, even one held in the South, was unnecessary. "There are getting to be entirely too many meetings of this kind and extension personnel is being pulled out of the State too much for this sort of thing," Brehm complained.[55] P. O. Davis stated his opposition in far more racialized terms. At the root of the meeting in Washington, Davis argued, was the "inclination [of African American extension] to 'ape' what the white people are doing. It seems that if the white people hold an extension meeting there is a feeling that the Negroes too must come along and hold a meeting, not necessarily because a meeting is needed but because the white folks have met."[56] African American extension leaders, Davis claimed, viewed whether to hold meetings as an issue of equality and justice, rather than as a question of efficient extension—a perspective Davis thought was unwise.[57]

Given this context, it was hardly surprising that Davis rejected the idea of a national gathering for African American 4-H. Before even discussing the issue with J. C. Ford, director of Negro extension for Alabama, Davis issued a blunt, if understated, reply to Brigham: "My dear Reuben. . . . I hope that the suggestion about a Negro 4H club congress will not be pushed. Frankly, I am very doubtful about the net value of those already being held."[58] Davis's reply framed his opposition in terms of efficiency—how money was best spent—but Davis's reaction was informed by his accusation that African American extension was "ape[ing]" white extension in a quixotic and mindless grab for racial justice (an issue that he addressed with apathy). From Davis's perspective, a national gathering for African American 4-H would be more about symbolically affirming African American equality than about advancing the interests of the agricultural extension service. Since Davis doubted that any funds spent on African American extension were funds well spent, it is difficult to separate his perspective from underlying racist assumptions that African Americans were too ignorant and lazy to be efficient workers. "I believe that the lowest return we are getting on extension work per dollar expended is that being spent on Negro extension personnel. My conclusion is that it is very difficult to get efficiency into Negro extension workers," complained Davis to Brigham in January 1941.[59]

Opposition from the SDE was enough to prevent the proposal from advancing in 1941, and the declaration of war in December quashed any further efforts. War made travel difficult and potentially dangerous, funds unrelated to the war scarce, and the work expected of extension agents more voluminous. Given those concerns, the USDA suspended the annual 4-H National Camp in Washington. (The National 4-H Club Congress continued to meet in Chicago during the war.) In addition, within the USDA and in state extension services, the commencement of the war pushed all other considerations from the agenda and focused attention exclusively on war planning. At the conclusion of the war, however, Campbell, John W. Mitchell, and other leaders in African American extension once again raised the issue, this time with support from M. L. Wilson, then undersecretary of agriculture, and Erwin Shinn, a senior agriculturalist at the USDA, as well as several other figures well placed in Washington. In 1946, the USDA and the LGCA gave tentative approval to a regional camp for African American 4-H, to be hosted by the Tuskegee Institute.[60]

Even as Campbell and his allies worked to organize the Regional Camp, the African American press aggressively questioned 4-H's separate-but-equal approach. In May 1946, John L. Hicks, a reporter for the National Negro Publisher Association, interviewed Gertrude Warren about plans for the 1946 National 4-H Club Camp. When pressed on why no black 4-H'ers would attend, Warren claimed that the presence of African American 4-H'ers at the camp would mean that "white Southerners would refuse to attend." She claimed that this reality was not by design but that, "like Topsy, the 4-H movement just grew up that way."[61] Hicks penned an article on the situation that was carried widely by African American newspapers, including the *Chicago Defender*, the *Minneapolis Spokesman*, the *Pittsburgh Courier*, and the *Washington Star*. In preparation for the camp, the *Defender* also contacted Ralph Fulghum, a CES official, about the propriety of the planned "lily-white" club congress in December. Fulghum asserted that the situation had the full endorsement of Campbell and Mitchell. Fulghum further claimed that invitations to the camp and congress were left to individual states and that the USDA had no formal policy banning African American attendance.[62]

Warren's and Fulghum's comments only heightened criticism from the African American press. The *Chicago Defender* described the 1946 National Club Camp as a "Jim Crow spectacle planned by hate-conditioned government officials." Attending campers risked being "thoroughly conditioned to believe segregation is correct," and thus, "our national government is helping develop a coming generation of farm citizens thoroughly imbued with reactionary theories of racism." In fact, "fascist government officials" were "ruin[ing] this important youth organization."[63] A letter to the *Washington Star* by E. B. Henderson made an identical case: "To me and many others, the whole 4-H program is no more valuable in its citizenship training than any one of [Adolf] Hitler's or Benito [Mussolini's] fascist youth projects."[64] News that the USDA would host a separate "meeting for Negroes that would be 'equivalent' to a national camp" only intensified the criticism from the black press and civil rights activists. Mary McLeod Bethune, president of the National Council of Negro Women and among the most prominent activists in the nation, informed the *Defender* that she would "fight to last ditch any attempt on the part of the Extension Service to hold a separate national encampment program for Negroes. We will not have it."[65] The *Defender* pressed Guy Noble to clarify whether the "Jim Crow selections" had the National Committee's sanction, but Noble stonewalled the newspaper, and all-white congresses were again held in 1946 and 1947.[66] The *Defender* memorialized the 1947 congress with "4-H Congress Observes 26th Year of Bias," an article that excoriated 4-H's democratic pretensions. The article bitterly noted: "Ironically, the young farmers were urged to raise more food to help build democracy—in Europe."[67]

The USDA moved forward with its own plans for separate national and regional camps, despite pressure from the *Defender*, Bethune, and their allies.[68] As a result of the negative publicity, both the secretary of agriculture, Clinton Anderson, and the White House's special assistant for minority problems, Phileo Nash, independently contacted M. L. Wilson to inquire about the situation. In both cases, as historian Carmen V. Harris notes, Wilson clung to the states'-rights position developed by Warren and Fulghum and "tacitly sanction[ed] state-level discrimination through federal passivity."[69] Despite announcing their intention to host a regional camp at the Tuskegee Institute in 1947, the USDA could prod the SDE to action only in 1948. Finally, the SDE appointed a committee with seven members, including Campbell and chaired by L. I. Jones, to organize a camp for African American 4-H in August 1948 at Southern University.[70]

Camp organizers navigated between the racist sensibilities of the SDE and the logistics of a positive and well-publicized event. As a result, the camp material uniformly presented arguments that deferred to the racist mind-set of the SDE. W. C. Abbott, the state club leader for Louisiana, warned the CES to eschew any thorny mention of civil rights or racial discord.[71] Instead, organizers created a program that studiously avoided the very debates about equality that had raged in the *Defender*, even as, paradoxically, they selected citizenship as the central theme of the camp: "Creating better homes today for a more responsible citizenship tomorrow." Camp organizers framed the issue of better homes as an issue of domestic health and hygiene and linked it directly to the able performance of citizenship. Two of the three daily themes for the camp focused on issues of health: "Better health for better living" on Wednesday and "Good nutrition and food build strong citizens" on Thursday. On Wednesday, delegates heard an address by Dr. Roscoe Brown from the U.S. Public Health Service; on Thursday, they listened to Patsy Graves, a home economist at the Farm Home Administration, give a speech on the relationship between nutrition and health.[72]

Camp material defined African American citizenship almost exclusively in terms of obedience to government authority. Organizers distributed a pamphlet, "The Code of the Good American," to each camper. It consisted of eleven laws and provided a succinct description of what citizenship required of African American youth. Most of its laws codified banal proscriptions in terse prose. "The Good American does his duty," explained the entirety of the fifth law, "The Law of Duty." Laws of "Kindness," "Sportsmanship," "Self-Reliance," "Truth," "Good Workmanship," and "Teamwork" received similarly concise explanations. Laws of "Self-Control" and "Reliability" were slightly more in-depth, in each case adding a sentence to reaffirm the link between their particular virtue and national well-being. "The Law of Good Health," a relatively verbose missive, encouraged readers to "gain and keep good health" and asserted that "the welfare of our country depends upon those who are physically fit for their daily life." The final law, "The Law of Loyalty," rendered all the previous laws superfluous. "The good American is loyal," explained the eleventh law. "He who obeys the Law of Loyalty obeys all of the other ten laws of the Good American."[73]

M. L. Wilson inaugurated the camp with an address on August 24, 1948, that illustrated a view of African American citizenship rooted in promises of economic opportunity and material comfort. Notably, this view provided positive incentives for obedience. Wilson stressed that the quality of life enjoyed by even the poorest Americans soared above that of most people outside the United States, and he cited his own tour of Europe and Tom Campbell's tour of Africa. "When people like Mr. Tom Campbell and I get back from those other countries," argued Wilson, "we can't help but appreciate how fortunate we in this country are. When we sit down and say 'Give us this day our daily bread,' we know that none of us will have to starve." More than current prosperity, claimed Wilson, America also provided opportunity to all its citizens, and the success of African American 4-H'ers proved it: "It's things like those which you boys and girls are doing in 4-H Club work that prove what a real land of Opportunity our country is. In the United States, every boy who is willing to use his head, heart, health, and hand, can succeed in making the best better." In return for prosperity and opportunity, Wilson suggested, African Americans owed America good citizenship—their loyalty and service—and no better model existed for good citizenship than Tom Campbell, a career public servant. Wilson's speech reiterated to the African American audience that the difference that mattered was not between white and black but between America and the world.[74]

Wilson's address was only the first of many to follow, though he was the camp's most distinguished speaker. Fortunately, like their counterparts at the white 4-H National Camp, attendees could expect a variety of tours and social activities to enliven the camp and offset the dense addresses of the various scheduled luminaries and club organizers. Even if the various tours did not directly advance the themes of the camp, organizers hoped that they would entertain and educate the delegates. Among other events, organizers made time for tours of the Louisiana State Capitol Building, the University of Louisiana, and the Standard Oil Refinery. In addition, campers could look forward to a trip to the New Orleans Zoo. Poor planning and the trenchant racism of the segregated South, however, transformed what should have been the most delightful part of the camp into an ordeal. After an eighty-mile bus ride in the August heat, campers found large parts of the zoo closed to them because of their race. In addition, camp organizers failed to investigate the available restroom and dining options. Predictably, the zoo managers refused to accommodate the eighty-two campers and their chaperones, forcing the entire group to endure an uncomfortable bus ride all the way back to Baton Rouge for relief.[75]

In the aftermath of the camp, L. I. Jones and Tom Campbell solicited feedback from attendees. 4-H members who responded were universally glowing in their praise of the camp.[76] The zoo trip, however, remained a sore point for many attendees.[77] Other attendees criticized the organizers explicitly for exposing the campers to segregation in New Orleans. Camilia Veems of

Georgia State College, for example, politely thanked Jones and Campbell for their efforts before recommending that "tours if possible should be planned to unsegregated places . . . where the children and leaders with them would not be embarrassed." It was not, Veems argued, that campers would be unaccustomed to segregation. To the contrary, their treatment in New Orleans, like the intense poverty among rural blacks they witnessed in the Louisiana countryside, reminded them too much of home. To Veems's thinking, the camp should inspire 4-H youth and expose them to different ways of living and thinking and, ideally, a world in which they would be treated with respect, dignity, and equality. She paraphrased a conversation she overheard among some of the camp attendees at the camp's conclusion:

> We really did enjoy our trip and we thank every body who made it possible for us to go and all of the 4-H delegates said that they learned many, many interesting and helpful things that will do us good in the years to come. But you know, we have seen very little that was any different from what we have seen all of our lives? We saw houses that looked just like the farm houses that we see in our communities back home; we saw cotton, corn, cane, gardens, poultry, cows, and other animals just like those in Georgia; we saw colored people working hard in the fields and of course they were getting little or nothing in return for their hard work; we saw prejudice and segregation just like we see at home. Oh! if we could only go somewhere we could see something different from what we see every day and from what we have seen all of our lives. We really like Louisiana and the people were indeed lovely to us and did everything nice to make us happy. Why we cannot go to Virginia, or to Washington, or to some place up that way where we can see something different.

Veems then apologized for the "radical" nature of her suggestion but urged the camp organizers to consider it, nevertheless, as an honest response to the camp.[78]

Veems articulated a vision of African American citizenship that clashed directly with Wilson's speech and "The Code of the Good American." Where Wilson and the code saw only responsibilities for African Americans and offered an empty promise of prosperity in exchange for obedience, Veems demanded more from society and the government. She linked the poverty of rural African Americans directly to prejudice and segregation, identified segregation as a humiliating and dehumanizing practice, indicted Southern agriculture as exploitative, and implicitly dismissed explanations for rural black poverty that tried to elide the issue of white racism. In sum, Veems's letter bristled with discontent with racism and the complacency that the USDA, Jones, and Campbell had shown in holding the camp in a segregated community. More important, it suggested that African American 4-H'ers as citizens were owed something more.

Veems's invocation of citizenship was somewhat indirect and implicit, but L. A. Toney, the state leader of Negro work in West Virginia, made the connection as explicitly as possible. Toney was incensed by the "affair" at the zoo. "It was exasperating to know that there were no toilet facilities or other reasonable provisions made for the accommodation and enjoyment of our future leaders, representing the best young people in the nation," wrote Toney. "The whole affair was a disgrace to democracy and I trust it will never happen again in the history of 4-H club work." Worse still, Toney reported that many delegates, not simply those from West Virginia, had "expressed themselves despairingly" about the incident, and he worried that it had undercut directly the whole purpose of the camp. "No tour should be planned to any place," argued Toney, "where restrictions will be practiced which will thwart the ambitions and desires of our young people and cause them to question our sincerity in the general theme of the camp." The incident at the zoo, from Toney's perspective, had exposed the hollowness of speeches about African American citizenship.[79]

Reactions to the 1948 Regional 4-H Camp exposed the possibilities as well as the limitations implicit in all 4-H citizenship programming. By staging a citizenship camp for African Americans, federal and state organizers intended to develop loyalty to the American nation-state, improve rural African American health, and promote African American extension. That vision of citizenship—impoverished as it was—found no contradiction in promoting African American citizenship amid the denial of substantive African American social and political equality. In recognizing and denouncing that contradiction, Toney, Veems, and the various youth delegates they cited advanced a different vision of citizenship, in which gestures at equality, liberty, and tolerance were more than cynical rhetoric.

*   *   *

Segregation continued unabated in 4-H until the mid-1960s. Prior to the Civil Rights Act of 1964, two African Americans attended national 4-H functions—once in 1960 and once in 1962. Facing only federal "passivity" on the issue, Southern states continued to exclude African American 4-H'ers from the Washington and Chicago events. The struggle to desegregate 4-H lagged substantially behind the simultaneous struggle to desegregate public education in the South. As historian Carmen V. Harris notes, federal bureaucrats selectively eschewed responsibility for 4-H segregation, hiding behind the excuse that the states chose their own delegations. "White federal officials had the greatest influence in overturning 4-H exclusionary practices," writes Harris, "but these bureaucrats lacked the will to do so. Instead, CES officials decided to collaborate with Southern extension directors, even after federal law made such collaboration questionable."[80] But even eventual desegregation hardly hailed equality. Through the 1960s and 1970s, African American youth actually saw diminishing opportunities for scholarships and awards in 4-H. As Mississippi home demonstration agent Alberta Dishmon put it: "We did not get integration, we got disintegration, a feeling that you would gradually disappear and that someone else would be in charge."[81]

The USDA's indifferent response suggests that by 1950, the cultural norms that had defined the complex relationship between state power, rural reproduction, and 4-H had hardened. It was not that M. L. Wilson or the other bureaucrats at the USDA were uninterested in the problem of racial inequality. It was that they could not and would not conceive of 4-H as an instrument of racial justice. Rather, agrarian futurism dictated that 4-H was a mechanism to optimize rural social reproduction, and agrarian futurism's vision of normal social reproduction was that of landed, white heteronormativity with clear gendered divisions of labor. When the state contributed to the agrarian futurist vision of a normal countryside, it disappeared from view as a political actor. When the state disrupted normal reproduction—when it allowed the National Committee to import urban corruption or when it disrupted rather than reinforced racial hierarchy in the South—its presence could be noted, recorded, and rejected. Put differently, despite its obvious relationship to the American state—indeed, despite its constant service to the decisively biopolitical objectives of that state—4-H constantly disowned its own political effect and, instead, portrayed the outcome of the state's rural modernization project as apolitical and inevitable—the natural outcome of generational change. By 1950, 4-H had quietly wed the highly contingent political economy of postwar American agriculture to a naturalized image of a family farm composed of a farmer and a farmer's wife.

As African American activists struggled to desegregate 4-H in the 1950s, 4-H maintained its image as an organization capable of reproducing a healthy countryside. It was precisely this cultural capital that African American activists sought to access: a place for black youth in the rural imaginary that accreted around public discussions of 4-H. The "Jane Ellison" series, written by popular juniors' novelist Anne Emery, offered a symptomatic example of exactly how 4-H's public image had, despite that activism, cohered around white rural heteronormativity by the 1950s. Her three romance novels—*County Fair: A 4-H Romance* (1953), *Hickory Hill* (1955), and *Sixteen* (1956)—went through dozens of printings into the 1970s.[82] They traced the trials and tribulations of a sandy-blond Indiana girl and her two great romances: one with farm life and the other with Chuck Ransome, a hunky, blue-eyed farm boy and 4-H'er. The Ransomes were a poor family of tenant farmers, and Chuck was hope for the future. Mr. Ransome sneered at the techniques that Chuck learned in 4-H. "Milk records, feed records, cost records, butter fat—what does it all amount to, anyway?" carped Mr. Ransome about Chuck's scribbling. Mrs. Ransome, a cheerful, masterful homemaker, chastised her husband's backward attitude. Chuck, she explained, was "going to be a businessman as well as a farmer. . . . If he doesn't make money running a farm, he's going to know why."[83] Although Jane lived in the nearby town of Marquette, she joined Chuck's 4-H club to spend more time with him and learn about farm life. Mrs. Ransome, as a leader of the club, instructed Jane in baking, sewing, and room decoration, and Jane even embarked on a disastrous dairy project (ignoring the warnings of her family and the club leaders). Jane's father, a doctor, provided the club with health advice and helped the club girls lose unwanted pounds. Jane eventually persuaded Dr. Ellison to relocate the entire family from Marquette to a farm near the Ransomes. Dr. Ellison, of course, could not run the farm. Instead, the Ellisons were landlords, and a family of tenants, the Wallaces, worked the farm.

In Emery's rural Indiana, farm tenancy was not an exception or even a problem worth solving. It was not wrought of mechanization, farm consolidation, and asymmetrical access to capital exacerbated by regressive subsidy regimes. Nor was farm tenancy a cornerstone of racial inequality and white supremacy, as it was throughout the South. Rather, in Emery's text, the residents of Marquette accepted farm tenancy as a normal and unlamented part of the landscape. The Ransomes could not escape tenancy only because Mr. Ransome was stubborn and ignorant. Generational change by way of Jane's blond beau was all that was needed. Similarly, Dr. Ellison assumed that the Wallaces, hardworking and unambiguously supportive of 4-H and its progressive agriculture, would save enough money to buy a large farm in a few years. Emery portrayed this political economy as seamlessly knit into the prevailing liberal order. Dr. Ellison dismissed rural political dissenters

as reactionary antistatists indifferent to the interests of the community—
"the old diehards out along Road M . . . squawking about government and
taxes."[84] Later, the 4-H club campaigned for a school bond issue, and Jane
used the romantic affections of Fred, a ne'er-do-well son of one such Road
M farmer, to help ensure the bond's victory.[85] In all this, the term "USDA"
appeared not once, though the county agent dropped in to compliment Jane
at a 4-H orchestra performance.[86]

In place of a racialized political economy shaped by government policy,
an intimate economy of white, youthful romance structured both the present
and future of Emery's countryside.[87] The club socialized its members along
the predictable gendered lines. Boys learned to be gracious economic com-
petitors; girls learned how to be attractive and attentive homemakers. These
paths were mutually exclusive, as Jane learned. Her father demanded to know
about her plans for the future, and she responded that, although she could
not run a farm herself, she would like to employ a tenant or marry a farmer.
Her father spelled out the precise contours of such a marriage: "If you're a
farmer's wife you'll have to know more about cooking and preserving and
sewing and housekeeping than about dairy cattle or agriculture."[88] As the
boys and girls learned to be farmers and farmers' wives, the club rippled with
adolescent yearning—not just between Jane and Chuck but between all the
4-H'ers. The 4-H club was their primary social nexus and thus an incubator
for numerous romances at meetings, dances, parties, and games. When Jane
strayed from the club's romantic offerings to date Fred, her grades slipped,
she had to quit the cheerleading squad, and she fell in with a group of fast and
easy girls. In Jane's example, Emery presented 4-H clubs as sure footing for
rural youth's ascent into normal heterosexual maturity.

Under these signs of rural normalcy lurked a range of perverse identifications forged precisely by Emery's effort to articulate Jane's heterosexual
desires. Consider how Emery narrated Jane's unfolding and visceral affections for Chuck. Jane first met Chuck when she accompanied her father on
a call to the Ransome farm. She was "immediately interested" in the "well-
built boy with keen blue eyes, blond hair, freckles, and a serious expression
about his mouth." Emery detailed Jane's visceral arousal, noting that Jane
"studied him with growing interest . . . and she felt her face grow hot."[89] Later,
at different moments when she steals glimpses of Chuck overflowing with
"secret adoration," Emery describes Jane's palpable reactions.[90] Jane's heart
"trip[ped]," "ached," "jump[ed]," "turned over," and "flipped."[91] As Jane left
Chuck's farm—as she saw Chuck walk off toward the barn—Emery describes
Jane feeling "attacked again with a deep desire to live on a farm and work

with animals and growing things." In that moment, Jane's erotic attachment
to Chuck is transferred to a larger fantasy of farm life. Set aside, for the time
being, the specific political economy of that fantasy—its normalization of
farm tenancy, capital-intensive production, and gendered divisions of labor.
As a depiction of open erotic attachments posing as a closed articulation
of heterosexual desire, Emery eroticizes the idea of being husbanded by a
farmer and of participating in his fecund spaces.[92]

In the novels, agricultural spaces fashioned unexpected identifications
and undercut the certainty that the reader would know precisely who or
what would be reproduced on the family farm. Jane, for example, forged an
obvious identification with her heifer, Daisy. She scrutinized Daisy's gendered performance "for attractive individuality, vigor, femininity, impressive
style, attractive carriage, graceful walk."[93] At the county fair, the very sight of
Chuck "grooming his Jersey heifer" causes Jane's "heart to drop with a quick
thump."[94] Was this nervous anxiety or jealousy? Later, as Jane watches Chuck
putting his heifer through the paces for the judges, she struggles with a
"dream" of "both of them walking down the aisle in the little country church."
But precisely who constituted the "both" in Jane's dream? The ambiguity of
identification in the passage was incumbent to a desire that emerged from a
space of promiscuous, multispecies reproduction.[95]

This ambiguity recalls Judith Butler's observation that heterosexuality is
always a failing "effort to imitate its own idealizations." In Emery's text, to
quote Butler, Jane's heterosexuality "create[d] more than it ever meant to, sig-
nifying in excess of any intended referent." Emery merely echoed the line of
agrarian futurist commentators who, in the name of normal rural reproduction, had forged various bestial connections among boys, cows, and corn.
Much like Oscar Benson's ambition to "to raise a crop of young farmers,"
Jane's heterosexual desire always exceeded itself. This was because in both
agricultural spaces and in the fantasy of Emery's text, human and nonhuman
reproductions functioned as mutually constituting metaphors and as systems
of material coproduction. It was hardly surprising, then, that Jane found
farming to be a bewildering, if arousing, space of charged reproductive possibilities rather than merely the foundation for a stable heterosexual identity.[96]

Jane's ambiguous desires underscored the distances between the idealized
rural normalcy that 4-H ostensibly produced and the peculiar bedfellows that
it actually made. Just as this idealized vision of rural normalcy ascended, the
USDA turned its attention from rural America to a global countryside. In the
immediate aftermath of World War II, the USDA reevaluated its own ambitions for 4-H and schemed to export youth club work to war-torn societies

around the globe. If 4-H could produce modern citizens in rural America, experts at the USDA reasoned, it might also effectively develop the human resources of rural communities the world over. Through the Foreign Training Division (FTD) at the USDA graduate school in Beltsville, Maryland, the USDA aggressively promoted agricultural extension and youth club work as essential components of postwar reconstruction. By 1960, graduates of the FTD programs had founded 4-H organizations in dozens of countries, and 4-H claimed an annual enrollment of more than 6 million youth worldwide. 4-H shadowed American military forces abroad: Japan, Germany, Korea, and, after 1955, Vietnam all claimed functioning 4-H organizations. In each instance, 4-H joined a host of other development programs financed, directly and indirectly, by the U.S. government. 4-H supplemented these other efforts at state building by explicitly strengthening relationships between the nation-state and rural youth, by modernizing agricultural practices, and by fostering national democratic spirit. Less explicitly, 4-H wound itself into the complex of international development organizations that constituted a vital part of America's projection of power abroad.

CHAPTER SIX

International 4-H in the Cold War

> . . . for my club, my community, my country,
> and my world.
>
> —The 4-H Pledge

In April 1946, Gertrude Warren took a tropical tour on behalf of the USDA. She traveled to Cuba and Jamaica, where she was charged with observing, advising, and encouraging agricultural youth club movements in both countries. The Jamaican and Cuban youth organizations took their inspiration and names from American 4-H: the Cuban clubs, first organized in 1931, were called 5-C clubs—for *Cuba, cabeza* (head), *corazón* (heart), *capacidad* (ability), and *cooperación* (cooperation)—and the Jamaican clubs even called themselves 4-H.[1] During her stay, the Cuban ministry of agriculture invited Warren to observe the ninth annual 5-C Congress in Holguín and requested that she appear in a promotional film on behalf of 5-C, in which she would be shown "taking the hand of a 5-C Club boy in the presence of the President of the Republic or the Minister [of Agriculture]."[2] Speaking to the congress through a translator, Warren praised the accomplishments of 5-C and hoped that it could also enact the goals of her own organization in the Cuban context—to cultivate "young citizens imbued with the desire to do, to earn, and to serve." If the American and Cuban club organizations could engineer such "a deep and sympathetic understanding of our common ideals and aspirations," they could help build "an enduring world peace."[3] Warren's rhetoric reiterated the symbolism of the hand-taking ceremony and promised a prosperous future rooted in cooperation and exchange between a mature North and a developing South.

Despite Warren's optimism, Enrique Bello, director of 5-C, held a more conflicted view of the club organizations outside the United States. He had taken a parallel journey through the United States and was well acquainted with the methods and accomplishments of 4-H there. Bello held that the robust American 4-H network was more than merely "an institution of learning of fixed methods." Thanks to their "ideological, ambient air," 4-H clubs in the United States were "a forge on which future citizens are molded." By contrast, 5-C was a poor imitation. It had insufficient funds and staff to match the American example or to reach the rural poor. The majority of the work was wasted, and the clubs were too obsessed with flashy expositions and thus incapable of "reach[ing] the heart of the people," Bello complained to the congress. 5-C had "broken away from the main body" of Cuba and was connected only enough that "the body feeds and keeps the soul and the brain of a future generation alive." That future generation, Bello hoped, "will be the pliable material for a social structure which will benefit" ensuing generations thereafter. Indeed, although 5-C struggled now, he believed that its current and former members, who numbered thirty thousand, would one day issue "a voice . . . today or tomorrow . . . which with patriotic feeling will ask for the children."[4] Bello designated rural children as the keys to the Cuban future, even as the specific path to that future seemed murky at best.

Warren's comments reflected the USDA's growing postwar interest in the rural spaces beyond the United States, but Bello's comments incisively foreshadowed the generational structure of many of the USDA's international development endeavors in the following decades. 4-H programs during the global Cold War were designed to use agricultural modernization to escort juvenile developing nations into Northern maturity. This chapter focuses on a handful of programs that represented the variety of approaches taken by international 4-H in the postwar period: the Japanese Agricultural Training Program; the Programa Interamericano para la Juventud Rural (PIJR); and the Vietnamese 4-T. Although these programs operated in very different ways and in very different landscapes, they were united by how they envisioned rural youth as the decisive elements of social and economic development—a view that Bello succinctly expressed to the Cuban 5-C. Indeed, Bello identified two critical, interlocking features of youth-oriented programs that nearly all 4-H development technicians would cite: First, youth were a productive focus for development programs because, unlike their parents, they were a pliable material; second, youth development programs were definitionally generational—that is, investments in youth could pay dividends only in the distant future.

These two features imbued youth with the power to coordinate between development's heterogeneous, contradictory elements: agribusinesses premised on both capitalist enterprise and statist technocracy; democracies

built on both liberal tolerance and violent anticommunism; and an international order structured by both the equality of nations and U.S. interventionism. Youth's coordinating, generational power served as the black
box of development discourse by which development technicians could
bridge the temporal gaps between the impoverished present and an imagined prosperous future.[5] Based on the precedent of 4-H's experiment in the
rural United States, these development technicians crafted 4-H programs
for the developing world that imagined American capital, technology, and
knowledge flowing into and enriching the bodies of rural youth in the global
South. Much as O. H. Benson, C. B. Smith, and Gertrude Warren had done
a half-century earlier, development technicians imagined that pliable, young
bodies were the most fecund soil for cultivating a prosperous future. This
pliability enabled the thorny translation of developmental lessons from
north to south. "Though the financial resources are from North America,
the bulk of human resources are from Latin America, and this is one reason we can claim PIJR is 'Latin-centered,'" wrote PIJR director Theodore
Hutchcroft about his organization. "Another is that the concept and services
of PIJR have been developed to fit 'the system' in Latin America and the
Caribbean."[6] Yet this imagined flow contained the seeds of its own destruc-
tion. As development technicians eventually discovered, that narrative was
premised on a series of false assumptions: that capital and technology would
flow without end; that the political context within the nations of the global
South would remain amenable to such a flow; and that the bodies of youth
were not only pliable but also docile and passive. As each of these assumptions unraveled, the imagined future that 4-H international programs hoped
to cultivate seemed only ever more distant by 1980.

*   *   *

In the two decades following World War II, U.S. policymakers looked with
increasing interest and anxiety at the rural spaces of the global South as
sites of geopolitical conflict. Envisioning communist rebels fueled by rural
poverty, American planners deployed rural development schemes first
to preempt insurgency and then, increasingly, as an active component of
counterinsurgency initiatives. This vision of development tied rural prosperity to input- and capital-intensive export monocultures fed by vertically
integrated agribusinesses, as well as a bureaucratic state that guaranteed
property rights, subsidized scientific research, and prioritized economic

infrastructure above redistribution and social welfare. Actors in thrall of this vision spanned U.S. government agencies. They also included quasi-state institutions such as the International Monetary Fund, International Bank for Reconstruction and Development, and United Nations' Food and Agriculture Organization, as well as philanthropic agencies like the Rockefeller Foundation and the Ford Foundation and even major multinational corporations invested in rural markets and agricultural commodities. These would-be modernizers drew lessons from the rural United States in crafting their various prescriptions for rural poverty, drawing universal lessons from an agrarian futurist interpretation of the American past. The Roosevelt administration's rural development and mobilization projects provided immediate templates for foreign development. Thus, amid large-scale infrastructure projects advocated by "modernization theorists" like Talcott Parsons and Walt Whitman Rostow, development programs also looked to cultivate human infrastructure in rural spaces through agricultural extension programs.[7]

In September 1944, scores of government officials, agricultural technicians, and university professors met in Washington, D.C., to discuss the role of agricultural extension in the reconstruction of nations devastated by World War II. The conference explored how to restore afflicted regions to prewar levels of prosperity but also ambitiously pondered how to cultivate societies amenable to peace. Secretary of Agriculture Claude Wickard explained to attendees: "[T]here is little chance of establishing permanent peace so long as great numbers of rural families throughout the world are seriously lacking in income, education, housing, health, and other living standards." Agricultural extension would help create the "prosperous, efficient, well-kept farms, and bright, attractive, happy rural homes" necessary to "keeping the entire world happy and peaceful."[8] Leading USDA extension and planning officials, including M. L. Wilson, Carl Taylor, C. B. Smith, and Gertrude Warren, addressed the conference on the possibilities and practicalities of this approach. Wilson and Taylor emphasized the "cultural approach": an insistence that "*development* has to come from within and cannot be forced from without." What counted as "inside" and "outside" was, however, a matter of perspective. An indigenous extension system employed native workers, respected local culture, and appeared homegrown rather than contrived, but it still fundamentally aspired to develop rural cultures through universally applicable scientific and democratic "basic principles." By respecting local culture and proceeding "from within," agriculture extension promised to be "not only consistent with the democratic pattern of culture but to become a powerful educational instrument in the development of a democratic world society."[9]

Drawing from the American precedent, conference speakers argued that youth-oriented extension work overseas played a vital role in this "development from within" because it allowed extension workers to reach the fundamental unit of rural life the world over: the "farm family." The United States, Wilson explained, "owe[d] much to . . . 4-H clubs." They "interest[ed] young people in the activities" of that fundamental unit. Thus, 4-H clubs "buil[t] democratic citizenship and [ensured] increased farm production and better farm living as well." Wilson endorsed Henry A. Wallace's perspective on the issue. Wallace "emphasized the great importance of the family unit on United States farms. He saw it as the core of rural democracy and progress in the age of science."[10] The conference report presented Wilson's family unit as a near-universal and inviolable characteristic of rural societies around the globe, but one that needed to be integrated into a democratic scheme of governance. Thus, extension workers in locales as far-flung as the Middle East, Germany, and the Philippines needed knowledge of and respect for "the family . . . as a basic unit."[11] As with American extension pioneers in the early twentieth century, respect for the family entailed an extension program addressed to women and youth, not just to adult men who might be particularly "resistant to change." In the context of international development, club work promised to bypass a global class of resistant farmers and produce a generation open to and responsible for "desirable ideals and standards of farming, homemaking, community life, and citizenship," as Warren put it.[12]

To assist in the creation of functional systems of agricultural extension abroad, the USDA maintained a training school for foreign extension workers in Beltsville, Maryland. Initially, the program was jointly administered by the USDA and the State Department's Institute of Inter-American Affairs and was designed to promote "the improvement of farming efficiency, living standards, and health of rural people" in Central and South America only. The initial class of seventy-eight trainees from twelve Latin American nations received intensive instruction in extension methods, with many living and working with county agents in rural communities in what the program referred to as "in-service" training.[13] In 1944, the USDA took exclusive responsibility for the program, made it available to extension workers from all over the world, and renamed it the Foreign Training Division (FTD). More than six hundred foreign nationals graduated from the program and returned to their native countries to establish or expand extension systems before 1950.[14] In 1960, FTD graduates numbered six thousand from more than a hundred countries on every inhabited continent. Between 1950 and 1970, FTD extension graduates labored in nearly all the battlefields of the global Cold War: Korea, Cuba, Taiwan, Colombia, El Salvador, the Philippines, and scores of others.[15]

In each location, FTD graduates also organized 4-H organizations, frequently with the assistance of the U.S. military apparatus. 4-H organizations sprouted across Asia and the Pacific Rim in every nation with a sustained American military presence, including Korea, Vietnam, Japan, and the Philippines. In Korea, Colonel Charles Anderson, military governor of Kyunggi Province, first established 4-H clubs in 1947 before turning the organization over to Korean extension workers. Korean 4-H expanded "at a remarkable rate," using "American resources and Korean initiative," historian Gregg Brazinsky states. The American embassy directed financial and technical support to the clubs. By 1967, 760,000 Korean youth had enrolled and recited the official creed: "I believe in my country, my province and my community and in my responsibility for their development."[16] In Central and South America, FTD graduates founded 4-H organizations (usually called 4-S, 4-F, or 4-C clubs) in nearly every nation. Through the 1950s, however, most of these organizations were haphazard affairs, enrolling only a few thousand members and culling support almost exclusively from national ministries of agriculture. In 1963, the USDA claimed, "There are 76 countries with 4-H or 4-H-type organizations," enrolling more than 6.3 million youth worldwide, including more than 4 million youth outside the United States.[17]

The existence of 4-H organizations around the globe introduced the possibility of more sustained transnational interactions between youth from abroad and youth in the United States. Beginning in 1948, the National 4-H Foundation, in cooperation with the USDA and the State Department, arranged for American 4-H'ers to live abroad through the International Farm Youth Exchange (IFYE). Initial cohorts journeyed to the United Kingdom and Western Europe; by the 1970s, IFYE had placed American youth in Latin America, East Asia, and even the Soviet Union.[18] In return, tens of thousands of foreign nationals came to the United States and lived in rural communities and on farms for extended stays. While the USDA and the National 4-H Foundation designed this exchange to allow bodies to flow both ways, the ideal of development supported by these programs flowed only north to south. American youth sent abroad were expected to learn about foreign cultures and cultivate goodwill toward the United States, but 4-H officials never justified the program in terms of foreign expertise or practices enriching or improving American agriculture. By contrast, support for foreign youth living in the United States was premised on the idea that such exchanges would improve the quality of farming and rural living in the home countries. Ideally, youth living in the United States through IFYE would learn about modern agriculture and homemaking and, upon returning to their home countries, would become pivotal agents of rural modernization.

This ambition became explicit with the creation of the Agricultural Training Program (ATP) in the mid-1960s. In 1965, following the passage of the Immigration and Nationality Act, the U.S. secretary of labor terminated a special program that had allowed three thousand laborers from rural Japan to work on American farms.[19] Seeking to find an alternative flow of labor, as well as to mollify U.S. farmers and the Japanese government, the Department of Labor approached the National 4-H Foundation and concocted a scheme by which a cohort of Japanese older youth could live and work on farms in the United States for up to two years. After laboring on American farms, trainees would return to their home countries—with a nest egg, one hoped, of funds saved from an allowance they received in lieu of wages. The first ATP in 1966 brought two hundred young men, mostly between the ages of eighteen and twenty, from Japan. (A parallel program for young women, called the Homemaker Training Program, was proposed in 1969 but was never launched.)[20] By 1974, about 1,400 trainees had worked in the United States through the Japanese ATP. Based on the success of the program, additional ATPs were organized for Korea, Taiwan, and the Philippines and, with détente between the United States and the Soviet Union in the 1970s, Hungary and Poland.[21]

Although the proximate cause of the ATPs was the disruption to the flow of laborers from Japan to American farms, the National 4-H Foundation explained that the primary benefit of the program was that it modernized agriculture abroad by sidestepping resistant adult farmers. In its initial justification for the program, the National 4-H Foundation noted that "adherence to traditional methods of farming" in Japan had ensured that agriculture "lags far behind other sectors." There was, however, a burgeoning interest in farming "as a business as well as a family tradition" and a serious demand for youth who could "demonstrate the advantages of modern scientific production techniques." ATPs would thus "assist the Japanese in changing segments of their agriculture toward an industrial orientation through modern, scientific techniques."[22] A 1970 overview of the program contrasted between the suffering wrought of traditional agriculture and the prosperity that modern agricultural technology and the Green Revolution promised. But adult farmers, the report contended, were "generally firmly rooted in the past and are preservers of tradition. Youth, on the other hand, aspires to build a new world. In youth lies the world's hope for freedom from hunger and malnutrition."[23] A 1967 study of the Japanese ATPs by academic sociologists similarly concluded that the program could erode the "submissiveness" and deference to "traditionalism" that plagued Japanese rural family life. "As the trainees progressed in their training and obtained experience in modern, American style of dairying," the study stated, "their attitudes toward traditional Japanese customs and relationships became less submissive and more oriented to their individual needs."[24]

For development technicians, the potential for ATPs to transform Japanese rural family life as well as agricultural practice suggested that Japanese social reproduction and agricultural productivity were inseparable. Just as 4-H had done in the United States, the Japanese ATP understood the "basic producing unit" of Japanese agriculture to be the "family or clan."[25] This was not, however, the modern democratic family unit that joined a commercial-oriented father to an expert homemaker, each party with respective spheres of influence and authority. Rather, the primordial "clan" organization of rural Japan bespoke stubborn rural patriarchs who dominated their wives and children and overstepped their boundaries. This dysfunctional family model, a holdover from Japan's feudal past, rendered rural society immune to innovation and could lead to social and economic stagnation or even regression. Crucially, this factor helped technicians place Japan in a developmental framework for which it was otherwise ill suited. By drawing Japanese youth from their backward rural villages into the developed American hinterlands, development technicians devised a way to develop Japanese youth from without *before* developing their villages from within. The American countryside offered possibilities for growth for all types of youth, regardless of nationality, and it was the essential, shared pliability of all youth that structured such a possibility.

The ATP system was only one model for development inspired by 4-H programs and was particularly well suited to the capacities and needs of the governments in Japan and Korea (the two nations that enjoyed the most active ATPs). The hope of modernizing farming and family life in rural Japan was ambitious but was a far more modest goal than those set forth by development agencies in Latin America. In Latin America, the positions of both the United States and the agribusiness and finance interests that underwrote 4-H were substantially more tenuous. In Latin America, development agencies looked to 4-H not just as a way to improve agricultural productivity but also to build rural support for capitalism, democracy, and U.S. geopolitical hegemony amid a rapidly polarizing and militarizing political environment.

*   *   *

ATPs and the USDA FTD tried to develop rural youth, extension systems, and agriculture around the world by drawing foreign youth to the rural United States, but a different scheme prevailed in Latin America. Although many Latin American countries maintained exchanges with the United States through IFYE, those exchanges brought only a handful of youth to the United States in a given year—about four hundred in total over the first two decades of the IFYE.[26] Moreover, the majority of Latin American 4-H club members did not have the means for, or an interest in, traveling to the United States. Although most Latin American youth could not come to the rural United States, a private development agency, the PIJR, hoped to bring the rural United States to Latin America through 4-H clubs. Between 1960 and 1975, the PIJR knit together a diverse array of interests—American capitalists and corporations, Latin American modernizers, the U.S. federal government, and millions of Latin American rural youth—all in the service of its vision of development "from within." The PIJR's vision and its alliance of interests hinged on the "pliability" of Latin American youth. "Our efforts should be dedicated to youngsters . . . who easily assimilate the training and innovations and who do not have to break through the barriers of tradition," explained former Ecuadoran president Galo Plaza to a meeting of Ecuador's National 4-F Foundation. "This is the essence of the 4-F Club Program: education and training for future farmers and housewives."[27] While Plaza naturalized the flexibility of youth, the PIJR used youth's pliability to coordinate between the radical economic, technological, and gendered transformations that constituted development politics.

Howard Law, an American international development technician working in Venezuela, identified the paucity of support for youth club work as a major obstacle for successful rural development throughout Latin America. Law, a former rural credit supervisor in the New Deal USDA, spent most of the 1950s directing the Consejo de Bienestar Rural, a Venezuelan rural development agency financed by Nelson Rockefeller's American International Association (AIA).[28] In Venezuela, the ministry of agriculture had, since the late 1930s, been running agricultural youth clubs called 5-V clubs, modeled after American 4-H clubs. FTD graduates expanded the program in the 1950s, but budget problems and a lack of attention to rural development in general had stymied Venezuelan club work.[29] Through his related rural development work, Law became increasingly familiar with 5-V and convinced of its potential. Echoing Wilson's conception of youth as agents of a development "from within," Law wrote that young Venezuelans involved in 4-V clubs carried "new ideas into the home—a transmission that is often possible in no other way."[30] However, he worried that 5-V's overreliance on government agencies limited its growth and departed too substantially from American 4-H's tested model of public-private hybridity. With ample private corporate and philanthropic support, Law maintained that 5-V clubs could more successfully train "the individual in modern agricultural practices, in homemaking, in the fundamental credit and sound business practices and, perhaps most heartening of all, in the orderly democratic process of solving group problems."[31] To that end, he lobbied the AIA for funds to establish an independent National 5-V Foundation, which would gather financial support from the domestic and international business community, including "General Motors, Ford, several tractor companies, General Electric, Westinghouse, Sears, fertilizer companies, oil companies, tire companies and many others."[32]

With Rockefeller support, Law scaled upward from Venezuela. In 1960, he received funding from the AIA and office space at the Inter-American Institute of Agricultural Sciences (IICA) to create an umbrella organization for Latin American 4-H clubs, the PIJR.[33] Based in the Costa Rican offices of the institute, the PIJR soon opened additional regional offices in Brazil and Venezuela, run by extension specialists Santiago "Jimmy" Apodaca and Edgar Matta. From those offices, the PIJR sought to knit the inchoate and underfunded Latin American rural youth clubs into an efficient, well-funded, transnational movement through a series of initiatives. In each nation, the PIJR gathered supporters for a private foundation that could raise funds and supplement the activities of the ministries of agriculture. The PIJR also ran training workshops for extension staff and volunteer youth club leaders and organized international 4-H competitions, conferences, and exchanges designed to award outstanding club work and to garner positive attention for member organizations. With the PIJR's support, 4-H in South and Central America grew from fewer than fifty thousand members in 1960 to more than 410,000 by 1974.[34]

Law served as the director of the PIJR until 1970, when he handed the reins to Theodore Hutchcroft. Hutchcroft was born in Iowa in 1931 and, after two years in army intelligence, worked in succession for the Iowa Farm Bureau Federation, the USDA, and as information director for the National 4-H Foundation.[35] In its leadership and programming template, the PIJR operationalized a perceived common pliability of rural youth through arrangements between agribusiness, state-run extension agencies, U.S. federal agencies, and agricultural scientists. In other words, the PIJR promoted a particular brand of grassroots development that connected rural youth to international sources of capital and technology.

The PIJR's method bypassed resistant rural adults as well as fickle ministries of agriculture. Law explained how this process worked in practice, by describing an experimental 4-H program in rural Uruguay. Extension specialists affiliated with the PIJR and the IICA selected a small "pilot zone" south of Montevideo where the "soil was fair to poor" and "the people had a reputation of resisting change." The extension specialists then assumed control of an existing but dysfunctional youth club in the community, Movimiento de la Juventud Agraria. They retained the teachers who led it but gave them special training in "democratic" leadership that would "guide them away from being autocratic." In addition, they organized a hybrid corn contest and provided club members with access to hybrid seed and fertilizer. The winning contestants produced an astounding yield of over 5,000 kilograms per hectare. "This had its effect on the farmers," explained Law. "It was . . . the 'softening up' of the resistance, the entrance to the farmers. . . . The youth with the highest yield had parents that were completely against the use of hybrid seed. His success convinced them to his side." In addition to introducing hybrid corn to the region, the project also had a salutary effect on the community's politics, according to Law. Rather than blaming industrialists, landowners, and middlemen for their poverty, "the farmers and homemakers have already begun to take responsibility for solving their own problems." Indeed, Law continued, "from inside the home (of the youth of the family in club work) it has been possible to overcome prejudices that the agent couldn't combat directly."[36] Success could be measured as much through shifts in political sentiments as it could through enhanced crop yields.

Law's reference to "the farmers and homemakers" pointed out how Latin American 4-H clubs aimed to develop rural society through the gendered labor of their members. Boys were encouraged to enroll in corn and livestock projects. Girls pursued various homemaking projects, including sewing and nutrition. If that gendered division had poorly fit the reality of rural life in the United States a half-century earlier, it was equally distant from the daily labor of many poor, rural Latin American women, who often contributed vital agricultural labor to rural households. Nevertheless, like their U.S. ante-cedents, Latin American 4-H clubs served as instruments of gendered reform that targeted a rural family unit composed of a farmer father, a homemak-ing mother, and children developing toward these gendered polarities. For example, one Colombian extension worker, Beatris Vargera, described how she tried to replicate the gendered arrangements she had witnessed in the rural United States as an IYFE participant among poor subsistence farmers outside Bogotá. She was intent on trying "to teach women how to use better methods in the kitchen." To that end, she organized youth clubs for girls and young women through which she demonstrated modern homemaking tech-niques, feminine hygiene, and proper nutrition.[37]

As with the Japanese ATPs, gendered labor reforms were aimed at a broader transformation of extant dysfunctional rural families and, through them, dysfunctional rural societies. Vargera reported that, thanks to her homemaking innovations, the "Indian women" of the community had to spend less time on domestic drudgery and therefore had more time for nurturing. "I have more time to take care of my husband and children," she reported one woman as saying. "My husband is no longer stubborn and always griping as I have more time to make him happy." Of course, happy husbands were sometimes a long-term, rather than immediate, product of the work. As a part of feminine hygiene, Vargera taught the girls and young women about "the birds and the bees" as well as when women should "keep the hus-band away" to avoid pregnancy. This, in turn, had caused "a few family fights because the wife is refusing the husband . . . and because he is frustrated . . . he hits the wife and she the children." This resulting strife was grounds for more education—education for the husband about proper "family relations." The image of family life that emerged from Vargera's efforts suggested that the Colombian family unit needed gendered labor reform—women needed to be better nurturers and men better providers—as well as access to the expertise of family relations specialists who could assuage and mediate the conflicts wrought of that reform. Club work, as part of that program, could also medi-ate conflicts between, as well as within, families. Vargera announced that a vital goal of her homemaking program was "to bring the rich and poor closer together and to have the rich cooperate in relieving some of the problems of the poor." This did not mean economic redistribution, however. Paralleling her approach to domestic violence, class conflicts were best eased through education. Epitomizing this approach, Vargera boasted that she had per-suaded a previously unsympathetic rich woman in the community to lead a club on art and music for the poorest children of the community.[38] In this rendering, the gendered terms of rural modernity that 4-H programs articulated had the potential to cross-cut divides of race, class, and even indigeneity.

Like Vargera, PIJR technicians believed that Latin American 4-H provided a generational solution to political radicalism by offering rural youth with community solidarity, happy family life, and rural leadership. Law described the clubs as being "free from political overtones," but the ambition to produce robust "rural citizenship" implicitly criticized revolutionary programs that threatened property rights and foreign investment.[39] The AIA maintained that political instability was a "strong deterrent" to economic growth and blamed the "history of political strife" in many Latin American countries for the absence of foreign and domestic investment.[40] Ironically, the same development technicians also ascribed poverty in rural communities to ignorance, complacent farming techniques, and a nebulous "resistance to change."[41] They suggested that the problems of Latin America were paradoxically rooted in both too much and too little stability. The dominant concepts of youth and adolescence also complicated this view. As Isaac Azofeifa of the University of Costa Rica explained in an article in *Extensión en las Americas*, a publication of the IICA, adolescence was characterized by "rebelliousness, defiance against adults and violent criticism of the adult world."[42] Left untended, adolescence could feed political instability; but it could be also be controlled and vented productively if youth were properly organized. The youth of Latin America needed an insurrection, announced IICA director general José Araujo, but "I am not speaking about insurrection expressed by the tragedy of drug consumption, dressing in rags and making a cult of laziness" or of "throwing stones instead of talking." Rather, "I am speaking about rebellion against the traditional values . . . a revolution of knowledge and of will power."[43] In this call to revolution, PIJR technicians found themselves confronted with the local particularities of youth cultures, even as they banked on a more general, transnational vision of flexible youth subjects.

PIJR technicians suggested that, when paired with the angry energy of adolescence, 4-H clubs offered international development agencies a middle way between political radicalism and stagnant agriculture. 4-H could be "a potential element in the pacific and democratic, but radical and accelerated change that is needed in Latin America," Araujo explained.[44] As Law also suggested, the cultivation of future rural "leaders and citizens" in 4-H clubs could solve a sweeping range of problems, from "poor health" to "primitive agricultural practices."[45] "Leaders and citizens," unlike radicals and revolutionaries, found ways to spur economic growth and solve community problems that were constructive—rather than destructive—and amenable to private property and commercial exchange. Similarly, Oscar Tord Romero, Hernan Jorge Ojeda, and Pajuelo Malleux Storck, leaders in Peru's 4-H affiliate, the CAJP, explained that peasants frequently believed that a "simple" land redistribution "is a form of social justice that can only be accomplished by a strong left-wing government" because of "incessant extremist propaganda." Club work, they maintained, would help rural youth to understand that agrarian reform "is not a process of violent transformation in which the landless become landholders overnight." Rather, agrarian reforms should be "scientifically analyzed and not the partisan ideas of particular political ideologies" and would, thus, require sacrifices and "a reasonable amount of time."[46] Scientific development discourses framed club work as apolitical; but in practice, club work wedded youth to antiradical and anticommunist reform schemes.

The PIJR's claim that Latin American 4-H created robust rural citizenship, then, existed within a broader political field in which prudent development required education, the passage of time, and nonviolence rather than immediate redistributive social justice or insurrection. Club literature created by the PIJR frequently asserted that citizenship was a fundamental goal of club work and argued that the uniquely deliberative, cooperative model of the clubs would enable members to be "useful to society and to perpetuate democracy." "Members of 4-S know how to live with others and they know their rights and the rights of others," stated an article in an IICA magazine. They "learn to behave properly within a group, to have intellectual discussions while respecting the opinions of others, to keep the rules and regulations of their groups, which makes lasting and successful societies."[47] Indeed, by encouraging small-group discussion and coordination, PIJR technicians claimed that they were providing valuable "democratic practice" that could be replicated when the youth were adults.[48] Law and the other PIJR technicians explicitly contrasted this approach to development with expensive brick-and-mortar infrastructure projects and claimed that only human investment could provide the citizens necessary for continued "economic and social improvement." "Great sums of money have been spent in capital outlay for 'things,'" complained a 1964 PIJR report. "Are we dedicating a proportionate share of investment capital in rural people?"[49]

Even if club members noticed the profound distance between the rhetoric of democratic citizenship and the violent repression of counterrevolutionary governments, the PIJR's model of development "from within" also aspired to create material incentives for youth's cooperation with capital. For this reason, the PIJR concentrated intently on expanding credit facilities for club members by building relationships with American corporations, banks, foundations, and development agencies. The PIJR solicited funds from various international sources but left the loans to be jointly administered by the national club foundations and the various extension services. Participating entities were a diverse lot but shared a commitment to U.S. hegemony and commercial agribusiness development. Major American banks, including the Bank of America and Chase Manhattan, offered loans, as did national banks and the Inter-American Development Bank. Large multinational corporations based in the United States, seeking new customers in Latin America, contributed funds: Sears, Eli Lilly, Purina, Esso, Ford, General Mills, and International Harvester all provided significant support. The charitable foundations of those corporations—the Sears Foundation, the Ford Foundation, and the Johnson Foundation—also contributed monies. Finally, the U.S. government channeled support through the United States Agency for International Development (USAID) after its creation in 1961, and indirectly through the thicket of development agencies that USAID subsidized. By the mid-1960s, the PIJR was also working with several national governments and the U.S. State Department to establish "4-H Peace Corps Projects" in Brazil, El Salvador, Uruguay, and Venezuela. 4-H Peace Corps projects placed U.S. nationals with experience in club work in rural Latin American communities, where they would organize and supervise youth credit projects funded by USAID and U.S.-based corporations.[50] Of course, these credit projects gave rural youth firsthand experience with agribusiness financial instruments. But by focusing on rural youth, such projects also created a terrain to connect a host of private and public international actors. Through 4-H, multiple, occasionally competing, agents of rural modernization entered the Latin American countryside, gathered around the bodies of participating youth, and cohered as development programs.

The PIJR drew its primary public support within Latin America from a number of prominent center-left politicians. Such nationalist social democrats occupied a precarious middle ground between the antidemocratic Right and the anticapitalist Left. This middle ground often entailed ambitious modernization programs, opened economies to foreign investment, and expanded social spending—all policies that were designed to alleviate the poverty that fed communist insurgencies while protecting property rights and capital investment. Figures such as Juscelino Kubitschek, Rómulo Betancourt, José Figueres, and Galo Plaza traded support with both the United States government and the same multinational corporations that invested in rural youth through the PIJR. This dynamic was especially evident in the growth of Brazilian 4-S clubs—*saber* (to know), *sentir* (to feel), *servir* (to serve), and *saúde* (health). 4-S clubs originated first in the Brazilian state of Minas Gerais in 1952 as a scheme of a rural credit organization funded by the AIA. When Minas Gerais governor Kubitschek ascended to the Brazilian presidency in 1956, he nationalized the credit organization, renamed it the Associação Brasileira de Crédito e Assistência Rural (ABCAR), and placed the now-national 4-S clubs under its control.[51] In December 1961, Kubitschek, then ex-president, accepted a position on the PIJR executive committee, along with Nelson Rockefeller; José Figueres, Associação president João Napoleão de Andrades; Betancourt's secretary of health and social assistance, Arnoldo Gabaldón; and the U.S. secretary of agriculture, Orville Freeman.[52]

Despite its broad array of political backers, PIJR development technicians held the in-country extension services and ministries of agriculture at a distance. Law and Hutchcroft consistently complained that Latin American extension services were too poorly funded and suffered from high rates of staff turnover. Decades of investment in an extension system, or decades spent currying favor with a particular bureaucrat, might be undone in a fortnight of political revolution. Rather than spending their energies on winning over bureaucrats and extension workers, PIJR technicians concentrated on developing independent support for club work through what they called "private support entities." Such entities, like the National 4-H Foundation in the United States, served as institutional intermediaries between the formal club organization run by national governments and the sources of domestic and international capital. Usually composed of prominent members of the business community, private support entities like the Patronato of Panama and the JUNACH of Chile, Hutchcroft explained, were "a balancing factor to some of the governmental instability" and sustained "continuity" in an era of "reorganization, restructuring and redistribution."[53] Even when political violence made the operation of the state-run extension systems impossible, or when counterrevolutionaries set their sights on gutting rural development programs that were contrary to the interests of large landholders, Law and Hutchcroft imagined that well-heeled businessmen could continue to direct resources to rural youth through such organizations.[54] 4-H opened onto a wide array of political actors but also offered a stable backbone for the PIJR. Built upon the supposed essence of youth, 4-H was a constant amid such dynamic political jockeying, and this combination of dynamism and stability was its core appeal.

Although PIJR technicians frequently averred that the weakness of many Latin American states necessitated the creation of private support entities,

they also tried to alter the structure of those states to fit their model of development. Development "from within" meant connecting rural youth to international sources of finance through private support entity intermediaries, but
the legal systems in many Latin American nations forbade precisely those
sorts of relationships. As Law noted, many nations needed special legislation
to permit the incorporation of tax-exempt private support entities. Such lobbying, in turn, recapitulated the same conflicts of interest that the USDA had
struggled to contain with the National Committee forty years earlier. The PIJR
recommended that the boards of the private support entities be drawn from
members of the business community, but this insistence rankled national
extension officials, who perceptively noted that such an arrangement might
mean ceding control of the club organizations to corporations, agencies, and
interests from abroad. Extension officials countered that they should have rep-
resentation in any entity that intended to guide a state-run rural youth organization. As a result, such lobbying was often slow going and met with regular
setbacks. Of the twenty-three national private support entities in existence
in 1974, nine operated without any legal sanction. Beyond lobbying to create
the legal infrastructure for such foundations, the PIJR found itself embroiled
in banking regulation reforms. For example, Costa Rica's national banking
system had stringent regulations that prohibited rural youth from obtaining loans. Hutchcroft explained that the Costa Rican Fundación Nacional
de Clubes 4-S had initially served as a supplemental finance system and provided credit to youth to whom the national bank would not loan. Then, with
the PIJR's assistance, the Fundación Nacional had "worked with the national
banking system to amend its regulations."[55]

    PIJR technicians rarely admitted that there were any trade-offs between
their vision of development and the autonomy of the nations that would be
developed. "PIJR must be two-faced in its programming," Hutchcroft confessed to his U.S.-based backers. "While on the one hand we must be meeting the needs of our clientele, on the other hand we must serve the interests
of the National 4-H Foundation (which itself serves the interests of the U.S.
extension service and the business community)."[56] Nevertheless, Hutchcroft
contended that the state ceding some control of youth organizations to private partners was a necessary step that "enrich[ed] the official rural youth
program beyond that possible with public funds alone." He argued that the
situation in Costa Rica was emblematic of this point. "The ready availability
of credit" guaranteed by the Fundación Nacional "attract[ed] young people
to 4-S" and "expand[ed] the effectiveness of the rural extension training"
far beyond what the state had previously accomplished. Just as important,

Hutchcroft continued, youth clubs provided "an important opportunity for a cooperative relationship between official and private-sectors that benefits all participants."[57] The PIJR maintained, despite the misgivings of extension officials, that public-private partnerships amplified the effectiveness of development schemes rather than impaired them. When framed in that way, the PIJR's programs were not merely designed to educate rural youth about the benefits of credit-financed, capital-intensive agriculture; they were also designed to educate developing states about the benefits of cooperation with foreign and domestic capital. Describing the situation in the region, Hutchcroft announced that there was no real precedent for the sort of public-private partnerships that the PIJR was forming. Rather, "PIJR can point-with-pride to the establishment of this idea throughout the hemisphere."[58]

The "pliability" of youth—youth's seemingly limitless potential to innovate, grow, and fashion new connections across the yawning chasms of culture and distance—remained the conceptual pivot upon which the PIJR and its allies turned. As Galo Plazo told the PIJR-organized 1974 Inter-American Rural Youth Conference, rural youth were still a "terrain . . . almost virgin," whose allegiances would dictate the future, good or ill, of Latin America.[59] Or, as Hutchcroft put it, without attention from planners, impressionable youth might just as well be "drawn to destructive activities." Curiously, Hutchcroft recognized that the characteristics of malleability and flexibility were features that the PIJR actually shared with rural youth. Thanks to its status as a "private agency, the PIJR ha[d] an informality due to a minimum of structure and tradition, giving it the opportunity to be flexible, for innovation, and individuality of action." It was, he conceded, "an unconventional institution; connective linkages may appear to be confusingly complex, almost to the point of being impossible." Those connective linkages were such strong threads that they could bind "widely divergent interests"—American corporations, the USDA, Brazilian technocrats, and Guatemalan youth—into a seamless network. A belief in the strategic "importance and value of the rural boys and girls of the Americas," Hutchcroft announced, mobilized this array of actors and joined them in common cause. Youth were not just potential embodiments of an imagined prosperous future for development technicians. They were also the durable thread that bound together their projects and the very terrain that made development at its multiple scales—biological, social, national, regional, and global—possible.[60]

Yet this approach also meant that the PIJR connected rural youth to actors for whom democracy meant little more than opposition to communism. In

July 1964, the PIJR, with the support of the National 4-H Foundation and the Puerto Rican Extension Service, invited 4-H representatives from all over Latin America to attend a conference on "the responsibilities of 4-H members in our democracy." Conference material reiterated the PIJR's conflation of democratic governance with transnational capitalist development models, promising to help participants further their "development as a citizen of a democracy" and to introduce them to Puerto Rican "leaders of . . . banking and commerce."[61] This vision of *buenos ciudadanos* cooperating with capital was, in fact, nearly identical to the way the Salvadoran president and his minister of agriculture celebrated the clubs at a Central American 4-H gathering in autumn 1963. Speaking to two thousand club members, leaders, and onlookers drawn from Guatemala, El Salvador, Panama, and Costa Rica, Colonel Julio Adalberto Rivera, the unelected figurehead of the Salvadoran military junta, hailed Salvadoran 4-C Clubs as a marvel of "private enterprise and government . . . pool[ing] forces." The Salvadoran minister of agriculture told the crowd that 4-C was led by men and women of "exemplary civic conscience" who were clearing an "ambitious but most necessary" path in rural Latin America and exposing rural youth to "a new slant on education, responsibility and cooperation."[62]

After the speeches, 4-H members took the lead and offered the spectators a series of demonstrations of everything that they had learned. President Rivera, exhibiting an uncanny sense for good publicity, called one club member—a particularly photogenic Guatemalan 4-S member—to demonstrate for him the correct way to inoculate a chick.[63] This moment exemplified the competing notions of citizenship that infused Latin American 4-H clubs. On the one hand, the gesture of reciprocity between the Salvadoran national father and the Guatemalan boy hinted at a Latin American citizenship defined by transnational, cross-class, and transgenerational cooperation—adults learning from youth and Salvadorans sharing the bounties of American agriculture with their Guatemalan neighbors. But that imagining of the future also placed the undemocratic present in stark contrast. The exchange between a poor rural youth and an unelected junta figurehead made clear that the envisioned democracy was a democracy of dreams and gestures of tomorrow, not of votes or redistribution today. The unnamed Guatemalan youth who instructed Rivera also had the opportunity as a 4-S member to parade through the streets of Guatemala City the following year in support of Enrique Peralta's government, newly installed by a military coup d'état.[64] In such moments, the true diversity of interests ensnared by the PIJR came into sharpest relief and exposed the fragility of the PIJR's vision of citizenship.

Figure 9. Salvadoran president Colonel Julio Adalberto Rivera receives
instructions on chicken inoculation from a Guatemalan 4-S member in 1963.
Courtesy of the Rockefeller Archive Center.

*   *   *

If the pliability of rural youth throughout Central and South America connected U.S. corporations and Latin American modernizers—as well as agricultural transformation and anticommunist politics—it assembled an even
more curious cast of players in Southeast Asia. Funded and organized by
the U.S. government and the Republic of Vietnam, between 1956 and 1975,
Vietnamese 4-T clubs worked to foment popular anticommunism and to
introduce agricultural technology and practices to the villages and hamlets
of rural Vietnam. Over those two decades, hundreds of thousands of Vietnamese boys and girls participated in 4-T clubs—growing rice, raising pigs,
sewing, and signaling their support for the South Vietnamese government
and its U.S. backers.

4-T was part of a much broader Vietnamese "modernization" program
embarked upon by American interests in the late 1950s. In 1956, the conflict

between the U.S.-backed Government of the Republic of Vietnam (GVN) in the South and the communist Democratic Republic of Vietnam in the North was still in its infancy. Only two years earlier, France had withdrawn from Vietnam, and the Geneva Accords had established the two independent Vietnamese zones. Formal American military presence was still limited to the U.S. embassy (United States Operations Mission, or USOM), which advised the ruthless, nationalistic Ngô Đình Diệm on how to solidify his rule, build the South Vietnamese state, deal with a flood of refugees, and forestall communist activities in the South. Between 1956 and 1960, USOM directed $1.5 billion to a "modernization" program supervised by a team of experts from Michigan State University. Historian James M. Carter describes this program as "economic aid, educational programs, technological initiatives, humanitarian relief aid, and innumerable cultural transmissions" that "involved the resources of the government, military, private corporations, and nongovernmental organizations."[65] Among those programs, USOM funded 4-T, an organization of youth clubs modeled directly after 4-H. 4-T's first leader, Buu Loan, trained at the FTD in 1955 and spent several months observing 4-H clubs around the United States. Then, in the joint employment of USOM and the GVN's extension service (VES), Loan built a rural youth organization designed to simultaneously produce economic prosperity and fealty to the national state.[66]

4-T launched with fanfare and official applause. In September 1956, several hundred 4-T members staged a rally to celebrate the youth movement's first year. Select club members met at the botanic gardens in Saigon on a Saturday morning and journeyed by bus to the campground near Bảo Lộc, two hundred kilometers northeast of the city. After registration, they enjoyed refreshments and a movie. On Sunday, Ngô Đình Diệm gave a short speech, and the national director of extension presented him with a gift as a token of thanks from the campers. The campers gave demonstrations to display all that they had learned. For the next four days, the rally continued in a similar vein: a flag ceremony and a pledge to dedicate their *trí*, *tâm* , *tay*, and *thân* (roughly translated as mind, heart, hand, and body) to the organization and nation; more speakers; a tour of a plant nursery; singing and square-dancing; demonstrations on how to build a rabbit hutch and a talk on "insects and parasites" by an entomologist; and, on the last night of camp, a talent show. The sum of these activities, wrote Loan, would expose rural youth to greater "methods for developing ideals and standards for farming, home making, family, and community life and national citizenship."[67]

Buu Loan replicated the same apolitical, "scientific" rhetoric that 4-H clubs in the Americas used, but the relationship of 4-T to the political trauma

Figure 10. Illustration from the 1956 4-T national rally pamphlet.

of Vietnamese nation-making was all too apparent in the camp's program. The director of the U.S. embassy to Vietnam and a representative of the South Vietnamese army both addressed the camp. On Tuesday night, the campers dined with the "Father in charge" of a nearby "resettled village" comprising some of the near half-million refugees fleeing from the North. And on that final night, those local "Tribesmen" and refugees saluted the youth by staging the talent show "in recognition of [the] achievement[s of] 4-T members." Such gestures placed rural youth at the symbolic center of the larger struggle for Vietnam's future. Through 4-T, the GVN, the U.S. operations mission, and Buu Loan all aspired to breed a Vietnamese strain of rural modernity: rural subjects who could symbolize the recently concocted nation of "South Vietnam" by heeding Western technocratic expertise, opposing communism, and laboring for the South Vietnamese state.[68]

For most of the first decade of its existence, the educational pretenses of the rally aside, USOM and the GVN used 4-T primarily for nationalist mobilization. Diệm's lieutenant and eventual GVN foreign minister, Tran

Chanh-thanh, praised 4-T as "a very successful way of fighting communism," but the value of the homemaking and agricultural education elements of the organization were suspect.[69] Operating a rural youth organization amid Vietnam's growing "political unrest and insecurity," as USAID put it, proved difficult: the VES had hardly any means to communicate with clubs in remote villages, and the clubs' leadership and older members were frequently drafted into military service. Thus, despite alleged "enthusiasm" and superficially impressive enrollments, many clubs had no leadership and no discernible strategy for how to direct the interest and labor of the youth momentarily in their thrall. As American USAID technicians confessed, the overwhelming majority of sixty thousand 4-T members in 1962 carried no projects and rarely, if ever, attended meetings.[70] In this sense, there was little distinction between 4-T and its much larger sibling, the similarly village-focused Republican Youth Movement. Both claimed to represent "enthusiastic" rural youth who were clamoring to volunteer for a pro-GVN youth movement.[71]

Unlike other components of the Diệm-era modernization program, which deteriorated or fell into disrepute with the increased militarization of the conflict in the 1960s, the value of 4-T increased over the decade. In autumn 1963, a cadre of military officers supported by the U.S. military assassinated Diệm, and the U.S. military began to assert greater control over the handling of both military counterinsurgency and general governance. At the same time, Vo Quang Tam replaced Buu Loan as head of the ministry of agriculture's rural youth section and declared that 4-T would count only youth who carried a project and regularly attended meetings. As a result of that change, official membership fell by 80 percent, to only twelve thousand members, but the remaining members engaged substantively with the educational components of the 4-T program. Indeed, as 4-T's USAID advisers put it, "little or no 'deadwood'" remained, and the youth organization was free to concentrate on practical development activities instead of mere nationalistic ritual.[72]

By 1966, the VES employed a total staff of 384, with the overwhelming majority conducting some fieldwork that involved 4-T.[73] In theory, VES staff took responsibility for "organizing 4-T clubs, training volunteer leaders, appointing district 4-T workers, supervising provincial 4-T program, obtaining technical assistance for subject matter for 4-T projects, and general supervision of the Rural Youth program." USAID and U.S. military technicians would offer advice, promote 4-T rallies, and, most critically, "procure essential commodities, training aids, promotional material, 4-T record books, subject matter leaflets, commodities such as cement, fertilizer, seed, cloth, sewing kits, pigs, chickens and rabbits."[74] U.S. experts intended this division of responsibilities to build grassroots support for the GVN. As one manual written "for Americans who are interested in helping the rural youth of Vietnam" explained, 4-T would attract the support of local hamlet chiefs because the clubs taught youth "to be loyal, respectful and to support [the chief's] office and [the] GVN" and discouraged "riots, demonstrations, idleness, and law breaking by rural youth." It was also paramount that "the Hamlet, Village, and District officials and most important of all, the local volunteer 4-T leader, should believe and know the local 4-T club is their very own and the club's welfare and future is entirely dependent on the people in the Hamlet." Offers of free commodities from "non-Vietnamese" actors poisoned this sense of local and indigenous ownership, and the manual strongly "discouraged" a "give away system" from the various U.S. agencies cooperating with the clubs. To be sure, capital and technology provided by USAID and the U.S. military—what the manual euphemistically referred to as "improved methods of farming and home making"—attracted local support and participation. But because U.S. officials also prioritized the cultivation of a local leadership loyal to the GVN, they emphasized that U.S. cooperators needed to be silent—or, at least, quiet—partners in the alliance.[75]

The increasing violence of the conflict, of course, rendered such goals hopelessly unrealistic. U.S. agricultural advisers complained that the Vietcong targeted effective VES agents for violence and harassment, and, without additional military support, successful extension projects were bound to be short-lived. Organizers struggled to maintain continuity in 4-T clubs because seasoned 4-T members and trained extension staff might be "arbitrarily draft[ed]" for military service and prevented from continuing work. Replacements "needed to be retrained" and "often [had] no relevant experience." Similarly, "the widows and orphans of military casualties" enjoyed priority in hiring for home improvement staff positions and crowded out "qualified" applicants.[76] More broadly, the GVN and VES, American officials complained, lacked the effective capacity to work with Vietnamese youth, a fact that actively corroded the pliable character of the young. At a 1967 meeting of a U.S. military Voluntary Civic Action Committee, Thomas Recknagel, chief of USOM's political section, argued that, due to "so much conflict and political confusion," Vietnamese youth exhibited distressing relativism—too much pliability—and did "not fully accept the legitimacy of the Government of Vietnam." This chaotic situation posed real dangers to U.S. efforts in Vietnam. Ray Van Cleef, the USAID youth affairs officer, noted that youth had been "instrumental in overthrowing Diem, Khanh, and Huong." But the

GVN's neglect of youth ensured that "apathy, discouragement, and the lack of an ethical and moral base characterize[d] the attitudes of most of Vietnamese youth." Similarly, Bill Ackerman, a USAID project officer, credited Vietnamese youth with "considerable spirit and vitality" but noted that the GVN's "reluctance to assist youth organizations" and "bureaucratic delays" left youth "disillusioned." In sum, just as in Latin America, the pliability of Vietnamese youth was a volatile but valuable resource, if only it could be correctly developed.[77]

The GVN's "weakness" and the perceived increasing strategic value of Vietnamese youth dictated that USAID and U.S. military officials frequently exercised de facto supervision of 4-T organizers through the Civil Operations and Revolutionary Development Support (CORDS) program. Accompanying the "Americanization" of combat forces in the mid-1960s, U.S. military strategists such as Robert W. Komer argued that, to effectively undercut popular sympathy for the Vietcong, military operations needed to be better integrated with civilian governance and nation-building programs. Initiated in 1966, CORDS dedicated military resources and logistical support to civilian modernization projects and various governance initiatives, thus reframing counterinsurgency and previous "pacification" efforts as "revolutionary" economic and civil-society "development" projects. By design, CORDS would economically integrate rural and urban Vietnam through a program that operated through military rather than GVN infrastructures, even as increasing stability and prosperity would build popular support for the American-backed regime. CORDS's five thousand civilian and military operatives dispersed funds, credit, and commodities in rural hamlets, as U.S. military forces tried to guarantee the security of rural economic development projects. Nevertheless, as historian Michael Latham writes, "if CORDS was 'revolutionary,' it promoted a revolution from above. Rather than empowering peasants or promoting local autonomy, it sought to tie remote villages into a firm hierarchical structure enforced by the military and anchored in Saigon."[78]

Along these lines, CORDS authorized "assistance in kind" (AIK) pacification funds to be used on 4-T. CORDS officers wielded wide discretion in the use of AIK funds, which operated, loosely, as a kind of counterinsurgency slush fund to pay for bounties for captured weapons and intelligence on Vietcong activities. But CORDS also used AIK funds to purchase commodities for 4-T clubs and even to pay salaries for 4-T agents and leaders.[79] In Kien Tuong, a province in the Mekong Delta along the Cambodian border with substantial Vietcong activity, a 4-T staffing concern illustrated the operational priorities that this kind of funding dynamic created. In June 1969, CORDS's officer Richard White terminated the employment of Pham Thi Thuy, Thai Thi Nam, and Truong Thi Phang, three 4-T home economics agents in Kien Binh district, and ordered them to surrender their CORDS-issued bicycles. By September, the provincial 4-T home improvement supervisor, Mai Thi My Nhung, requested that CORDS rehire for the positions. She suggested that new hires receive English training, since it would "help the [agent] fell [*sic*] closer to CORDS rather than to Agriculture Service so that it will be easier to carry out program under our wants and also easier for controlling their activities." William Faulkner, the provincial CORDS supervisor, agreed with Nhung that English proficiency was desirable for the hires but that training would "take too long"; he urged Nhung to find a worker with English qualifications. Nevertheless, Nhung's request revealed that, contrary to 4-T's official narrative, CORDS operatives quietly tried to wrest 4-T from the VES's ineffectual grasp and impose their own control over the organization.[80]

CORDS modernization schemes that were run through 4-T spanned the kinds of rural credit facilities championed by the PIJR and, in addition, a wide variety of projects promoting experimental commodities. USAID's then-adviser to 4-T, John Noland, boasted in 1970 that the clubs had assisted the introduction of a variety of new agricultural products to Vietnam, including Tamworth-Yorkshire hogs, sugar baby watermelons, granex onions, and IR-8 rice.[81] IR-8 "miracle" rice was an experimental rice breed originally developed by scientists at the International Rice Research Institute in the Philippines, an institute funded by the Ford and Rockefeller Foundations. By the late 1960s, the U.S. military had begun to introduce the high-yielding dwarf grain in rural Vietnam. To sustain its miraculous yields, IR-8 required inputs of fertilizer and pesticides, and pacification strategists reasoned that creating demand for those inputs would, in turn, knit rural populations into the national market economy.[82] 4-T fit seamlessly into this larger pacification strategy. USAID and CORDS distributed IR-8 "kits" with seed, fertilizer, pesticides, and instructions to 4-T members. A 1969 USAID report bragged that 4-T members in Phong Dinh Province averaged yields of six tons of rice per hectare and that one member had even "realized 10 metric tons per hectare. . . . Several 4-T youths in Phong Dinh Province have made sufficient profit in selling their agricultural products to enable them to purchase their own land under the current GVN Land Distribution Program."[83] By 1970, more than 1,100 4-T members were farming seventy hectares of rice through 4-T rice projects.[84] In addition, CORDS-financed rice institutes, like the Plain of Reeds Agricultural Development Center at Hoc Hoa in Kien Tuong Province and the National Rice Production Training

Center at Hiep Hoa in Bien Hoa Province, trained 4-T leaders and members in IR-8 cultivation.[85]

Mirroring the approach taken in the United States and Latin America, 4-T created parallel programs for rural girls that would focus on gendered reform. In 1969, about a quarter of the 4-T's twenty thousand members were female and carried various agricultural projects. In addition, a parallel organization operated by the VES's home economics specialists, known as 4-T Home Improvement, enrolled about eight thousand girls and focused on the "homemaking" labor of rural women and girls.[86] Mai Thi Nhung, for example, described 4-T's Home Improvement work as directed at an idealized "family composed of father, mother and kids" in which "only the father will make living for the family." 4-T Home Improvement work made other family members "productive" and efficient in their domestic labor. Nhung's description reflected the broader goal of 4-T to reform rural family life along the lines of the farmer/homemaker ideal but also was designed to discourage polygamy in rural areas. The Diệm government had outlawed polygamy in 1959, and, since many of the home economists were drawn from the Christianized colonial elite, they perceived polygamy as a serious obstacle to rural progress. The imperative to remove it, however, created tension within the broader 4-T program. 4-T's male leader, Vo Quang Tam, had several wives, a fact that irritated Nguyen Ngoc Anh, the VES's chief home economics extension leader. She contended that a practicing polygamist should not lead rural girls and, on that basis, successfully lobbied the minister of agriculture to have the boys' and girls' programs separated. Noland disapproved of the separation, as did Mel Thompson, the National 4-H Foundation technician who coordinated the foundation's support for 4-T with USAID. Whatever his marital arrangement, Thompson wrote in a memo, Vo Quang Tam was "respected, and capable of handling the job."[87]

Vo Quang Tam and Nguyen Ngoc Anh never reconciled, but the national bifurcation of 4-T mattered less where USAID and CORDS operatives handled local coordination. Thus, 4-T and 4-T Home Improvement members participated together in a variety of health and citizenship initiatives. During National 4-T Health Week, USAID, CORDS, the VES, and cooperating health agencies arranged a broad-based health campaign through 4-T during which villagers "visit[ed] the X-ray mobile to be vaccinated, destroy mosquitoes, rats; [took anti-] polio pills; [and] clean[ed] up unsanitary places in the village. Clinics were held to examine teeth and eyes by medical teams under the sponsorship of the local 4-T Club." In addition, even amid wartime carnage, 4-T promised to train Vietnam's future "citizens" and improve community relations. For example, in Tam Ky Province, 4-T members built eighteen bamboo clubhouses that they offered to their communities for general use and to house village councils. More broadly, in 1969, during the inaugural 4-T Citizenship Week, the VES brought two 4-T delegates from each province to Saigon for "a week of training in citizenship." Noland reported: "This new activity was most successful in that each delegate learned to appreciate and understand the different function of the Vietnamese government and the part he plays as a leader of the junior citizens."[88] As with Latin American 4-H, the goal of "training" future leadership also provided opportunities for transnational cooperation. In 1967 and 1968, USAID sent the top 4-T agents to train in the United States for six months, and, in 1971, two 4-T members, Ho Thi Hien and So Chau Ba, traveled to the United States through IFYE.[89]

In 1967, a team of USDA youth work experts known as the Rural Youth Survey Team traveled to South Vietnam to review 4-T.[90] At a conference with representatives of the GVN in December 1967, the team recommended that the GVN expand rural youth programs and substantially increase its investment in extension-based programs like 4-T. The survey team suggested that the U.S. government should continue to be a major investor, "provid[ing] technical, advisory and financial assistance and support." 4-T clubs provided a vital link between rural youth and the central state and helped to materially develop the Vietnamese countryside through IR-8 cultivation. Despite being administered by the GVN and bankrolled by the United States, 4-T clubs should nevertheless disavow "political and secular involvements" so that the program could be "available to all citizens."[91] On this last point, the USDA's team recommended that 4-T maintain an apolitical edifice to hide the manifestly political objective of aligning rural Vietnamese youth with the GVN and its U.S. backers.

In the United States, speaking without representatives of the GVN, American policymakers made a similar case for strengthening 4-T's reputation as a homegrown movement without any connection to the United States. In September 1969, representatives from the White House, USDA, USAID, the State Department, the Society for International Development, and several other organizations convened at the National 4-H Foundation's Chevy Chase headquarters to discuss the GVN's youth programming and its relationship to the goal of international "development." Dana Reynolds, vice president of special operations for the Society for International Development, compiled a report based on notes from the two discussion sessions. The report identified youth as the "single most strategic group in Vietnam's future." If the GVN and the United States were to prevail, they would need to win the hearts and minds of

Vietnam's youth from its primary competition, the communist National Liberation Front (NLF). Current efforts, the report suggested, were insufficient. The NLF wisely recruited members by intensively cultivating youth leaders and obtaining mass participation through a "simple problem, or functional, approach." This approach identified basic "problems" of social equality and enrolled youth through action-oriented agendas like land and finance reform. This strategy enabled the NLF to delay the controversial and complicated task of ideological indoctrination until after Vietnamese youth were already practically invested in the communist agenda. 4-T took a similar approach, of course, eschewing ideological discussions in favor of practical projects that generated material results for rural communities. But 4-T was too small in comparison with the NLF and still inadequately funded. Among other recommendations, the report suggested that a "Southeast Asia 4-H Committee" be formed. Support from the U.S. government, philanthropic foundations, and interested corporations could then be amply provided without "any suggestion of U.S. domination" and without damaging the organization's image as Vietnamese youth working for the future of South Vietnam. To support the idea, the report cited the model of the PIJR.[92] Despite the vast distances and cultural difference that separated San Juan from Saigon, the 4-H network extracted its lessons and deployed them ever optimistically anew. Hope in the generative powers of youth sprang eternal.

*   *   *

The spiraling violence of the Vietnam War, the U.S. withdrawal from Vietnam beginning in 1973, and the fall of the GVN in 1975 all spelled doom for 4-T. Despite the enthusiasm of the Rural Youth Survey Team and USAID, the war's escalation and the "Vietnamization" of the military conflict left 4-T in shambles. Absent a sustained American military presence, the dreams of assembling South Vietnam's future through the bodies of rural youth quickly dissipated. At the end of 1971, the National 4-H Foundation announced that it would not continue to sponsor Vietnamese IFYE participants. "Certainly, we are not sending any U.S. delegates over," wrote John Martin, the National 4-H Foundation's Vietnam program liaison. "Frankly, this is one program we let ride until things are bit more settled."[93] Martin and his colleagues at the National 4-H Foundation would have to wait indefinitely, but the voices of 4-T members occasionally echoed through the foundation's archives. In 1981, Mel Thompson, still working for the National 4-H Foundation, received a letter from Ho Thi Hien, who had traveled to the United States in 1971 as one of the last two Vietnamese IFYE participants. Living now in Ho Chi Minh City, Ho Thi Hien reported that she worked in a government seed-distribution office and was married with three children. Her salary was inadequate for her family, and now that her husband and mother were very ill, she faced total ruin. She implored her 4-H friends to send money and medicines. The connections between development technicians and rural youth—frayed and tortured though they were—lingered in testimony to the painful distances between development dreams and realities.[94]

4-T's last chance to breed a modern future for rural Vietnam perished with the GVN in April 1975 but managed to outlive the PIJR by several months. The PIJR, despite its status as a model of development to be emulated in Vietnam, dissolved at the beginning of 1975.[95] Unlike 4-T, which failed because of the defeat of the United States and its allies in Vietnam, the PIJR failed primarily because of the ascendancy of the United States' allies in Latin America. Due to a series of U.S.-backed military coups d'état in Latin America in the late 1960s and early 1970s, many Latin American polities endured increasing political polarization and violent counterrevolutionary political movements. The PIJR's plan to battle communism through development from within failed to inspire the interest of right-wing dictatorships in the same way that it had energized center-left modernizers. Although the military governments occasionally used 4-H organizations for symbolic purposes, most dictatorships were far more interested in jeeps and guns than in economic development schemes. Nor were the military dictatorships particularly interested in the kinds of credit programs that the PIJR had put at the center of those schemes. To the contrary: across Latin America, military dictatorships planned to control rural spaces by reinforcing the power of the largest landholders, not by addressing rural capital inequalities. Crucially, when Cuban support for left-wing guerillas proved less ample than hoped and military dictatorships systematically routed rural guerilla movements, both the Left and the Right turned their attention to urban insurgencies. Even in 1970, the PIJR's promise to quash rural communist insurgencies through youth-focused economic development rang anachronistic.[96]

PIJR technicians witnessed this polarization with alternating frustration and stoicism. "Should the extreme socialistic and nationalistic trend continue, the concepts encouraged by PIJR no longer may be acceptable, nor will a privately supported institution be welcome to operate," wrote Hutchcroft in 1971. "One of our guidelines must be to try to work within the political system whenever possible. At times this may be very frustrating and even appear to be poor politics, yet the development of effective rural youth programs goes beyond politics. We must not give up at the mere change of government. In fact, some of the more nationalistic systems may be more responsive to youth education than were their predecessors. Our responsibility in those cases is to try to guide these programs in a more acceptable direction over the long range."[97]

Yet such a balance was impossible to strike. As Hutchcroft noted in the same report, the PIJR's connections to the USDA and to the U.S. business community meant that cooperation with "some radical though rather logical elements of the Latin American scene might sever [the PIJR's] 'life line.'" Moreover, those "collective-type" movements actually interested in alleviating rural poverty would have little interest in the PIJR's procapitalist approach.[98] Thus, the PIJR could realistically work only with conservative elements that had no real interest in rural development and that wanted to use 4-H organizations only to shore up government support in rural areas.

This dynamic was most evident in the PIJR's relationship with the Brazilian 4-S clubs, which deteriorated following Brazil's 1965 military coup. In the early 1960s, Brazil's 4-S enjoyed the largest enrollments and best funding of any club organization in South America, and the PIJR frequently boasted about 4-S's contributions to Brazilian rural development. The military government, however, took "great efforts to restructure its 4-S program in a more 'nationalized' image . . . not wanting to merely accept hand-me-downs from the U.S.," Hutchcroft explained.[99] In practice, this meant that, though 4-S enrollments continued to grow, the clubs did little more than circulate propaganda—or "mass mail and no follow-up," as Ted Williams of the National 4-H Foundation put it—that reflected the military government's conservative Catholicism, a change reflected in the clubs' new motto, "TO KNOW to better FEEL; HEALTH to better SERVE—GOD, country, family, community and my 4-S club."[100] The autocratic demeanor of 4-S's new leadership made cooperation with the PIJR and other Latin American 4-H organizations difficult. For example, Williams attended a disastrous 1973 international PIJR leadership conference in São Paulo and complained bitterly about the ruinous "defensiveness," "self-aggrandizement," and "dominat[ing]" behavior of the large cadre of Brazilian leaders in attendance. "The Brazilians completely dominated the discussions and the participants from the other 11 nations for whatever reasons chose to withdraw and make no statements," he reported.[101]

Worse, the PIJR's U.S.-based supporters began to lose interest as well. In 1968, Nelson Rockefeller shuttered the AIA, transferred administration of the PIJR to the National 4-H Foundation, and began to phase out financial support. Hutchcroft managed to win a four-year grant from the Kellogg

Foundation in 1970 that replaced the lost funding, but the terms of the grant took the PIJR into new terrain for which it was not particularly well prepared. While the organization had previously focused on expanding rural credit facilities, the Kellogg grant was targeted at alleviating malnourishment in Latin America. The PIJR rapidly expanded a variety of food-production projects and endeavored to make technical education more central to its programs but found most of the national club organizations too understaffed to execute the programs. By 1974, the final year of the grant, Latin American 4-H organizations enrolled more than 400,000 members annually, but Hutchcroft candidly admitted that the national extension services were overburdened and ill equipped to handle so many members.[102]

By the early 1970s, Hutchcroft and the PIJR were facing a sea change in both public and elite American attitudes toward economic development abroad. Disgruntled by the debacle of the war in Vietnam and facing a recession in 1973, the American public soured on any program that had even the faintest whiff of foreign adventurism. The catastrophic costs of Vietnam had also discredited modernization theory across the political spectrum of American intellectuals. On the right, neoconservatives chastised modernization theory's "utopian" pretenses and pushed for American foreign policy to focus on market reforms, structural adjustment, and the vigorous paring of the "welfare state." The Left, by contrast, gravitated toward "dependency theory" critiques that held that development programs like the PIJR tended to create relationships of economic dependency that further impoverished laborers in the global South. Crucially, the Nixon, Ford, and Carter administrations all pursued a policy of détente with the Soviet Union that shifted some funding from development spending in the global South to direct aid to the Soviet Union and its satellites. The foreign policy establishment doubled down on its support for military dictatorships in Latin America, reasoning that robust police states coupled with probusiness economic policies would forestall communist insurgencies more effectively than wave after wave of development projects.[103]

In aggregate, this climate proved poisonous for the PIJR and U.S. support for Latin American 4-H. In 1974, Hutchcroft failed to renew the Kellogg grant and to find a suitable grant to replace it. The National 4-H Foundation had no interest in carrying the PIJR through its financial difficulties, choosing instead to renovate its Chevy Chase headquarters, maintain the IFYE, and expand the ATPs. Witnessing the PIJR's rapidly deteriorating financial conditions, the organization's remaining Latin American supporters, with the National 4-H Foundation's consent, arranged to have an IICA body known as the Consejo Asesor Interamericano para la Juventud Rural (Inter-American Rural Youth Advisory Council, or CAIJR) assume the PIJR's transnational organizing responsibilities, but the national organizations were left to fend for themselves.[104] In the meantime, the National 4-H Foundation closed the PIJR's San José office at the end of 1974 and terminated the organization as a whole at the beginning of 1975. The CAIJR proved no more capable of raising funds than the PIJR and, because it was financed primarily by voluntary dues from participating national organizations, fared much worse. In 1977, "due to the lack of follow-up and organization," only Haiti and Costa Rica paid their dues, and the CAIJR ground to a halt.[105] By 1980, most of the 4-H-type organizations of Latin America had ceased operation altogether.[106]

Although 4-H-type organizations persisted in many places beyond the Americas and Vietnam—most notably, in Korea, Japan, the Philippines, Kenya, and Botswana—the 1970s were a difficult period for 4-H's internationalizing ambitions. Of all the Cold War–era programs that used 4-H networks to develop the populations, economies, and polities of countrysides around the world, ATPs fared the best. Yet in the case of the Japanese ATP, the success of the program was rooted in the already existing similarities between Japan and the United States. Although the National 4-H Foundation deployed the language of development to justify the program, Japanese rural youth already enjoyed relatively easy access to modern agricultural technology and ample credit in one of the most affluent and stable industrial democracies of the postwar world. In fact, many of the youth who enrolled in the Japanese ATP joined to become more familiar with American customs and to improve their English language skills, not to absorb the lessons that masterful American farmers might deign to offer them.

These divergent understandings of the benefits of the ATPs were all too evident in how ATP participants reacted to their experiences. Rather than celebrating the lessons learned from their labors on American farms, Japanese youth often expressed skepticism about whether American agricultural models were suited for Japan. American farmers, they complained, worked long hours and used machinery "not properly adaptable to Japan." The Japanese youth found that the lauded American family model gave farmwives too much power and encouraged children to be disobedient and disrespectful to their elders. In addition, a study commissioned by the National 4-H Foundation found that 90 percent of the ATP participants would have liked more language training and that an astounding 100 percent of ATP participants were dissatisfied with their level of exposure to the "American way of life." Indeed, this dissatisfaction may well have been rooted in the fact that the participants were sometimes treated by their sponsors as hired hands and no more. A common complaint exposed by the study was that sponsors had often left ATP participants to work on the farm while their host families went to church. Such a complaint presupposed that the youth in question had been included in a "family" in the first place. A group of participants assigned to a "corporation type citrus farm in Arizona" found that almost all the people they interacted with were Mexican. "They searched for American friends through bowling and church, but did not find them," the study lamented. "The Mexicans were friendly but were not helpful to learn American culture."[107] Even if the Japanese youth could not recognize it as such, their interactions with Mexican laborers offered a brief glimpse of the realities of American farming concealed by the ossified myths of family farms circulated by the National 4-H Foundation and its allies in the international development complex. Beyond the vague promises of gendered order and rural prosperity wrought of American family farms transplanted in Japanese soil lurked the stark truth of 4-H's real harvest: dispossessed workers selling their labor to large capital-intensive, heavily mechanized farms. This was, in earnest, a very American way of life and certainly the most honest vision of the future of agriculture and rural America.

Still, some ATP participants learned this lesson well, and dramatic rewards awaited them in Japan. A 1972 publication recorded the accomplishments of returning ATP trainees. In each case, the vital lessons learned were uniformly about scale, specialization, and mechanization. Shibuyo Kazuo of Gunma prefecture took the lessons he had learned on a Nebraska livestock farm and developed a plan to produce a thousand fattened hogs every six months, their feces to be stored in an open-air reservoir near his newly constructed "fattening sheds." Miyake Yoshiharu of Ehime prefecture aimed to raise 100,000 chickens, and Hoshii Eiji hoped to become the largest carnation grower in Japan, thanks to the familiarity with greenhouses he had obtained on a farm in Washington State. Ozeki Sumio of Shizuoka explained that his ATP experience had encouraged him to rid his family's operation of rice, tea, tangerine, and vegetable production and to focus exclusively on broiler chicken production. He had begun to build new poultry houses, and by the time they were completed, his annual shipments would amount to 200,000 birds.[108]

Some trainees derived benefits from the ATPs that the program's architects never could have imagined and only incompletely recorded. A series of unexpected missives in the National 4-H Foundation's Korean ATP files provide a particularly suggestive example. On October 31, 1971, a young Korean ATP trainee, Young Sup Shin, failed to appear at the National 4-H

Foundation's Chevy Chase headquarters to complete his "final consultation" before returning to Korea. Mel Thompson contacted Shin's host families in Maryland and Ohio, but no one had seen or heard from the young
man. Concerned that an accident or a crime had transpired, Thompson contacted the Bureau of Missing Persons.[109] A few days later, through the Korean
embassy, Thompson received word that Shin was safe and sound; a few days
after that, he received an apologetic letter from a deeply conflicted Shin. His
stay in America had brought both "sorrow" and "pleasure," but he did not
want to return to Korea to operate a farm, as the National 4-H Foundation
had clearly intended for him to do. Instead, he planned to stay in the United
States, marry a young woman, and study computer science. In fact, his refusal
of 4-H's narrow reproductive ambitions was a fait accompli: he was writing
from his honeymoon.[110]

Shin's actions resolutely refused to conform to the narratives of exchange
and flow between north and south, developed and developing, that framed
international 4-H programs. The Korean ATP, like the Japanese ATP, was premised on the notion that trainees could become the vessels of modernization
for Korean agriculture. Exposed to the gendered order and mechanized pre-
cision of American farms, they would build families and farms in the Korean
countryside that transplanted American rural modernity in foreign soil. But
Shin imagined—and then created—a very different future for himself: one
that resisted each element of that narrative. He had no desire to return to
Korea. He did not want to be a farmer. And his new wife and family would be
in the United States, not Korea. He recognized the role that the National 4-H
Foundation had designated him to play, and he declined it. Their imagined
future was not a future he desired or one that he would labor to create.

*   *   *

During the global Cold War, the USDA, the American military, and affiliated development agencies created 4-H organizations around the world. As
these organizations, agencies, and youth became interwoven, international
4-H became a lattice of development—an infrastructure upon which modern economies and polities could grow. Through this infrastructure, development lessons migrated from the American countryside to Latin America and
the Caribbean, from the Costa Rican offices of the PIJR to the Saigon offices
of the VES, and from Colombian villages to Mekong Delta hamlets. Each
encounter between development technicians and the objects of development

generated new information and called for a reconsideration of strategies and tactics—a recalibration of development "from within." But just as the focus on the developmental potential of youth had ordered the "diverse array of interests" captured by the PIJR, the same vision of the pliability and limitless generative possibilities of youth constructed this still-grander global edifice. To be sure, the lattice was not as stable as its architects believed, or even as stable as they had hoped it would be. The lattice was fragmented and partial, and overgrown vines covered the gaps beneath. But to its planners, the infrastructure of youth still offered limitless possibilities for development in rural Vietnam, Latin America, and all the rural spaces between.

What did these places share? Beyond the United States' interest and attention amid the global Cold War, they shared youth and thus the ostensible means to erase culture, difference, and distance. Development technicians took the biological fact of youth—the certain knowledge that humans, the world over, aged from infancy to adulthood—and constructed a broader narrative of social and economic development around that fact. Within development discourses, youth functioned simultaneously as a stabilizing factor and as a generative possibility. On the one hand, the biological fact of youth permitted development technicians to aggregate diverse and culturally dissimilar populations under unified theories of development. Broad conceptual categories like "Latin American youth" or "third world youth" erased cultural differences, national boundaries, spatial distances, and geopolitical inequalities and, in their place, created a pliable, homogenous substance upon which development technicians could act. On the other hand, the model of development as an ongoing biological process—tempestuous but continuous—provided technicians with a way to think about development as a process of waiting for deferred, generational rewards. Within that model, development planning was a necessarily futurist act. Investments were predicated on the planner's imagined future—a future necessarily too distant to behold but never too distant to imagine.

More broadly, faith in the generative pliability of youth connected not only development practices in Vietnam to those in Central and South America; it also connected the work of early twentieth-century 4-H club organizers like Otwell, Warren, and Benson to development technicians like Noland, Law, and Hutchcroft a half-century later. The notion that the gendered bodies of youth provided the cultural key to an emergent "agricultural welfare state," as political scientist Adam Sheingate called it, was not without precedent. It was an established tenet that emerged not from the ether but from the USDA's domestic development projects of the first half of the twentieth century—a development project that, if judged by the level of cultural deference awarded to state-subsidized, capital-intensive commercial agriculture in postwar America, was a success. That such success was not remotely replicable hints at the fragility of youth, the hopelessly grandiose pretenses of the would-be modernizers, and, most acutely, the painful distances between a supposed science of agricultural development and development as it was practiced. Yet it is also a testament to the power of the agrarian futurist imaginary that 4-H continually captured the enthusiasm and investments of so many minor mandarins of the future.

Future Farmers of Afghanistan:
Agrarian Futurism at the Twilight of Empire

A sign tells me that I am eleven miles from a place called Romney when I begin to lose the radio station out of Indianapolis. I am on my way to meet Bob, a former high-ranking appointee in George W. Bush's USDA.[1] Bob has generously invited me to his northwestern Indiana farm to discuss the details of the U.S. Army's Agribusiness Development Teams (ADTs) and the youth clubs that those ADTs have been organizing in Afghanistan, known as "Future Farmers of Afghanistan." He was involved in agricultural development in Afghanistan until 2006. The ADTs are a somewhat more recent invention that Bob helped create only after he left the USDA. The ADTs act essentially as an Afghan extension service organized and partially staffed by the U.S. military. Each individual ADT is created as a National Guard unit and has an attachment of Guard members with agricultural backgrounds and training. The ADTs travel to rural Afghan communities and organize agricultural improvement projects, of which the Future Farmers of Afghanistan is one. Although their name riffs on American FFA, the clubs are something of a hybrid between a school-based and an extension-based model: they also draw from 4-H. As Bob's narrative suggests, the ADTs deploy 4-H's logic of generational transformation through youth outreach and call into question the visibility of the American state in even its most imperial moments.

I park behind Bob's farmhouse, flanked by a row of livestock sheds. The odor of hogs burdens the air, and a mechanical whine emits from the sheds. Bob comes out of the house and issues a firm handshake. A sturdy white man in his sixties with a thick silvery beard, he is friendly enough but also serious and somber. He escorts me to his home office, where, among books, papers, memorabilia, bird figurines, and photos of Bob with notable people, I sit on a couch. Bob sits in a chair richly upholstered in a flower print. I had come expecting to have a conversation narrowly focused on the ADTs and Future Farmers of Afghanistan. Instead, our talk sprawls over four hours and we cover a wide range of topics—from farming to development, and from political philosophy to military strategy. And we talk about 4-H, as Bob narrates his path from his Indiana farm to architect of the ADTs and, through them, the Future Farmers of Afghanistan.

Bob grew up on a poor farm in Indiana, so poor that he never wanted to be a farmer when he grew up. But to make ends meet during college, he got a job at a modern, highly productive operation and found that he enjoyed it. After college, he first rented and then bought a farm of his own—the very farm on which he still resided. "The weeds were so high you could only see the roof from the road," he reminisces. Through hard work and determination, he turned the broken-down farm into an economic success, even amid the farm crisis of the 1980s. He won a major award for farm leadership in 1982, which placed him on the radar of Republican leaders in Indiana and around the country. In 1989, he joined George H. W. Bush's Environmental Protection Agency, concentrating on environmental regulations in farming. He thrived in the job but opted not to stay in Washington as a lobbyist after Clinton was elected. He worked the farm through the nineties, and came back to Washington in 2001 with George W. Bush. He had only been on the job for two months when, in September 2001—in the aftermath of the attacks on the World Trade Center and the Pentagon—he was given responsibility for the USDA's food security systems. "They dropped a $300 million budget in my lap and I caught hell when I couldn't spend it all," he tells me.

Finding a way to systematically secure the food system was daunting. The American food system is extremely diffuse and interconnected, Bob explains, and once a toxin or bacteria has gained entry—accidentally or intentionally—it will disperse rapidly and uncontrollably. He made a "threat matrix" for the food system and discovered that the threats and the potential vulnerabilities of the system were far too numerous to be secured without cost-prohibitive or invasive measures. Instead of approaching the problem on American terrain, Bob reframed food security overseas: "We needed to do something there rather than here." He endeavored to bring the USDA "into the mix" when it came to America's military operation in Afghanistan. Rather than a war of "conquest" or "extraction," he said that the Bush administration was determined to develop a strategy of reconstruction and rebuilding. Given the centrality of agriculture to the Afghan economy, Bob immediately grasped the role that he wanted the USDA to play and even had a strong precedent in mind. "I went back in time. I asked, how did we

rebuild this country after the Depression?"—meaning the rural modernization programs of the CES and the land-grant colleges that "took scientific
knowledge" back "to the land."

Beginning in 2003, Bob traveled frequently to Afghanistan to tour the
countryside and speak with Afghan farmers. From farmers as well as the
ministry of agriculture, he learned that Afghanistan had enjoyed a sophisticated agricultural sector and an extension service until the Soviet invasion
in 1978. The farmers had sharp memories of pre-invasion agriculture—the
almond and pistachio groves—and they wanted to farm that way again. Bob
endeavored to rebuild the Afghan extension service and the school of agriculture at Kabul University, over the objections of USAID. He monetized a
PL-480 strategic soy reserve by selling it in southern Afghanistan (undercutting the expensive, heavily adulterated Pakistani oils that dominated the
market there). He then contributed $30 million from that "monetized soy" to
rebuild the schools of agriculture and veterinary science at Kabul University.
Still, effective "knowledge-producing institutions" in Kabul meant little to the
poor farmers in the rugged peripheries. As Bob sees it, the flaw of American
development initiatives in Afghanistan, like the Soviet ones before them, was
an absence of connectivity in terms of the physical infrastructure—modern
factories without power and roads to nowhere—and in terms of the complex
interpersonal relationships between economic actors, state agencies, and private citizens that undergird contemporary capitalism.

Emboldened by his success with Kabul University, Bob redoubled his
efforts to resurrect the Afghan extension service. His initial efforts were
quickly stymied by USAID, but his persistence began to pay off. In 2005, he
stepped down from the USDA but continued to advise the Afghan ministry
of agriculture and pushed American authorities to fund extension. That same
year, he coauthored a proposal with Obaidullah Ramin, the Afghan minister
of agriculture, that made a strong case for extension funding. "The adoption
of this program," the proposal explained, "realizes the great need to provide
highly visible 'government' mentors—commonly referred to as extension
agents—who will reside in rural Afghanistan, teaching and demonstrating
new skills for farming and even basic skills for living." Although the proposal conceded that rural Afghans could expect to receive similar technical assistance from the host of international development nongovernment
organizations, the extension agent system offered to "extend the reach . . . and
visibility of the central government" through a permanent "human capacity."
It was thus "educationally sound for long-term development" and "politically
sensible" for the Karzai government.[2]

The proposal emphasized "investing in youth." Of all Afghanistan's desperately needed investments, the proposal asserted, "none is more important or will bring more stability to the country than to focus on this next generation."[3] Bob said that the war had "severely interrupted" the "generational transfer of knowledge" that had historically sustained Afghan farmers.[4] With nearly half of all Afghans being under the age of sixteen, such a disruption meant that malleable youth might easily be drawn into the Taliban's influence. Youth extension was vitally important, if only to supplement and stabilize the "generational transfer of knowledge" that made peaceful rural life possible. This was particularly true in the context of post-occupation Afghan agriculture, where poppy production had rapidly overtaken all other forms of commercial agriculture. Most Afghan youth had only lived during a period when poppy was the exclusive cash crop, driven by a voracious international market and intense pressure from warlords as well as the Taliban. But more than just a way to stabilize social conditions for youth—and implicitly to buttress support for the Karzai government—Bob considers youth-focused extension a great "opportunity . . . to transfer rapidly new knowledge" about modern farming and to have that naturalized system of "commercial" agriculture become an organically perpetuating model of rural life that could be seamlessly "transferred from generation to generation."[5] "You plant the seed early on," he says, deploying a basic agrarian futurist trope. Extension planted the seed in youth; but once planted, the commercial model would grow, self-sustaining, and blossom of its own accord.

The proposal explicitly invoked 4-H as a model and potential partner for youth-focused extension programs. "4-H . . . has an international presence," according to the proposal, "and can provide project activities that include developing simple farming skills or technologies, exposure to small business management, practical vocational skills as well as leadership development." (Ironically, Bob and Ramin were unaware that the Afghan extension service had briefly organized 4-H clubs in the early 1970s, only to abandon the program for lack of interest.)[6] 4-H leaders would be "trained catalysts," and, through 4-H, "these trained facilitators will develop the next generation of leaders that understand a different Afghanistan and will be dedicated to making the country a place where pride and progress toward democracy is the centerpiece."[7] As with 4-H technicians in other contexts, this vision of a new generation of rural leaders imagined a strategic alliance between the Afghan government, farmers, agribusinesses, and the bodies of rural youth enrolled in 4-H clubs.

Bob and Ramin's arguments persuaded Hamid Karzai and Donald Rumsfeld to take the proposal to George W. Bush in 2005. Bush initially approved the project, but Bob claims that USAID's director, Andrew Natsios, managed to have the project silently scuttled, forcing Bob to bypass USAID and the State Department altogether.[8] The framework of counterinsurgency provided one particularly compelling means to do so. By arguing that an Afghan extension service would expand counterinsurgency capacities, Bob believed that he could run the project through the Department of Defense. In coming to this conclusion, he drew explicitly from the example of CORDS and other Vietnam-era programs that blurred the lines between economic development and military operations. With the help of Kit Bond, then-senator from Missouri, Bob was able to persuade the Department of Defense to create special U.S. Army National Guard Units that would act in lieu of an Afghan extension service. In 2007, the 935th Missouri Army National Guard Unit became the first such unit to deploy to Afghanistan.[9] By 2012, the U.S. Army had deployed similar units from nearly a dozen states, among them Iowa, Indiana, Kentucky, Texas, Arkansas, and California. The units were named ADTs. As Bob explains, "agribusiness" did not simply include farmers; agribusiness describes the long chain of actors who would, in the future that the ADTs would cultivate, connect Afghan farmers to consumers around the world, as well as to steady sources of capital, inputs, and agricultural technology.

The Indiana ADT, the 3-19th, focused part of its efforts on youth programs in Khost Province, a mountainous, primarily Pashtun, area that borders Pakistan. Before deploying, members of the 3-19th toured a variety of Indiana schools and farms, including Bob's, and solicited club project plans from Indiana FFA members. Once in Khost, the 3-19th educational officer, Jeremy Gulley, designed a youth-oriented development program called "Future Farmers of Afghanistan" in cooperation with a local university, Shaikh Zayed University, with which previous ADTs had also worked. The university agreed to train 120 high school teachers and thirteen extension agents to build and operate greenhouses and chicken coops, with the ADT providing support and supplies. After an intensive twelve-day seminar for teachers and agents, Shaikh Zayed University graduate students offered six weeks of on-site mentorship to students and teachers at the high schools where the "agricultural kits" had been installed. To assist that mentorship, Gulley relayed lesson plans prepared by Indiana agricultural education leaders and FFA members. After seven months of work, the Future Farmers of Afghanistan project trained 117 teachers and thirteen extension agents, who, in turn, enrolled more than five hundred, mostly male, high school students. Students from all six participating high schools had begun to sell produce in local markets, and the Future Farmers of Afghanistan had already generated $419 in sales.[10]

Gulley emphasized that a lack of human infrastructure posed the greatest challenge to Afghan development, and his project was therefore designed to avoid those perils: "We can't build our way out of Afghanistan. We have been building schools, building hospitals, building roads, and building facilities throughout the country. There's no doubt we have improved the lives of countless Afghans, but it has not brought stability. If we measure progress by 'clinics built,' 'roads paved,' 'dollars spent,' or 'enemy killed' we miss the most important metric in a war against insurgency; the connection between the government and its people."[11]

To generate those connections, Gulley hoped to use "Indiana's vast ag-education knowledge. . . . Anyone who has seen the impact that 4H and FFA has had on multiple generations of Hoosier youth can see the possibilities in this approach. Kids are kids no matter where they are from."[12] While Afghan FFA would be good for those kids, Gulley emphasized that the project would also be an instrument of counterinsurgency. "To use a military term," Gulley noted, "the civilian connections, relationship-building skills, and life experiences that ADT teams possess, can act as 'combat multipliers' that generate creative and adaptable possibilities on the ground. . . . [ADT teams] may create on-the-ground possibilities that can be exploited for tactical advantage within the counterinsurgency (COIN) strategy, while planting the seeds for a future that the average Afghan is willing to harvest."[13] In the case of Gulley's project, the "seeds of the future" were Afghan youth, and the harvest would be an Afghan countryside unanimous in its opposition to the Taliban and free of poppy production but still rich in other varieties of licit commercial agriculture.

Back in his office, Bob's visionary optimism about Afghanistan is offset with somber resignation when he discusses matters closer to home. He calls his approach to development "generational." Generational projects are those that require investment in youth today, fully cognizant of the fact that benefits will not be measurable for decades. Bob believes that nothing he did in Afghanistan generated results that he would see in his lifetime. In the meantime, despite his confidence in that distant Afghan future, he is deeply pessimistic about the U.S. present. He finds recent political trends deeply disturbing. "Can democracy as it was established stand the test of time?" he wonders. His worries about the health of American democracy are fed by what he considers America's global geopolitical decline and a looming resource crisis driven by competition from China and India.

Bob's adult son enters the room and interrupts the interview. I take the moment to catch my breath—we've been at it for almost three and a half hours by now—and listen to their brief conversation concerned not with development programs but with banal farm practicalities: they discuss a problem with the machine that generated the whine that I heard on my way into the house. Bob assures his son that he'll look at it later. After his son leaves, he tells me that they are experimenting with an engine that runs off of waste biomass—corn-husks, in fact. Bob's concern about resource scarcity is more than just talk; he is already preparing for the impending resource crisis of the future. In that moment, there is an uncanny juxtaposition: he has spent the better part of the last decade cultivating a generational project in an outpost of empire, a generational project that he believes, earnestly and confidently, will flower in distant decades in the form of a modern Afghan countryside. That vision of Afghanistan seems to be a necessary counterweight to Bob's heavy pessimism about American empire. As American empire fades into the twilight, he envisions a rich Afghan harvest. Youth lost; youth reborn.

A Clover Out of Place

I have chosen in this epilogue to focus on a program that places the familiar 4-H clover in a context that will seem radically unfamiliar to many readers. When I conducted my interview with Bob in the fall of 2011, the ADT program was in its infancy and only a tiny component of a larger project of Afghan state building and U.S. military counterinsurgency. The ADTs will surely not outlive America's rapidly diminishing military presence, much as 4-T could not survive the U.S. military withdrawal from South Vietnam. Gulley's and Bob's attention to cultivating this youth infrastructure responded to a logistical problem with which they grappled: when the (American) boots had departed, who would carry the torch for the Afghan extension service and, with it, their vision of a rich Afghan harvest?

The engineers of Future Farmers of Afghanistan, like other agrarian futurists before them, saw youth as a flexible, universally malleable medium suitable for generating connections among government institutions, civil society, and the factories, farms, and warehouses needed for profitable agriculture. To envision youth as a solution to connectivity in this context—as the material that binds disparate elements of a tribal, agrarian Afghan society into a modern, democratic whole—is to imagine youth as agribusiness. It also demonstrates that the demarcation of state and society is one fraught with historical contingency and open to decisive political negotiation. The heavy-handed American state—a state that interns, renditions, relocates, and sterilizes according to its monumentalist designs—has always coexisted with an American state that nudges, coaxes, subsidizes, educates, and seduces its subjects through its "weak" powers. U.S. military units organizing voluntary agricultural youth clubs in occupied Afghanistan are an ultimate testament to the coexistence of American states, both strong and weak.

That issue has lingered around 4-H throughout its history, just as it haunts discussions of the Future Farmers of Afghanistan. 4-H has always been a complex and shifting alliance of actors: it captured the interests of progressive reformers and educators before it captured the interest of the USDA. USDA participation attracted diverse capitalist interests but also opened the alliance to critiques animated by partisan and pecuniary interests and gendered responsibilities. With capital investment and USDA expertise, 4-H brought the actual bodies of millions of rural youth into the alliance and, through the cultivation of healthy, white rural bodies, advertised the USDA's biopolitical expertise. The gendered and racial contours of that expertise shaped and tested the terms of the alliance and initiated an ongoing negotiation of the line between state and civil, public and private. The demands of the wartime state, with its heightened need for bodily availability, again reshuffled the alliance.

The proposal for the Afghan extension service contends that programs like Future Farmers of Afghanistan make the state visible today so that its favored model of capitalist agriculture will be politically invisible tomorrow. This is Bob's generational project. The Afghan extension service will make visible in the periphery a state apparatus that is otherwise assumed to be distant and ineffectual. It will also mobilize voluntary actors and set in motion a model of economic self-regulation that will be "transferred from generation to generation." This transfer slowly shifts the line of demarcation between state and civil. It politically naturalizes a contingent political economy. It casts certain ways of relating to the state as organic and authentic, others as artificial and unnatural. Actors who might previously represent the designs of a distant, monolithic, and forbidding state come to merely express the collective moral commitments of the community. In this, the generational transfer that Bob envisions becomes a way of constituting a political amnesia as much as a way of generating final knowledge about the rigid and impermeable boundaries of the correctly constituted liberal state.

Future Farmers of Afghanistan—a clover out of place—can tell us much about clovers in more familiar environs where a similar amnesia already persists. When a rural Oklahoma county greets visitors with 4-H emblem and name, we should not dismiss it as a provincial affectation or nostalgia. That clover also testifies to the power and success of a pervasive invented tradition, engineered by the agrarian futurist alliance that this book describes, which is equally powerful in urban and rural imaginations. On left and right, from urban locavores to agribusiness executives, from agrarian philosophers and food sovereignty activists to secretaries of agriculture and food marketers, the very sorts of family farms that 4-H publicly popularized stand in for wholesome, healthy, and permanent agriculture. The fecund family farm is a model of envisioned rural permanence—permanent agriculture, permanent families, and a permanent landscape—with each ensuing generation of healthy farm kids reinvigorating the rural landscape anew. This agrarian futurist imaginary structures not only how we see rural America but also how Bob, Howard Law, and other promoters of international 4-H saw (and continue to see) the problems of a largely rural global South, where agricultural development is again posited as a curative for hunger, poverty, and political extremism.

This invented tradition of folk virtue, environmental permanence, gendered order, and healthy reproduction displaces a rich, if painful, history of dislocation, suffering, and impermanence wrought of the very same processes and often by the very same actors. Farmers have always been at both the cutting edge of North American settler colonialism and among its first victims. To tell the story of rural America is not to tell a story about permanence. It is often to tell a story about dislocation and loss. As America continues its imperial project—Bob's doubts about its sustainability notwithstanding—the political stakes of this misremembering continue to rise. When we look at the 4-H clover, we should be reminded of the alliances that it makes visible as well as those that it conceals—and the stakes of forgetting either.

NOTES

Introduction

1. Foucault defined biopolitics as a political strategy centered on the "the basic biological features of the human species" (*Security, Territory, Population,* 1) that "consists in making live and letting die" (*Society Must Be Defended,* 247). For Foucault's major writings on biopolitics, see Michel Foucault, *The History of Sexuality,* vol. 1: *An Introduction* (New York: Vintage, 1990); idem, *Society Must Be Defended: Lectures at the Collège de France, 1975–1976* (New York: Picador, 2003); idem, *Security, Territory, Population: Lectures at the Collège de France, 1977–1978* (New York: Picador, 2009); idem, *The Birth of Biopolitics: Lectures at the Collège de France, 1978–1979* (New York: Picador, 2010).

2. 4-H has been the subject of several articles, book chapters, and master's theses, though they have focused on particular components of the program. See Marilyn I. Holt, "From Better Babies to 4-H: A Look at Rural America, 1900–1930," *Prologue* 24 (1992): 252–253; idem, "I Wouldn't Leave the Farm, Girls," in *Linoleum, Better Babies and the Modern Farm Woman, 1890–1930* (Lincoln: University of Nebraska Press, 2005), 141–168; and, especially, Carmen V. Harris, "States' Rights, Federal Bureaucrats, and Segregated 4-H Camps in the United States, 1927–1969," *Journal of African American History* 93 (summer 2008): 362–388; Amrys O. Williams, "Head, Heart, Hands, and Health: 4-H, Ecology, and Conservation in Wisconsin, 1930–1950" (MA thesis, University of Wisconsin, 2007). Histories commissioned by the organization and written by nonacademic historians include Franklin Reck, *The 4-H Story: A History of 4-H Club Work* (Chicago: National Committee, 1951); Marilyn Wessel and Thomas R. Wessel, *4-H, An American Idea, 1900–1980: A History of 4-H* (Chevy Chase, MD: National 4-H Council, 1982); James William Clark, *Clover All Over: North Carolina 4-H in Action* (Raleigh, NC: NCSU, 4-H & Youth, 1984). 4-H is briefly referenced in a number of explorations of rural America and broader surveys of American culture. For illustrative recent examples, see R. Douglas Hurt, *American Agriculture: A Brief History* (West Lafayette, IN: Purdue University Press, 2002), 258–259; Lu Ann Jones, *Mama Learned Us to Work: Farm Women in the New South* (Chapel Hill: University of North Carolina Press, 2002), 109, 127, 181; Melissa Walker, *All We Knew Was to Farm: Rural Women in the Upcountry South, 1919–1941* (Baltimore: Johns Hopkins University Press, 2002), 140, 183; Deborah Fitzgerald, *Every Farm a Factory: The Industrial Ideal in American Agriculture* (New Haven, CT: Yale University Press, 2003), 53, 54; Katherine Benton-Cohen, *Borderline Americans: Racial Division and Labor War in the Arizona Borderlands* (Cambridge, MA: Harvard University Press, 2009), 247, 264–265; Miriam Forman-Brunell, *Babysitter: An American History* (New York: New York University Press, 2009), 168; David Ekbladh, *The Great American Mission: Modernization and the Construction of an American World Order* (Princeton, NJ: Princeton University Press, 2009), 177; Sally Gregory Kohlstedt, *Teaching Children Science:*

Hands-On Nature Study in North America, 1890–1930 (Chicago: University of Chicago Press, 2010), 215. For an examination of contemporary 4-H programs in global context, see Kiera Butler, *Raise: What 4-H Teaches Seven Million Kids and How Its Lessons Could Change Food and Farming Forever* (Berkeley: University of California Press, 2014).

3. By "cultural," I mean attentive to the analytic tools of cultural studies and, particularly, how formal legal, political, and economic institutions are embedded within and mutually constituted by historical norms of race, gender, sexuality, and nationality. For example, my approach follows the important work of historians of rural women such as Mary Neth, Katherine Jellison, Melissa Walker, and Rebecca Sharpless in suggesting that the gendering of agricultural labor was central to the political economy of agriculture in post–Civil War America. See Mary Neth, *Preserving the Family Farm: Women, Community, and the Foundations of Agribusiness in the Midwest, 1900–1940* (Baltimore: Johns Hopkins University Press, 1998); Katherine Jellison, *Entitled to Power: Farm Women and Technology, 1913–1963* (Chapel Hill: University of North Carolina Press, 1993); Walker, *All We Knew Was to Farm*; Rebecca Sharpless, *Fertile Ground, Narrow Choices: Women on Texas Cotton Farms, 1900–1940* (Chapel Hill: University of North Carolina Press, 1999). More broadly, I challenge the stability and permanence of some of the foundational conceptual binaries of political economy like public/private and state/civil. To a degree, this challenge echoes sociologist Philip Gorski's suggestion that scholars of governance pay attention to the work of "diffuse ideological power" in democratic societies, particularly as they cohere as "tactics of seduction and a politics of pleasure," as well as "for the mute practices and rituals through which ideology acts on the body." Philip Gorski, "Mann's Theory of Ideological Power: Sources, Applications and Elaborations," in *An Anatomy of Power: The Social Theory of Michael Mann*, ed. John A. Hall and Ralph Schroeder (Cambridge: Cambridge University Press, 2006), 130. This position, of course, has been more extensively elaborated by feminist and queer theorists of contemporary political culture. Scholars like Lauren Berlant, Elizabeth Povinelli, and Ann Stoler place the regulation of intimacy, body, and affect at the center of contemporary political formations and, in particular, the constitution of American empire. See Lauren Berlant, *The Queen of American Goes to Washington City: Essays on Sex and Citizenship* (Durham, NC: Duke University Press, 1997); Ann Stoler, *Carnal Knowledge and Imperial Power: Race and the Intimate in Colonial Rule* (Berkeley: University of California Press, 2002); Elizabeth Povinelli, *The Empire of Love: Toward a Theory of Intimacy, Genealogy, and Carnality* (Durham, NC: Duke University Press, 2006); Ann Stoler, ed., *Haunted by Empire: Geographies of Intimacy in North American History* (Durham, NC: Duke University Press, 2006); Elizabeth Povinelli, *Economies of Abandonment: Social Belonging and Endurance in Late Liberalism* (Durham, NC: Duke University Press, 2011).

4. See Neth, *Preserving the Family Farm*; Hal S. Barron, *Mixed Harvest: The Second Great Transformation in the Rural North* (Chapel Hill: University of North Carolina Press, 1997); Ronald Kline, *Consumers in the Country: Technology and Social Change in Rural America* (Baltimore: Johns Hopkins University Press, 2002). For Southern agriculture, see Jack Temple Kirby, *Rural Worlds Lost: The American South, 1920–1960* (Baton Rouge: Louisiana State University Press, 1987); Mart A. Stewart, *What Nature Suffers to Groe: Life, Labor, and Landscape on the Georgia Coast* (Athens: University of Georgia Press, 1996); Pete Daniel, *Breaking the Land: The Transformation of Cotton, Tobacco, and Rice Cultures Since 1880* (Champaign: University of Illinois Press, 1986).

5. For irrigated agriculture in the West, see Donald Worster, *Rivers of Empire: Water, Aridity and the Growth of the American West* (New York: Oxford University Press, 1992); Richard

White, *The Organic Machine* (New York: Macmillan, 1996). For California specifically, see David Vaught, *Cultivating California: Growers, Specialty Crops, and Labor, 1875–1920* (Baltimore: Johns Hopkins University Press, 1999); Steven Stoll, *The Fruits of Natural Advantage: Making the Industrial Countryside in California* (Berkeley: University of California Press, 1998); Douglas Cazaux Sackman, *Orange Empire: California and the Fruits of Eden* (Berkeley: University of California Press, 2005).

6. Fitzgerald, *Every Farm a Factory*, 23.

7. On the emergence of the "farm bloc" and the politics of "cooperation," see John Mark Hansen, *Gaining Access: Congress and the Farm Lobby, 1919–1981* (Chicago: University of Chicago Press, 1991); Victoria Saker Woeste, *Farmer's Benevolent Trust: Law and Agricultural Cooperation in Industrial America, 1865–1945* (Chapel Hill: University of North Carolina Press, 1998). For the Southern case, see Monica Richmond Gisolfi, "From Crop Lien to Contract Farming: The Roots of Agribusiness in the American South, 1929–1939," *Agricultural History* 80, no. 2 (spring 2006): 167–189.

8. I calculated these figures by comparing state enrollments with the rural populations by state, compiled in the 1930 and 1940 decennial censuses. See "Boys and Girls Enrolled, Number Completing, by States, 1923–1960," 4-H Series, Records of the CES, Record Group 33, National Archives, College Park, MD (NACP1), Box 16, "Statistical Records of 4-H Club Work, 1910–1960"; *Fifteenth Census of the United States: Census of Population* (Washington, DC: Census Office, 1931); *Sixteenth Census of the United States: Census of Population* (Washington, DC: Census Office, 1941).

9. See annual reports in NACP1, Box 16a, "Statistics."

10. See salary data in H. W. Conway to G. L. Noble, August 4, 1947, NACP1, Box 1c, "Bankhead-Jones—amended, June, 1945." See Debra Ann Reid, *Reaping a Greater Harvest: African Americans, the Extension Service, and Rural Reform in Jim Crow Texas* (College Station: Texas A&M Press, 2007); Carmen V. Harris, "'The Extension Service Is Not an Integration Agency': The Idea of Race in the Cooperative Extension Service," *Agricultural History* 82 (spring 2008): 193–219.

11. See 4-H club material in Box 336, Records of the Alabama Cooperative Extension Service (ACES), Special Collections, Ralph Draughon Library, Auburn University, Auburn, Alabama.

12. For African American 4-H'ers by year, see the state enrollments in Box 16. For a broader analysis of the relative growth of African American 4-H enrollments, see Erwin Shinn, "Statistical Analysis of Negro 4-H Club Work with Special Reference to 1936," 1938, NACP1, Box 16, "Statistical Records of 4-H Club Work, 1910–1960."

13. For the New Deal USDA, see Sarah T. Phillips, *This Land, This Nation: Conservation, Rural America, and the New Deal* (New York: Cambridge University Press, 2007); Donald Worster, *Dust Bowl: The Southern Plains in the 1930s* (New York: Oxford University Press, 1979).

14. C. B. Smith, "Preparedness and 4-H Work," 1941, ACES, Box 43, "Defense Memos (1)."

15. Joseph L. Anderson, *Industrializing the Corn Belt: Agriculture, Technology, and Environment, 1945–1972* (De Kalb: Northern Illinois University Press, 2008). For the full integration of national agribusinesses firms into agricultural production, see Shane Hamilton, *Trucking Country: The Road to America's Wal-Mart Economy* (Princeton, NJ: Princeton University Press, 2008); Paul Conkin, *A Revolution Down on the Farm: The Transformation of American Agriculture Since 1929* (Lexington: University of Kentucky Press, 2009).

16. On framing, see Cary Wolfe, *Before the Law: Humans and Other Animals in a Biopolitical Frame* (Chicago: University of Chicago Press, 2012).

17. Wendy Brown, *Regulating Aversion: Tolerance in the Age of Identity and Empire* (Princeton, NJ: Princeton University Press, 2005), 81.

18. For links necessary between life-making and death-making in contemporary biopolitical systems, see Achille Mbembe, "Necropolitics," *Public Culture* 15, no. 1 (2003): 11–40. Cf. "thanatopolitics" in Giorgio Agamben, *Homo Sacer: Sovereign Power and Bare Life* (Stanford, CA: Stanford University Press, 1998), 142; Roberto Esposito, *Bios: Biopolitics and Philosophy* (Minneapolis: University of Minnesota, 2008), 110–144.

19. Nick Cullather, *Hungry World: America's Cold War Battle with Poverty in Asia* (Cambridge, MA: Harvard University Press, 2010).

20. Angus Wright, *The Death of Ramon Gonzalez: The Modern Agricultural Dilemma* (Austin: University of Texas Press, 2005).

21. Richard White, *"It's Your Misfortune and None of My Own": A New History of the American West* (Norman: University of Oklahoma Press, 1991), 58.

22. See Ariel Ron, "Developing the Country: Scientific Agriculture and the Roots of the Republican Party" (PhD diss., University of California at Berkeley, 2012); Richard John, *Spreading the News: The American Postal System from Franklin to Morse* (Cambridge, MA: Harvard University Press, 1998); Alan L. Olmstead and Paul W. Rhode, "An Impossible Undertaking: The Eradication of Bovine Tuberculosis in the United States," *Journal of Economic History* 64, no. 3 (2004): 734–772; Kenneth Finegold and Theda Skocpol, *State and Party in America's New Deal* (Madison: University of Wisconsin Press, 1995).

23. See Daniel Immerwahr, *Thinking Small: The United States and the Lure of Community Development* (Cambridge, MA: Harvard University Press, 2015); Ekbladh, *The Great American Mission*; S. Hamilton, *Trucking Country*; Bethany Moreton, *To Serve God and Wal-Mart: The Making of Christian Free Enterprise* (Cambridge, MA: Harvard University Press, 2009).

24. Charles Postel, *The Populist Vision* (New York: Oxford University Press, 2007); Ron, "Developing the Country."

25. Limited scholarship on sexuality in rural communities in the United States is rooted in the metronormative assumptions of historians of sexuality and its overwhelming focus on urban sexual subcultures. On metronormativity, see Judith Halberstam, *In a Queer Time and Place: Transgender Bodies, Subcultural Lives* (New York: New York University Press, 2005); Scott Herring, *Another Country: Queer Anti-Urbanism* (New York: New York University Press, 2010). For crucial exceptions to this tendency, see John Howard, *Men Like That: A Southern Queer History* (Chicago: University of Chicago Press, 2001); Colin R. Johnson, *Just Queer Folks: Gender and Sexuality in Rural America* (Philadelphia: Temple University Press, 2013).

26. Rural-oriented state-building programs and the political economy of agriculture have been major topics of study in American political development (APD), a historicist subfield within the academic discipline of political science. In fact, 4-H's parent agencies, the USDA and the CES, are central to APD debates about when, where, and how the modern American state began to amass substantive regulatory powers. Nevertheless, this line of scholarship has tended to ignore the relationship between the growth of governing capacities and the regulation, policing, and production of sexuality and intimacy. See David E. Hamilton, *From New Day to New Deal: American Farm Policy from Hoover to Roosevelt* (Chapel Hill: University of North Carolina Press, 1991); Finegold and Skocpol, *State and Party in America's New Deal*; Elizabeth Sanders, *The Roots of Reform: Farmers, Workers, and the American State* (Chicago: University of Chicago Press, 1999); Daniel P. Carpenter, *The Forging of Bureaucratic Autonomy: Reputations, Networks, and Policy Innovations in Executive Agencies, 1862–1928* (Princeton, NJ: Princeton University

Press, 2000); Adam Sheingate, *The Rise of the Agricultural Welfare State: Institutions and Interest Group Power in the United States, France, and Japan* (Princeton, NJ: Princeton University Press, 2002); Bill Winders, *The Politics of Food Supply: U. S. Agricultural Policy in the World Economy* (New Haven, CT: Yale University Press, 2010).

27. Michael Mann, "The Autonomous Power of the State," *Archives Européennes de Sociologie* 25 (1984): 113. See also William Novak, "The Myth of the Weak American State," *American Historical Review* 113 (June 2008): 752–772, and the roundtable responses in *American Historical Review* 115 (June 2010): 766–800.

28. My interpretation of the state diverges from Mann on this point. As useful as Mann's attention to logistics is, it conceptualizes state/civil relationships in a way that presumes a monumentalist state standing astride society and "actually penetrating" it. By contrast, as Gilles Deleuze notes, for Foucault, "The state appears as the overall effect or result . . . of a 'microphysics of power.' . . . Far from being a source of power relations, the State already implies them." If Mann offers the state unity and causal priority in its dealing with civil society, Foucault contends that the two, state and civil, are both the effects of power. Yet does this mean that talk of the state as a historical object is meaningless or, at least, a diversion from the real issues at play? For my part, this is not the case. The state/civil distinction is a politically potent means of both licensing some forms of violence and manufacturing some kinds of consent. The state can be a strategy of alliance as much as a warehouse of sovereignty. For this reason, mapping a diffuse "microphysics of power" illustrates how the demarcation between state and civil becomes unstable and interpenetrating. See Gilles Deleuze, *Foucault* (Minneapolis: University of Minnesota Press, 2006), 25, 76. On the strategic malleability of state/civil demarcations, see also Timothy Mitchell, "Society, Economy, and the State Effect," in *State/Culture: State Formation After the Cultural Turn*, ed. George Steinmetz (Ithaca, NY: Cornell University Press, 1999), 76–97.

29. James Atkinson, "Raising a Crop of Young Farmers," 1909, NACP1, Box 1a, "4-H Early Development (Folder 2)," 1.

Chapter 1

1. Dick Crosby, "Boys' Agricultural Clubs," in *Yearbook of the United States Department of Agriculture, 1904* (Washington, DC: Government Printing Office, 1905). On corn structures, modernization, and white masculinity in late nineteenth-century America, see Kelly J. Sisson Lessens, "Master of Millions: King Corn in American Culture" (PhD diss., University of Michigan, 2011), 127–211.

2. Josiah Strong, *The New Era; Or the Coming Kingdom* (New York: Baker & Taylor, 1893), 173; Walter M. Rogers, "Vermont's Deserted Farms," in *Stray Leaves from a Larker's Log* (Concord, NH: Republican, 1897), 27–29. The poem, in fact, is a "commercial rhyme" endorsing Bradley's Phosphate, an artificial means to replenish the land's waning fertility.

3. Carpenter, *The Forging of Bureaucratic Autonomy*; Worster, *Rivers of Empire*; William Cronon, *Nature's Metropolis: Chicago and the Great West* (New York: W. W. Norton, 1991); Richard White, *Railroaded: The Transcontinentals and the Making of Modern America* (New York: W. W. Norton, 2012); Frieda Knobloch, *The Culture of Wilderness: Agriculture as Colonization in the American West* (Chapel Hill: University of North Carolina Press, 1996).

4. See *Twelfth Census of the United States: Census of Agriculture* (Washington, DC: Census Office, 1902).

5. See Alan Olmstead and Paul Rhodes, *Creating Abundance: Biological Innovation and American Agricultural Development* (New York: Cambridge University Press, 2008).

6. See Roy Scott, *The Reluctant Farmer: The Rise of Agricultural Extension to 1914* (Champaign: University of Illinois Press, 1971), 145; David Danbom, *Born in the Country: A History of Rural America* (Baltimore: Johns Hopkins University Press, 1995), 173.

7. Michael McGerr, *A Fierce Discontent: The Rise and the Fall of the Progressive Movement in America, 1870–1920* (New York: Oxford University Press, 2003), 30.

8. *Thirteenth Census of the United States: Census of Agriculture* (Washington, DC: Census Office, 1912), 27–28.

9. See Frederick Jackson Turner, "The Significance of the Frontier in American History," *Annual Report of the American Historical Association* (1893), 199–227.

10. Edward A. Ross, "The Causes of Race Superiority," *Annals of the American Academy of Political and Social Science* 18 (July 1901): 88–89.

11. Theodore Roosevelt to Bessie Van Vorst, October 18, 1902, in *The Letters of Theodore Roosevelt: Volume 3: The Square Deal, 1901–1905*, ed. Elting E. Morrison (Cambridge, MA: Harvard University Press, 1951), 355–356.

12. Gail Bederman, *Manliness and Civilization: A Cultural History of Gender and Race in the United States, 1880–1917* (Chicago: University of Chicago Press, 1995), 204–205.

13. On rural degeneracy, see Maria Farland, "Modernist Versions of the Pastoral: Poetic Inspiration, Scientific Expertise, and the 'Degenerate' Farmer," *American Literary History* 19, no. 4 (winter 2007): 905–936.

14. Ross, "The Causes of Race Superiority," 72; Orator F. Cook, "Agriculture: The Basis of Education," *The Monist* 17, no. 3 (July 1907): 352–353.

15. Edward A. Ross, "Folk Depletion as a Cause of Rural Decline," *Publications of the American Sociological Society* 11 (1916): 21–30. Ross suggested that "folk depletion" was an alternative to a "rural degeneracy" theory. His point was not to deny a role to inferior breeding in rural decline; rather, it was to link that genetic deterioration to demographic migration. Cook, "Agriculture," 354.

16. Richard Louis Dougdale, *The Jukes: A Study in Crime, Pauperism, Disease and Heredity* (New York: G. P. Putnam, 1877); Henry Goddard, *The Kallikak Family* (New York: Macmillan, 1912); Arthur Estabrook and Charles Davenport, *The Nam Family: A Study in Cacogenics* (Lancaster, PA: New Era, 1912); Florence Danielson and Charles Davenport, *The Hill Folk: Report on a Rural Community of Hereditary Defectives* (Lancaster, PA: New Era, 1912).

17. Charles Otis Gill and Gifford Pinchot, *Six Thousand Country Churches* (New York: Macmillan, 1919), 15–16.

18. See Aldrid Scott Warthin, *The New Pathology of Syphilis* (Philadelphia: J. B. Lippincott, 1920); Albert Gallatin Love and Charles Davenport, *Defects Found in Drafted Men: Statistical Information Compiled from the Draft Records Showing the Physical Condition of the Men Registered and Examined in Pursuance of the Requirements of the Selective-Service Act* (Washington, DC: Government Printing Office, 1920), 348–403. For relative prevalence of venereal diseases, in particular, see 353.

19. George Walter Fiske, *The Challenge of the Country* (New York: YMCA, 1912), 16.

20. Liberty Hyde Bailey, *The State and the Farmer* (London: Macmillan, 1908), 70, 73.

21. See Jeffrey Moran, *Teaching Sex: The Shaping of Adolescence in the 20th Century* (Cambridge, MA: Harvard University Press, 2002); Steven Mintz, *Huck's Raft: A History of American Childhood* (Cambridge, MA: Harvard University Press), 185–199.

22. Fiske, *The Challenge of the Country*, frontispiece and 18.

23. Beverly T. Galloway, "Seaman Asahel Knapp," in *Yearbook of the United States Department of Agriculture, 1911* (Washington, DC: Government Printing Office, 1912), 151–154; Wayne

D. Rasmussen, *Taking the University to the People: Seventy-Five Years of Cooperative Extension* (Ames: Iowa State University Press, 1989), 34–45; Carpenter, *The Forging of Bureaucratic Autonomy*, 227–235.

24. S. A. Knapp, "A Work for the Girls," 1910, NACP1, Box 1, "Records of Development of Early Phases of Development"; Hanchey E. Logue, "Alabama 4-H Trail," 1961, NACP1, Box 2, "State Histories of 4-H Club Work, Volume 1: Alabama to Montana"; Carpenter, *The Forging of Bureaucratic Autonomy*, 233–235.

25. Crosby, "Boys' Agricultural Clubs," 489.

26. Ibid., 489–490.

27. Alvin Dille, "The Reorganization of the Country School," in *Yearbook of the United States Department of Agriculture, 1919* (Washington, DC: Government Printing Office, 1920), 289.

28. Horace Culter and Julia Madge Stone, *The Rural School: Its Methods and Management* (New York: Silver, Burdett, 1913), 3.

29. See Tracy Steffes, "The Rural School Problem and the Complexities of National Reform," in *School, Society, and State: A New Education to Govern Modern America* (Chicago: University of Chicago Press, 2012), 47–82. See also Barron, *Mixed Harvest*; Wayne Fuller, *The Old Country School: The Story of Rural Education in the Middle West* (Chicago: University of Chicago Press, 1985); David Danbom, "Rural Education Reform and the Country Life Movement, 1900–1920," *Agricultural History* 53 (April 1979): 462–474.

30. *Report of the Commission on Country Life* (New York: Sturgis & Walton, 1917), 121–122.

31. Ibid., 122–127.

32. O. J. Kern, "Extracts from Among Country Schools," 1906, NACP1, Box 1a, "4-H Early Development (Folder 2)"; A. B. Graham and J. Phil Campbell, "Action Programs in Education," 1941, 65–71, NACP1, Box 1b, "Misc. Talks."

33. Crosby, "Boys' Agricultural Clubs," 492–493.

34. See also Lessens, "Master to Millions," 357–440.

35. A. B. Graham, "The Objectives of Boys' and Girls' Agricultural Clubs," 1905, NACP1, Box 1, "Principles and Policies Governing 4-H Club Work."

36. Graham and Campbell, "Action Programs in Education," 66–68; Carpenter, *The Forging of Bureaucratic Autonomy*, 233.

37. "Extracts from Letters of Boys' Corn Club Members," NACP1, Box 1, "Records of Development of Early Phases of Development."

38. Selene Armstrong Harmon, "Why Theodore N. Vail Backed O. H. Benson," *World's Work* (March 1921): 517–520.

39. Andrew Feffer, *The Chicago Pragmatists and American Progressivism* (Ithaca, NY: Cornell University Press, 1993), 134.

40. O. H. Benson, "Organization and Instruction in Boys' Corn Club Work" [1912?], 1–27, NACP1, Box 1, "Part 1—Organization and Supervision of 4-H Club Work," 6.

41. Graham and Campbell, "Action Programs in Education," 67. Another Iowa school superintendent, Jessie Fields, was actually a much more ardent advocate of club work than Benson. As superintendent of education in Wright County, Benson focused more on in-school agricultural education, though he also organized clubs. See Paul C. Taff, "A Brief History of the Origin and Development of the 4-H Clubs in Iowa," 4, 1961, NACP1, Box 2, "State Histories of 4-H Club Work, Volume 1: Alabama to Montana"; Atkinson, "Raising a Crop of Young Farmers."

42. Benson, "Organization and Instruction in Boys' Corn Club Work," 5–6.

43. O. H. Benson, "Education for Rural Life," 1911, 1–5, NACP1, Box 1c, "Early Talks, Papers, Articles," 1–3.

44. O. H. Benson, "Boys' and Girls' Club Work, Its Principles, Policies and Requirements," 1915, NACP1, Box 4, "Significant Talks and Addresses on 4-H Club Work, Volume 1: 1904–1929," 2–3.

45. Wilbur J. Fraser, "Conservation of Energy and Its Relation to the Dairy Man," *Berkshire World and Corn Belt Stockman*, August 1, 1910, 42; "Why Boys Leave the Farm," *Prairie Farmer*, February 1, 1910, 5; J. J. G., "Why One Boy Left the Farm," *National Rural and Family Magazine*, December 1, 1898, 24.

46. J. J. G., "Why One Boy Left the Farm"; Warren H. Wilson, "Conservation of Boys," *Prairie Farmer*, January 15, 1912, 41; "A Boy Headed the Wrong Way," *Wallaces Farmer*, April 19, 1912, 6.

47. Benson, "Boys' and Girls' Club Work, Its Principles, Policies and Requirements."

48. Benson, "Organization and Instruction in Boys' Corn Club Work," 10.

49. O. H. Benson and Gertrude Warren, "Organization and Results of Boys' and Girls' Club Work," 1918, NACP1, Box 3a, "Unmarked Folder," 22; USDA National Agricultural Statistics Service, "Indiana Historical Data: Corn Acreage, Yield, Production, Value of Production, and Marketing Year Average (1866–2001)," http://www.nass.usda.gov/Statistics_by_State/Indiana/Historical_Data/Crops/hcorn1.txt (accessed September 1, 2009); "Our Boys and Girls," *Ohio Farmer*, March 18, 1911, 22.

50. Benson and Warren, "Organization and Results of Boys' and Girls' Club Work," 22–23.

51. Frank Lever, *Report from the Committee on Agriculture to Accompany H.R. 7951* (Washington, DC: Government Printing Office, 1914), 5–6.

52. *Bicentennial Edition: Historical Statistics of the United States, Colonial Times to 1970* (Washington, DC: Government Printing Office, 1975), 1115.

53. See Finegold and Skocpol, *State and Party in America's New Deal*; Sanders, *The Roots of Reform*; Carpenter, *The Forging of Bureaucratic Autonomy*.

54. Frank Lever, *Congressional Record*, 63-2, 1997.

55. John Adair, *Congressional Record*, 2067–2068.

56. John Works, *Congressional Record*, 2824.

57. Frank Brandegee, *Congressional Record*, 2822.

58. John Joseph Fitzgerald, *Congressional Record*, 2000.

59. Franklin Lane, *Congressional Record*, 3068.

60. Thomas Sterling, *Congressional Record*, 3244.

61. Dudley Hughes, *Congressional Record*, 1997–1998.

62. Albert Cummins, *Congressional Record*, 2907.

63. *Congressional Record*, 3242.

64. James Sharp Williams, *Congressional Record*, 2904.

65. Moses Clapp, *Congressional Record*, 3144.

66. See Leslie Paris, *Children's Nature: The Rise of the American Summer Camp* (New York: New York University Press, 2008); Susan Miller, *Growing Girls: The Natural Origins of Girls' Organizations in the United States* (New Brunswick, NJ: Rutgers University Press, 2007); Abigail van Slyke, *A Manufactured Wilderness: Summer Camps and the Shaping of American Youth, 1890–1960* (Minneapolis: University of Minnesota Press, 2006); Clifford Putney, *Muscular Christianity: Manhood and Sports in Protestant America, 1880–1920* (Cambridge, MA: Harvard University Press, 2003); Thomas Winter, *Making Men, Making Class: The YMCA and Workingmen, 1877–1920* (Chicago: University of Chicago Press, 2002); Anthony Rotundo, *American Manhood: Transformations in Masculinity from the Revolution to the Modern Era* (New York:

Basic Books, 1994); David MacLeod, *Building Character in the American Boy: The Boy Scouts, YMCA, and Their Forerunners, 1870–1920* (Madison: University of Wisconsin Press, 1983).

67. Harris and Ewing, "Population Centre Moving East, Cities Lead," *New York Times*, May 23, 1920; "54,796,100 in Cities; Country Has 50,972,000," *Chicago Daily Tribune*, October 1, 1920.

68. Frederic J. Haskin, "The Drift to the City," *Los Angeles Times*, October 2, 1920.

Chapter 2

1. For examples of the labels, see O. H. Benson, 4-H Brand Labels [1917?], NACP1, Box 1, "Records of Development of Early Phases of Development"; Oscar Baker Martin, *The Demonstration Work: Dr. Seaman A. Knapp's Contribution to Civilization* (Boston: Stratford, 1921), 76–78.

2. O. B. Martin to Warburton, June 3, 1931, ACES, Box 10, "M Corr."; Martin, *The Demonstration Work*, 76. There was at least one earlier version of the pledge, and probably several. For example, Milton Danziger reported in 1919 the pledge as "I pledge the service of my Head, Heart, Hands and Health, thru boys and girls' club work, to make American agriculture and home life the best in the world." See Milton Danziger, "Application of Terms Used in Boys' and Girls' Club Work," 1919, NACP1, Box 4, "Significant Talks and Addresses on 4-H Club Work, Volume 1: 1904–1929," 5.

3. Kenyon L. Butterfield, *The Farmer and the New Day* (New York: Macmillan, 1919).

4. On the populists as modernists and capitalists, see Postel, *The Populist Vision*, an important revision of previous interpretations of the populists as reactionaries and traditionalists. That interpretation is largely owed to the enduring legacy of Richard Hofstadter. See Richard Hofstadter, *The Age of Reform: From Bryan to FDR* (New York: Knopf, 1955); idem, *Anti-Intellectualism in American Life* (New York: Knopf, 1963).

5. See Richard M. Valelly, *Radicalism in the American States: The Minnesota Farmer-Labor Party and the American Political Economy* (Chicago: University of Chicago Press, 1989); Robin D. G. Kelly, *Hammer and Hoe: Alabama Communists During the Great Depression* (Chapel Hill: University of North Carolina Press, 1990); D. Hamilton, *From New Day to New Deal*.

6. Albert Mann, quoted in G. Walter Fiske, "The Development of Rural Leadership," *Publications of the American Sociological Society* 11 (December 1916): 54–70; "Whole Cooperative Movement Depends upon Loyal Support of Members, Says Sec. Jardine," *The Co-Op* 5, no. 4 (April 20, 1925): 1.

7. Wayne Rasmussen, *Taking the University to the People: Seventy-Five Years of Cooperative Extension* (Ames: Iowa State University Press, 1989), 70–75.

8. See, e.g., "Hoover Opposes Government Aid to Farm Exporting" *New York Times*, June 26, 1921, 1; R. Douglas Hurt, *Problems of Plenty: The American Farmer in the Twentieth Century* (Chicago: Ivan R. Dee, 2002), 43–47; Fitzgerald, *Every Farm a Factory*, 19–20.

9. Fitzgerald, *Every Farm a Factory*, 23.

10. On the history of rural sociology and its relationship to the USDA, see Olaf F. Larson and Julie N. Zimmerman, *Sociology in Government: The Galpin-Taylor Years in the U. S. Department of Agriculture, 1919–1953* (University Park: Pennsylvania State University Press, 2003).

11. Claud Scroggs, "Historical Highlights," in *Agricultural Cooperation*, ed. Martin Abrahamsen and Claud L. Scroggs (Minneapolis: University of Minnesota Press, 1957), 21; Morton Keller, *Regulating a New Economy: Public Policy and Economic Change in America, 1900–1933* (Cambridge, MA: Harvard University Press, 1990), 155; Aaron Sapiro, "True Farmer Cooperation," *The World's Work* 46, no. 1 (May 1923): 89. On the history of Capper-Volstead, see Donald

A. Frederick, "Antitrust Status of Farmer Cooperatives: The Story of the Capper-Volstead Act," *Cooperative Information Report* 59 (September 2002): i–361; J. C. Thompson, "Agricultural Cooperatives in the United States: Origin and Current Status," *Agricultural Administration* 11 (September 1982): 1–22.

12. Keller, *Regulating a New Economy*, 152.

13. Maurice Burritt, *The County Agent and the Farm Bureau* (New York: Harcourt, Brace, 1922), 190–191; B. H. Crocheron, "A Real Farmers' Club," *Journal of Agriculture* 4, no. 4 (February 1917): 207.

14. See Nancy Berlage, "Organizing the Farm Bureau: Family, Community, and Professionals, 1914–1928," *Agricultural History* 75, no. 4 (autumn 2001): 406–437; Burritt, *The County Agent*, 228. On the "farmer's wife," see Jellison, *Entitled to Power*. For transformations in rural women's labor, see Neth, *Preserving the Family Farm*.

15. See Laura Lovett, "'Fitter Families for Future Firesides': Florence Sherbon and Popular Eugenics," *Public Historian* 29, no. 3 (summer 2007): 69–85.

16. William Lloyd, "Report of the Annual Conference of Leaders in Boys' and Girls' Club Work and Junior Extension Work, Northern and Western States," 8, NACP1, Box 1, "Records of Development of Early Phases of Development"; O. H. Benson, "Educational Philosophy of Boys' and Girls' Club Work" [1919?], NACP1, Box 1, "Principles and Policies Governing 4-H Club Work."

17. O. H. Benson, "Suggestion for Boys' and Girls' Club Interstate Pageant Programme" [1917?], NACP1, Box 1, "4-H Club Activities and Programs," 1; Rasmussen, *Taking the University to the People*, 71. For club enrollments and specific project enrollments, see NACP1, Box 16a, "Statistics." For other material on urban garden clubs, see George E. Farrell, "Plan of Organization and Supervision for Boys' and Girls' City Garden and Marketing Club Project" [1920?], NACP1, Box 1, "Part 1—Organization and Supervision of 4-H Club Work."

18. Simcox, "Report of the Annual Conference of Leaders in Boys' and Girls' Club Work and Junior Extension Work, Northern and Western States," 46–48, 22.

19. Cooper, "Report of the Annual Conference of Leaders in Boys' and Girls' Club Work and Junior Extension Work, Northern and Western States," 35.

20. Benson and Warren, "Organization and Results of Boys' and Girls' Club Work," 12.

21. Danziger, "Application of Terms Used in Boys and Girls' Club Work".

22. Benson, "Boys' and Girls' Club Work, Its Principles, Policies and Requirements."

23. Ibid., 9.

24. Gertrude Warren, "Development of Local Volunteer Leadership," 1925, NACP1, Box 1, "Part 1—Organization and Supervision of 4-H Club Work," 1.

25. Sheridan, "Report of the Annual Conference of Leaders in Boys' and Girls' Club Work and Junior Extension Work, Northern and Western States," 17.

26. Warren, "Development of Local Volunteer Leadership," 8.

27. See "Report of the Standardization Committee," 1928, NACP1, Box 1a, "4-H Goals."

28. See, e.g., A. B. Ballantyne, "1927 Annual Report, Supervisional and Boys' and Girls' 4-H Club Work, State of Arizona," 1927, Reports of the Arizona Agricultural Extension Service, 1921–1963 (UAL), Main Library Special Collections, University of Arizona. Tucson.

29. Benson, "Boys' and Girls' Club Work, Its Principles, Policies and Requirements," 9–10.

30. "Try Growing Iceberg in a New Hampshire County," *Chicago Packer*, January 7, 1928, 9.

31. George E. Farrell, "How to Organize Boys' and Girls' Clubs" [1920?], NACP1, Box 1, "Part 1—Organization and Supervision of 4-H Club Work."

32. Milton Danziger, "The Demonstrational Value of Club Work," 1920, NACP1, Box 1, "Part 2—Principles and Policies Governing 4-H Club Work," 5.

33. For estimates of county agent time, see Barnard Joy, "25 Years of 4-H Club Work: Analysis of Statistical Trends with Special Reference to 1938," 1939, NACP1, Box 16, "Statistical Records of 4-H Club Work, 1910–1960"; Laurel K. Sabrosky, "Statistical Analysis of 4-H Club Work, 1914–43," 1945, NACP1, Box 16, "Statistical Records of 4-H Club Work, 1910–1960."

34. Ballantyne, "1927 Annual Report," 9; H. J. Baker and M. C. Wilson, *Relative Costs of Extension Methods Which Influence Changes in Farm and Home Practices* (Washington, DC: US Government Printing Office, 1929), 21.

35. Lloyd, "Report of the Annual Conference of Leaders in Boys' and Girls' Club Work and Junior Extension Work, Northern and Western States," 11.

36. J. D. McVean, "How Bankers Can Start Pig Clubs—What They Mean to Bank and Boy," *Banker Farmer* (September 1, 1917): 12–13; "Boys' Pig Club Contest at Kentucky State Fair," *Berkshire World and Corn Belt Stockman*, October 1, 1915, 33.

37. Benson, "Educational Philosophy of Boys' and Girls' Club Work," 1–2.

38. Gertrude Warren, "Value of the Demonstration," 1918, NACP1, Box 4, "Significant Talks and Addresses on 4-H Club Work, Volume 1: 1904–1929," 4.

39. "Boys' and Girls' 4-H Club Work, a New Factor in the Nation's Educational System," 1925, NACP1, Box 1, "Principles and Policies Governing 4-H Club Work," 3.

40. David Nasaw, *Schooled to Order: A Social History of Schooling in the United States* (New York: Oxford University Press, 1977), 156.

41. David Snedden, *Vocational Education* (New York: Macmillan, 1920), 150; idem, *Educational Sociology* (New York: Century, 1922), 638; Mabel Carney and Fannie Dunn, in "Course of Discussions on Club Work," 1927, NACP1, Box 1b, "Misc. Conferences—4-H (1914–1928 period)."

42. Robert Foster, "Course of Discussions on Club Work," 17–35.

43. C. B. Smith, "How Bankers May Cooperate in Agricultural Extension Work," 1919, NACP1, Box 4, "Significant Talks and Addresses on 4-H Club Work, Volume 1: 1904–1929," 7.

44. A. C. True, "The Place of 4-H Clubs in the American System of Public Education," 1928, NACP1, Box 1, "Records of Development of Early Phases of Development," 4.

45. "Hard Work Plus Profit Equals Satisfaction" *Wallaces Farmer*, January 2, 1920, 8; "Financial Independence Won by Club Boys and Girls," *Farm Home*, December 1, 1919, 15; Mary E. Kramer, "Boys' and Girls' Garden Clubs in Cook County," *Prairie Farmer*, November 6, 1915, 13.

46. "Boys' Boom Baby Beef," *Chicago Livestock World*, November 29, 1916, 10; Caroline Eyring, "My Experiences as a Local Club Leader," in Ballantyne, "1927 Annual Report"; O. C. Croy, "Boys' and Girls' Club Work in Ohio," *Ohio Farmer*, July 30, 1921, 3.

47. "Where Is Your Wandering Boy?," *Wallaces Farmer*, April 28, 1928, 3, 10; "A True Story," *Banker Farmer*, September 1, 1919, 14.

48. "Farm Problems Interest Banks," *New York Times*, September 14, 1912; "For Better Farming," *New York Times*, September 22, 1912.

49. Smith, "How Banks May Cooperate in Agricultural Extension Work," 6.

50. G. L. Noble, untitled article, *Banker Farmer*, 1921, NACP1, Box 1a, "4-H Early Development (Folder 2)."

51. E. L. Austin, "Club Work Is Good Business for Banker," *Banker Farmer*, January 1, 1925, 4.

52. See, for examples, E. L. Quaife, "Boys, Girls and Purebreds," *Wallaces Farmer*, May 14, 1920, 7.

53. See R. A. Ward, *The Bank Agricultural Department* (New York: Bankers, 1923); idem, "Banking Service in the Rural Community," *Bankers Magazine* (November 1921); "Says Farm Club Aid Is Best Investment," *New York Times*, April 29, 1923.

54. E. B. Harshaw, "Bank Co-operation in Community Extension Work," *Bankers Magazine* (April 1925); idem, "The Community Development Phase of Bank Agricultural Work," *Bankers Magazine* (May 1925).

55. A. B. Ballantyne, "Annual Report: Boys' and Girls' Club Work, State of Arizona, December 1, 1922–December 1, 1923," 1923, UAL, 3; "Special Club Prizes," 1927, Wisconsin 4-H Records, Series 9/5/2—General Correspondence Files, Box 3, University of Wisconsin at Madison, Memorial Library, Special Collections (UWSC).

56. "The Banker and the Boy," *Wallaces Farmer*, December 8, 1916, 5; "A True Story," 14; McVean, "How Bankers Can Start Pig Clubs," 12–13.

57. F. C. Claflin to T. L. Belwick, July 29, 1929, Box 3, UWSC. See also T. L. Belwick to F. C. Claflin, July 19, 1929; T. L. Belwick to F. C. Claflin, August 1, 1929; F. C. Claflin to T. L. Belwick, August 2, 1929.

58. T. L. Belwick to F. C. Claflin, August 1, 1929.

59. Austin, "Club Work Is Good Business for Banker," 4.

60. See Gertrude Warren, "Glimpses of the Life and Accomplishments of Dr. Clarence Beaman Smith" [1938?], NACP1, Box 1b, "CB Smith."

61. C. B. Smith and George Farrell, "Boys' and Girls' Clubs Enrich Country Life," 1920, NACP1, Box 3, "4-H Club Work Printed Bulletins, 1910–1960."

62. C. B. Smith, "The Responsibility of Expanding the Boys' and Girls' Club Movement in Its Field of Work," 1925, NACP1, Box 4, "Significant Talks and Addresses on 4-H Club Work, Volume 1: 1904–1929," 8–9.

63. Noble, untitled article, *Banker Farmer*, 1921. The National Committee officially styled itself as I have indicated in the text—with "on" instead of "for" and with no apostrophes after the words "boys" and "girls"—but it is occasionally referred to in some sources as the National Committee *for* Boys and Girls Club Work and the National Committee on Boys' and Girls' Club Work.

64. Guy Noble to T. T. Martin, April 7, 1932, NACP1, Box 1c, "Capper-Ketchum."

65. Noble, untitled article, *Banker Farmer*, 1921.

66. "Coolidge Encourages Farm Boys and Girls," *New York Times*, December 4, 1923.

67. See R. A. Turner, "Report of the First International 4-H Training School," 1923, NACP1, Box 1b, "Misc. Conferences—4-H (1914–1928 period)."

68. "Boys' and Girls' 4-H Club Work: Present and Future Development," 2, NACP1, Box 1, "Principles and Policies Governing 4-H Club Work.

69. Harold Carmony, "The Proper Club Spirit—I," *Ohio Farmer*, November 18, 1922, 30; O. H. Benson, "Boys' and Girls' Club Projects as a Means of Industrial Education in Our Rural Schools," 17–19, 1921, NACP1, Box 4, "Significant Talks and Addresses on 4-H Club Work, Volume 1: 1904- 1929."

70. C. J. Galpin, "4-H Club Work—Old and New Objectives," 1930, NACP1, Box 1, " Records of Development of Early Phases of Development," 5.

71. C. B. Smith, "The Outlook in Agriculture in Relation to 4-H Club Work," 1931, NACP1, Box 1b, "CB Smith."

72. Rachel Nelson, "Reminisces as a Member of the Girls' Own Room Club," in Ballantyne, "1927 Annual Report." For plans and representations in home furnishing projects, see, e.g., Alice

Dodge, "Personality in the Girl's Room," July 1924, 4-H Club Work Extension Service Publications, Iowa State College Extension Service Records, Parks Library University Archives, Iowa State University, Ames (ISU1).

73. "The Housewife Keeps Score," *University of Wisconsin Extension Service Circular* (May 1920).

74. L. C. Boggs, "Boys' and Girls' Club Work: Poultry Clubs," *University of Arizona Extension Service Circular* (December 1924): 14.

75. Warren, "Value of the Demonstration"

76. D. Anderson, "The 4-H Club Girl: Her Book," *North Dakota Agricultural College Extension Circular* (February 1925): 3.

77. Helen Parsons, "Score Cards for Children," *University of Wisconsin Extension Service Circular* (1924).

78. Robert G. Foster, "A Guide to the Development of Boys' and Girls' 4-H Club Leadership," 1926, NACP1, Box 1, "Principles and Policies Governing 4-H Club Work," 2–3; Warren, "Development of Local Volunteer Leadership," 21–22.

79. "Boys' and Girls' 4-H Club Work: Present and Future Development," 3.

80. Farrell, "How to Organize Boys' and Girls' Clubs," 9.

81. Boggs, "Boys' and Girls' Club Work: Poultry Clubs," 14.

82. Ballantyne, "Annual Report: 1923," 15.

83. Smith, "The Responsibility of Expanding the Boys' and Girls' Club Movement," 1, 14.

84. Liberty Hyde Bailey, "Remarks," 1914, NACP1, Box 1, "Records of Development of Early Phases of Development," 1–3.

Chapter 3

1. Report of the Committee on Girls' Work, White House Conference on Child Health and Protection, 1930, NACP1, Box 1, "Records of the Development of Early Phases of the 4-H Clubs," 1, 17–18.

2. Gertrude Warren, "What Do We Want Local Club Leaders to Do in Homemaking Club Work?," NACP1, Box 1b, "Misc. Conferences—4-H (1914–1928 period)," 2–3. See also idem, "The Social and Economic Problems of Farm Youth," 1931, NACP1, Box 1b, "Gertrude Warren."

3. Mary E. Sweeney, "A Call to Service," *Bulletin of the American Home Economics Association* 7, no. 1 (March 1921). For the history of home economics, see Megan J. Elias, *Stir It Up: Home Economics in American Culture* (Philadelphia: University of Pennsylvania Press, 2010); Carolyn M. Goldstein, *Creating Consumers: Home Economists in Twentieth-Century America* (Chapel Hill: University of North Carolina Press, 2012).

4. *Report of the Commission of Country Life*, 104.

5. *Social and Labor Needs of Farm Women, Report 103* (Washington, DC: USDA, 1915); *Domestic Needs of Farm Women, Report 104* (Washington, DC: USDA, 1915); *Educational Needs of Farm Women, Report 105* (Washington, DC: USDA, 1915); *Economic Needs of Farm Women, Report 106* (Washington, DC: USDA, 1915).

6. Stella Mather, "Talk Given at Annual Meeting of the State Federation of Women's Clubs," 5, in "Annual Report of Home Demonstration Work in Arizona, December 1, 1924–December 1, 1925," UAL.

7. For children's contributions to farm labor, see Pamela Riney-Kherberg, *Childhood on the Farm: Work, Play, and Coming of Age in the Midwest* (Lawrence: University of Kansas Press, 2005).

8. Charles F. Powlison, "Child Welfare in the Rural Community," *Public Health* 8 (January 1920): 170.

9. National Child Labor Committee, *Rural Child Welfare* (New York: Macmillan, 1922), 92.

10. Ibid., 85.

11. See, e.g., Willystine Godsell, *The Education of Women: Its Social Background and Its Problems* (New York: Macmillan, 1923), 301.

12. William Arch McKeever, *Farm Boys and Girls* (New York: Macmillan, 1913), 188.

13. Roy Hinman Holmes, *The Farm in a Democracy* (Ann Arbor, MI: Edwards, 1922), 15–16.

14. Ibid., 16.

15. John Herbert Quick, *The Fairview Idea* (Indianapolis: Bobbs-Merrill, 1919), 199–207.

16. Orrin Giddings Cocks, *The Social Evil and Methods of Treatment* (New York: Association Press, 1912), 18.

17. Orie Latham Hatcher, *Rural Girls in the City for Work* (Richmond, VA: Garrett and Massie, 1930).

18. National Child Labor Committee, *Rural Child Welfare*, 92–93.

19. Quick, *The Fairview Idea*, 215.

20. The statistics in this section are derived from annual reports that can be located at NACP1, Box 16a, "Statistics."

21. See "Garment Making Club: Part 1—Preparatory Work," March 1915, ISU1; "Garment Making Club: Part 1—Preparatory Work," October 1915, ISU1; "Garment Making Club: Part 2," September 1915, ISU1; "Garment Making Club: Part 3—Dressmaking," November 1916, ISU1; "Garment Making Club: Part 4—Making a Wool Dress," November 1917, ISU1; "Garment Making Club: Part 1—Preparatory Work," December 1917, ISU1; "Garment Making Club: Part 1—Preparatory Work," September 1918, ISU1.

22. See "Food Preparation Club," May 1915, ISU1; "Food Preparation Club: Part 2—Bread Making," September 1915, ISU1; "Food Preparation Club: Part 2—Bread Making," April 1916, ISU1; "Food Preparation Club: Part 3—Vegetables, Fruits and Cereals," September 1915, ISU1; "Nutrition Primer" [1917?], ISU1.

23. See Gertrude Warren, "The Cultural Side of 4-H Club Work," *Rural America* (February 1936): 16; idem, "The Older Girl in Extension Work," *Rural America* (February 1927): 9; idem, "4-H Club Work and Its Work," *National Republic* (October 1927); idem, "The Ideal Girl," *Country Gentleman* (March 1935): 48; idem, "Character Building," *Country Gentleman* (June 1935): 21; idem, "Grandfather's Young Folks and Ours," *The Southern Planter* (January 1930): 14; idem, "The Radio in 4-H Club Work," *American Farming* (October 1929): 10; idem, "4-H Club Work," *Journal of Social Hygiene* (November 1937): 411; idem, "Boys' and Girls' Club Work," *Journal of Home Economics* (May 1921): 207; idem, "The National 4-H Club Camp," *Journal of Home Economics* (September 1929): 652; idem, "4-H Club Work with Rural Girls," *Journal of Home Economics* (August 1932): 686.

24. Gertrude Warren, "Cooperative Extension Problems in Relation to the Farm Home," 1923, NACP1, Box 4, "Significant Talks and Addresses on 4-H Club Work, Volume 1: 1904–1929," 5–10.

25. Jeffrey Moran, *Teaching Sex: The Shaping of Adolescence in the 20th Century* (Cambridge, MA: Harvard University Press, 2002), 20.

26. Crista DeLuzio, *Female Adolescence in American Scientific Thought, 1830–1930* (Baltimore: Johns Hopkins University Press, 2007), 134.

27. Gertrude Warren, "Some Suggestions on Methods of Work with Club Girls," 1925, NACP1, Box 1, "Principles and Policies Governing 4-H Club Work," 3.

28. Gertrude Warren, "The Junior Mind in Relation to Boys' and Girls' Club Work," February 1925, NACP1, Box 3, "General Circulars on 4-H Club Work," 1–3. See Edward Asbury Kirkpatrick, *Genetic Psychology: An Introduction to an Objective and Genetic View of Intelligence* (New York: Macmillan, 1909); idem, *Individual in the Making: A Subjective View of Child Development with Suggestions for Parents and Teachers* (New York: Houghton Mifflin, 1911); idem, *Mental Hygiene for Effective Living* (New York: Appleton-Century, 1934).

29. Warren, "The Junior Mind," 4–5.

30. Ibid., 6–7.

31. Ibid., 7.

32. "4-H Club Refreshments," July 1924, ISU1; "Our Club Girl's Birthday Party," August 1924, ISU1; "Iowa 4-H Music Memory Selections," 1925, ISU1.

33. See "Attractive Home Breakfasts," June 1924, ISU1; "Under Garments," June 1924, ISU1; Irma Camp Graff, "Personality in Dress," July 1924, ISU1; Alice Dodge, "Personality in the Girl's Room"; "Home Furnishing Primer for the Girl's Room," July 1924, ISU1; "4-H Bread Primer," June 1926, ISU1; "The Iowa 4-H Club Uniform," June 1926, ISU1; "4-H Health Primer," June 1926, ISU1; "A Primer for Clothing," June 1926, ISU1; "4-H Bread Primer," May 1930, ISU1; "4-H Canning for Good Nutrition," June 1930, ISU1.

34. "Attractive Home Breakfasts," 1–5.

35. Mildred Simon, "Food Selection—Preparation and Serving: First Year," November 1928, ACES, Box 336, "Projects for 4-H Club Girls," 38–41.

36. Irma Camp Graff, "Personality in Dress," 2–4.

37. Florence Forbes, "Home Furnishing Primer," 1931, ISU1, 1–9. Forbes's work echoes almost directly an earlier manual by Alice Dodge. See Dodge, "Personality in the Girl's Room," July 1924.

38. "The Complete 4-H Outfit" [mid-1930s?]. ISU1.

39. Dorothy Dean, "Clothing for Health," October 1929, ACES, Box 336, "Projects for 4-H Club Girls," 2.

40. Mildred Simon, "Foods for 4-H Clubs," October 1929, ACES, Box 336, "Projects for 4-H Club Girls," 5.

41. "Meal Planning and Table Service," July 1924, ISU1, 3.

42. Forbes, "Home Furnishing Primer," 3, 12; "Iowa 4-H Efficiency Primer," ISU1, 10–12.

43. "4-H Canning for Good Nutrition," 1.

44. Warren, "Some Suggestions on Methods of Work with Club Girls," 3.

45. "Decide Healthiest Juniors: Physical Specimens from Crawford and Story Counties," *4-H Club News* 5 (August 28, 1924): 1.

46. "Health," *1930 Annual Report, 4-H Series*, RS 16/1/1, Iowa State University Parks Library Special Collections, Ames (ISU2), 129.

47. "The Perfect Boy and Girl," *Washington Post*, February 8, 1925, SM3.

48. Edith Barker, "History of 4-H Club Work in Iowa," *1939 Annual Report, 4-H Series*, ISU2, 6; "Counties Conducting County Wide Health Contests: 1927," *1927 Annual Report, 4-H Series*, ISU2.

49. "Iowa Health Score Card," *1924 Annual Report, 4-H Series*, ISU2.

50. "Excerpts from County Agent Reports," *1927 Annual Report, 4-H Series*, ISU2; "Health, A Definite Part of Club Program," *1928 Annual Report, 4-H Series*, ISU2.

51. "From Field Agent's Annual Report–1930," *1930 Annual Report, 4-H Series*, ISU2.

52. "Interesting Results of the Health Work Is Reported from All Counties," *1927 Annual Report, 4-H Series*, ISU2.

53. See "General and Historical Information about the National 4-H Club Congress," 1950, National Committee Program Files Series, Records of the CES, Record Group 33, National Archives, College Park, MD (NACP2), Box 1, "[Unmarked Folder]," 1. The National 4-H Congress is also sometimes referred to as the National 4-H Club Congress.

54. W. W. Bauer, "Contesting for Better Health," NACP2, Box 1, "1933 Club Congress" Folder, 3.

55. For health-club enrollments, see the statistical compilations found at NACP1, Box 16a, "Statistics."

56. Miriam Birdseye, "Grow Finer Club Members," 1929, NACP1, Box 1, "Principles and Policies Governing 4-H Club Work," 2.

57. Miriam Birdseye, "Suggested Plans for Growth in Connection with Boys' and Girls' Clubs," 1926, NACP1, Box 1, "Principles and Policies Governing 4-H Club Work," 6.

58. Birdseye, "Suggested Plans," 8.

59. Birdseye, "Grow Finer Club Members," 3–5.

60. "Pick Healthy Specimens of Boys and Girls," *Oelwein (IA) Daily Register*, December 3, 1924, 1A.

61. For examples, see "The Perfect Boy and Girl," SM3; "Huskiest Farm Boy Is a Kentucky Lad," *New York Times*, December 1, 1926, 16; "Dakota Girl, 17, Wins National Health Contest," *Chicago Daily Tribune*, December 5, 1928, 14; "South Dakota Girl, Michigan Boy Chosen Nation's Healthiest in Chicago Contest," *New York Times*, December 5, 1928, 4; "Healthiest Boy and Girl Picked," *Los Angeles Times*, December 5, 1928, 1.

62. "So. Dakota Girl Gets 99 Rating in Health Tests," *Waterloo Evening Courier*, December 5, 1928, 9; "America's Healthiest Girl," *Alden (IA) Times*, May 24, 1924, 2.

63. "Floridan Is Healthiest Girl in U.S.," *Mason City Globe-Gazette*, December 4, 1929, 5.

64. C. Harris, "States' Rights, Federal Bureaucrats."

65. Excerpts of field agent reports, *1927 Annual Report*, *4-H Series*, ISU2.

66. Noble to Smith, January 2, 1925, NACP1, Box 1a, "4-H Goals." See also the announcement in the *National Boys and Girls Club News*, January 10, 1925, NACP2, Box 13, "National 4-H Club News, 1924–1935."

67. Smith to Noble, January 10, 1925, NACP1, Box 1a, "4-H Goals"; telegram, Smith to Noble, January 5, 1925, NACP1, Box 1a, "4-H Goals."

68. William M. Jardine to H. L. Russell, April 28, 1925, NACP1, Box 1a, "4-H Goals"; Warburton to Smith, February 18, 1925, NACP1, Box 1a, "4-H Goals"; Smith to Warburton, February 20, 1925, NACP1, Box 1a, "4-H Goals."

69. T. T. Martin to A. J. Meyer, May 21, 1924, NACP2, Box 1, "1924 Club Congress." See also "The Montgomery Ward Offer," *National Boys and Girls Club News*, January 10, 1925, NACP2, Box 13, "National 4-H Club News, 1924–1935, and "Memorandum on Montgomery Ward," 1923, NACP2, Box 1, "1923 Club Congress."

70. "Swift Company Prize Memo," 1924, NACP2, Box 1, "1924 Club Congress"; "Armour Gives to State Livestock Champs," *National Boys and Girls Club News*, January 10, 1925, NACP2, Box 13, "National 4-H Club News, 1924–1935; "Program of Wilson & Co.," *National Boys and Girls Club News*, January 10, 1925, NACP2, Box 13, "National 4-H Club News, 1924–1935; "Grain Marketing Company Aids Corn Champs," *National Boys and Girls Club News*, January 10, 1925, NACP2, Box 13, "National 4-H Club News, 1924–1935; "'Electrolux' Sponsors Food Contest," *National Boys and Girls Club News*, May–June 1935, NACP2, Box 13, "National 4-H Club News, 1924–1935; "IHC Sponsors Farm Account Contest," *National Boys and Girls Club News*,

December 1933–January 1934, NACP2 Box 13, "National 4-H Club News, 1924–1935"; "National State and Local Prizes Offered Poultry Club Members," *National Boys and Girls Club News*, August 20, 1929, NACP2, Box 13, "National 4-H Club News, 1924–1935."

71. "Memo from Chicago Great Western Railroad Co.," 1923, NACP2, Box 1, "1923 Club Congress"; "Agreement with Sante Fe Railroad," 1923, NACP2, Box 1, "1923 4-H Club Congress"; "Agreement with Rock Island Railroad," 1923, NACP2, "1923 4-H Club Congress"; "Fare and One-Half Granted 4-H Congress: Reduced Rates to Chicago Made by Passenger Associations," *National Boys and Girls Club News*, October 10, 1925, NACP2, Box 13, "National 4-H Club News, 1924–1935; "Rock Island Railway In," *National Boys and Girls Club News*, January 10, 1925, NACP2, Box 13, "National 4-H Club News, 1924–1935; "More Aid to 4-H Work from Railways," *National Boys and Girls Club News*, January 10, 1925, NACP2, Box 13, "National 4-H Club News, 1924–1935; "Grain Marketing Company Aids Corn Champs," *National Boys and Girls Club News*, April 10, 1925, NACP2, Box 13, "National 4-H Club News, 1924–1935; "Railway Presidents Add 24 Congress Trips," *National Boys and Girls Club News*, May 10, 1925, NACP2, Box 13, "National 4-H Club News, 1924–1935.

72. For examples, see "The Perfect Boy and Girl"; "Huskiest Farm Boy Is a Kentucky Lad"; "Dakota Girl, 17, Wins National Health Contest"; "South Dakota Girl, Michigan Boy Chosen Nation's Healthiest in Chicago Contest"; "Healthiest Boy and Girl Picked."

73. "Huskiest Farm Boy Is a Kentucky Lad."

74. "The Perfect Boy and Girl."

75. Warburton to Noble, February 27, 1925, NACP1, Box 1a, "4-H Service Com. & Ext. Rel."; Noble to Warburton, March 3, 1925, NACP1, Box 1a, "4-H Service Com. & Ext. Rel."; Warburton to directors of extension, March 10, 1925, NACP1, Box 1a, "4-H Service Com. & Ext. Rel."; R. S. Wilson to Warburton, March 5, 1925, NACP1, Box 1a, "4-H Service Com. & Ext. Rel."; W. A. Conner to Warburton, March 4, 1925, NACP1, Box 1a, "4-H Service Com. & Ext. Rel."; Arizona to Warburton, March 3, 1925, NACP1, Box 1a, "4-H Service Com. & Ext. Rel."; Harry Umberger to Warburton, April 1, 1925, NACP1, Box 1a, "4-H Service Com. & Ext. Rel."; T. O. Walton to Warburton, March 7, 1925, NACP1, Box 1a, "4-H Service Com. & Ext. Rel." See collected responses of the state directors in NACP1, Box 1a, "4-H Service Com. & Ext. Rel." See also discussion of the article in correspondence between Warburton and Smith in NACP1, Box 1a, "4-H Goals."

76. See statement by William Jardine of *Hearing Before the Committee on Agriculture and Forestry, United States Senate, Seventieth Congress, First Session on S. 1285* (Washington, DC: Government Printing Office, 1928), 3–5.

77. For examples, see Resolution of the AFBF, November 14, 1922, NACP1, Box 1c, "Capper-Ketchum"; Resolution of the Executive and Advisory Committees, National Association of Farm Equipment Manufacturers, January 11, 1923, NACP1, Box 1c, "Capper-Ketchum"; Declaration of the Administrative Committee of the ABA, December 1922, NACP1, Box 1c, "Capper-Ketchum"; Declaration of the Extension Committee of the Land Grant College Association, 1923, NACP1, Box 1c, "Capper-Ketchum." The file folder at the National Archives incorrectly uses the spelling "Ketchum," but the correct spelling of both the act and its sponsor is, as in the text, "Ketcham."

78. See Mary Belle King Sherman, *Hearing Before the Committee on Agriculture and Forestry, United States House of Representatives, Seventieth Congress, First Session, on H.R. 6074* (Washington, DC: Government Printing Office, 1928), 24; Noble to T. T. Martin, April 7, 1932, NACP1, Box 1c, "Capper-Ketchum."

79. See statements of support collected by Noble in NACP1, Box 1c, "Capper-Ketchum."

80. Resolution of the National Grange, NACP1, Box 1c, "Capper-Ketchum." See also Oscar G. Mayer to House Committee Members, February 1, 1927, NACP1, Box 1c, "Capper-Ketchum"; statement by National Swine Growers Association [1927?], NACP1, Box 1c, "Capper-Ketchum."

81. In particular, the 1927 version of the bill mandated an immediate increase in the federal appropriation by $480,000, split evenly between the states, and authorized an appropriation increase of $500,000 each year for eleven years. The 1928 version doubled the initial payment to $960,000 but was otherwise identical. See statement of Chester H. Gray, *Hearing Before the Committee on Agriculture and Forestry, United States Senate, Seventieth Congress, First Session on S. 1285* (Washington, DC: Government Printing Office, 1928), 13–15.

82. Editorial, *Minneapolis Tribune* [1927?], NACP1, Box 1c, "Capper-Ketchum."

83. Statements of Viola Yoder, John Visny, Mrs. D. B. Phillips, and Guy Noble, in *Hearing Before the Committee on Agriculture and Forestry, United States Senate*, 23, 24–26, 28–30, 30–35.

84. *Hearing Before the Committee on Agriculture and Forestry, United States Senate*, 35–36.

85. Sherman, *Hearing Before the Committee on Agriculture and Forestry, United States House of Representatives*, 23.

86. "Sherman Asks Wider Farm Extension Law at Meeting," *Atlanta Constitution*, January 10, 1928; Sherman, *Hearing Before the Committee on Agriculture and Forestry, United States House of Representatives*, 23–24. While Sherman's larger point about employment disparities between male agricultural agents and female home demonstration was completely accurate, her portrayal of the relationship between male agricultural agents and female club members was not. As Clyde Warburton pointed out during the hearings, agricultural projects accounted for less than 2 percent of all female enrollments and girls were becoming less, not more, likely to enroll in an agricultural project. See C. W. Warburton, *Hearing Before the Committee on Agriculture and Forestry, United States House of Representatives*, 4.

87. Statement of Mrs. John S. Sippel, *Hearing Before the Committee on Agriculture and Forestry, United States House of Representatives*, 29.

88. James Aswell, *Hearing Before the Committee on Agriculture and Forestry, United States House of Representatives*, 4.

89. See, for examples, Noble to R. A. Pearson, May 28, 1928, NACP1, Box 1c, "Capper-Ketchum"; Noble to Arthur Capper, May 28, 1928, NACP1, Box 1c, "Capper-Ketchum"; Noble to John Ketcham, May 28, 1928, NACP1, Box 1c, "Capper-Ketchum."

90. Guy Noble, "Progress Report: Giving Results of the Capper-Ketcham Act," 1929, NACP1, Box 1c, "Capper-Ketchum."

91. Warburton to Noble, February 27, 1925, NACP1, Box 1a, "4-H Service Com. & Ext. Rel."

92. Bailey, "Remarks," 1.

Chapter 4

1. O. E. Baker, "Rural-Urban Migration and the National Welfare," *Annals of the Association of American Geographers* 23 (June 1933): 92.

2. O. E. Baker, "The Outlook for Rural Youth," 1935, NACP1, Box 6, "4-H Club Studies, Volume 3," 27.

3. C. B. Smith, "Our Enlarging Extension Objectives," 1938, NACP1, Box 1b, "CB Smith," 12; idem, "The Outlook in Agriculture in Relation to 4-H Club Work," 1–6.

4. Baker, "Rural-Urban Migration and the National Welfare," 122.

5. For an excellent account of Depression conditions in rural America, see Danbom, *Born in the Country*, chap. 9. For excellent regionally focused studies, see Catherine McNicol Stock,

Main Street in Crisis: The Great Depression and the Old Middle Class on the Northern Plains (Chapel Hill: University of North Carolina Press, 1997); Kirby, *Rural Worlds Lost*. For the classic work on the Dust Bowl, see Worster, *Dust Bowl*.

6. Sheingate, *The Rise of the Agricultural Welfare State*, 103–107; D. Hamilton, *From New Day to New Deal*, 26–147; Alonzo Hamby, *For the Survival of Democracy: Franklin Roosevelt and the World Crisis of the 1930s* (New York: Simon & Schuster, 2004), 81.

7. Sheingate, *The Rise of the Agricultural Welfare State*, 107; Finegold and Skocpol, *State and Party in the New Deal*, 66–89.

8. See M. L. Wilson and O. B. Jesness, *Farm Relief and the Domestic Allotment Plan* (Minneapolis: University of Minnesota Press, 1933).

9. For the clearest explanation of how the AAA functioned at a local level, see Worster, *Dust Bowl*, 155–158.

10. Richard Kirkendall, *Social Scientists and Farm Politics in the Age of Roosevelt* (Columbia: University of Missouri Press, 1973), 91.

11. "Wallace Decries Inflation Cure-All," *New York Times*, September 21, 1933.

12. On Duncan's use of the extension system for political influence, see Hugh McElderrey to L. B. Braden, March 21, 1930, ACES, Box 4, "Mc Misc."; "Failed to Click," *Wiregrass Journal*, October 19, 1933, ACES, Box 14, "Newspaper Clippings"; "Doc Conner," *Birmingham Post*, November 3, 1933, ACES, Box 14, "Newspaper Clippings."

13. "Adjustment Act Brings Benefits for Alabamans," *Anniston Star*, May 27, 1934, 8.

14. Brian Balogh, *A Government Out of Sight: The Mystery of National Authority in Nineteenth-Century America* (New York: Cambridge University Press, 2009), 391.

15. M. L. Wilson, quoted in Phillips, *This Land, This Nation*, 101.

16. See Phillips, *This Land, This Nation*; Sara Gregg, *Managing the Mountains: Land Use Planning, the New Deal, and the Creation of a Federal Landscape in Appalachia* (New Haven, CT: Yale University Press, 2010); Neil Maher, *Nature's New Deal: The Civilian Conservation Corps and the Roots of the American Environmental Movement* (New York: Oxford University Press 2008); Michael Johnston Grant, *Down and Out on the Family Farm: Rural Rehabilitation in the Great Plains, 1929–1945* (Lincoln: University of Nebraska Press, 2002).

17. Henry A. Wallace, *New Frontiers* (New York: Reynal & Hitchcock, 1934), 241.

18. Maher, *Nature's New Deal*, 199.

19. See Jellison, *Entitled to Power*, 67–106.

20. Phillips, *This Land, This Nation*, 108.

21. See Laura Lovett, *Conceiving the Future: Pronatalism, Reproduction, and the Family in the United States, 1890–1938* (Chapel Hill, NC: University of North Carolina Press, 2007) and Wendy Kline, *Building a Better Race: Gender, Sexuality, and Eugenics from the Turn of the Century to the Baby Boom* (Berkeley: University of California Press, 2005).

22. On the sexual anxieties around "degenerate" hobos, see Frank Tobias Higbee, *Indispensable Outcasts: Hobo Workers and Community in the American Midwest, 1880–1930* (Urbana: University of Illinois Press, 2003).

23. Wallace, *New Frontiers*, 243.

24. Gertrude Warren, "Youth Movements Abroad," 1935, 2, NACP1, Box 3, "General Circulars on 4-H Club Work."

25. C. B. Smith, "Summary and Goodbye," 1933, NACP1, Box 33, "National 4-H Club Camp, June 15–21, 1933," 3.

26. T. A. Sims, "Summary of Boys 4-H Club Work: Oct. 1 to Nov. 1, 1934," ACES, Box 19, "S–Si Correspondence"; I. O. Schaub, "Can Extension Continue and Educational Program and

Administer Enforcement and Regulatory Measures?," 1934, ACES, Box 19, "S–Si Correspondence." For nationwide 4-H enrollments, see NACP1, Box 16a, "Statistics."

27. See C. F. Sarle, "Operation of the Farm Adjustment Act with Corn and Hogs," NACP1, Box 33, "National 4-H Club Camp, June 15–21, 1933"; B. B. Derrick, "Operation of the Farm Adjustment Act as Applied to the Dairy Industry," NACP1, Box 33, "National 4-H Club Camp, June 15–21, 1933"; Dorothy Emerson, "Relation of the New Adjustment Act to the Farm Home," NACP1, Box 33, "National 4-H Club Camp, June 15–21, 1933"; Elaine E. Massey, "How the New Agricultural Adjustment Act Will Benefit the Home," NACP1, Box 33, "National 4-H Club Camp, June 15–21, 1933"; Eugene Merritt, "Organized Action," NACP1, Box 33, "National 4-H Club Camp, June 15–21, 1933"; V. B. Hart, "The Relation of the Present Price Situation to Organization of 4-H Club Programs," NACP1, Box 33, "National 4-H Club Camp, June 15–21, 1933"; L. J. Taber, "Rural Readjustment and Our Farm Youth," NACP1, Box 33, "National 4-H Club Camp, June 15–21, 1933."

28. Smith, "Summary and Goodbye," 3.

29. Gertrude Warren, "4-H Club Work Has a Place in the Adjustment of Agriculture," 1934, NACP1, Box 4, "4-H Newsletters to State Club Leaders, 1930–1952."

30. George Farrell, "4-H Club Leadership at Work," 1933, NACP1, Box 4, "4-H Newsletters to State Club Leaders, 1930–1952."

31. See the accusations of A. B. Moore in ACES, Box 7, "JM & AB Moore."

32. See G. B. Phillips to club members, April 8, 1932, ACES, Box 10, "P Corr."; and "Proposed Bill," April 23, 1931, ACES, Box 6, "P Corr."

33. Charles Brockway to club members, May 5, 1931, ACES, Box 6, "B Corr."

34. Luther Duncan to O. B. Martin, July 24, 1931, ACES, Box 10, "M Corr."

35. "Farmers Urged to Keep Records," 1935, ACES, Box 22, "Newspaper Clippings"; "22 County Farm Leaders Evolve Program for '36," *Montgomery Advertiser*, January 2, 1936; J. C. Lowery, memorandum to Luther Duncan, December 17, 1935, ACES, Box 22, "L Correspondence"; Luther Duncan to H. M. Dixon, December 20, 1935, ACES, Box 22, "L Correspondence."

36. Clyde W. Warburton, "A New Year's Greeting to the 4-H Clubs," January 6, 1934, NACP1, Box 4, "4-H Newsletters to State Club Leaders, 1930–1952."

37. "County Leads in AAA and Club Work, Too," *National Boys and Girls Club News*, March 1934, NACP2, Box 13, "National 4-H Club News, 1923–1935."

38. See 1930's personal account books, 4-H material, Clay County Historical Society, Clay County, Iowa.

39. "Report of the Sub-Committee on 4-H Personal Accounts: American Home Economics Association," December 1933, NACP1, Box 4, "4-H Newsletters to State Club Leaders, 1930–1952."

40. C. B. Smith, "How Extension May Participate in the Various Plans for Conservation," 1936, NACP1, Box 34, "National 4-H Club Camp, June 18–24, 1936," 7.

41. For other descriptions of conservation programs, see Ruth Lohmann, "A Suggested Program in Wildlife Conservation for the 4-H Clubs," 1936, NACP1, Box 1b, "Misc. Talks"; C. B. Smith, "Rural Life and Nature," 1938, NACP1, Box 4, "Significant Talks and Addresses on 4-H Club Work, Volume 2: 1930–1960"; Gertrude Warren, "The Intangible Values of the 4-H Club Program" [1938?], NACP1, Box 1b, "[Gertrude Warren Folder]."

42. "Ohio Tree Planting Three-Fourths Done," *Piqua Daily Call*, May 26, 1936, 6.

43. Roy Westley, "1936 Report of the Specialist in Agronomy and Irrigation," 1936, UAL.

44. "Nearly 300 Attend Camp," *Hutchinson (KS) News*, August 30, 1938, 5.

45. Charles Peterson, "County 4-H Club Representative Meet Gives Resume Conservation," *Brainerd (MN) Daily*, October 14, 1935, 3.

46. "4-H Members to Take Part in Rural Electrification," *Emmetsburg (IA) Democrat*, June 11, 1936, 2; "Rural Electrification," *National 4-H Club News*, January 1937, 2.

47. Gertrude Warren, "Why 4-H Clubs Welcome Rural Electrification," 1939, NACP1, Box 3, "General Circulars on 4-H Club Work." See also idem, "Rural Electrification and 4-H Clubs," *4-H Horizons* (March 1939): 10; "Instruction Meet on Electrification Set for New Week," *Burlington (NC) Daily Times-News*, September 7, 1939, 10; "Linton's National 4-H Winner Had Big Project," *Bismarck Tribune*, January 9, 1939, 2; "4-H Clubs Continue Electrification Work," *La Crosse Tribune and Leader-Press*, March 15, 1937, 11; "Rural Lighting Is Contest Subject," *Evening Huronite*, June 17, 1937, 13; "Give Awards on Electrification," *Sandusky Register*, April 14, 1928, 5.

48. Maude Wallace, "Ways in Which the Spirit of Service Has Been Developed in the Local Club and Rural Community Through 4-H Club Work," 1935, NACP1, Box 34, "National 4-H Club Camp, June 13–19, 1935," 2, 5.

49. C. B. Smith, "Our Enlarging Extension Objectives and What of Extension?," 1938, NACP1, Box 1b, "CB Smith Folder," 10–11.

50. Robert Foster, "Social Relations and Family Life," 1931, NACP1, Box 32, "National 4-H Club Camp, June 17–23, 1931," 10.

51. Warren, "The Social and Economic Problems of Farm Youth," 25.

52. Gertrude Warren, "Young People and the Rural Home," 1937, NACP1, Box 1b, "Gertrude Warren," 1.

53. Smith, "Our Enlarging Extension Objectives," 11.

54. Robert A. Polson, "Views of an Extension Sociologist on the Rural Youth Problem," 1934, NACP1, Box 34, "National 4-H Club Camp, June 14–20, 1934."

55. Eugene Merritt, "The Farm Young People: A Memorandum to Accompany the Land Grant-Rural Youths' Committee Report," 1936, NACP1, Box 6, "4-H Club Studies, Volume 3," 5; Gertrude Warren, "Meeting the Needs of Older Rural Girls," 1933, NACP1, Box 1b, "[Gertrude Warren Folder]," 5.

56. A. B. Graham, "Reasons for Losses in Club Membership," June 1934, NACP1, Box 1b, "Misc. Talks," 2.

57. Merritt, "The Farm Young People," 6.

58. For Dimock's definition of heterosexuality as both biological and socially constructed, see Hedley S. Dimock, "A Research in Adolescence: The Social World of the Adolescent," *Child Development* 6, no. 4 (December 1935): 285–305.

59. Hedley S. Dimock, untitled talk, *Proceedings of the 1934 National 4-H Club Congress* (Chicago: National Committee, 1935), 9–10. Dimock's talk was apparently a hit; Guy Noble asked him to return the following two years. See Hedley S. Dimock, untitled talk, *Proceedings of the 1935 National 4-H Club Congress* (Chicago: National Committee, 1936), and *Proceedings of the 1936 National 4-H Club Congress* (Chicago: National Committee, 1937).

60. Peterson, "County 4-H Club Representative Meet."

61. See UAL, 1939, 1941–1942. The issues that I quote from are included in the reports of the club specialist as addenda and are not regularly paginated. They are titled *Roundup News* in 1939 and 1941 and *Camp News* in 1942. In *Roundup News*, specific contributors are irregularly named; but in *Camp News*, comments appear in an anonymously authored section known as the "Dust Pan."

62. *4-H Roundup News* in "Club Specialist Report, 1941," 10–11.

63. *Camp News*, in "Club Specialist Report, 1942," 3.

64. Warren, "Meeting the Needs of Older Rural Girls," 5.

65. Margaret Latimer, " Planning an Extension Program for Older Girls," October 1933, NACP1, Box 6, "4-H Club Studies, Volume 3," 14.

66. C. B. Smith, "Older Rural Youth: Some Successful Solutions of Their Problems by County Extension Workers," 1936, NACP1, Box 6, "4-H Club Studies, Volume 3."

67. Hallie Hughes, "Self Management," 1931, NACP1, Box 33, "National 4-H Club Camp, June 17–23," 1.

68. Foster, "Social Relations and Family Life."

69. Gertrude Warren, "Development of Happy Family Relationships Through 4-H Club Work" [1937?], NACP1, Box 1b, "[Gertrude Warren Folder]," 1.

70. Robert G. Foster, "The Place of Marriage and Family Relationships in the 4-H Club Program," 1933, NACP2, Box 1, "1933 Club Congress"; Gertrude Warren, "Work of 4-H Clubs in Child Development and Education for Family Living," *Parent Education* (May 15, 1935): 29; Ruth Durrenburger, "Contributions of 4-H Club Work to Good Family Living with Suggestions for Increasing These Contributions," 1938, NACP1, Box 9a, "National 4-H Fellowship Program"; Lydia Lynde, "How 4-H Club Members Help to Plan Family Life," 1938, NACP1, Box 34, "National 4-H Club Camp, June 16–22, 1938."

71. "This Will Start a Discussion," *National 4-H Club News*, January 1938.

72. Genevieve K. Tippett, "Little Mothers," *National 4-H Club News* (January 1940), 8, NACP2, Box 13, "National 4-H Club News 1940–1942."

73. "Senior Girls' 4-H Handbook," April 1947, ACES, Box 336, "Projects for 4-H Club Girls," 80. See also Lynde, "How 4-H Club Members Help to Plan Family Life."

74. R. E. Parry, "What Is the Future for the Doctor and 4-H Girl," *1936 Annual Report*, ISU2.

75. *1939 Annual Report*, ISU2, 4.

76. "Wisconsin Boys and Sex Education," *Journal of Social Hygiene* 25, no. 4 (April 1939).

77. See "Food Nutrition and Health Unit 1," 1941, NACP1, Box 3a, "State 4-H Publications (Primarily Subject-Matter)."

78. Ibid., 2–3.

79. See Henry Jackson Waters and Franklin George King, *Animal Husbandry* (New York: Ginn, 1925); Leon F. Whitney, *The Basis of Breeding* (New Haven, CT: Earle C. Fowler, 1928); James E. Russell, *Heredity in Dairy Cattle: Lessons in Breeding and Herd Development for 4H and FFA Dairy Clubs and Other Beginners* (Peterborough, NH: American Guernsey Cattle Club, 1944); M. E. Ensminger, *Beef Cattle Husbandry* (Danville, IL: Interstate, 1951).

80. Harry H. Cook, *Like Breeds Like* (Ontario, CA: Research Department, Sans Aloi's Jersey Farm, 1931), 283, 374–375.

81. Russell, *Heredity in Dairy Cattle*, 133.

82. M. L. Wilson, "Making the Most of Our Rural Heritage," 1937, NACP1, Box 34, "National 4-H Club Camp, June 17–23, 1937," 2.

83. William F. McDermott, "Rebirth of the Barefoot Boy and Girl," *The Rotarian* (November 1937): 26.

84. Robert H. Reed, "Here's How to Keep Them Down on the Farm," *Saturday Evening Post*, March 29, 1941.

85. Neil M. Clark, "A Challenge to the Cities," *Saturday Evening Post*, November 30, 1946.

86. Arthur Hyde, "Recommended Policies Governing 4-H Club Work," 1935, NACP1, Box 1a, "4-H Goals," 1.

87. R. A. Turner, "A Brief Review of Negotiations Between Representatives of the Extension Service and the National Committee on Boys' and Girls' Club Work," 1948, NACP1, Box 1a, "4-H Service Com. & Ext. Rel," 3.

88. "Offer Trip to Paris as Prize," *National Boys and Girls Club News*, August 20, 1929, NACP2, Box 13, "National 4-H Club News 1924–1935."

89. Memo, Gertrude Warren to Clarence Smith, March 20, 1930, NACP1, Box 1a, "4-H Service Com. & Ext. Rel," 1–3.

90. Ibid., 4–6.

91. C. B. Warburton to Luther Duncan, May 29, 1930, ACES, Box 5, "CW Warburton."

92. D. P. Trent to C. B. Smith, April 30, 1930, ACES, Box 5, "CW Warburton"; C. B. Warburton to Trent, May 29, 1930, ACES, Box 5, "CW Warburton"; Luther Duncan to C. B. Warburton, June 30, 1930, Box 5, "CW Warburton."

93. O. B. Martin to C. W. Warburton, June 3, 1931, ACES, Box 10, "M Corr."

94. Luther Duncan to I. O. Schaub, August 14, 1931, ACES, Box 10, "S Corr."

95. See material in ACES, Box 10, "S Corr."

96. See Hyde, "Recommended Policies Governing 4-H Club Work."

97. See Charles Potter, "Developments in Relation to the Report of the Special 4-H Club Committee Appointed Following 1937 National Club Camp," 1948, NACP1, Box 1a, "4-H Service Com. & Ext. Rel."

98. See "Report of the 4-H Club Committee," 1937, NACP1, Box 1a, "4-H Service Com. & Ext. Rel." See also Turner, "A Brief Review of Negotiations." See also HR 913, 4-H Emblem Act, 1939, NACP1, Box 1, "Records of Development of Early Phases of Development"; Extension Committee on Organization and Policy, "A Procedure for Developing a National 4-H Club Activity Involving a Plan of Award by a Non-Governmental Agency," 1939, NACP1, Box 1, "4-H Club Activities and Programs"; Extension Committee on Organization and Policy, "Prizes and Awards in 4-H Club Work," 1939, NACP1, Box 1, "4-H Club Activities and Programs"; Extension Committee on Organization and Policy, "Brief Report on Relationships of Extension Service to National Committee on Boys' and Girls' Club Work," 1939, NACP1, Box 1, "4-H Club Activities and Programs"; Extension Committee on Organization and Policy, "Digest of Conference on Relationships," 1939, NACP1, Box 1, "4-H Club Activities and Programs"; C. W. Warburton, "Relations with National Committee on Boys' and Girls' Club Work," March 20, 1939, ACES, Box 29, "4-H Club Work"; "Resolution on Further Steps to Be Taken on Relationships Between Agricultural Extension Services and the National Committee on Boys' and Girls' Club Work in Contest Awards," March 1939, ACES, Box 29, "4-H Club Work"; "A Summary of the Progress on Clarifying Relationships Between the Extension Service and the National Committee on Boys' and Girls' Club Work," March 1939, ACES, Box 29, "4-H Club Work." For the (mixed, at best) attitudes of the state directors of extension toward the *Club News*, see the extended correspondence in NACP1, Box 1a, "4-H Service Com. & Ext. Rel."

99. Potter, "Developments in Relation to the Report," 4; Turner, "A Brief Review of Negotiations," 15.

100. For ongoing problems of cooperation between the USDA and the National Committee, see "Report of the 4-H Subcommittee," 1945, NACP1, Box 1a, "4-H Service Com. & Ext. Rel," 6.

101. Guy Noble to Hickman Powell, July 25, 1944, NACP1, Box 1c, "Misc. Bills Introduced Before Congress."

102. "Stars in Queen Film," *Galveston (TX) Daily News*, March 14, 1942; "Young America," *Hutchinson (KS) News-Herald*, February 1, 1942; "Jane Withers in 4-H Club Story," *Laredo Times*, April 28, 1942.

103. "Sex Delinquency Among Girls," *Journal of Social Hygiene* 28, no. 8 (November 1943): 496.

104. "The Program in Action in the States and Communities," *Journal of Social Hygiene* 28, no. 5 (May 1942): 294.

105. Elena Bonilla, "Action on the Home Front," *Journal of Social Hygiene* 30, no. 4 (April 1944): 205–206.

106. See Laura Briggs, *Reproducing Empire: Race, Sex, Science, and U.S. Imperialism in Puerto Rico* (Berkeley: University of California Press, 2002).

Chapter 5

1. A. Powell Davies, "The Atomic Age—What Is It?," 1946, 4–6, NACP1, Box 34, "National 4-H Club Camp, June 11–18, 1946."

2. "4-H Citizenship Oath Mockery at Jim Crow Meet," *Chicago Defender*, June 29, 1946, 1.

3. "Education for Fascism," *Chicago Defender*, July 13, 1946, 14.

4. M. L. Wilson, "4-H Club Citizenship Inaugural Ceremony for Rural Youth of Voting Age," 1940, NACP1, Box 5, "4-H Clubs in Wartime, 1939–1950."

5. Jess Gilbert, "Agrarian Intellectuals in a Democratizing State: A Collective Biography of USDA Leaders in the Intended New Deal," in *The Countryside in the Age of the Modern State: Political Histories of Rural America*, ed. Catherine McNicol Stock and Robert D. Johnston (Ithaca, NY: Cornell University Press, 2001), 236. For the USDA philosophy programs, see Andrew Jewett, "The Social Sciences, Philosophy, and the Cultural Turn in the 1930s USDA," *Journal of the History of the Behavioral Sciences* 49, no. 4 (autumn 2013): 396–427.

6. For elaborations of the purpose of democratic education and the "cultural approach," see M. L. Wilson, "The Democratic Processes and the Formulation of Agricultural Policy," *Social Forces* 19 (October 1940); idem, "Problem of Poverty in Agriculture," *Journal of Farm Economics* 22, no. 1 (February 1940): 10–29; idem, "Rural America Discusses Democracy," *Public Opinion Quarterly* 5, no. 2 (June): 288–294.

7. See also Jess Gilbert, "Low Modernism and the Agrarian New Deal: A Different Kind of State," in *Fighting for the Farm: Rural America Transformed*, ed. Jane H. Adams (Philadelphia: University of Pennsylvania Press, 2003); Jess Gilbert, "Eastern Urban Liberals and Midwestern Agrarian Intellectuals: Two Group Portraits of Progressives in the New Deal Department of Agriculture," *Agricultural History* 74 (spring 2000): 162–180; David Lachman, "Democratic Ideology in Agricultural Policy: 'Program Study and Discussion' in the U.S. Department of Agriculture, 1934–1946" (MS thesis, University of Wisconsin, 1991).

8. George Farley, "What More Can We Do to Teach Citizenship?," 1940, NACP2, Box 2, "1940 Club Congress."

9. Gertrude Warren, "Contributions That Can Be Made by the 4-H Clubs to National Defense," 1940, 9–18, ACES, Box 43, "Defense Memos(3)."

10. "Brief Resume of Activities Concerning 'Citizenship Training' in the Several States," 1941, ACES, Box 42, "Sims TA"; "Report Training in Citizenship," 1942, 8, NACP1, Box 4, "Reports of State Club Leaders' Conferences, 1912–1946."

11. "Iowa 4-H Girls' Club Citizenship Program," *1940 Boys and Girls Club Annual Reports*, ISU2.

12. "4-H Girls' Panel Discussions," *1940 Boys and Girls Club Annual Reports*, ISU2, 8; "Discussion Helps," *1940 Boys and Girls Club Annual Reports*, ISU2, 8.

13. "Rural Urban Exchange—New York Trip," *1941 Boys and Girls Club Annual Reports*, ISU2, 1–3.

14. "Brief Statements by the Girls Themselves," *1941 Boys and Girls Club Annual Reports*, ISU2.

15. "Rural Urban Exchange—New York Trip," 8.

16. Ruth Ann Hermanson dossier, *1941 Boys and Girls Club Annual Reports*, ISU2, 1–3; "Iowa 4-H Club Leaders Explore the Vastness of New York City," *1941 Boys and Girls Club Annual Reports*, ISU2.

17. William F. Ogburn, untitled speech, *Proceedings of the 1935 National 4-H Club Congress* (Chicago: National Committee, 1936), 29–45.

18. "Report of Committee on 4-H Club Work: Extension Conference, December 13–16, 1939," 1, 7, NACP1, Box 1b, "Miscellaneous State 4-H Leader Conferences."

19. See, e.g., Ella Gardner, "Flag Raising Ceremonies Suggested for Six Days in Camp," 1941, NACP1, Box 1, "4-H Club Activities and Programs"; "4-H Achievement Pays Education Dividends to 4," *Chicago Daily Tribune*, December 1, 1941, NACP2, Box 2, "1941 Club Congress"; "A Ceremony for Sunday Evening at 1943 National 4-H Club Congress," 1943, NACP2, Box 2, "1943 Club Congress"; "4-H Club Ceremony: Looking to the Hilltop," 1943, NACP2, Box 2, "1943 Club Congress"; "4-H Club Ceremony," 1944, NACP2, Box 2, "1944 Club Congress"; "The 4-H Citizenship Oath," wartime, NACP1, Box 5, "4-H Clubs in Wartime, 1939–1950." For the increasing emphasis on citizenship programming, see "Education for Citizenship and Democracy—and Preparation for Life," 1940, NACP1, Box 5, "4-H Clubs in Wartime, 1939–1950"; "Report: Training in Citizenship," 1941, NACP1, Box 5; Farley, "What More Can We Do to Teach Citizenship?."

20. Gertrude Warren, "4-H Ceremonials," 1951, NACP1, Box 1, "4-H Club Activities and Programs"; "Citizenship Inaugural Ceremony for Senior 4-H Members," 1939, NACP1, Box 5, "4-H Clubs in Wartime, 1939–1950." For later National 4-H Citizenship Ceremonies, see M. L. Wilson, "4-H Club Citizenship Inaugural Ceremony for Rural Youth of Voting Age," 1940, NACP1, Box 1, "4-H Club Activities and Programs"; M. L. Wilson, "The Meaning of Citizenship," 1941, NACP1, Box 5, "4-H Clubs in Wartime, 1939–1950."

21. Wilson, "The Meaning of Citizenship."

22. "1942 Rally Days," *1942 Boys and Girls Club Annual Reports*, ISU2; "Suggestive Rally Day Program," *1942 Boys and Girls Club Annual Reports*, ISU2; "4-H Girls' Service Review," *1942 Boys and Girls Club Annual Reports*, ISU2.

23. G. J. Fowler, "There's Much to Be Thankful For," *Alabama 4-H Club News* (November 1942), ACES, Box 355, "Alabama 4-H Club News."

24. "Democracy in the Present Crisis," 1941, NACP1, Box 5, "4-H Clubs in Wartime, 1939–1950." See also "Suggested Plan for Group Discussions Regarding Democracy in the Present Crisis," 1941, NACP1, Box 5, "4-H Clubs in Wartime, 1939–1950."

25. P. O. Davis to 4-H club members, *Alabama 4-H Club News* (January 1942), ACES, Box 355, "Alabama 4-H Club News"; P. O. Davis to 4-H club members, *Alabama 4-H Club News* (April 1943), ACES, Box 355, "Alabama 4-H Club News."

26. "Suggested Wartime Program for the Local 4-H Club Meeting," *1943 Boys and Girls Club Annual Reports*, ISU2.

27. "I'm Gonna Buy a Bond," *Alabama 4-H Club News* (July 1943), ACES, Box 355, "Alabama 4-H Club News."

28. George Gilbertson, "Bug Blitz Skit," *1943 Boys and Girls Club Annual Reports*, ISU2.

29. P. O. Davis to 4-H club members, *Alabama 4-H Club News* (July 1943), ACES, Box 355, "Alabama 4-H Club News."

30. "Hands Around the World," 1946, NACP2, Box 2, "1946 Club Congress"; Joyce Lee Remsberg, "What Democracy Means to a 4-H Member," 1946, NACP2, Box 2, "1946 Club

Congress"; Roy Burkhart, "Contributions That Community and Spiritual Values Make for Better Home and World Communities," 1947, NACP2, Box 2, "1947 Club Congress"; M. L. Wilson, "4-H Responsibilities in Enriching the Community Life of Our Democracy," 1947, NACP1, Box 34, "National 4-H Club Camp, June 11–18, 1947"; Joy Elmer Morgan, "Individual Responsibility for Citizenship," 1947, NACP1, Box 34, "National 4-H Club Camp, June 11–18, 1947"; Clinton P. Anderson, "Talk," 1947, NACP1, Box 34, "National 4-H Club Camp, June 11–18, 1947"; Albert Hoefer, "The 4-H Club Member and World Affairs," 1948, NACP2, Box 2, "1946 Club Congress."

31. P. O. Davis to 4-H club members, *Alabama 4-H Club News* (April 1942), ACES, Box 355, "Alabama 4-H Club News."

32. Observance of Rural Life Sunday by 4-H Clubs: "Moral Responsibility and National Unity," 1942, NACP1, Box 1b, "4-H and Church Programs"; "The Spiritual Influence in the American Way of Life," 1943, NACP1, Box 1b, "4-H and Church Programs"; "Serving God and Country," 1944, NACP1, Box 1b, "4-H and Church Programs"; "Serving as Citizens in Maintaining World Peace," 1946, NACP1, Box 1b, "4-H and Church Programs"; "Working Together for a Better Home and World Community," 1947, NACP1, Box 1b, "4-H and Church Programs."

33. "Thousands of Flags in the Making," 1950, NACP1, Box 5, "4-H Clubs in Wartime, 1939–1950"; "Outline for Dramatic Setting to Use for Introducing the United Nations Flag Project," 1950, NACP1, Box 5, "4-H Clubs in Wartime, 1939–1950."

34. *Alabama 4-H Club News* (February 1943), ACES, Box 355, "Alabama 4-H Club News"; Smith, "Preparedness and 4-H Work."

35. Claude R. Wickard, "The Challenge to Farm Youth in 1943," 1942, NACP2, Box 2, "1942 Club Congress."

36. *Alabama 4-H Club News* (October 1942), ACES, Box 355, "Alabama 4-H Club News."

37. Visual aids, ACES, Box 46, "Visual Aids for Ag. Defense Program."

38. "Naming and Launching of a Liberty Ship," 1943, NACP1, Box 1b, "4-H and War Reports"; Liberty Ships press release, 1944, NACP1, Box 5, "4-H Clubs in Wartime, 1939–1950"; notes about doomed liberty ships, 1948, NACP1, Box 5, "4-H Clubs in Wartime, 1939–1950."

39. *Alabama 4-H Club News* (October 1943), ACES, Box 355, "Alabama 4-H Club News"; "4-H Clubs of Alabama on Flying Fortress," *Alabama 4-H Club News* (December 1944), ACES, Box 355, "Alabama 4-H Club News."

40. Lawrence R. Samuel, *Pledging Allegiance: American Identity and the Bond Drive of World War II* (Washington, DC: Smithsonian, 1997), 37; "National 4-H Victory Program," 1942, NACP1, Box 1b, "4-H and War Reports"; "National 4-H Mobilization Week," 1943, NACP1, Box 1b, "4-H and War Reports"; "4-H Mobilization Week," 1944, NACP1, Box 1b, "4-H and War Reports"; "4-H Victory Loan Drive," September 14, 1945, NACP1, Box 5, "4-H Clubs in Wartime, 1939–1950"; "National 4-H Mobilization Week," 1944, NACP1, Box 5, "4-H Clubs in Wartime, 1939–1950"; "600 Carloads," undated but wartime, NACP1, Box 1b, "4-H and War Reports."

41. The figure of 600,000 is derived from an extrapolation of the figures provided in Z. L. Galloway, "Feed a Fighter in 1943," 1943, NACP1, Box 1b, "4-H and War Reports."

42. "Extension Activities and Accomplishments, 1941–1949," and "Statistical Results of Cooperative Extension Work, 1924–1940," NACP1, Box 16a, "Statistics."

43. M. L. Wilson, "The Wartime Objectives of 4-H Club Work," 1943, 1, NACP1, Box 5, "4-H Clubs in Wartime, 1939–1950"; idem, "4-H Service for Human Freedom," 1942, NACP2, Box 2, "1942 Club Congress." For an exhaustive account of agricultural policy and strategy during World War II, see Bureau of the Budget, *The United States at War: Development and*

Administration of the War Program by the Federal Government (Washington, DC: Government Printing Office, 1946), chap. 11.

44. "Report of the National Conference on Voluntary Local Leadership," ACES, Box 46, "Wilson ML (2)."

45. H. W. Hochbaum, "A Special 4-H Club Leader in Each Neighborhood," 1942, NACP2, Box 2, "1942 Club Congress."

46. Wilson, "The Wartime Objectives of 4-H Club Work," 2.

47. Warren, "Contributions That Can Be Made by the 4-H Clubs to National Defense," 1942, 8.

48. Radio script, ACES, Box 392, "Radio Scripts (1)"; Harriet Elliot, quoted in M. L. Wilson, "Nutrition's Role in Total Defense," 1941, ACES, Box 43, "Defense Memos."

49. Lewis B. Hershey, "Building Strength for a Strong America," 1946, 1–6, 4–6, NACP1, Box 34, "National 4-H Club Camp, June 11–18, 1946."

50. Ibid., 5.

51. Edith Barker, "4-H Girls' World Famine Emergency Bulletin," *1946 Boys and Girls Club Annual Reports*, ISU2.

52. L. A. Toney to L. I. Jones, September 15, 1948, NACP1, Box 10, "Negro 4-H Club Programs, Early History, Volume 1," 3. On the civil rights movement and the 1940s, see Glenda Elizabeth Gilmore, *Defying Dixie: The Radical Roots of Civil Rights, 1919–1950* (New York: W. W. Norton, 2008).

53. For a broader and more detailed account of segregation in 4-H camps, see C. Harris, "States' Rights."

54. Reuben Brigham to L. R. Simons, December 9, 1940, ACES, Box 38, "Reuben Brigham"; Reuben Brigham to H. H. Williamson, December 9, 1940, ACES, Box 38, "Reuben Brigham."

55. C. E. Brehm to Reuben Brigham, December 26, 1940, ACES, Box 38, "Reuben Brigham."

56. P. O. Davis to Reuben Brigham, December 31, 1940, ACES, Box 38, "Reuben Brigham."

57. P. O. Davis to Reuben Brigham, December 18, 1940, ACES, Box 38, "Reuben Brigham."

58. P. O. Davis to Reuben Brigham, December 19, 1940, ACES, Box 38, "Reuben Brigham"; P. O. Davis to J. C. Ford, December 19, 1940.

59. P. O. Davis to Reuben Brigham, January, 16, 1941, ACES, Box 38, "Reuben Brigham."

60. C. Harris, "States' Rights," 367.

61. "US Department Bars Negroes at 4-H Meet," *Chicago Defender*, May 18, 1946, 1.

62. "4-H Congress Bars Negroes," *Chicago Defender*, June 8, 1946, 12.

63. "Education for Fascism," 14.

64. E. B. Henderson, "Four-H Program Fascist," quoted in C. Harris, "States' Rights," 369. See also "4-H Clubs Open Jim Crow Convention," *Chicago Defender*, June 22, 1946, 1.

65. "Jim Crow 4-H Meet US Plan, Youths Claim," *Chicago Defender*, June 29, 1946, 6.

66. "4-H Congress Still Jim Crow," *Chicago Defender*, July 20, 1946.

67. "4-H Congress Observes 26th Year of Bias," *Chicago Defender*, December 13, 1947.

68. For lingering publicity on the issue, see "Jim Crow in 4-H Probed," *Chicago Defender*, July 13, 1946, 6; "U.S. Studies Plan for Negro 4-H Conference," *Chicago Defender*, May 24, 1947, 4; "Plan National Meet for 4-H Club Youth," *Chicago Defender*, June 7, 1947, 2.

69. C. Harris, "States' Rights," 370.

70. Camp program, 1948 Southern Regional 4-H Camp, 1948, NACP1, Box 10, "Negro 4-H Club Programs, Early History, Volume 1."

71. C. Harris, "States' Rights," 376.

72. Ibid.

73. "The Code of the Good American," camp program, 10, 1948 Southern Regional 4-H Camp, 1948, NACP1, Box 10, "Negro 4-H Club Programs, Early History, Volume 1."

74. M. L. Wilson, "Our Daily Bread," ACES, ML Wilson (1), Box 55, 1–2.

75. Camp program, 1948 Southern Regional 4-H Camp, 1948, NACP1, Box 10, "Negro 4-H Club Programs, Early History, Volume 1"; L. A. Toney to L. I. Jones, September 15, 1948, NACP1, Box 10, "Negro 4-H Club Programs, Early History, Volume 1."

76. Bessie L. Walton to L. I. Jones, September 15, 1948, NACP1, Box 10, "Negro 4-H Club Programs, Early History, Volume 1"; John Henry Brown to Wayman Johnson, September 25, 1948, NACP1, Box 10, "Negro 4-H Club Programs, Early History, Volume 1."

77. P. H. Stone to T. M. Campbell, September 7, 1948, NACP1, Box 10, "Negro 4-H Club Programs, Early History, Volume 1"; W. H. Williamson to T. M. Campbell, September 4, 1948, NACP1, Box 10, "Negro 4-H Club Programs, Early History, Volume 1."

78. Camilia Veems to L. I. Jones, September 16, 1948, NACP1, Box 10, "Negro 4-H Club Programs, Early History, Volume 1."

79. L. A. Toney to L. I. Jones, September 15, 1948, NACP1, Box 10, "Negro 4-H Club Programs, Early History, Volume 1," 3.

80. C. Harris, "States' Rights," 383.

81. Quoted in ibid., 382.

82. Anne Emery, *County Fair: A 4-H Romance* (Philadelphia: Macrae Smith, 1953); idem, *Hickory Hill* (Philadelphia: Macrae Smith, 1955); idem, *Sixteen* (Philadelphia: Macrae Smith, 1956). On the popularity of Emery's novels, see Joyce Litton, "Dinny Gordon: Proto-Feminist" *Journal of American Culture* 29, no. 1 (March 2006): 43–51; Jillian Anderson, "Looking Together in the Same Direction: Girls' Intellectual Desire in Anne Emery's Postwar Junior Fiction." As Anderson notes, Emery was popular enough that her novels occasionally landed reviews in the *New York Times*. For the *Times* review of *Hickory Hill*, see Elizabeth Youman, "The Simple Life," *New York Times Review of Books*, January 22, 1956, 26. For a review of *County Fair*, see "For Teen Girls," *Chicago Daily Tribune*, November 15, 1953, pt. 4, sec. 2, p. 53.

83. Emery, *Hickory Hill*, 80.

84. Emery, *Sixteen*, 21.

85. Ibid., 139.

86. Emery, *County Fair*, 126.

87. Race is predictably unaddressed explicitly in the books, though the cultural markers of whiteness are ubiquitous. It's worth noting that *Hickory Hill's* major plot arc involves Marquette High School's trip to the state finals of the Indiana High School basketball tournament, Chuck as a player and Jane as a cheerleader, where the team is eventually vanquished by Frankfort High School. In reality, Crispus Attucks High School in Indianapolis, led by future NBA Hall of Famer Oscar Robertson, won the first of back-to-back state titles in 1955. Attucks was the first all-black high school in the nation to accomplish that feat and did so despite regular racist harassment from rival teams, coaches, referees, and a hostile white public.

88. Emery, *Sixteen*, 44.

89. Emery, *County Fair*, 15.

90. Ibid., 128.

91. Ibid., 22, 29, 128; idem, *Hickory Hill*, 73, 89.

92. Emery, *County Fair*, 20.

93. Emery, *Hickory Hill*, 70.

94. Emery, *County Fair*, 27.

95. Ibid., 29.

96. Judith Butler, *Bodies That Matter: On the Discursive Limits of Sex* (New York: Routledge, 1993), 125, 122; Atkinson, "Raising a Crop of Young Farmers," 1.

Chapter 6

1. Theodore Hutchcroft, "The Evolution of '4-H Type' Rural Youth Educational Programs in the America," 1973, 1, 1973 Folder, Box 3, *PIJR Series*, Records of the CES, Record Group 33, National Archives, College Park, MD (NACP3).

2. Enrique Bello to Gertrude Warren, March 22, 1946, NACP1, Box 12, "International 4-H Programs, Volume."

3. Gertrude Warren, "Greetings to the Leaders and Members of the 5-C Clubs of Cuba," April 1946, NACP1, Box 12, "International 4-H Programs, Volume 1," 1–2.

4. Enrique Bello, "Visit of the Chiefs of the 5-C Clubs to the 4-H Clubs of the United States of America," 1946, NACP1, Box 12, "International 4-H Programs, Volume 1," 1–2.

5. On the black box, see Bruno Latour, *Science in Action: How to Follow Scientists and Engineers Through Society* (Cambridge, MA: Harvard University Press, 1987).

6. Theodore Hutchcroft, "Some Questions and Responses About PIJR in the 1970s," 2, "PIJR in the 1970s," Box 2, NACP3.

7. On New Deal programs as models for international development programs, see Ekbladh, *The Great American Mission*; Immerwahr, *Thinking Small*; Elizabeth Borgwardt, *A New Deal for the World: America's Vision of Human Rights* (Cambridge, MA: Harvard University Press, 2007). For modernization theory, see Nils Gilman, *Mandarins of the Future: Modernization Theory in Cold War America* (Baltimore: Johns Hopkins University Press, 2007); David C. Engerman et al., eds., *Staging Growth: Development, Modernization, and the Global Cold War* (Amherst: University of Massachusetts Press, 2003).

8. Claude Wickard, "Extension's Contribution Toward World Peace," in *Conference Report on the Contribution of Extension Methods and Techniques Toward the Rehabilitation of War-Torn Countries*, ACES, Box 53, E Correspondence, 191–192.

9. M. L. Wilson, "Objectives of the Conference," and Carl Taylor, "The Cultural Approach to Extension," in *Conference Report*, 6–7, 194–196.

10. Wilson, "Objectives of the Conference," 3.

11. "Committee Report on Western Europe," in *Conference Report*, 90.

12. Gertrude Warren, "4-H Club Work as Integral Part of Extension in the United States," in *Conference Report*, 227.

13. "Training Program in Extension Methods for Latin Americans," September 1944, NACP1, Box 12, "International 4-H Programs, Volume 1," 1.

14. "Quadrennial," *Trainee Trails*, November 7, 1949, NACP1, Box 12, "International 4-H Programs, Volume 1," 1.

15. "Trainees Worldwide," *Trainee Trails*, April 1958, NACP1, Box 12, "International 4-H Programs, Volume 1," 1.

16. Gregg Brazinsky, *Nation Building in South Korea: Koreans, Americans and the Making of a Democracy* (Chapel Hill: University of North Carolina Press, 2009), 209–217.

17. "The 4-H Idea Around the World" 1963, NACP1, Box 12, "International 4-H Programs, Volume 1," 6.

18. The Soviet exchange program was a product of détente and primarily funded by Chase Manhattan Bank and International Harvester. It was also plagued by a variety missteps and bad publicity—most notably, when the KGB arrested International Harvester's representative in Moscow on charges of spying on the eve of an announcement of its sponsorship of the exchange. See material in *4-H US-Soviet Exchange Series*, Records of the CES, Record Group 33, National Archives, College Park, MD (NACP4).

19. National 4-H Foundation, minutes of the executive committee meeting, April 28, 1966, *Agricultural Training Program Series*, NACP5, Box 1, JATP.

20. National 4-H Foundation, Homemaker Training Program proposal, February 27, 1969, NACP5, Box 1, JATP.

21. Memorandum, Andrew Eure to Grant Shrum and Francis Pressly, August 9, 1965, NACP5, Box 1, JATP; National 4-H Foundation, "Background Statement: Japanese Agricultural Training Program," March 3, 1969, NACP5, Box 1, JATP; National 4-H Foundation, "Prospectus: Agricultural Training Programs for Farm Youth," October 10, 1970, NACP5, Box 1, JATP; National 4-H Foundation, "Prospectus for Japanese Agricultural Trainee Program," 1965, NACP3, Box 1, JATP. For Poland and Hungary, see POLATP and HATP in NACP5, Boxes 2–8.

22. National 4-H Foundation, "Prospectus for Japanese Agricultural Trainee Program," 1965.

23. National 4-H Foundation, "Prospectus: Agricultural Training Programs for Farm Youth," October 10, 1970.

24. Robert Glenn Matthews, Jr., Glenden Oltie Asbury, and Peter Shen Kuo Chi, "A Study of Agricultural Trainees in a Program of Educational and Cultural Exchange," November 21, 1967, NACP5, Box 1, JATP, 104.

25. National 4-H Foundation, "Prospectus for Japanese Agricultural Trainee Program."

26. "Inter-American Rural Youth Program Gains Important U.S. 4-H Resources," December 13, 1967, Folder 22, Box 3, American International Association Archives, Rockefeller Archive Center (AIA-RAC), 3.

27. "Report of Mr. Galo Plaza, President of the National 4-F Foundation at the Annual 1968 Ordinary Meeting," 1968, Folder 22, Box 3, AIA-RAC, 1.

28. "Announcement," March 2, 1970, Folder 199, Box 25, Record Group 4, Series B, Rockefeller Family Archives, Rockefeller Archive Center (RFA-RAC). For this history of the AIA, see Darlene Rivas, *Missionary Capitalist: Nelson Rockefeller in Venezuela* (Chapel Hill: University of North Carolina Press, 2002).

29. See also "Organización, Funcionamiento y Actividades de la Sociedad Civil Pro-Clubes 5-V de Venezuela," 1962, *PIJR October/December 1962 Quarterly Report*, Folder 270, Box 35, AIA-RAC.

30. Howard Law, "A Venezuelan 5-V Foundation," December 1957, Folder 100, Box 10, Record Group 4, Series B, RFA-RAC, 1.

31. Ibid.

32. Ibid., 5.

33. *PIJR January/March Quarterly Report 1960*, Folder 255, Box 33, AIA-RAC.

34. For a useful breakdown, see "The 1964 Report of Rural Youth Club Programs in the Americas: Part 1 of the Proceedings of the 1964 Inter-American Rural Youth Leaders' Conference," 1964, Folder 101, Box 10, Record Group 3, Series B, RFA-RAC, 4.

35. "Announcement," 1; Theodore Hutchcroft, "Resume," Folder 3490, Box 579, AIA-RBF, 1–2.

36. "Talk Given by Howard E. Law at South American Extension Conference, Bogotá, Colombia, July 2–15, 1961," *PIJR July/September Quarterly Report 1961*, Folder 259, Box 33, AIA-RAC.

37. W. Francis Pressly, "Visit with Beatris Vargera," October 25, 1965, Folder 22, Box 3, RFA-RAC, 1.

38. Ibid., 1–2.

39. Law, "A Venezuelan 5-V Foundation," 2.

40. "American International Association for Economic and Social Development: Proposal for Future Support of Rural Development in Latin America," December 1963, Folder 288, Box 30, Record Group 4, Series B, RFA-RAC, 36.

41. "The 1964 Report of the Rural Youth Club Programs in the Americas," 2.

42. Isaac Azofeifa, "The Adolescent, the Adult, and the Community," 1963, Folder 298, Box 13, RFA-RAC, 3.

43. José Emilio G. Araujo, "Summary of Remarks Presented at the Inaugural Ceremony," October 1970, NACP3, Box 2, "Argentina Conference—Recommendations," 2.

44. Ibid.

45. Howard Law, "Talk on the Present Situation and the Potential for the Rural Youth Work in Latin America," 1960, *PIJR October/December Quarterly Report 1960*, Folder 255, Box 33, AIA-RAC, 2, 9; "Talk Given by Howard E. Law at South American Extension Conference," 3.

46. Oscar Tord Romero, Hernan Jorge Ojeda, and Pajuelo Malleux Storck, "La Ayude que le Puede Prestar la Juventud Rural Organizada a la Reforma Agraria," 1962, *PIJR October/December Quarterly Report*, 1962, Folder 270, Box 35, 73.

47. "Los Clubes 4-S y la Democracia," 1964, *PIJR January/March Quarterly Report 1964*, Folder 280, Box 37, AIA-RAC, 1.

48. "Some Methods and Tools to Increase Interest, Participation, and Teaching Effectiveness," Folder 258, Box 33, AIA-RAC.

49. "The 1964 Report of the Rural Youth Club Program in the Americas," 1.

50. See "Proposed Brazil 4-S Club Peace Corps Project," *PIJR April/June Quarterly Report 1961*, Folder 258, Box 33, AIA-RAC; "Inter-American Rural Youth Program Gains Important U.S. 4-H Resources," 3.

51. See Santiago Apodaca, "Rural Youth Clubs in Brazil," Folder 22, Box 2, AIA-RAC. For more on AIA, ABCAR, and Kubitschek, see Margaret B. Boardman, "The Man, the Girl and the Jeep AIA: Nelson Rockefeller's Precursor Non-Profit Model for Private U.S. Foreign Aid," *Mexico and the World* 6, no. 1 (winter 2001); Elizabeth Ann Cobbs, *Rich Neighbor: Rockefeller and Kaiser in Brazil* (New Haven, CT: Yale University Press, 1992).

52. Organization of American States press release, December 22, 1961, Folder 885, Box 93, RG 4, Series L, RFA-RAC.

53. Theodore Hutchcroft, "1974 Report of the Status of Rural Youth Educational Programs in Latin America and the Caribbean," 1974, NACP3, Box 3, "Inter-American RYL Conf.—1974—PIJR," 8–9.

54. Hutchcroft, "Some Questions and Responses About PIJR in the 1970s," 7.

55. Hutchcroft, "1974 Report," 8–11. For a similar arrangement in Ecuador, see "Report of Mr. Galo Plaza, President of the National 4-F Foundation at the Annual 1968 Ordinary Meeting," 1–2.

56. Hutchcroft, "Some Questions and Responses About PIJR in the 1970s," 3.

57. Hutchcroft, "1974 Report," 9–10.

58. Hutchcroft, "Some Questions and Responses About PIJR in the 1970s," 7.

59. "Message from Galo Plaza," October 1974, NACP3, Box 4, "Inter-American RYL Conf.—1974—PIJR," 1.

60. Hutchcroft, "3rd Annual Report to CAIJR," September 1973, NACP3, Box 4, "Inter-American RYL Conf.—1974—PIJR," 11–12.

61. "Programa Conferencia Estatal 4-H: Responsabilidades del Socio 4-H en Nuestra Democracia," July 26–31, 1964, Folder 281, Box 37, AIA-RAC.

62. Julio Adalberto Rivera, "Palabras del Señor Presidente de El Salvador, Colonel Julio Adalberto Rivera, en la Inauguración de la Quinta Concentración Anual de Clubes 4-C e Intercambio de Juventudes Rurales de México y Centro America," Folder 279, Box 37, AIA-RAC; Mario Sol Bang, "Palabras del Señor Ministro de Agricultura de El Salvador, Ing. Mario Sol, en la Inauguración de la Quinta Concentración Anual de Clubes 4-C e Intercambio de Juventudes Rurales de México y Centro America," Folder 279, Box 37, AIA-RAC.

63. Edgar Arias, *Quarterly Report October/December 1963*, Folder 275, Box 36, AIA-RAC, 9. For full texts of the speeches, see Rivera, "Palabras del Señor Presidente de El Salvador," and Bang, "Palabras del Señor Ministro de Agricultura de El Salvador."

64. See photographs in *PIJR Quarterly Report October/December 1964*, Folder 284, Box 38, AIA-RAC.

65. James M. Carter, *Inventing Vietnam: The United States and State Building, 1954–1968* (New York: Cambridge University Press, 2008), 16. For Diệm, see Seth Jacobs, *America's Miracle Man in Vietnam: Ngo Dinh Diem, Religion, Race, and U.S. Intervention in Southeast Asia* (Durham, NC: Duke University Press, 2004).

66. "Vietnam on the Move," *Trainee Trails*, March 1956, NACP1, Box 12, "International 4-H Programs, Volume 1," 8; "Footprints on the Stepping Stones," *Trainee Trails*, April 1957, NACP1, Box 12, "International 4-H Programs, Volume 1," 12; "Rural Youth Activities Around the World," *Trainee Trails*, April 1958, NACP1, Box 12, "International 4-H Programs, Volume 1," 7.

67. Buu Loan, "First National 4-T Rally in Vietnam," 1956, NACP1, Box 12, "International 4-H Programs, Volume 1."

68. Ibid., 3–5.

69. Quoted in Anne Raffin, *Youth Mobilization in Vichy Indochina and Its Legacies, 1940 to 1970* (Lanham, MD: Lexington, 2008), 209–210.

70. Harold Christie and Dang Van Loc, "4-T Clubs: Rebuilding on Firm Foundation," *Vietnam Agricultural Newsletter* 1, no. 6 (October 1966); "Vietnam Country File," 1, 7–8, in *4-H Country File Series*, Records of the CES, Record Group 33, National Archives, College Park, MD (NACP6).

71. Raffin, *Youth Mobilization*.

72. Christie and Loc, "4-T Clubs," 7.

73. Memorandum, "Republic of Vietnam, Ministry of Agriculture, Directorate of Agricultural Affairs, Agricultural Extension Service: Activity Report of Agriculture Extension in 1966," 1967, 2, *U.S. Forces in Southeast Asia, 1950–1975 Series*, Record Group 472, National Archives, College Park, MD (NACP7), Entry #A1 701, Advisory Team 701, Box 556, "4-T Clubs 1968."

74. Memorandum, "Office of Agriculture: Extension Branch Policy Guidelines," June 1, 1967, 5, NACP7, Entry #A1 701, Advisory Team 701, Box 556, "4-T Clubs 1968."

75. "4-T Handbook" [1967?], 2, NACP7, Entry #A1 701, Advisory Team 701, Box 556, "4-T Clubs 1968."

76. Leonard B. Williams, "Briefing Paper," 4–6, NACP7, Entry #A1 701, Advisory Team 701, Box 556, "4-T Clubs 1968."

77. Memorandum, "Minutes of the Voluntary Civic Action Committee," January 1968, 2–4, NACP7, Entry #A1 701, Advisory Team 701, Box 557, "Youth and Sports—1968."

78. Michael Latham, *The Right Kind of Revolution: Modernization, Development, and US Foreign Policy from the Cold War to the Present* (Ithaca, NY: Cornell University Press, 2011), 141. For an in-depth explanation of CORDS from the perspective of U.S. military analysts, see Dale Andrade and James H. Willbanks, "CORDS/Phoenix: Counterinsurgency Lessons from Vietnam for the Future," *Military Review* 86, no. 2 (2006): 9.

79. See "USAID/Vietnam: Office of Domestic Production, Agricultural Production Memo," June 17, 1968, NACP7, Entry #A1 701, Advisory Team 701, Box 556, "4-T Clubs 1968."

80. Memorandum, Mai Thi My Nhung to William H. Faulkner, "Home Economic and 4-T Program," September 9, 1969; Richard W. White to Pham Thi Thuy, Thai Thi Nam, and Truong Thi Phang, June 25, 1969, NACP7, Entry #A1727, Advisory Team 85 (Kien Tuong Province Advisory Team), Administrative and Operational Records, 1967–1973, Box 1458, "Agriculture, 1968/1969."

81. John Noland, "4-T Program in Vietnam," 1970, NACP6, "Vietnam Country File," 2.

82. See Nick Cullather, *The Hungry World: America's Cold War Battle Against Poverty in Asia* (Cambridge, MA: Harvard University Press, 2010).

83. "USAID/Vietnam Weekly Report," June 12, 1968, NACP7, Entry #A1727, Advisory Team 85 (Kien Tuong Province Advisory Team), Administrative and Operational Records, 1967–1973, Box 1460, "USAID/ Wkly. Repts."

84. Noland, "4-T Program in Vietnam."

85. See material on Plain of Reeds Agricultural Development Center, in "Agriculture, 1968/1969" and "Training Center, 1969" folders in NACP7, Entry #A1727, Advisory Team 85 (Kien Tuong Province Advisory Team), Administrative and Operational Records, 1967–1973, Box 1458; W. L. Averill, "Agricultural Production Memo," May 15, 1968, NACP7, Entry #A1 701, Advisory Team 701, Box 557, "Agriculture Production Memos 33–100, 1968."

86. John Noland, "4-H Statistics in 1969," 1970, NACP6, "Vietnam Country File."

87. Mel Thompson, memorandum, February 26, 1969, NACP6, "Vietnam Country File."

88. Noland, "4-T Program in Vietnam," 6.

89. John R. Martin to Nguyen The Thieu, July 16, 1971, NACP6, "Vietnam Country File"; John R. Martin to Nguyen The Thieu, July 2, 1971, NACP6, "Vietnam Country File"; John R. Martin to Nguyen The Thieu, May 20, 1971, NACP6, "Vietnam Country File"; John R. Martin to Charles Brown, February 25, 1971, NACP6, "Vietnam Country File"; John R. Martin to Vo Quang Tam, January 27, 1971, NACP6, "Vietnam Country File."

90. See "Work Sheet and Discussion Outline for Considering Expansion of Extension Rural Youth Work in Vietnam," "Recommendations of the Rural Youth Survey Team," and "Outline of Program for the Vietnamese 4-T Team," in NACP1, Box 12, "International 4-H Programs, Volume 2."

91. "Recommendations of the Rural Youth Survey Team," 1.

92. "Building a Base for Vietnam-Asia Development," NACP1, Box 12, "International 4-H Programs, Volume 2."

93. John R. Martin, "Status Report," September 1971, NACP6, "Vietnam Country File."

94. Ho Thi Hien to Mel Thompson, November 19, 1981, NACP6, "Vietnam Country File"; Mel Thompson to Ho Thi Hien, February 17, 1982, NACP6, "Vietnam Country File."

95. See documents in Folder 3490, Box 579, Record Group 3.1, RBF-RAC; Theodore Hutchcroft to José Emilio Araujo, February 17, 1975, NACP3, Box 3, "IICA Agreement, etc."

96. See Hal S. Brands, *Latin America's Cold War* (Cambridge, MA: Harvard University Press, 2010).

97. Hutchcroft, "Some Questions and Responses About PIJR in the 1970s," 1971, NACP3, Box 2, "PIJR in the 1970s," 6.

98. Hutchcroft, "Some Questions and Responses About PIJR in the 1970s," 16.

99. Ibid., 11.

100. Speech, Major J. V. Ruy Barbosa, October 1970, NACP3, Box 2, "PIJR in the 1970s."

101. Ted Williams, trip report, November 1973, NACP3, Box 3, "II Inter-American Seminar for Support Entities—Nov. 4–11, 1973, Brazil."

102. Theodore Hutchcroft, "Fourth Annual Report to the Inter-American Rural Youth Advisory Council by the Directory of the Inter-American Rural Youth Program," April 1974, NACP3, Box 3, "IICA Agreement, etc.," 6.

103. For the demise of modernization theory, see Latham, *The Right Kind of Revolution*, chap. 6; Gilman, *Mandarins of the Future*, chaps. 6–7.

104. See Rafael Segovia Atencia, "Institutionalization of CAIJR," December 23, 1977, NACP3, Box 3, "IICA Agreement, etc." Initially, the CAIJR was intended merely to provide guidance to the PIJR, but, in anticipation of the dissolution of the PIJR, the OAS and IICA altered its mission to have it assume all the activities of the PIJR. However, while the PIJR had an average budget of $200,000, the CAIJR had almost no regular funds and no real possibility of successfully assuming the PIJR's programs.

105. Atencia, "Institutionalization of CAIJR," 5.

106. "Project to Reinforce Rural Youth Programs in Latin America and the Caribbean," 1983, NACP3, Box 3, "1980s."

107. Joseph Beeson, "Evaluation of the Effectiveness of the Japanese Agricultural Training Program," November 29, 1968, NACP3, Box 1, JATP.

108. National 4-H Club Foundation of America, "Activities of Returned Japanese Agricultural Trainees, 1972," NACP3, Box 2, JATP.

109. Mel Thompson, memorandum on Young Sup Shin, November 16, 1971, NACP5, "Korea Country File"; Beatrice Cleveland to Mel Thompson, November 8, 1971, NACP5, "Korea Country File."

110. Young Sup Shin to Mel Thompson, November 15, 1971, NACP5, "Korea Country File."

Epilogue

1. "Bob" is a pseudonym.

2. "The National Agricultural Program: A Concept Paper," in author's possession, August 26, 2005, 3. The proposed resurrection of the Afghan extension service was part of a broader effort on Bob's part to restructure the Afghan ministry of agriculture. Many of Bob's other suggestions, in fact, were adopted. See "Afghanistan Agriculture: A Way Forward," in author's possession, April 14, 2005; "Water Basin Authorities: An Organizing Principle in Restructuring the Afghan Ministry of Agriculture and Encouraging Comprehensive Natural Resource Management and Administration," in author's possession, 2005.

3. "The National Agricultural Program," 8.

4. E-mail to the author, October 26, 2011.

5. Ibid.

6. See material in "Afghanistan Country File," NACP5.

7. "National Agricultural Program," 6.

8. After Natsios's departure from USAID in January 2006, Bob was able to persuade the Bush administration to deploy him as a consultant to the Afghan ministry of agriculture, where he continued to push for funding for extensions. See "Proposal of Work," in author's possession, February 11, 2006.

9. See *Handbook: Agribusiness Development Teams* (Fort Leavenworth, KS: U.S. Army Combined Arms Center, 2009).

10. Jeremy Gulley, "It's in Their Hands Now," posted July 14, 2011, jeremygulley.blogspot.com (accessed October 18, 2011).

11. Jeremy Gulley, "The Way Ahead," posted November 4, 2010, jeremygulley.blogspot.com (accessed October 18, 2011).

12. Jeremy Gulley, "Soldier as Teacher," posted September 4, 2010, jeremygulley.blogspot.com (accessed October 18, 2011).

13. Ibid.

INDEX

Page numbers in italics indicate images.

Great Depression: farm crisis and rural
hardships, 9, 121–23; youth crisis of the
early 1930s, 127–28, 134. *See also* 4-H
in the 1930s; New Deal agricultural
programs
Green Revolution, 12, 192–93
Guatemalan 4-S clubs, 204, *205*
Gulley, Jeremy, 227–28
GVN. *See* Republic of Vietnam (GVN)

Hall, G. Stanley, 96–97
Harris, Carmen V., 176, 181
Harrison, Carrie, 54
Harshaw, E. B., 75
Haskin, Frederic J., 52
Hatch Act (1887), 25
Hatcher, Orie Latham, 93
Head, Walter William, 79
health programs, 4-H, 7–8; and African
American extension, 107; boys and,
105–6, 110–11, 140–44; and citizenship programs, 170–72; Colombia, 197;
competitive health contests, 82, 103–7,
110–11; contrasting healthy bodies with
sick and hungry bodies, 170; girls and,
101–8, 110, 140, 197; health examinations, 104–5, 140; international 4-H, 197,
212–13; nutrition projects, 82, 101–2; and
physical attractiveness/perfect bodies,
106–7, 110–11; scorecards, 82, 103–5; sex
education, 140–44, 152, 197; venereal
disease education, 152; Vietnam, 212–13;
World War II mobilization, 166, 169–72
Heflin, James, 113
Heredity in Dairy Cattle (Russell), 144
Hermanson, Ruth Ann, 159–60
Hershey, Lewis B., 170–71, 173
heterosexuality: agrarian futurism and
rural reproduction, 13, 120, 181; camp
romances, 136–37, 183–84; farm families and rural reproduction (1930s),
7–8, 18, 119–21, 126, 134–45, 152; girls'

training for happy marriages (1930s),
131, 136–40, *139*; heteronormativity, 10,
13, 14–15, 120, 126, 181; international
4-H and the rural family model, 190,
193, 197, 212, 218–19; racial inequality
and rural normalcy (1950s), 182–84,
260n87; self-management training/
cultivation of a pleasing personality for
the opposite sex, 138–39; sex education, 140–44, 152, 197
Hickory Hill (Emery), 182, 260n87
Hicks, John L., 175
Hitchcock, Gilbert, 49
Ho Thi Hien, 213, 215
Hochbaum, H. W., 169
Hofstadter, Richard, 241n4
Holden, P. G., 38–39
Holmes, Roy Hinman, 92
home economics: and child labor/rural
girls' overwork, 91–93; Colombian
clubs, 197–98; girls' programs in the
1920s, 7, 68–69, 73, 94–95, 98–99, *99*,
114–16; land-grant college departments,
91; and late nineteenth-century domes-
tic economy movement, 90–91; New
Deal agricultural programs, 125; and
rural reformers of the 1920s, 90–94,
117–18; and Smith-Hughes Act, 91; and
Smith-Lever Act, 91; Vietnamese 4-T
clubs, 212
The Homestead, 19–20
Homestead Act (1862), 25
Hoover, Herbert, 79, 122
How to Keep America Out of War (Page),
158
Hughes, Dudley, 48, 50
Hutchcroft, Theodore, 188, 195–96, 201,
202–3, 215–17
Hyde, Arthur, 145, 149

IFYE. *See* International Farm Youth
Exchange (IFYE)

ACKNOWLEDGMENTS

I'll start with some big debts. The most faithful friends to this book have been Mari Jo Buhle, Margot Canaday, and Robert Lockhart. Mari Jo patiently waded through many drafts of my writing. That she did so deftly and with such grace speaks to her unparalleled skill as a mentor and scholar. This isn't news to anyone: if you stacked all the books that Mari Jo has shaped and enriched, you would have a very tall, structurally unstable tower of erudition. Meanwhile, I suspect that Margot was initially attracted to the book because of her Iowa roots, but she proved an indefatigable ally and among its most constructive critics. Her ample and generous suggestions dramatically improved the book. As my editor at the University of Pennsylvania Press, Bob had the difficult task of reining in some of my academic excesses. My mother, a long-standing foe of esoteric jargon, may have wounded the words "enthymeme" and "autochthonous," but it was Bob who ultimately slew them. Bob has been a patient hand, a meticulous editor, and a good friend to both the book and me. Thank you to all of them.

A number of institutions provided support for the writing and researching of this book. I am grateful for the support of Brown University, the Program in Women's Studies and the Office of the Dean of Arts and Sciences at Duke University, the Program in Agrarian Studies at Yale University, the Rockefeller Archive Center, and the German Historical Institute. In addition, my research would have been impossible without the generous assistance of the librarians and archivists in the special collections at the Parks Library at Iowa State University, the Ralph Draughon Library at Auburn University, the University of Arizona Library, the James B. Hunt Library at North Carolina State University, the Memorial Library at the University of Wisconsin, the National Archives at College Park, the National Agricultural Library, and the Rockefeller Research Archive.

Brown University was a happy home for many years. Thanks are due to the university community for supporting me and providing me with a rich intellectual home. I am deeply grateful to Karl Jacoby and Michael Vorenberg.

Karl patiently guided me through American environmental history, while Mike shared his enormous wealth of knowledge about the history of the American state. At Brown, I also had the pleasure and good fortune of learning from the late Jack Thomas. It was an experience that I will always cherish. Deborah Cohen, Mary Gluck, Elliott Gorn, Joan Richards, Amy Remensnyder, and Kerry Smith showed me by example what excellence in research and teaching entailed. Carolyn Dean taught me a tremendous amount about the philosophical traditions central to this book's argument. I also learned much from a circle of outstanding friends and scholars there. In particular, Erik Anderson, Farid Azfar. Caroline Boswell, Marcia Chatelain, Lara K. Couturier, Christopher Brick, Matthew Dunne, Natalina Earls, Nicole Eaton, Sara Fingal, Gillian Frank, Lauren Faulkner, Robert Fleegler, Paige Meltzer, Sheyda Jahanbani, James Kabala, Jooyoung Lee, Oded Rabinovitch, Adam Ringguth, Mark Robbins, Erica Ryan, Derek Seidman, William Tatum, Stacie Taranto, Jason C. White, and Jennifer Wilz put up with me, taught me, and sometimes celebrated with me. I couldn't have asked for better friends and colleagues. To our collective sorrow, Adam Ringguth did not survive to complete his PhD. We miss him dearly.

I drove across the United States in an old Taurus doing research for this book. During my travels, a number of people sheltered me, fed me, and gave me comfort and friendship. Dan and Vicki Bunnell, Allen and Cindy McGranahan, Devan McGranahan and Megan Kirkwood, John and Nancy Pielemeier, Gina Stilp, John Ryan and Wes Chenault, and Jansen Tsiongson all have my sincere thanks for opening their homes to me.

The Program in Agrarian Studies at Yale University was an ideal base for a year while I worked on this book. James C. Scott and Kalyanakrishnan Sivaramakrishnan provided intellectual hospitality for that year, as well as personal support and mentoring. The year would have been lovely regardless, but it was improved further by the other scholars whom Jim and Shivi assembled as fellows. Matthew Bender, Janam Mukherjee, Rishabh Kumar Dhir, and Juno Parreñas offered me great company, tenacious minds, and the chance to read their innovative scholarship. I benefited from conversations with a number of scholars during that year, including Ned Blackhawk, Uday Chandra, Joe Fischel, Todd Holmes, Rachel Purvis, Joanna Radin, William Rankin, Paul Sabin, Sara Shneiderman, Michael Stone, Linn Marie Tonstad, and Jeremy Wallace.

At Duke University, my colleagues in the Program in Women's Studies have been vital allies. Elizabeth Grosz, Frances Hasso, Ranjana Khanna, Kimberly Lamm, M. Kathy Rudy, Kathi Weeks, and Ara Wilson made me feel right at home and provided me a thrilling intellectual community. Kathy has been a friend, counsel, sage, and pack leader. Ara, Kathy, Kathi, and Elizabeth also read and commented on portions of the book, enriching it significantly with their formidable intellects. Many other colleagues at Duke have been generous with their time and minds. I am grateful, in particular, to Anne Allison, Edward Balleisen, Dirk Bonker, Sarah Deutsch, Ralph Litzinger, Diane Nelson, Carlos Rojas, Adriane Lentz-Smith, and Priscilla Wald. Other scholars have enriched my intellectual life and improved my writing through the Working Group on Feminist History and the Triangle Writing Group, including Morgan Adamson, GerShun Avilez, Emily Burrill, James Chappel, Miles Greer, Anne-Maria Makhulu, Kathyrn Mathers, Tomas Matza, Eli Meyerhoff, Jessica Namakkal, Seraphima Rombe-Shulman, Harris Solomon, Matthew Watson, and Shannon Withycombe.

I've had the privilege to learn from an eclectic and brilliant set of minds. Daniel Immerwahr and Mischa Honeck are two of my regular coconspirators, and Daniel read the whole manuscript on at least two occasions. He did this because he is a true mensch. Ariel Ron and Gillian Frank have also been unusually generous with their well-formed thoughts. From those people who have contributed to this book by sharing ideas, encouraging my research, and offering timely wisdom, I could raise a great army. Gratitude is owed to Michael Adas, Vanessa Agard-Jones, Kristine Alexander, Joseph Anderson, Beth Bailey, Paula Baker, Brian Balogh, Hal Barron, Eileen Boris, Ryan Cartwright, Marcia Chatelain, David Danbom, Pete Daniel, Todd Dresser, Erika Dyson, Elise Edwards, Betsy Erbaugh, Paula Fass, Sara Fieldston, Mark Finlay, Jess Gilbert, James Giesen, Janet Golden, Mary Gray, Sean Guillory, Julie Guthman, David Hamilton, Shane Hamilton, Mark Hersey, Andrew Isenberg, Katherine Jellison, Colin Johnson, Jennifer Klein, Amnon Lev, Kriste Lindenmeyer, Laura Lovett, Mike McGovern, Devan McGranahan, Betsy More, Jeff Miner, Susan Miller, Tamara Myers, Christina Norwig, Andrew Jewett, Alan Olmstead, Tore Olsson, Leslie Paris, Emily Pawley, Adrienne Petty, Sarah Phillips, Charles Postel, Debra Reid, Paul Rhode, Pamela Riney-Kehrberg, Elizabeth Sanders, Adam Sheingate, Kelly J. Sisson Lessens, James Sparrow, Whitney Strub, Mary Summers, Paul Sutter, Robin Turner, Jeremy Vetter, Jeannie Whayne, and Amrys Williams. I pray that I will never need this army for anything but purely academic purposes, for it would be an army intellectually prolific but martially hapless.

Old friends can sometimes teach the lessons colleagues cannot. Michael Hayes, Noe Montez, Alexander Nakhnikian, Geoffrey Swenson, and Joseph Walsh all know what they've done, and it's been quite an instructional example. Meanwhile, I couldn't have written this book without the support and care of many others. Gestures of kindness and comity sustained me as I wrote the book, and I have some extraordinary friends. Thank you to Tim Delaney, Jon Dunlop, Kiera Feldman, Brian Gaylord, Julio Gray, Andy Hagan, Emma Hayes, Jeff Miner, Katina Boosalis Miner, Shaun Southworth, Courtney Wertz-MacIntyre, and Eric Zobel.

My schoolmates regarded my family as a quarrelsome and peculiar brood, partly because we are prone to contentious debates at the dinner table that are often settled only by recourse to a dictionary or an encyclopedia. This has led to a lifelong affection for intellectual sparring and awkward, public nerdishness in me and my brother and sister, Daniel and Erin Rosenberg. Having brilliant, assertive older siblings was good preparation for academia but occasionally the source of headaches. I pin the blame entirely on my parents, Louis Rosenberg and Sheila Farrell Rosenberg. They both read large portions of this book, and then argued with me about it. Their love and support made this book possible. Now that my brother and his wonderful wife, Mindy Rosenberg, have added another generation, who knows how long the dinner debates will last. Ruthie, Barry, Abe, and Jack all show signs of the pugnacious Farrell-Rosenberg intellect.

The joke among academics is that effusive, performative declarations of romantic love in an acknowledgments section are always inversely correlated to the strength, depth, and health of a relationship. So, to conclude, thank you, Harris Solomon.